INTRODUCTION TO FEMINIST JURISPRUDENCE

Cavendish Publishing Limited

London • Sydney

INTRODUCTION TO FEMINIST JURISPRUDENCE

Hilaire Barnett BA, LLM
Queen Mary and Westfield College
University of London

Cavendish
Publishing
Limited

London • Sydney

First published in Great Britain 1998 by Cavendish Publishing Limited,
The Glass House, Wharton Street, London WC1X 9PX, United Kingdom
Telephone: +44 (0) 171 278 8000   Facsimile: +44 (0) 171 278 8080
e-mail: info@cavendishpublishing.com
Visit our home page on http://www.cavendishpublishing.com

© Barnett, H 1998

All rights reserved. No part of this publication may be reproduced, stored in a retrieval system, or transmitted, in any form or by any means, electronic, mechanical, photocopying, recording, scanning or otherwise, except under the terms of the Copyright, Designs and Patents Act 1988 or under the terms of a licence issued by the Copyright Licensing Agency, 90 Tottenham Court Road, London, W1P 9HE, UK, without the permission in writing of the publisher.

Barnett, Hilaire A
Introduction to feminist jurisprudence
1. Feminist jurisprudence

I. Title
340.1'15'082

ISBN 1 85941 237 8

Printed and bound in Great Britain by
Biddles Ltd, Guildford and King's Lynn

In loving memory of my mother

PREFACE

Nothing evidences a subject's maturity so convincingly as the emergence of introductory texts. It may be said that over the past two decades feminist legal theory and jurisprudence[1] has come of age. The literature is now both extensive and impressive, although sometimes inaccessible to many students because it is dispersed amongst international journals. It is the objective of this book to introduce students to the major themes of inquiry and scholarship with which feminist scholars, many of whom are lawyers, are concerned. Feminist jurisprudence has many objects of inquiry, and seeks to answer many difficult, sometimes intractable, questions about law and society. If there is one single, unifying strand of thought amongst feminist legal scholars, it may be interpreted as the unmasking of the many inequalities based on gender, deriving from nature and culture and encapsulated in the law. Equally important are the practical implications of this area of study – nothing less than the search for equality for women under the law. The project is thus ambitious and all embracing, encompassing the unmasking of gender-based inequality in the substantive law, and the unravelling of the traditional exclusion of women in legal theory and jurisprudence. Feminist jurisprudence is at one and the same time an academic, legal and political enterprise.

While the focus of this book is necessarily legal, insights into the law derive from many other disciplines. Thus anthropology, economics, history, philosophy, politics, psychology and sociology all inform the many discourses of law. That law and legal theory cannot exist in a cultural or political vacuum is a simple truism, but its implications are complex. Feminist jurisprudence is no exception: its sweep is not only multidisciplinary but also universal, although crossing disciplines and geographical boundaries provides its own difficulties and pitfalls for the researcher. Feminist jurisprudence has evolved and continues to evolve at dramatic pace. It is hoped that this work will provide, for those interested in equality and justice, a window on the diversity and richness of feminist legal thought.

In Part I of the book, the foundations of feminist jurisprudence are discussed. The evolution of feminist jurisprudence and the methods employed by feminist scholars are discussed, as are the inequalities, both historical and contemporary, from which women have suffered. Chapter 3 introduces the concept of patriarchy and patriarchal manifestations in society and law. In Part II, the manner in which women have been marginalised or excluded from traditional or conventional masculine jurisprudence is considered. Because it is not assumed that all readers will be lawyers or that they will have studied conventional jurisprudence as an academic discipline, a brief overview – inevitably an unsatisfactory enterprise in an introductory work – of the central tenets of jurisprudential theories and schools of thought

---

[1] Legal theory is concerned with theoretical constructions of the law; jurisprudence is concerned with theoretical explanations about law.

is offered. In Part III the focus is on the schools of thought which have dominated feminist legal scholarship. Part IV is devoted to key issues in feminist jurisprudence: women and medicine; women, violence and the legal system; women and pornography. Where relevant, reference is made to the *Sourcebook on Feminist Jurisprudence*, 1997, in which extracts from cited works will be found.

My thanks are due to many. To the Law Librarian, Bob Burns, for his calm and constructive responses to my several anxiety attacks, and to all the librarians, and particularly Susan Richards and her staff on Inter-Library Loans, for their efficiency and patience. My thanks also go to colleagues and friends, Ros Goode, Wayne Morrison and David Toube for reading assorted chapters and making constructive criticisms. To Jo Reddy and Sonny Leong and staff at Cavendish Publishing, my thanks for their patience and support. My thanks also, and yet again, to family and friends who have been understanding and allowed me the space in which to think and write. And to Matthew, my thanks, for 'being [t]here'.

Hilaire Barnett
Queen Mary and Westfield College
University of London
April 1998

CONTENTS

Preface   vii

PART I   THE FOUNDATIONS OF FEMINIST JURISPRUDENCE

1   Introduction   3

THE EVOLUTION AND SCOPE OF FEMINIST JURISPRUDENCE AND FEMINIST LEGAL METHODS	3
THE FEMINIST GENDER DEBATE	14
What is a woman? The gender question	14
Woman as 'Other'	15
FEMINIST LEGAL METHODS	19
Consciousness raising	19
Asking the 'woman question'	21
Feminist practical reasoning	23

2   Gender Inequalities and Law   29

EMPIRICAL EVIDENCE OF CULTURAL PATRIARCHY	31
Chinese footbinding	31
Female circumcision	32
Hindu suttee	33
European witch-murders	33
Wife sale in England	34
Women in marriage	35
Gender-based violence against women in contemporary society	35
LAW'S DEPENDENCE ON CULTURE: THEORETICAL EXPLANATIONS	36
Karl von Savigny, Eugen Ehrlich, William Graham Sumner	36
EARLY STRUGGLES FOR EQUALITY IN WESTERN SOCIETY	38
Rights for women	38
THE FRANCHISE	40
The franchise in the United Kingdom	40
The franchise in the United States of America	43
EDUCATION FOR WOMEN	45
Science and medicine	46
The legal profession	49
THE TWO WORLD WARS AND WOMEN'S EQUALITY	49
THE POSITION OF WOMEN IN CONTEMPORARY SOCIETY	51
Participation in employment	51
Occupational differences	52
Part time work	53
Women's pay	53
The British Central Statistical Office Report 1995	53
Women's earnings	54
Occupational data	54

3 Patriarchy — 57

EXPLAINING PATRIARCHY — 57
  Theoretical explanations of the origins of patriarchy — 58
    Early political conceptions of patriarchy — 58
    Lawful patriarchy within the family in earlier times — 61
CONTEMPORARY PATRIARCHAL MANIFESTATIONS — 64
  The 'public' sphere — 64
  The 'private' sphere — 65
  The invisibility of women — 65
  Extending the private sphere? — 67
INEQUALITY IN THE PUBLIC AND PRIVATE SPHERES — 69
  The Subject of law: woman as 'Other' — 71
    Physical violence against women — 72
    Sexual harassment — 74
    Pornography — 75
PATRIARCHY AND ESSENTIALISM — 76
CONCLUSION — 79

PART II CONVENTIONAL JURISPRUDENCE AND FEMINIST CRITIQUE

4 Conventional Jurisprudence and Feminist Critique: I Ancient Greek Political Thought and Natural Law Theory — 83

INTRODUCTION — 83
THE GREEK PHILOSOPHERS — 83
  Reason in Greek philosophy — 84
  Plato — 84
  Aristotle — 88
NATURAL LAW THOUGHT — 89
  Natural law in ancient Greece and Rome — 89
  Christian natural law thought — 90
  Natural law and positive law — 92

5 Conventional Jurisprudence and Feminist Critique: II Positive Law and Social Contract Theory — 95

THE ORIGINS OF POSITIVISM: THE AGE OF MODERNITY — 95
LIBERALISM — 96
  The rise of legal positivism — 99
  The elements of positivist thought — 100
SOCIAL CONTRACT THEORY — 110
  Knowledge and ignorance behind the 'veil of ignorance' — 111
  The principles of justice — 112
  The communitarian critique of liberalism — 115

The public and private spheres of life	128
THE FAILURES OF TRADITIONAL JURISPRUDENCE	117

PART III SCHOOLS OF FEMINIST JURISPRUDENTIAL THOUGHT

6 Schools of Feminist Jurisprudential Thought: I Liberalism and Marxism — 121

INTRODUCTION	121
The liberal tradition in Western democracy	121
The public and private spheres in liberal philosophy	123
The feminist critique of liberalism	127
MARXIST-SOCIALIST FEMINISM	135

7 Schools of Feminist Jurisprudential Thought: II Difference feminism/cultural feminism — 143

Feminist developmental theories	143
Carol Gilligan's psychological/developmental research	145
French feminism	146
Luce Irigaray	148
Luce Irigaray and the charge of 'essentialism'	158
Drucilla Cornell	159

8 Schools of Feminist Jurisprudential Thought: III Radical Feminism — 163

Catharine MacKinnon's dominance theory	165
Radical feminism and the critiques of 'essentialism'	173

9 Postmodernism and Critical Legal Studies — 177

INTRODUCTION	177
The age of modernity	177
The age of postmodernism	178
Michel Foucault	182
Jean-Francois Lyotard	183
Jacques Derrida	185
CRITICAL LEGAL STUDIES	188
FEMINISM, POSTMODERNISM AND CRITICAL LEGAL STUDIES	189
POSTMODERN FEMINIST JURISPRUDENCE	195
The construction of gender	195
Postmodernism/poststructuralism and Critical Legal Studies: unravelling law's claim to rationality and objectivity	200
FEMINISM AND THE CLS DISTRUST OF RIGHTS	202
DECONSTRUCTING THE SUBJECT OF LAW	204

PART IV KEY ISSUES IN FEMINIST JURISPRUDENCE

10 Women and Medicine   211
INTRODUCTION   211
THE MEDICAL PROFESSION IN WESTERN SOCIETY   213
   Obstetrics and gynaecology   215
THE MEDICALISATION OF REPRODUCTION   216
STERILISATION   219
   The case law   220
COURT ORDERED CAESAREAN SECTIONS   223
   Treatment under the Mental Health Act 1983   225
INFERTILITY TREATMENT   227
ABORTION RIGHTS   229
   Introduction   229
   The evolution of abortion law in England   230
   'Foetal rights'? and the law   232
   The Warnock Committee Report   233
   The legal position of the father of the child   233
   The interaction between abortion, contraception and sterilisation   234
   Abortion rights in the United States of America   234
WOMEN'S REPRODUCTIVE RIGHTS IN
   INTERNATIONAL DIMENSION   240
   The religious and cultural inheritance and influence   240
   Population control programmes   241
NON-CONSENSUAL TREATMENT OF PATIENTS SUFFERING FROM
   ANOREXIA NERVOSA   244
   Competence and the 'mature minor'   246

11 Women, Violence and the Legal System   251
INTRODUCTION   251
   Defining gender-based violence   251
   Measuring gender-based violence   252
   International data   252
   Violence against women in the United Kingdom   255
   Explaining gender-based violence   256
   The problem of the liberal analysis of the 'public' and 'private'
      spheres of life   258
   A woman's traditional 'place': the home   259
      Marital rape   259
   Evolution of the English law relating to domestic violence   261
   The criminal law   261
   Reconceptualising 'domestic' violence   263

Contents

Female victims and the legal system	264
The failure of traditional defences to a charge of murder for women victims of violence	265
Provocation	266
Diminished responsibility	268
Recognising the impact of domestic violence	270
Battered woman syndrome	270
R v Ahluwalia, R v Thornton	272
Battered woman syndrome in Australia and Canada	273
R v Lavallee: success for self-defence and battered woman syndrome	273
Women on trial: rape	275

12 Pornography and Prostitution — 281

INTRODUCTION	281
PORNOGRAPHY	281
The evolution of the pornography industry	281
Defining pornography	282
Legal definitions	283
Differing constitutional contexts	284
Empirical evidence concerning pornography	287
Reformulating pornography from a feminist perspective	289
Alternative theoretical approaches to pornography	290
FEMINIST APPROACHES TO PORNOGRAPHY	291
Radical feminism	291
Racial discrimination and pornography	293
The Dworkin (Andrea) and MacKinnon Indianapolis and Minneapolis Civil Rights Ordinances	295
Freedom of expression reconsidered	297
'Speech act' theory	298
THE LIBERAL APPROACH: ABSOLUTE AND MODIFIED	301
An alternative interpretation of John Stuart Mill's 'harm' principle	304
THE CONSERVATIVE APPROACH TO PORNOGRAPHY	307
ALTERNATIVE AND POSTMODERN PERCEPTIONS CONCERNING PORNOGRAPHY	309
Arguments for and against the legal regulation of pornography	312
CONCLUSION	314
PROSTITUTION AND LAW: AN OUTLINE	315
Alternative legal responses to prostitution	317
Competing arguments concerning prostitution	317

Bibliography	321
Index	341

PART I

THE FOUNDATIONS OF FEMINIST JURISPRUDENCE

CHAPTER 1

INTRODUCTION

THE EVOLUTION AND SCOPE OF FEMINIST JURISPRUDENCE AND FEMINIST LEGAL METHODS

The debate concerning the status of women dates back to the Ancient Greeks. Plato[1] and Aristotle[2] both sought to analyse the actual and appropriate role of women in society and from their writings may be discerned many of the ideas which continue to exercise feminist scholarship.[3] In ancient Greek thought can be found many of the ideas which have endured in later thought: the concepts of public and private life which are allegedly distinguishable, with the confinement of women to the private sphere;[4] considerations of equality based on gender; the concept of patriarchal ownership of, and/or authority and power over women.[5]

However, it is eighteenth, nineteenth and early twentieth century feminist campaigns[6] for the elimination of discriminatory laws which prevented women from participating fully in civic life which mark the origins of contemporary feminist thought.[7] The struggle for the franchise and the battle to be admitted to universities and the professions represented a seminally important, and ultimately largely successful, campaign on which subsequent work towards the full emancipation of women in society was founded.

In Europe, the First World War, the depression of the inter-war years, the Second World War and the subsequent struggle for economic recovery and the rebuilding of a viable peaceful society, resulted in a quiet phase for feminist endeavours, with one principal exception: in the United Kingdom the struggle for the vote for women over the age of 30 was finally achieved in 1918, and the full franchise for women on a basis of equality with men in 1928.

In 1949, Simone de Beauvoir's seminal work, *The Second Sex*, was published[8] and the movement revitalised. Simone de Beauvoir's work still

---

[1] c 427–347 BC.
[2] 384–322 BC.
[3] Subjected to feminist analysis, however, both Plato and Aristotle reveal a deep misogyny, as discussed in Chapter 4.
[4] See Chapters 5 and 6.
[5] See Chapter 3.
[6] See Chapter 2 for further discussion of the early struggles for equality for women.
[7] See Wollstonecraft, M, *Vindication of the Rights of Women* (1792), 1967, New York: WW Norton.
[8] de Beauvoir, S, *The Second Sex* (1949), Parshley, H (ed and trans), 1989, London: Picador.

forms a foundation for much feminist analysis and a focus for differing approaches to the question of gender and its significance. The core theme running through de Beauvoir's work is that of women being the 'Other' (sex). By this de Beauvoir means that the construction of society, of language, thought, religion and of the family all rests on the assumption that the world is male. It is men who control the meaning given to society: man is the standard against which all is judged. Women, on the other hand, are excluded from these constructions: women is the 'Other'. Through nurturance and socialisation a female child learns to become a woman. Women, de Beauvoir argues, are socially constructed rather than biologically determined: '[O]ne is not born, but rather becomes, a woman.'[9] Being a woman – the Other – is reflected in law's construction. Law is male; the subjects of law are male. As de Beauvoir wrote:

> She is defined and differentiated with reference to man and not he with reference to her; she is the incidental, the inessential as opposed to the essential. He is the Subject, he is the Absolute – she is the Other.[10]

The categories of Self and Other, de Beauvoir instructs, are as 'primordial as consciousness itself'. In all societies, there exists the essential and the inessential; the Self and Other, and all societies reflect this duality.[11] Considering this phenomenon in relation to law, it can be seen that traditionally law has been a male construct and that the subject of law is male. Women, being the Other, have been for long at worst oppressed, and at best ignored by the law. For women to be included as subjects of law, their voices have to be listened to and, more importantly, to be heard and acted upon. For too long the law, legal theory and jurisprudence has presented itself as a rational objective ordering of gender-neutral persons, while at the same time subconsciously addressing only the essential male.

Feminist scholars in the liberating 1960s were dedicated to the political struggle for the equality of women in the family, in the work place and in politics. By identifying sites of exclusion and oppression, feminist scholars, whether writing from a social or political science or philosophical base, demonstrated further the supremacy which men have traditionally assumed and maintained in society. Feminist legal scholarship became a natural and integral part of this movement, although lagging behind the general movement.[12] Feminist jurisprudence is both simultaneously challenging and alternative, and reflects the demands of women – irrespective of race, class, age, or ability – to be recognised as an equal party to the social contract which is underpinned by law and legal systems.

---

[9] *Op cit*, de Beauvoir, fn 8, p 293.
[10] *Op cit*, de Beauvoir, fn 8, p 16.
[11] See, further, Chapters 6 and 10.
[12] See, further, Naffine, N, *Law and the Sexes*, 1990, Sydney: Allen & Unwin.

Introduction

Subsumed within the quest for equality there exist many lines of inquiry. From what origins, for example, have the inequalities which have for long been enshrined in law derived? Or to rephrase the question, *why* is society and law – from a feminist perspective – a reflection of masculine power and authority? One aspect of feminist scholarship – whether engaged in from a political or legal perspective – seeks to understand and to develop a secure theoretical base of knowledge from which to press for reform. Other scholars have long been, and remain, primarily concerned with the analysis of specific inequalities based on gender. Thus, for example, the criminal justice system, the law relating to the family, employment law and other substantive areas of law form the focus for study with a view to the eradication of often subtle but pervasive gender-based inequalities.

Feminist legal scholarship is frequently presented as having differing phases or waves, although none of these is totally distinct or isolated from other phases.[13] First phase feminism which may be dated from mid Victorian times to the present time, although most vociferous from the 1960s through to the mid 1980s, is dedicated to unmasking the features which exclude women from public life. As Ngaire Naffine has written '... the first phase can be characterised by its concern with the male monopoly of law'.[14] The quest is for equality, whether in employment generally, or in the professions or in politics. First phase feminists work within the existing system in order to remove the inequalities of the system, without necessarily questioning the system itself. This liberally inspired enterprise undertaken by the women's rights' movement accepted law as traditionally portrayed: the rational, objective, fair, gender-neutral arbiter in disputes over rights which applied to undifferentiated but individual and autonomous legal subjects. The objections voiced by feminists in this phase was to not law *per se* but to 'bad law': law which operated to the exclusion or detriment of women.[15]

'Second phase feminism', which dominated the late 1970s and 1980s, addresses not so much the substantive (legal) inequalities under which women exist – although these remain a focus for action – but rather the legal and societal structure which perpetuates inequalities. Here the focus is less on the male monopoly of law and the correlative inequalities of women, but on understanding, 'the deep-seated male orientation which infects all its practices'.[16] First phase feminists had made many remarkable advances for female equality. However, despite these achievements, it remained the case

---

[13] Feminist scholars differ on the interpretation of these phases, which may be no more than different emphases on differing aspects of the movement.

[14] *Op cit*, Naffine, fn 12, p 2.

[15] See, eg, on the male monopoly of law and the legal profession, Sachs, A and Hoff Wilson, J, *Sexism and the Law*, 1978, Oxford: Martin Robertson; Atkins, S and Hoggett, B, *Women and the Law*, 1984, Oxford: Basil Blackwell.

[16] *Op cit*, Naffine, fn 12, p 2.

that women were treated differently and discriminated against. If women enjoy the same capacities and talents as men, and all that is required is an analysis, recognition and reversal of the existing inequalities, how is it that women remain, still, despite all the reforms, the 'second' and 'lesser sex'? The answer lies in the masculinity of law and legal systems. For second phase feminists, of differing political persuasions, the root problem with law lies in its pretended impartiality, objectivity and rationality. By assuming gender-neutral language, law masks the extent to which law is permeated by male constructs, male standards. The 'reasonable man' so beloved by the common law, does not include women. If women are to be 'reasonable', within the legal meaning of the term, they must adopt the male standard of reasonableness.

The analyses – and there is no single or simple analysis of this work – centres on the construction of society as patriarchal in its broadest sense. Radical feminists, Marxist/socialist feminists, all – in their differing manner – focus not on specific inequalities supported by law, but on the societal structure which forms the foundation for law.[17] Cultural, or difference feminism, on the other hand, focuses more specifically on the gender issue – on women's difference from men – and its ramifications. To take but one example for introductory purposes, radical feminists[18] argue that the true source of inequality lies not just in the failure of society (and law) to accommodate women on an equal basis, but rather that law and society is deeply gendered in all its aspects and that the relationship between the sexes is determined, not by some historical or cultural accident, but by the dominant position assumed by men which results in female subordination. Sexual relations – in the broadest sense – are explained not so much by biological or gender differences, but by the dominance of men and the subordination of women, a subordination supported, reinforced and maintained by men and which many women unconsciously also support. The patriarchal tradition may – as with so much of legal and political philosophy – be traced back to Ancient Greece. We find in Aristotle, for example, the clearest exposition of the view that the man is the head of the household; that it is he who holds authority over 'his' wife and children '... for the male is more fitted to rule than the female, unless conditions are quite contrary to nature ...'.[19]

This *assumption* about women's appropriate role, based on women's lesser physical strength and her role in childbearing, has carried forward throughout society, universally and from time immemorial, and remains a principal site of women's oppression. It is for reasons such as this that feminist Shulamith Firestone argued in the 1970s, that the essence of women's subordination

---

[17] For further analysis, see Chapters 6–9.
[18] See MacKinnon, C, *Feminism, Unmodified: Discourses on Life and Law*, 1987, Cambridge, Mass: Harvard UP; *Toward a Feminist Theory of the State*, 1989, Cambridge Mass: Harvard UP.
[19] Aristotle, *The Politics*, Sinclair, TA (trans), 1962, London: Penguin, 1259a37. (See *Sourcebook*, pp 281–86.)

Introduction

remains situated in women's biological role, and that until reproductive technology is developed to the point of freeing women from the oppression of the womb, women will never be truly free.[20] But, while medical science and technology come closer to the era of emancipating women from the tyranny of childbirth, and society recognises (even if it does not implement) the need for childcare facilities to release women's energies for other pursuits, there remains a deep social and political resistance to women abandoning or giving less priority to the traditional mothering role. Further, demands such as Firestone's, for the release of women from traditional roles, lead to spontaneous adverse reactions from those whose political agenda turns on the centrality of the family and 'family values' for the stability and health of society. Women making such demands are thus seen as threatening the traditional social order and the Moral Right is quick to deny the demands and cloak their denial in the rhetoric of biological determinism.

'Third phase feminism' goes beyond the analysis of law as male monopoly, and questions law's claim to objectivity and rationality:

> ... by maintaining the appearance of dispassionate neutrality, law is able quietly to go about its task of assisting in the reproduction of the conditions which subordinate women (as well as other social groups).[21]

Third phase feminism, while accepting the premise of law's maleness, questions whether – as second phase feminists submitted – law and legal systems operate in an *invariably* sexist manner. The perception of third phase feminists is that while law is gendered, and deeply so, this does not necessarily mean that law operates consistently, inevitably or uniformly to promote male interests. Rather, law is too complicated a phenomenon to be portrayed in this holistic manner. What needs to be understood, from this perspective, is the manner in which law responds to differing problems, and in its operation reveals its well concealed gender bias. The approach of third phase feminists is one which necessarily rejects the 'grand theories' of second phase feminism: law in the reflection of the society it serves, is as complex as that society. In Carol Smart's analysis of the family, for example, the author demonstrates that while the law relating to abortion,[22] the law relating to financial provision for women on divorce, and the law relating to domestic violence,[23] advance protection for women, it does so unevenly, and in a manner which conceals the patriarchal ordering of law and society.[24]

---

[20] See Firestone, S, *The Dialectic of Sex: The Case for Feminist Revolution*, 1972, New York: Bantam.

[21] *Op cit*, Naffine, fn 12, p 3.

[22] On which see Chapter 10.

[23] On which see Chapter 11.

[24] Carol Smart's writing is prolific: see, eg, Smart, C, *The Ties That Bind: Law, Marriage and the Reproduction of Patriarchal Relations*, 1984, London: Routledge and Kegan Paul; *Feminism and the Power of Law*, 1989, London: Routledge and Kegan Paul; *Law, Crime and Sexuality: Essays in Feminism*, 1995, London: Sage. See, also, Olsen, F, 'The family and the market: a study of ideology and legal reform' (1983) 96 Harv L Rev 7.

The dominant current phase of feminist thought reflects both the rejection of 'grand theory' and the uncertainties and doubts concerning the role of law. Arising out of the late 1980s and continuing through the 1990s, feminists adopt postmodernist philosophy which questions all 'meta-narratives' and denies the validity of global explanations. Postmodernist political and social theory is beset with doubt, uncertainty and fragmentation.[25] Grand theorising, whether in the form of liberalism or Marxist-socialist theory falls under attack, as do feminist theories which espouse monocausal explanations of women's inequalities.

Accordingly, and as is evident from the above introductory discussion, it cannot be assumed that feminist legal scholars adopt a united stance in relation to their subject over and above the unifying desire and quest for equality. Feminist jurisprudence, to use a much overused but nonetheless useful phrase, is a 'broad church'. As will be seen, within this 'church' co-exist, *inter alia*, liberal feminists, cultural or difference feminists, socialist feminists, Marxist feminists, radical feminists and feminists who centre their scholarship on particular issues raised by race and gender orientation.

The breadth of the avenues of inquiry should cause no surprise in a postmodern era in which traditional modes of thought about society and law have come under analytical scrutiny, leading to a denial that society can be understood through the 'grand theories' which have hitherto sought to explain the world. Fragmentation, individuation and uncertainty all portray postmodern thought. Within feminist scholarship, this postmodernist approach challenges the notion that women can be encapsulated within some single theory of society and law; denies that the interests of all women are the same, as if there is some 'essential women' imbued with the characteristics and needs of every woman, irrespective of age, race or class. There accordingly exists nowadays a rich diversity in feminist writings.

Given the contemporary dominance of postmodern thought, with its overarching critique of monocausal and essentialist social and legal theory, and the postmodern emphasis on analysis untainted by philosophy and all forms of meta-narrative, it can be argued that to attach the label feminist jurisprudence to legal scholarship is to perpetuate the modernist mode of thought in a postmodern age. Postmodern analysis thus poses a challenge to feminist jurisprudence, but also offers much potential. Insisting on analysis of the local, and the specific, realities of women's lives rather than postulating monocausal explanations of women's inequalities facilitates a broadening of the boundaries of feminist scholarship, and a more comprehensive, inclusionary understanding of the relationship between law and women's lives. The postmodern critique does not deny the value of social and legal theory cast in modernist terms. Feminist scholarship, particularly since the 1960s, with its focus on the inequality of women in law and society, has,

---

[25] See, further, Chapters 6 and 10.

notwithstanding its tendency to essentialism and monocausality, not only provided a wealth of theoretical analyses of women's condition, but also achieved much by way of achieving legal and political reform. The sheer growth in interest in feminist analyses within the academy is testament to the strength of feminist legal thought. Feminist scholarship, irrespective of its former modernist tendencies, has greatly advanced the equality of women across numerous spheres and retains, notwithstanding postmodern critiques, its critical force.

No school of thought can exist in an historical vacuum: each is dependent upon – and is a reaction against – preceding modes of thought. By way of example, Karl Marx could not have conceived his radical and original thesis which culminated in an enduring Marxist theory without a detailed analysis of industrialisation and the capitalist system. The charge that Marxism 'has not worked' and/or that this is now a 'post Marxist world' does not, however, signify the actual or imminent demise of the intellectual challenge posed by Marxist thought. Marxist theory continues to engage scholarship as a powerful challenge to and critique of liberalism. So too with feminism and feminist jurisprudence. The postmodern challenge denies the possibility of 'grand theory' and demands recognition that the construction of social reality is far more complex than any one modernist 'meta-narrative' could encompass. However, the meta-narratives of modern thought continue to exert their influence and to engage the imagination.

The postmodern challenge, while persuasive in its demand that feminist jurisprudence open itself up to the very differing conditions – social, economic and political – under which women exist, and recognise the diverse characteristics of different women – in terms of race, colour, age, class and gender orientation – does not, as will be argued further later in this book, necessarily lead to the inescapable conclusion that theorising on the grand scale has no continuing relevance to all women. As will be demonstrated throughout this work, women, as a class – though not a minority statistically – have been consistently subordinated throughout history by differing cultural, social, economic and political conditions, conditions which become supported by the governing legal regime. These forces, which may be subsumed within the term patriarchy, which is discussed principally in Chapter 3, continue to manifest themselves in the contemporary world, albeit under different guises. Within the Western industrial 'liberal' world, while women enjoy *de jure* equal economic opportunities, there nevertheless remain barriers to the *de facto* achievement of equality. Also within the Western 'liberal' world, women's rights to autonomy and equality are hampered by legal systems which reflect the characteristics of their predominantly male architects: the legislatures and judges.[26] A woman's right to control her own reproductivity – a primary

---

[26] See Chapters 2 and 11.

feature of individual autonomy, equality and freedom – is by no means guaranteed. Those rights are determined by the framework of legal rules and medical practices relating to contraception, abortion and sterilisation. Law, religion, social policy and the medical profession combine to ensure that matters relating to women's fertility and capacity to reproduce are regulated by the State, regulation justified by its defenders as necessary in the interests of health, procreation, and by the competing claims of the moral rights of the foetus.

It is impossible in a brief introduction to demonstrate the many and differing cultural and political forces at work which have ensured women's inequalities. Each society is, quite simply, culturally and historically different. However, by way of introductory illustration, if one considers further for a moment, and this is discussed more fully in Chapter 10, the issue of reproductive control, and the converse side of the coin, that of women's right to control their own fertility, it becomes rapidly apparent that women's rights in some societies are subordinated to State policy. Population control programmes, encouraged by the United Nations and adopted by many 'Third World' countries, involve not only the use of contraceptive devices which women in the industrialised West have rejected on the basis of lack of safety, but also policies such as China's one-child policy, and, particularly in India and Pakistan, the forced sterilisation of women and men in order to control reproductivity. In Roman Catholic countries, by contrast, Church and State combine to deny women full autonomy over their own fertility by the institutionalised opposition, on doctrinal grounds, to contraception and abortion on demand.

It may perhaps be argued that the only political scenario in which feminist activity can be effective is within Western liberal democracies. It is true that the most dramatic advances in the rights of women – particularly in the sphere of politics and the economy – have been achieved under such conditions. Throughout much of the Western world, women have secured *de jure* equality in the public sphere of employment. In Europe, the Court of Justice of the European Communities,[27] in its interpretations of the right to equality,[28] has ensured that employers do not, and cannot, discriminate between men and women in terms of pay and conditions of work. Feminists in the United States of America, with its written Constitution and Bill of Rights, have achieved dramatic improvements in women's rights. Sexual harassment in the 1980s became judicially accepted to be a form of discrimination against women, contrary to the 'equal protection' clause of the

---

[27] As the Court continues to be labelled, despite the Community now being singular and the advent of the European Union.
[28] Treaty of Rome, Art 119.

Constitution.[29] Equally, the (limited) right to abortion was secured under the constitutional guarantee of the right to privacy. Feminist lawyer Catharine MacKinnon and author and activist Andrea Dworkin have long campaigned to bring pornography within the confines of legal protection for women against the discrimination allegedly caused by pornography.[30] While this campaign to date has been unsuccessful in terms of legal reform, it reveals not only the potential power but also limitations of a written constitution as an agent for legal reform.[31]

However, whilst the legal and political climate of Western democracies offers the greatest likelihood of legal reform for women, it should not be concluded that reforms cannot be secured for and by women in very differing societies.[32] Whilst women in many societies are powerless to oppose the combined forces of law, patriarchy and religion, the agencies of the United Nations have done much to reveal the nature and extent of women's inequalities in such societies, and remain constant in the quest for the improvement of women's position in society. In a world increasingly characterised by globalisation, no longer do the injustices suffered by women remain behind 'closed doors'.[33] If women have secured much in the West, although as will be seen, not yet *de facto* equality, there remain vast and intractable difficulties for women in all parts of the world.[34] The task for feminist jurisprudence – in all its manifestations – is to research and analyse the conditions of women under law, fully cognisant of the differing cultural, legal and political contexts, in order to improve the status of women.

The success of the women's liberation movement from the 1960s onwards in exposing patriarchal control and demanding equality in all spheres of life, was received neither with equanimity nor without resistance. A backlash set in. Feminism was explicitly and implicitly attacked: the average great Western male – irrespective of class – collectively declared himself to be an endangered species. Women were threatening the 'natural order': invading the (male) workplace; 'deserting the home'; breaking up families and neglecting husbands and children. As Susan Faludi has persuasively argued, the reaction was uniform and universal: women needed to be put back in 'their' place – the

---

[29] See MacKinnon, C, 'Sexual harassment', in MacKinnon, 1987, *op cit*, fn 18; see, also, *op cit*, MacKinnon, 1989, fn 18.

[30] See, further, Chapter 12.

[31] The effect of differing constitutional arrangements in differing jurisdictions will become clearer in discussion of differing aspects of feminist jurisprudence.

[32] Of paramount importance, however, is also to recognise the dangers of Western cultural and political imperialism in relation to women in very differing societies.

[33] See, further, Chapter 2 for data published by the United Nations.

[34] See Cook, R (ed), *Human Rights of Women: National and International Perspectives*, 1994, Pennsylvania: Pennsylvania UP.

home. Whether analysing the film industry, television industry, the press, the fashion and beauty industry, Faludi presents the same depressing chronicle of men in power, throughout the 1980s backlash, excluding women, opposing their advance, seeking to portray women not as achievers who had acquired equal status but misguided creatures who, in their lust for equality, had sacrificed themselves on the altar of success, in the process losing much which is deemed to be sacred in women's lives (namely that which must be preserved if male supremacy is to be upheld).[35]

Feminism thus became blamed for women's perceived plight: that of spinsterhood, childlessness, psychological pressures: if only women had remained in 'their place', women – spurred on by the women's liberation movement – would not be suffering the stresses and strains of the contemporary, complex world (and men would continue to have enjoyed the luxury of the wife and mother at home, nurturing and caring for him and the children). But as Faludi argues, the march towards women's equality has never been a smooth passage, never enjoyed a continuum of success resulting in the achievement of full freedom and equality. Rather, the march has been disjointed and frustrated:

> An accurate charting of Western women's progress through history might look more like a corkscrew tilted slightly to one side, its loops inching closer to the line of freedom with the passage of time – but, like a mathematical curve approaching infinity, never touching its goal. Woman is trapped on this asymptotic spiral, turning endlessly through the generations, drawing ever nearer to her destination without ever arriving.[36]

The explanation for this erratic progress is fourfold. First, the early movement (especially before the Second World War), as with all political movements, depended on those vociferous activists who were prepared to challenge the existing social and legal order, and to pay a high price for so doing. The clearest evidence of this may be seen in relation to the struggle for the franchise, when members of the suffragette movement suffered harassment and imprisonment in pursuit of their goal of equality.[37] Secondly, in order to advance any political movement, there exists the need to raise the consciousness of those who are being oppressed. Feminism, like Marxism, adopts consciousness raising as a primary tool in the struggle for equality.[38] So ingrained has prejudice and discrimination against women been throughout history that the patriarchal order – the superiority of men and the inferiority of women – appears a 'natural' (and therefore 'right') ordering. Not only men but also women have needed to be made aware of the very deep-

---

[35] See Faludi, S, *Backlash: The Undeclared War Against Women*, 1992, London: Vintage.
[36] *Ibid*, p 67.
[37] For an overview of the movement, see, further, Chapter 2. See, also, Strachey, R, *The Cause* (1928), 1978, London: Virago.
[38] See below, pp 19–21.

Introduction

rooted nature of the social and legal discrimination which has operated against women's interests. Thirdly, women have for so long been denied equal access to public offices and equal opportunities in the market place that it has been particularly difficult for women to find their voices. Women were silenced by inequality, and the acceptance, by the majority of society, that this equality was somehow 'natural'. The removal of legal disabilities and legal discrimination has proved an uphill struggle. The struggle for formal legal equality has been, in the industrialised, democratic West largely, but not yet totally, successful. While the legal barriers to full equality are progressively dismantled, social and economic barriers remain. The continued reliance on women's unpaid labour in the home; the high proportion of women in unskilled, part time, employment; the small percentage of professional women who struggle through the 'glass ceiling' in their careers all evidence the continuing difficulties which women seeking equality must overcome. Fourthly, and finally, it must be recognised that feminist jurisprudence is not a coherent, monolithic, unified endeavour. As noted above, within feminist jurisprudence there exist many differing areas of interests, specialisms, objectives. Not all feminist legal scholars agree on aims and objectives, other than as to the removal of remaining discriminations against women. The differing schools of thought[39] are testimony to the diversity of feminist scholarship. This diversity should not be regarded as a disadvantage or shortcoming of feminist scholarship, or indicating that feminist jurisprudential scholarship has somehow 'lost its way', but rather represents the wide and healthy diversity of the ongoing debates.

Feminist jurisprudence has also faced a different challenge. It has been argued that a feminist jurisprudence cannot come into being, let alone exist, given the gendered nature of conventional, male jurisprudence which forecloses or excludes a feminist analysis of law from a jurisprudential perspective. One analysis of this dilemma is that to enter into the world of jurisprudence is tacitly to accept the legitimacy of law, which is essentially male, and legal theory which is founded on the law it seeks to explain.[40] Thus it is argued that feminist jurisprudence suggests complicity with masculine jurisprudence. However, alternatively viewed, a feminist jurisprudence – which reflects the scholarship of half of the academy – women – has much to offer both as a critique of masculine legal theory, and more importantly as theorising about law from the perspective of the constituencies of law which have been traditionally excluded.[41] Thus continued feminist engagement with

---

[39] Discussed in Part III.
[40] See West, R, 'Jurisprudence and gender' (1988) 55 Chicago UL Rev 1; Litteton, C, 'In search of a feminist jurisprudence' (1987) 10 Harvard Women's LJ 1; Grosz, E, 'What is feminist theory?', in Pateman, C and Grosz, E (eds), *Feminist Challenges: Law and Social Theory*, 1986, London: Allen & Unwin, p 190; cf Smart, C, *Feminism and the Power of Law*, 1989, London: Routledge and Kegan Paul.
[41] Constituencies, rather than constituency, is consciously formulated to avoid the impression that there is, can be, or should be, a universalising, totalising, meta-narrative feminist jurisprudence.

conventional jurisprudence, far from implying acceptance of its terms of reference, is both necessary and important. Feminist jurisprudence encompasses not 'just' 'women' – howsoever woman might be conceptualised[42] – but multivocal, multicultural, theorising of women within their own particular time and place. Jurisprudence is not, and never has been, a cohesive, coherent discipline. It has however, conventionally, been a male world. Feminist jurisprudence offers challenges to conventional male jurisprudence which that discipline cannot ignore.

THE FEMINIST GENDER DEBATE

While the aims and objectives of all feminist legal scholars are directed constantly towards the understanding of, and the removal of, inequalities and discriminations supported by law, as with any philosophical, political or legal movement differing approaches towards the subject can be discerned. The diversity within feminist jurisprudence – as with mainstream feminism – has significant implications for the analysis of women's condition in law and society. One of the most vociferous debates has taken place between feminists on perceptions about the nature of society, law and legal systems and the implications these bear for women's equality. Equally powerful has been the debate about gender: the analyses of the equality, sameness and/or difference of women from men and, more crucially, the difference that gender makes. This debate, which dominated the 1980s, emphasises the breadth of feminist scholarship while at the same time suggesting an ineradicable and inevitable diversity within feminist jurisprudence. Gender has been, and remains, an organising focus for feminist analysis. The gender question is thus central to all schools of feminist thought, whether liberal, Marxist-socialist, cultural, radical or postmodern.

What is a woman? The gender question

What is a woman? This question, posed by Simone de Beauvoir,[43] in her now seminal work, *The Second Sex*,[44] is answered by de Beauvoir, in part, in the following passage:

> ... humanity is male and man defines woman not in herself but as relative to him; she is not regarded as an autonomous being ... And she is simply what man decrees; thus she is called 'the sex', by which is meant that she appears essentially to the male as a sexual being. For him she is sex – absolute sex, no

---

[42] On the complexities of this see, further, Chapter 9.
[43] *Op cit*, de Beauvoir, fn 8, p 13.
[44] *Op cit*, de Beauvoir, fn 8.

less. She is defined and differentiated with reference to man and not he with reference to her; she is the incidental, the inessential as opposed to the essential. He is the Subject, he is the Absolute – she is the Other.[45]

Woman as 'Other'

The idea of woman as 'the Other' is representative of linguistic analysis which is premised on binary opposites. Each concept in language contains within itself a primary and subordinate characteristic. The meaning of a word cannot correctly be understood unless both the primary meaning and its (silent) opposite is considered. Thus to understand the word 'presence' an understanding of its opposite, 'absence' must be incorporated. When considering the term 'masculine', its oppositional 'feminine' must be incorporated; for 'man', 'woman'; for 'universality', 'specificity'; for 'unity', 'diversity'. As discussed further in Chapter 9, each term thus contains a binary opposite. In the analysis of poststructuralist Jacques Derrida, these opposites are both interdependent and hierarchically arranged, with the leading term being superior, the opposite being inferior and weaker. In order to fully comprehend the meaning of words and concepts, they must be deconstructed in order to tease out these oppositions.

From this perspective, 'woman' is socially constructed in relation to, and as inferior to, the superior male. The man – who from infancy has been nurtured to assume an unquestioned superiority[46] – defines women's role, creates and maintains a mythology of woman based on her femininity, weakness and subordination to his power. Citing de Beauvoir once more:

> One is not born, but rather becomes, a woman. No biological, psychological, or economic fate determines the figure that the human female presents in society; it is civilisation as a whole that produces this creature, intermediate between male and eunuch, which is described as feminine.[47]

Thus far 'woman' is defined as a socially constructed individual, differentiated from man. The characterisation of 'woman' in the linguistic tradition of binary opposites, as the polar opposite to man, represents woman as the 'alternative', 'weaker', 'Other', whose identity can only be determined in relation to the more powerful construct 'man' which stands as a referent for 'woman'.

In *The Second Sex*, the author analyses the manner and means by which women are considered the 'Other' (and inferior) sex. For de Beauvoir, the

---

[45] *Op cit*, de Beauvoir, fn 8, p 16.
[46] See, on this, *op cit*, de Beauvoir, fn 8, particularly Book II, Part IV, Chapter 1; see, also, Chodorow, N, *The Reproduction of Mothering: Psychoanalysis and the Sociology of Gender*, 1978, Berkeley, California: California UP, Part II.
[47] *Op cit*, de Beauvoir, fn 8, Part IV, Chapter 1, p 295.

standard by which all matters are judged is that of the male gender. If maleness is the automatic reference point for the assessment of societal status, it follows that woman 'being different' is the 'other' sex. To be a woman, de Beauvoir argued, is to be defined as a womb, an ovary, to be female, and to be so defined is 'to imprison her in her sex'. It is gender, the social construction of woman, as opposed to biological sex, which is the focus for feminist analysis.

The concept of woman as other explains much of the traditional and continuing stereotyping of women as the bearers of children, the nurturers of children, the homemakers and (unpaid) homekeepers. The categorisation based on sex facilitates the perpetuation of low expectations of and for women; explains the lesser involvement in all aspects of the workforce; the lower pay; the concentration in part time employment; the lesser chances of promotion – that glass ceiling through which so many women fail to pass. Society – or those with power in society – constructs gender by adopting the physical and psychological distinctions between men and women. Law, being largely the reflection of society, adopts the social construction of gender and translates it into legal norms.[48] In the course of the struggle for social and legal equality, the gender question was, predominantly in the late 1970s and 1980s, placed centrestage in the feminist debate, especially in the United States of America. While liberal feminists' primary focus had been on removing the social and legal obstacles to women's equal civil and political rights within the liberal democratic State, others turned attention on the analysis of de Beauvoir's perception of women as social construct and its relevance to the maintenance of women's inferior position within the patriarchal state. What cultural/social forces determine women's identity and role in society? How can the consequences of gender be determined?

While the distinction between 'sex' and 'gender' has provided and proven to be a useful tool for analysis for feminist scholarship – most particularly in modern thought – a postmodern deconstructionist analysis of gender reveals its own complexities and the disutility of the very term in socio-political and legal analysis.[49] As Judith Butler[50] states: '[T]he limits of the discursive analysis of gender presuppose and pre-empt the possibilities of imaginable and realisable gender configurations within culture.'[51] For the time being, however, to facilitate discussion of gender and its role in feminist jurisprudence, these analytical and theoretical difficulties are put aside, to be

---

[48] On the difficulties caused by legal determination of gender at birth for the purposes of marriage law in England, see O'Donovan, K, *Sexual Divisions in Law*, 1985, London: Weidenfeld and Nicolson, Chapter 3. (See *Sourcebook*, pp 171–76.)

[49] For a recent, in-depth postmodern analysis, see Heinze, E, 'Discourses of sex: classical, modernist, post-modernist' (1998) 67 Nordic Journal of International Law 37.

[50] At the time of writing, Associate Professor of Humanities, John Hopkins University.

[51] Butler, J, *Gender Trouble: Feminism and the Subversion of Identity*, 1990, New York: Routledge, p 9.

Introduction

returned to in Chapter 9. The consequences of gender identity are conceptually very different from the question as to how women are socially and legally constructed. Much of the feminist debate in the 1970s and 1980s, which focused on the analysis of women's 'sameness' or 'difference' (to/from men), concentrating on the issue of whether and how men and women are 'different' or 'equal' or 'the same', distracted attention from the major issue: what difference does gender make? To life? To law?

At the heart of the gender debate lie the questions 'what difference – if any – does gender difference make?' and 'to what does gender difference make a difference?' In the third century BC, Aristotle formulated his central concept of justice: namely that equal cases should be treated alike, and that unequal cases should be treated differently.[52] In the case of women, it will be seen, this doctrine has had the effect of treating women not only differently, but as second-class citizens.

At this point, a word of caution concerning the merits of the gender debate is perhaps appropriate. On the one hand, embroilment in the sameness/difference debate may divert attention and valuable analysis away from the central task of redressing legal and social inequalities. On the other hand, the gender 'sameness versus difference' debate is both important and inevitable in the pursuit of an understanding as to why society and law have consistently denied to women an equal role and status in society, and in the movement towards the eradication of the discrimination(s) endured by women over the centuries. Understanding the 'difference that difference makes' has also facilitated analysis of the manner in which the operation of law is critically affected by gender difference. By way of example, feminist legal scholars have analysed the criminal law and criminal justice system and demonstrated convincingly how the law and legal system operates against the interests of women – how the law and legal system 'excludes' women and women's particular characteristics from its operational ambit.[53]

The differing schools of feminist thought, considered in Part III, adopt differing approaches to the issue of gender. For liberal feminists, gender *per se*, is theoretically unproblematic: what is required is the removal of such formal legal inequalities which bar women from entering public life on the basis of full equality. Marxist-socialist feminists[54] adopt Marxist political philosophy and accordingly theorise women's inequality within the context of class stratification. Difference, or cultural, feminist theory,[55] on the other hand, albeit in differing ways, focuses on the perception that women and men have

---

[52] *Op cit*, Aristotle, fn 19.
[53] See the discussion, eg, on the law relating to provocation, rape trials and marital rape in Chapter 11.
[54] See Chapter 6.
[55] See Chapter 7.

differing modes of reasoning, and different socially-constructed roles, which are explanatory of women's inferiority and exclusion from the gendered, male, world. By contrast, radical feminism,[56] epitomised by Catharine MacKinnon's jurisprudence, conceptualises the question of gender in the light of power relationships, and the disparity of power between men and women, supported by law and society. From this perception, woman's role is determined by her socially constructed gender, which ensures her inequality and subordination in relation to law and society which is characterised by male dominance.

Alternatively, in postmodern feminist thought, the gender question is altogether more complex and uncertain.[57] As seen above, postmodern feminist thought rejects any form of universalising theory, including theories of gender. Gender thus becomes a site of contestation, not only as to its interpretation, but also as to its significance in legal and social theory. The deconstruction of gender, and the rejection of totalising theories, leads to an understanding both of the indeterminacy and fragility of the very concept of gender, and of the need for feminist jurisprudence to avoid theory which adopts an essentialist view of woman as its focus.

The complaint made by many contemporary feminists is that the emphasis placed on the equality versus difference debate in the 1980s, and the concomitant discussion of relevant differences between men and women (the binary opposites) has caused feminist theorists to fall into the trap of universality and superficiality in relation to what the all-encompassing word 'woman' means. One consequence of this error has been the exclusion of many women's voices. For feminists of colour, for working-class feminists, for lesbian feminists, the writing of many feminists – particularly before the late 1980s – ignored them, failed to give them a voice, and accordingly was guilty of precisely that which feminists critique in their analyses of masculine jurisprudence and theory: namely exclusion.

Radical feminist analysis,[58] for example, has been criticised as most accurately representing principally the demands and interests of white, middle-class women. These claims, if substantiated, represent a powerful challenge to feminist scholarship, and suggest that an essential plurality and diversity characterises feminist thought more accurately. However, as will be seen in Chapter 9, there are dangers with overemphasising the force of anti-essentialist arguments. At the same time, however, it is undeniable that feminist theory must be inclusionary, not exclusionary. The strength of the anti-essentialists' argument lies in opening up further the frontiers for

---

[56] See Chapter 8.
[57] See Chapter 9.
[58] See Chapter 9.

Introduction

research and knowledge: the constructive analysis of specific inequalities suffered by different groups of women. The arguments become destructive of a coherent feminist analysis, whether the approach taken is that of cultural feminism, radical feminism or liberal feminism, if that analysis turns its back on the central organising concept: that of woman. For all its deficiencies as a tool for analysis, the concept of woman is one which is central to an understanding of the inequalities perpetuated by patriarchal society and law. The term 'woman' is thus a central organising construct. It is as unrealistic to argue that the effect of pollution on trees cannot meaningfully be discussed without understanding the extent to which beeches, conifers, elms and oaks suffer from that pollution, as it is to abandon the intellectual and political quest for women's equality under law.

FEMINIST LEGAL METHODS

The Western liberal tradition, the laws which serve that tradition and legal theory which presents analyses of law, portray themselves as class-, age-, race- and gender-neutral. It is this well sustained myth of law's neutrality to gender (in particular) which feminist legal theorists seek to unmask and bring into the clear light of day in order to bring about societal change. As has been seen, the task is both legal and political. In order to achieve the objective of full equality for women, feminist legal scholars adopt a number of methods. Each of these, notwithstanding the complexity inherent in the analysis of gender, is inextricably linked to the issue of gender equality sameness and difference. These methods, which intersect and are by no means mutually exclusive, may be labelled:

(a) consciousness raising/unsilencing women;

(b) asking 'the woman question'/critique/textual deconstruction;

(c) theorising law's gendered nature;

(d) feminist practical reasoning.

Consciousness raising

Women will not demand, and will not achieve, substantive (as opposed to formal) equality unless and until the substantive and procedural legal disabilities under which women have laboured since time immemorial are understood. Consciousness raising is a process whereby women become aware, through discussion and debate of their own and others' situations and the disabilities which are imposed by society and law. There is again a parallel here with the techniques of Marxism – that of raising the awareness of those who accept the ordering of society as somehow 'natural' when in fact that ordering is the product of societal forces. In the case of Marxism, the explanation for the class structure, and the capitalist system which maintains that structure, is explained by the relations of production and the economic system prevailing at any point in time in history. This 'historical materialism' determines societal structure and an individual's place within that structure. Thus an understanding of class, and class domination, is explained by socio-historical economic development. Only when this is understood will the 'working class' – the proletariat – shake off an acceptance of the given order as 'natural' and press for the change necessary to free them from capitalist domination. With feminism, the process of consciousness raising is analogous. Unless and until women understand why their position in society has come to be, and why women's inferiority is both systematically sustained and sustainable, there will not exist sufficient awareness raised for pressure for change. In one sense, consciousness raising represents an overarching method under which other methods are subsumed.

In order to create the climate for change, women's voices must be heard: their experiences recounted and the commonalities and differences between those experiences perceived. Moreover, in the process of this 'story telling', the individual and the group becomes empowered through the release from isolation. Consciousness raising is a process which may take place in private group settings, but is also one which operates on a public, institutional level, in the analysis of, for example, the manner in which the State and its laws, discriminate against women, exclude them from the public domain, or, when including them, do so in a discriminatory and patriarchal manner. Leslie Bender describes the process as follows:

> Feminist consciousness raising creates knowledge by exploring common experiences and patterns that emerge from shared tellings of life events. What were experienced as personal hurts individually suffered reveal themselves as a collective experience of oppression.[59]

There are difficulties entailed in this analysis, not least the risk of 'essentialism' or 'ethnocentrism': that is to say the assumption that the experience of all women, irrespective of race, age, sexual orientation, ability or class may be 'represented' by one, or any one, woman.[60] As the self-styled black lesbian feminist socialist writer Audrey Lorde argued in 1984:

> ... [b]y and large within the women's movement today, white women focus upon their oppression as women and ignore differences of race, sexual preference class, and age. There is a pretence to a homogeneity of experience covered by the word sisterhood that does not in fact exist.[61]

---

[59] Bender, L, 'A lawyer's primer on feminist theory and tort' (1988) 38 J Legal Educ 3, p 9.
[60] For discussion, see Chapters 6, 9 and 10.
[61] Lorde, A, 'Age, race, class and sex: women redefining difference', in *Sister Outsider*, 1984, Trumansburg: Crossing, pp 114–15.

Introduction

And consciousness raising has given rise to disputes between feminists as to their commonality. As Katharine Bartlett has written:

> Feminists disagree, for example, about whether women can voluntarily choose heterosexuality, or motherhood; or about whether feminists have more to gain or lose from restrictions against pornography, surrogate motherhood, or about whether women should be subject to a military draft. If they disagree about each other's roles in an oppressive society, some feminists accuse others of complicity in the oppression of women.[62]

Notwithstanding these difficulties, consciousness raising provides a forum for women's voices which might otherwise have remained silent or unheard; it also provides the means by which the many common experiences of women – despite their diversity – such as sexual harassment, rape and other violence, may be shared. If the feminist movement of the 1960s and 1970s was rightly charged with 'essentialism', the corrective voices have surely now been heard and acknowledged. Heterosexual women may experience patriarchal domination within the family; lesbian women arguably do not. White women may be oppressed by gender and class, but they are not, in Western societies, oppressed also by race; women of colour on the other hand, experience oppression not just on the basis of gender but also on the basis of race and class. The value of consciousness raising, however, should not be lost within the feminist debate on essentialism and diversity: rather women's diversity must be accommodated within the debate in order to further the dismantling of inequality.

Asking the 'woman question'

The woman question demands explanations for women's exclusion from all areas of life: it demands justification from those who perpetuate women's exclusion. The woman question asks: why is it that despite more or less equal employment opportunities, it is still women who undertake the child-rearing and domestic responsibilities within the home? It asks, in relation to medical issues, by what right the law prohibits or limits abortion against a woman's wishes; or sanctions sterilisation of women without their consent; or sanctions coerced caesarean sections. The woman question also asks how politicians, in their role of law makers, constructs the image of woman in the law. Remaining within the field of law and medicine, an analysis of the parliamentary debates preceding the English Abortion Act 1967 reveals that women were constructed as, *inter alia*, 'irresponsible, immature and emotional', in contradistinction to the (predominantly male) doctors who were portrayed as, *inter alia*, 'responsible, mature, professional, rational and

---

[62] Bartlett, K, 'Feminist legal methods' (1990) 100 Harv L Rev 829. (See *Sourcebook*, pp 94–105.) On 'collaboration', see *op cit*, MacKinnon, 1989, fn 18, pp 637, 639.

objective'.[63] Only by asking the woman question, by deconstructing texts and institutional practices, can the position of women be revealed; can justifications and rationalisations be demanded and the discriminations and disabilities be removed.

The woman question is asked also when women demand explanations as to why it is that they may not serve in an equal capacity in the armed forces; or as prison guards; or (historically) why they were not allowed to vote, or to own private property after their marriage, or to have custody of their children, or to enter into contracts as free and independent individuals. The question is also addressed when, having gained formal access to previously excluded categories of employment, women find themselves subject to discrimination in the form of sexual harassment.[64]

Rules of law and institutional practices are most generally cast in gender-, race-, class- and age-neutral terms.[65] While the criminal law relating to crimes of violence ranging from assault through grievous bodily harm to murder are framed in gender-neutral language, when subjected to feminist analysis the law is deeply imbued with masculinity. Equally, the definition of crimes and defences to criminal charges are cast in neutral language. Thus, for the most part, the appearance which law presents is one of gender-blindness. The reality of law, however, is that it operates in many respects in a manner which places gender centrestage. As has been well documented, for example,[66] the English law of provocation which operates as a partial defence to a charge of murder, is constructed in such a manner as to be appropriate to male responses to threats of violence, but is wholly inappropriate in its application to women victims of violent assaults which most often occur within the family and are inflicted by a male spouse, father or other male relation.

As the recent cases of *R v Ahluwalia*[67] and *R v Thornton*[68] so eloquently testify, female victims of domestic violence who live in fear of their lives from assaults by their husbands, do not react in the spontaneous manner which the English law of provocation requires. Neither has English law, until recently,

---

[63] See Sheldon, S, 'Who is the mother to make the judgment? Construction of women in English abortion law' [1993] 1 Feminist Legal Studies 3. (See *Sourcebook*, pp 507–18.)

[64] In 1997, a former Navy wren was awarded £65,000 by an industrial tribunal for assault and harassment; another won £85,000 from the Ministry of Defence for sexual harassment, and a Lieutenant was given £100,000 by the Ministry of Defence in compensation for sexual harassment. Twenty three cases for sexual harassment are pending against the Ministry of Defence, and *The Sunday Times* estimated that a further 15 cases remain pending against the Navy: *The Sunday Times*, 4 January 1998.

[65] Exceptions of course exist. Under English law, eg, until 1994, the crime of rape could only be committed against a woman: see now the Criminal Justice and Public Order Act 1994, ss 142 and 143.

[66] And see, further, Chapter 12.

[67] [1992] 4 All ER 889.

[68] [1992] 1 All ER 306; (No 2) [1995] NLJ Rep 1888; (1995) *The Times*, 14 December.

Introduction

even acknowledged 'battered woman syndrome' and its relevance within the context of defences to a prosecution for murder.[69] 'Asking the woman question' involves, within this context, unmasking the 'maleness' of the defence of provocation and pressing for reform which makes such a defence applicable to both men and women on equal terms.

The criminal justice system – in terms of its procedures – has also fallen for analysis by asking the woman question. In rape trials, for instance, it is well documented that, whereas the male defendant is on trial for the offence, and his liberty is at risk, women's perception of the legal process is that it is they – the rape victims – who are in fact on trial. Whereas it is the man's actions and state of mind which are primarily in issue when the matter is perceived in gender-neutral terms, when the victim's perspective and perceptions are seriously considered it becomes apparent that it is she, the victim, whose lifestyle is under scrutiny, whose consent or non-consent to sexual intercourse is centrestage of the proceedings.

Feminist practical reasoning

Feminist practical reasoning furthers the enquiry into the operation of law by unmasking the juridical techniques employed in the courts: techniques which have the effect of reinforcing women's inequality.

Conventional (male) legal reasoning, like language, is characterised by abstraction, objectivity, rationality and deductive logic. Legal reasoning is also cast in a binary mould:[70] right and wrong, lawful and unlawful, just and unjust. Rules of law, while they have a 'core of certainty and penumbra of doubt',[71] and may be more or less specific, have certain definable boundaries. If applied in a mechanical fashion – irrespective of, or ignoring the individual subject of law – laws can operate harshly and unjustly. No form of legal reasoning takes place in a vacuum and the application of law must be placed within its wider context.[72] If the context within which law is analysed and applied is one constructed from one dominant perspective – man's – the law risks operating in an exclusionary fashion. We can return to the example of the law of provocation for an illustration of this phenomenon. As the case law reveals the application of (male) standards to the circumstances facing battered women, ignored or excluded their own particularised subjectivity. A genuinely gender-neutral law of provocation would find room to accommodate women's subjectivities: their differing reactions to a violent

---

[69] See Edwards, S, *Sex and Gender in the Legal Process*, 1996, London: Blackstone. See, also, Hordern, J, *Provocation and Responsibility*, 1993, Oxford: Clarendon, Chapter 9.
[70] On which see Chapters 6 and 10.
[71] See Hart, HLA, *The Concept of Law*, 1961, 2nd edn, 1994, Oxford: OUP.
[72] *Ibid*.

situation. The law would then be transformed from one which excludes women to one which includes them.[73]

Supposedly gender-neutral language became a defence in the late nineteenth and early twentieth century for the exclusion of women from the legal profession, from the franchise and from political office.[74] In England, as discussed in Chapter 2, the right to vote was won only after years of legal and political struggle. The view adopted by the court in *Chorlton v Lings*,[75] namely that as a matter of legal interpretation the word 'man' does not include 'woman' – contrary to normal canons of statutory interpretation as set out in the Interpretation Act 1889 – was a form of reasoning adopted by the Canadian courts when challenges were presented to the exclusion of women from the profession and from public office. In the case of *In re French*[76] the court explicitly enunciated its views on the 'proper' role of women, namely within the private, domestic sphere of life. The differences between men and women, Mr Justice Barker argued, were such that '[t]he natural and proper timidity and delicacy which belongs to the female sex evidently unfits it for many of the occupations of civil life'.[77] In Mary Jane Mossman's view, such reasoning was out of step with the demands of legal method: those of reliance on relevant evidence, the use of legal precedents and a 'rational conclusion supported by both evidence and legal principles'. What the dictum reveals, in her view, is that legal method gave way to Mr Justice Barker's perceptions of women's 'proper' role, perceptions which were instilled in him by the 'cultural and professional milieu in which he lived'. Not that precedent was ignored: indeed the court relied on the earlier case of *Bradwell v Illinois* decided in 1873,[78] and followed it without consideration of the social change occurring in relation to women and women's employment. It was to be in 1930 that the Privy Council finally laid to rest the mythical exclusion of women from public life. In the *Persons* case,[79] Lord Sankey stated that:

> The exclusion of women from all public offices is a relic of days more barbarous than ours, but it must be remembered that the necessity of the times often forced on man customs which in later years were not necessary.[80]

---

[73] But cf *op cit*, Hordern, fn 69, in which it is argued that the defence of provocation should be abolished.

[74] See the analysis of Mary Jane Mossman on the Canadian cases on entry to the legal profession and public office in 'Feminism and legal method: the difference it makes' (1987) Wisconsin Women's LJ. (See *Sourcebook*, pp 107–19.)

[75] (1868) LR 4 CP 374.

[76] (1905) 37 NBR 359.

[77] *Ibid*, p 365.

[78] 83 US (16 Wall) 130 (1873).

[79] *Reference re: Meaning of the Word 'Persons' in section 24 of the British North American Act* [1928] SCR 276; *Edwards v AG for Canada* [1930] 1 AC 124.

[80] [1930] 1 AC 124, p 128.

Introduction

What becomes clear from an analyses of these cases is that the judges were, until the Privy Council decision, concerned not just with the techniques of legal method – the rational, objective determination on relevant facts and the application of justifiable precedent – but by their own subjective intuitions about 'women's place'. A feminist deconstruction on the legal reasoning reveals the damaging assumptions and presumptions which led the judges to their discriminatory decisions.

In Chapter 7, Carol Gilligan's research on the differences in girls' and boys' moral and psychological development is discussed.[81] Sufficient here for the discussion of feminist legal methods, Gilligan's research findings revealed that whilst boys reason in a logical, deductive manner, the development of girls is more influenced by relational concerns, by their 'connectedness' with others. Despite the controversy surrounding Gilligan's findings, her research carries implications for feminist legal method. How, if as the research demonstrates, girls and boys reason differently, can such evidence be incorporated within law and the legal system? As every first year student of law knows, under common law legal systems, both the interpretation of statutes and the evolution of the common law are constrained by so called 'rules' of statutory interpretation and the doctrine of *stare decisis* (precedent). The law employs the adversarial method, as opposed to the civil law inquisitorial method. Legal reasoning is characterised by deductive logic, the identification of relevant facts and the application of precedent to those facts. Objectivity and rationality are the hallmarks of legal practice:

> Traditional legal methods place a high premium on the predictability, certainty, and fixity of rules. In contrast, feminist legal methods, which have emerged from the critique that existing rules overrepresent existing power structures, value rule-flexibility, and the ability to identify missing points of view.[82]

Feminist legal method does not ignore, nor exclude, the necessity of predictability and certainty in law which is facilitated by the application of rules and principles. Nor, necessarily, does feminist legal method offer an exhaustive alternative to 'traditional' legal methods. Rather, feminist legal method seeks to complement traditional legal method by incorporation of alternative views, experiences, perceptions and values which traditional method, in its insistence on logic and deductive thought, may exclude.

If, adopting the results of Gilligan's research, the findings are applied to law and legal practice, what difference, if any, would occur? This issue has been explored by Carrie Menkel-Meadow,[83] and Leslie Bender.[84] In 'Portia in

---

[81] Gilligan, C, *In a Different Voice: Psychological Theory and Women's Development*, 1982, Cambridge, Mass: Harvard UP.
[82] *Op cit*, Bartlett, fn 62.
[83] Professor of Law, University of California, Los Angeles.
[84] At the time of writing, Associate Professor, Syracuse University College of Law.

a different voice: speculations on a woman's lawyering process',[85] Menkel-Meadow considers the potential impact of the increasing number of women entering into the legal profession, and the impact which women's distinctive moral reasoning has on legal practice. As is documented in Chapter 2, women were long excluded from higher education and from the professions. While women comprise some 50 per cent of law graduates and entrants into the legal profession, there remain obstacles to their advancement at the same rate as their male colleagues even today. Nevertheless, with an increasingly significant proportion of women legal practitioners, it is legitimate to consider the impact women can and do make on legal practice. One question raised is whether women's distinctive voices will be heard at all, given that to succeed in the male dominated world of law it is necessary to absorb the ethos of law – a professional ethos fashioned by men in the previously exclusionary professional era. If, however, women are to make an impact on the legal process, Menkel-Meadow argues that it is most likely to be in influencing the adversarial process, in 'softening' the hard, cold logic of male reasoning, of incorporating Amy's[86] concern for fairness and for relationships. A more co-operative and conciliatory legal process could be the outcome.

In 'From gender difference to feminist solidarity: using Carol Gilligan and an ethic of care in law',[87] Leslie Bender acknowledges the charges levelled at difference theorists,[88] while accepting that gender remains an 'organising concept' in society. Rather than rejecting gender difference theory as both perpetuating women's inequality and stereotyping and arguably being 'essentialist', Bender argues that women's distinctive reasoning has an important and legitimate role to play in law. The concern for interconnectedness, for relationships through an 'ethic of care' has a valuable contribution to make to the justice system. A justice system based primarily on cold rationality will not benefit all in the community. A legal system which incorporates women's insights and experiences, women's ethic of care and responsibility, is far more likely to exhibit humanity and justice.

Gilligan's research findings place women in a paradoxical position. Some go further and regard such findings as (a) perpetuating the myth that women are equal but different, or (b) perpetuating a debate on difference in which the only referent is always male,[89] or (c) portraying an unacceptable essentialism by portraying 'women' as a homogeneous group the components of which share the essential characteristics of being white, heterosexual and

---

[85] [1985] Berkeley Women's LJ 39.
[86] Amy was one of Gilligan's research subjects.
[87] (1990) 15 Vermont L Rev 1.
[88] See, further, Chapter 7.
[89] See, eg, MacKinnon, C, 'Difference and dominance: on sex discrimination', in MacKinnon, 1987, *op cit*, fn 18.

privileged.[90] On the other hand, as the discussion above demonstrates, 'woman' as an organising concept is a constructive platform from which to advance arguments for equality and equal treatment under law. While the arguments against 'woman' as organising concept have substance, and the concept needs in particular to be an inclusionary and not exclusionary construct, it represents nevertheless a starting point for much of the analysis of social and legal disabilities.

---

[90] See, eg, Spelman, E, *Inessential Woman: Problems of Exclusion in Feminist Thought*, 1990, London: The Women's Press.

CHAPTER 2

GENDER INEQUALITIES AND LAW

Disadvantages and inequalities supported by law do not exist in a cultural vacuum. Before, therefore, consideration can be given to the many facets of feminist jurisprudence, it is both instructive to illustrate the cultural origins of inequalities, and to review the contemporary state of women's equality as a background to the feminist campaigns for equality. Inequalities, in differing societies, naturally take many different forms, dependent upon many factors: cultural, historical, political, religious and legal. It is both dangerous and presumptive to suggest that women's inequality has a single explanation, let alone manifests itself in uniform ways. However, from time immemorial, woman's reproductive and nurturing role has resulted in women being viewed as 'the Other' of the male: as different, as unequal.

In the 1920s, anthropologist Bradislaw Malinovski was to analyse the position of women, arguing that women from the earliest times had been assigned – by men in the position of power in society – a predominantly child-bearing and child-nurturing role.[1] Although matrilineal[2] societies have existed in the past, they have been few. Moreover, even where such a political arrangement existed, it did not have the same political implications as does a patrilineal society. Property, for example, was not vested in the female, but rather controlled by male kin. Thus, a brother or husband rather than the sister or wife would have the power over property. In the view of the nineteenth century Marxist political philosopher Friedrich Engels, it was the introduction of private – as opposed to communal – property which conclusively consigned women to the 'private sphere' of life, and denied them full participation in civic life.[3]

However, as feminist anthropologists have demonstrated, the relationship between kinship structures and gender is more complex than these introductory remarks might suggest. Whilst early social scientists focused on human reproduction as a 'natural' biological function which represented the universalist foundation of all societies, thus aligning women's social role with her maternal function, feminist anthropologists have more recently revealed the inadequacies of such causal explanations of women's inferiority. Anthropological explanations of gender relations, developed from empirical

---

[1] See Malinowski, B, *Sex and Repression in Savage Society* (1927), 1960, London: Routledge and Kegan Paul.
[2] That is to say, societies in which women hold political power and succession is determined through the female line.
[3] Engels, F, *The Origins of the Family: Private Property and the State* (1884), 1940, London: Lawrence & Wishart. See, further, Chapter 6.

research in multifarious societies exhibiting very differing levels of 'development', are relied upon by feminists and others who seek to unmask the universality of women's inequality, and to seek an answer to Simone de Beauvoir's fundamental question: '[W]hat is a woman?'[4] As Michelle Zimbalist Rosaldo has explained, Victorian social theorists such as Herbert Spencer,[5] Emile Durkheim,[6] and Georg Simmel[7] recognised that women's social position and role was determined by her biological function, and while variously recognising that this function resulted in inequalities in public life, nevertheless accepted the 'naturalness' of women's inferiority as a result of her biological function: thus woman is reduced to her 'essence', her biological function. Moreover, according to Rosaldo, more modern social theorists have adopted the assumptions of earlier theorists unthinkingly and thereby 'reproduce what many recognise as outdated contrasts and conceptually misleading terms'.[8]

In 1974, Michelle Rosaldo had argued that gender inequality could be explained by understanding that woman's 'natural role' in reproduction was not merely biological, but rather a social construction of women, and that the identification of women with the home (the private sphere of life) and that of men with the public sphere (with employment, politics, law and public administration) was a by-product of the assumptions made about women's 'natural' role.[9] Thus, at this point Rosaldo was postulating a universalist explanation of women's inferiority. However, in 'The use and abuse of anthropology',[10] Rosaldo recognises that whilst there remains 'much that is compelling in this universalist account', the 'two spheres' model – of the public and the private – 'assumes ... too much about how gender really works'.[11] Whilst Rosaldo, in her research, found that patriarchy was a universal phenomenon, and that 'human and cultural forms have always been male dominated', it does not follow from that conclusion that the manifestation of male dominance assumes the same form in every society. Thus universalising anthropological theory must give way to theory which is culturally specific, and which is based on empirical research in order to

---

[4] See, eg, de Beauvoir, S, *The Second Sex*, (1949), Parshley, H (ed and trans), 1988, London: Picador; Firestone, S, *The Dialectic of Sex: The Case for a Feminist Revolution*, 1974, New York: Bantam.
[5] Spencer, H, *Principles of Sociology*, 1892–93, New York: D Appleton.
[6] Durkheim, E, *Suicide* (1858), 1951, Glencoe, Illinois: Free Press.
[7] Simmel, G, *Conflict and the Web of Group Affiliations*, 1955, New York: Macmillan.
[8] Rosaldo, M, 'The use and abuse of anthropology: reflections on feminism and cross-cultural understanding' (1980) 5, 3 Signs: Journal of Women and Culture in Society 389, p 405.
[9] See Rosaldo, M, 'Women, culture and society: a theoretical overview', in Rosaldo, M and Lamphere, L (eds), *Women, Culture and Society*, 1974, Stanford: Stanford UP.
[10] *Ibid*, Rosaldo, fn 8.
[11] *Ibid*, Rosaldo, fn 8, p 399.

explicate the forms in which male dominance is manifested in any particular society. Gender inequalities therefore cannot be explained, as earlier anthropologists and social scientists theorised, by either the biological fact of women's role in mothering and nurturing, or in universal theorising about the consequent relegation of women to the private sphere of life. Biological roles must be understood within the context of the social milieu: inequalities are not determined by biology but rather as social and political constructions of women which deny women a role in political life and thereby reinforce male dominance, which is reflected in differing ways in differing societies but remains universal in its manifestation in some form.[12]

From this brief introduction to early political thought and later anthropological research it can be seen that power in society has been accorded to men and women have been traditionally confined to the domestic sphere of life. Society is thus 'patriarchal' – a central concept which will be further examined in Chapter 3. Bearing in mind Rosaldo's caution about generalisation in theory, it is interesting to note the differing means by which patriarchy has been expressed in differing societies at differing times.[13]

Patriarchy assumes many and varied forms. Patriarchal attitudes are evident in the violent treatment of women, whether this treatment takes the form of sexual violence outside the home, sexual harassment in the workplace, domestic violence, or pornographic representations of women in 'art', or 'literature'. Patriarchy exhibits itself also in the manner in which women have traditionally been denied full participation in public life, whether that participation is represented by unequal positions in the employment sphere, or in democratically elected legislative bodies. Each of these aspects of the subject will be more fully explored later in the book. Our current concern is to consider cultural practices which reveal deeply ingrained patriarchal attitudes which have been manifested, in different times and places.

EMPIRICAL EVIDENCE OF CULTURAL PATRIARCHY

Chinese footbinding

In China by the twelfth century, the practice of 'footbinding' – whereby young girls' feet are bound in order to limit the size of the foot – had become established as 'correct' among 'higher society' and the practice was slow to

---

[12] See, for more recent anthropological analyses, Fishburne Collier, J and Junko Yanagisako, S (eds), *Gender and Kinship: Essays Toward a Unified Analysis*, 1987, Stanford: Stanford UP.

[13] See Daly, M, *Gyn/Ecology: the Metaethics of Radical Feminism*, 1979, London: The Women's Press. (See *Sourcebook*, pp 26–35.)

pass. The traditional explanation for the practice was that women were kept 'pure', 'delicate' and 'precious', and therefore more 'desirable' with small feet which caused the body to sway in a 'feminine' manner as it moved. That the practice resulted in severe disfigurement and pain for the victims was of little consequence to the men who demanded 'delicate' womenfolk.[14] In *Gyn/Ecology*,[15] feminist theologian Mary Daly[16] evaluates the practice, and concludes that in reality footbinding involved masculine control over women and girls, a control which was hidden by the fact that women themselves engaged in the practice in relation to their own children, for to refuse to do so would imperil their children's chance of a 'good marriage'.

Female circumcision

Similar arguments concerning female 'purity' and hence desirability may be found in relation to female circumcision reportedly still practised throughout Africa, in the Middle East[17] and amongst Indian tribes in South and Central America.[18] Circumcision may take three differing forms: the removal of the tip of the clitoris (sunna circumcision); excision of the entire clitoris, labia minora and most of the external genitalia; excision and infibulation (Pharaonic circumcision), the excision of the entire clitoris, labia minora and parts of the labia majora and the joining together (through stitching) of the two sides of the vulva, or as an alternative to stitching, the binding of the limbs until the wound heals. The purpose of this practice, as with footbinding, is tied in with female 'purity'. With circumcision, the removal of the clitoris symbolises the removal of an organ of purely female sexual gratification. The binding of the vagina ensures that no one other than the chosen husband will have access to the woman. Girls' (sometimes as young as the age of two) and young women's purity is thus ensured. A further comparative feature of circumcision with footbinding is that of the female relatives involvement in the practice. Men do not carry out circumcision: mothers and female relatives do so, in order to ensure the future desirability of their child(ren). With the myth of purity so firmly entrenched, what mother would dare not to circumcise her child?[19]

---

[14] See, eg, Chan, J, *Wild Swans: Three Daughters of China*, 1991, London: HarperCollins.
[15] *Op cit*, Daly, fn 13.
[16] At the time of writing, Associate Professor, Boston College.
[17] Yemen, Saudi Arabia, Iraq, Jordan and Syria.
[18] The following African countries have been cited: Kenya, Tanzania, Ethiopia, southern Egypt, Sudan, Uganda, northern Zaire, Chad, northern Cameroon, Nigeria, Dahomey, Togo, northern Ghana, Upper Volta, Male, northern Ivory Coast, Liberia, Sierra Leone, Guinea, Guinea Bissau, the Gambia, Senegal, Mauritania; Hosken, F, 'Women's international news' 1976, cited in Daly, *op cit*, fn 13, p 161.
[19] In Somalia, failure to circumcise a daughter is a ground for divorce.

Hindu suttee

In Hindu culture, upper caste widows were traditionally denied the right to remarry and until 1829, when the practice was officially banned, burned to death on their husband's funeral pyre. Mary Daly describes this barbaric practice of female slaughter[20] and provides evidence that, whilst confined to the upper classes, the practice 'spread downwards' into the 'lower classes' and moreover, affected other female family members: mothers, aunts, sisters, mistresses, all in the name, according to one (male) interpreter of 'sending the family or part of it "into the other world along with the chief member"'.[21]

European witch-murders[22]

It is unnecessary, however, to travel to once distant parts of the world for evidence of cultural male dominance and the suppression of women as second-class citizens and property of their male kinsfolk. In England, Scotland and continental Europe in the sixteenth and seventeenth centuries, women were persecuted, prosecuted, convicted and put to death on charges of being witches. Witchcraft was regarded as the means to do evil through the use of occult powers, or the belief in *maleficium*.[23] Between 1542 and 1739, almost 1,000 women were executed for witchcraft.[24] Two principal explanations exist for the persecution of witches. The first explanation is the 'traditional male' explanation, namely that witches were a threat to the established order of society and to religious beliefs.[25] Thus, Kramer and Sprenger, authors of *The Malleus Maleficarum*[26] first published in 1486, state that '[A]ll witchcraft comes from carnal lust which is in women insatiable'. In 1597, King James VI of Scotland wrote that witches were a 'threat to the social order, and that they

---

[20] See *op cit*, Daly, fn 13, Chapter 3.
[21] Campbell, J, *The Masks of God: Oriental Mythology*, 1962, New York: Viking, p 62, cited in Daly, *op cit*, fn 13, p 116.
[22] See *op cit*, Daly, fn 13, and, also, Hester, M, *Lewd Women and Wicked Witches: A Study of the Dynamics of Male Domination*, 1992, London: Routledge and Kegan Paul. (See *Sourcebook*, pp 35–39.)
[23] See, eg, Thomas, K, *Religion and the Decline of Magic*, 1971, London: Weidenfeld and Nicolson; Cohn, N, *Europe's Inner Demons*, 1975, London: Chatto, Heinemann.
[24] See Ewen, L, *Witch Hunting and Witch Trials* (1929), 1971, Frederick Miller; MacFarlane, A, *Witchcraft in Tudor and Stuart England, a Regional and Comparative Study*, 1970, London: Routledge and Kegan Paul; Monter, E, *Witchcraft in France and Switzerland*, 1976, New York: Cornell UP cited in Hester, *ibid*, p 128.
[25] The last woman to be convicted of witchcraft in England was Helen Duncan, who in 1944 stood trial at the Old Bailey on charges under the Witchcraft Act 1735, and served a term of imprisonment of nine months. Her prosecution was prompted by the fear that she represented a threat to national security in wartime. The Witchcraft Act was repealed in 1951, to be replaced by the Fraudulent Mediums Act. Between 1980 and 1996 there were seven prosecutions under this Act, six of them leading to convictions.
[26] Kramer, H and Sprenger, J, *The Malleus Maleficarum* (1928) Summers, Rev M (trans), 1971, New York: Dover.

should preferably be eradicated'.[27] The second, and more radical interpretation, is feminist. The well documented phenomenon of the murder of women for witchcraft has been interpreted by Mary Daly, for example, as representing the 'purification' of society of women – especially spinsters and widows – who were outside patriarchal control and thus a threat to the established (male) supremacy.[28] Marianne Hester[29] agrees, stating that witch murder represented 'an instance of male sexual violence against women, relying on a particular sexual construct of female behaviour. The hunts were a part of the apparently on-going attempt by men to control women socially, and to reimpose the male-dominated status quo in a period of many changes including economic restructuring and pressure on economic resources. In other words, the witch-hunts of the sixteenth and seventeenth centuries were a part of the "dynamics of domination" whereby men at the time maintained dominance over women'.[30]

Thus, from a feminist perspective it may be argued that the witch-hunts provided one means of controlling women socially within a male supremacist society, using violence or the threat of violence, and relying on a particular construct of female sexuality. Only certain women – usually older, lower-class, poor, and often single or widowed – were directly affected. Witch murder was a form of social control over women who were outside the control of some man and therefore represented a threat to society.[31]

Wife sale in England[32]

There can surely be no more poignant example of the notion that women have traditionally been regarded as the property of their husbands than the practice of 'wife sale'. Immortalised in Thomas Hardy's *The Mayor of Casterbridge*,[33] wife sale represented a semi-formal means of transferring the 'property' in the wife to a new freeholder, where the marital relationship had broken down and where divorce was either unavailable or too costly.

---

[27] James VI, *The Daemonology* (1597), cited in Hester, *op cit*, fn 22, p 129. See, also, Larner, C, *Witchcraft and Religion*, 1984, Oxford: Basil Blackwell; Robbins, RH, *The Encyclopedia of Witchcraft and Demonology*, 1959, London: Peter Nevill.

[28] *Op cit*, Daly, fn 13, Chapter 6.

[29] University of Exeter.

[30] *Op cit*, Hester, fn 22, p 199.

[31] Extensive legislation was introduced in England to regulate witchcraft from the time of Henry VIII until 1736. The penalty for being found guilty of witchcraft in Europe and Scotland was death by burning; in England those sentenced to death were hanged.

[32] See Kenny, C, 'Wife selling in England' (1920) 45 LQR 496; Menafee, S, *Wives for Sale*, 1981, Oxford: OUP; Stone, L, *Road to Divorce: England 1530–1987*, 1992, Oxford: OUP, Chapter 43.

[33] Hardy, T, *The Mayor of Casterbridge* (1886), 1975, London: Macmillan, pp 32–36. (See *Sourcebook*, pp 39–43.)

The practice of wife sale varied. As Lawrence Stone records,[34] in some instances, the 'sale' would be effected with the consent of the wife who had formed another attachment. In other cases, however, the husband would unilaterally dispose of the wife, at an auction sale, to the highest bidder. In order to emphasise the property aspect of the transfer, the husband would attach a leather collar around the wife's neck and lead her ceremoniously to the auction.

Women in marriage[35]

Traditionally, women have been treated under English law in a manner which stresses the cultural, economic, political and legal supremacy of the husband. For example, English law regarded the fact of marriage as representing a woman's implied consent to intercourse with her husband whenever he so desired. Moreover, under English law, until 1882,[36] upon marriage the husband became the sole owner and manager of the previously held wife's property. The official ideological rationale for this latter rule lay in the perception of women having a 'special status' (for this read inferior status). Thus, for example, Sir William Blackstone in his *Commentaries on the Laws of England 1765–69*, was to comment that on marriage the husband and wife are 'one person in law: that is, the very being or legal existence of the woman is suspended during the marriage, or at least is incorporated into that of the husband: under whose wing, protection, and cover she performs every thing'. Here confirmed is Aristotle's concept of the woman as chattel. Furthermore, in order to protect the husband's property via the succession through legitimate heirs, any man found guilty of adultery with the wife could be sued for criminal conversion and substantial damages awarded; and any woman guilty of adultery could be divorced 'without more'.

Gender-based violence against women in contemporary society

One of the remaining inequalities against women remains that of violence. In Chapter 11, the international and United Kingdom data on gender-based violence is considered. However, as will be seen, while any precise measurement of the incidence of violence in society is problematic,[37] what is clearly established from all the research data is that gender-based violence is universal. Irrespective of geography or politics, discrimination against

---

[34] See *op cit*, Stone, fn 32, pp 141–47.
[35] See, further, Chapter 3.
[36] The Married Women's Property Act 1882.
[37] Due largely to under-reporting.

women, in the form of violence, is widespread. Gender-based violence, the evidence reveals, whether in the form of sexual harassment, assault, sexual offences or murder, is deeply embedded in society. Moreover, gender-based violence in all its manifestations, presents difficulties for analysis, in so far as explanations vary from psychological, economic, socio-structural to political. This embeddedness, and the lack of consensus among researchers of gender-based violence, presents its own difficulties for law. As has been well documented in the literature on 'legal transplants',[38] while law has a degree of autonomy from society, the prognosis for law's effectiveness in regulating conduct – particularly conduct in private – is particularly low when law seeks to change deeply engrained social attitudes.[39] As will be seen in Chapter 11, feminist analysis and campaigning has done much to raise the profile of gender-based violence against women, which, however, remains both universal and widespread within all societies.

LAW'S DEPENDENCE ON CULTURE: THEORETICAL EXPLANATIONS

Karl von Savigny, Eugen Ehrlich, William Graham Sumner

Towards the end of the nineteenth century and early in the twentieth century, three theorists sought to explain the evolution from culture to law. Whilst differing in their individual approaches and terminology, each writer sought to explain the need for law to rest on its societal foundations. For law to depart too greatly from the 'spirit of the people', or *volksgeist*,[40] or the '*mores*',[41] or '*living law*'[42] would spell disaster for the relevance of and respect for legal rules.

It has been well established by empirical research that there are limits to the utility of legal, as opposed to societal/cultural, reform, and these limits are no better demonstrated than in precisely the areas of reform which are the most culturally sensitive. In the nineteenth century, Karl von Savigny, seeking to impede hasty codification of the laws of Germany on unification, argued that before effective laws could be drafted and implemented, research needed to be undertaken in order to establish the common 'spirit' (the *volksgeist*) of the

---

[38] The 'transplanting' of laws from one society to another.
[39] See, *inter alia*, Allott, A, *The Limits of Law*, 1980, London: Butterworths; Cotterrell, RBM, *The Sociology of Law: An Introduction*, 1985, London: Butterworths.
[40] von Savigny, K, *On the Vocation of Our Age for Legislation and Jurisprudence*, 1831, Hayward A (trans), 1975, New York: Arno.
[41] Sumner, W, *Folkways* (1906), 1940, Boston, Mass: Ginn.
[42] Ehrlich, E, *Fundamental Principles of the Sociology of Law* (1936), 1975, New York: Arno.

peoples.[43] At the turn of the century, William Graham Sumner, in a wide ranging historical survey, argued that for the maximum effectiveness of law to be guaranteed, the laws must be rooted firmly in the *'mores'* of the people. Too great a divergence between law and culture would result in the failure of law.[44] In 1936, Eugen Ehrlich's *The Fundamental Principles of the Sociology of Law* was published. Here too Ehrlich argues for an understanding of the rules which regulate everyday life before State law could intervene and seek to impose effective legal regulation. Evidence of the dependence of law upon culture comes also from comparative lawyers who have sought to explicate the conditions under which laws from one society could be effectively grafted on to the legal system of another culture.[45] In each case, the point which shines through most clearly is that laws which affect the most intimate parts of life, aspects of life which are central to a culture, will be of limited success unless there exists either a correspondence between the substance of the law being introduced and the cultural mores of society, or there exists a demonstrated willingness on the part of the recipient society to accept the proposed changes.[46]

On the other hand, and to offset the otherwise pessimistic prognosis for law as an instrument of social change, it must be recognised that law has a significant role to play in both changing the attitudes and conduct of those it regulates. Law has a relative autonomy. Without legal reform, slavery would still persist.[47] Without legal reform, apartheid and other forms of racial discrimination would remain. Without legal reform, women would not have achieved the vote, achieved legal equality within marriage and in the workplace. In the United Kingdom, the Race Relations Act 1968, although generally agreed to be of limited practical utility, represented a starting point for the effective elimination of racial discrimination, as did the Sex Discrimination Act 1970 and the Equal Pay Act 1975 in relation to sexual discrimination. In the United States, the Supreme Court in *Brown v Board of Education of Topeka*[48] reversed its decision of 1896[49] and ruled that the segregation of schools violated the Constitution and could no longer be justified on the basis that educational and other segregation amounted to justifiable 'separate but equal' treatment. On this basis, law plays and must

---

[43] See *op cit*, von Savigny, K, fn 40.
[44] See *op cit*, Sumner, fn 41.
[45] See *op cit*, Allott, fn 39.
[46] Such 'universal' theorising about societal development is, from a postmodern perspective (discussed in Chapter 9), too generalised to reveal the particularities of the forces which coalesce to produce laws. Notwithstanding postmodern reservations about 'grand theory', such theories illustrate the interaction between cultural mores and law.
[47] See Lester, A and Bindman, G, *Race and Law*, 1972, London: Penguin.
[48] 347 US 483 (1954).
[49] See *Plessey v Ferguson* 163 US 537 (1896).

continue to play a pivotal role in the elimination of sexism in society. It must also be recognised, however, that it is easier to change overt conduct through law than to change attitudes which underlie that conduct. To make racial or sexual discrimination an offence, as such, may result in a change in conduct, a change brought about by the fear of sanctions under the law, but may leave the racial or sexist attitude in place, but more carefully concealed. However, law also acts as a symbol in society: a symbol of what society regards as appropriate conduct or treatment towards another person. On this reasoning, while initially conduct but not attitudes may change, it can be argued that there is a long term effect on society, and that in the long term attitudes will change to come more into line with the requirements for conduct under the law.[50]

Deeply entrenched cultural mores – such as sexism and patriarchy – prove strongly resistant to change. Without such change at a cultural level, the success of law as an instrument of reform will inevitably be limited to the regulation of conduct which can be evaluated under the law, whilst attitudes – so central to the real effectiveness of social change – remain either the same, or exceedingly slow to change. It for reasons such as these that radical feminists, whilst accepting and acknowledging the valuable work undertaken by liberal feminist legal scholars, question the tenets of liberalism with its insistence on formal equality under the law. Others, on the other hand, call for a recognition that law has limited utility and effectiveness as a mechanism for social change, and that an overemphasis on law – as opposed to social change – distorts the significance of law which is but one form of social regulation.[51]

EARLY STRUGGLES FOR EQUALITY IN WESTERN SOCIETY

Rights for women

One of the earliest English advocates for women's rights in relation to the franchise, education and laws relating to the family was Mary Wollstonecraft.[52] In *Vindication of the Rights of Women*,[53] written at the time of the French Revolution, Wollstonecraft argued for equality. Despite her radicalism, Wollstonecraft was imbued with the prevailing ideology of her time: that of the 'natural' inferiority of women to men. While reasoning that women's intellectual capacities were naturally equal to those of men, Wollstonecraft accepted the traditional role of women in the family. There is

---

[50] On the English Race Relations Act and Sex Discrimination Act, see Cotterrell, RBM [1981] PL 469.
[51] See, eg, Smart, C, *Feminism and the Power of Law*, 1989, London: Routledge and Kegan Paul.
[52] 1759–97.
[53] Wollestonecraft, M, *Vindication of the Rights of Women* (1792), 1967, New York, WW Norton.

accordingly a dualism in her work: women campaigning for full participation in civic 'public' life, and women in more conventional mode in the 'private' sphere: the home.

In the nineteenth century, one of the most influential women was the feminist writer Hariett Martineau.[54] Widely travelled, and an insightful social and political commentator, Martineau was as well known and regarded in the United States as in England.[55] Education for women was a constant campaign for Martineau for only through education could women participate fully in public life, on equal terms with men. Martineau observed, however, that while girls and boys having equal educational opportunities succeeded on equal terms, too often girls were not encouraged to complete their education, and then criticised for failing to achieve their true potential:

> She is taught to believe that solid information is unbecoming her sex, almost her whole time is expended on light accomplishments and thus before she is sensible of her powers, they are checked in her growth, chained down to mean objects, to risk no more; and when the natural consequences of this mode of treatment arise, all mankind agree that the abilities of women are far inferior to those of men.[56]

The right to vote was also central to Martineau's concerns and she was critical of the idea that democracy could exist without the participation of women.

Education for women,[57] full civil rights for women and the law relating to prostitution[58] represented two sites of political activity for the Victorian campaigner Josephine Butler.[59] The Contagious Diseases Acts represented one of the most discriminatory legal provisions of the nineteenth century. In an attempt to eradicate venereal disease among soldiers and sailors, the government enacted legislation which provided for designated army towns and ports, in which special police forces would identify women prostitutes. The prostitutes were then required to submit to regular medical treatment, or if they refused, to appear in court. The court had the power to order the examinations. The burden of proof relating to a charge of being a prostitute lay on the woman accused.[60]

---

[54] 1802–76.

[55] In the course of her life, Hariett Martineau wrote over 50 books and pamphlets and over 1,600 articles for the *Daily News* and a further 50 articles in periodicals such as the *Edinburgh Review* and *Westminster Review*.

[56] Martineau, H, 1823, cited by Weiner, G, 'Harriet Martineau: a reassessment', in Spender, D (ed), *Feminist Theorists*, 1983, London: The Women's Press, p 65.

[57] Butler was to become president of the North of England Council for the Higher Education of Women from 1868–73.

[58] In 1869, Butler headed the Ladies National Association campaign for the Repeal of the Contagious Diseases Acts of 1864, 1866, 1869.

[59] 1828–1906.

[60] The Acts were finally repealed in 1886.

Butler was keenly aware that the issue of prostitution was linked to women's inferiority in the labour market. In 1861 the census recorded three and a half million women working for subsistence pay. Butler attacked employers' practices which included qualifications for apprenticeships which women could not obtain, thus further pushing women down the economic scale to the position where women represented the lowest class in society.[61]

THE FRANCHISE

The franchise in the United Kingdom

Women were to remain disentitled from the right to vote until 1918, but the movement for women's right to vote predates the Representation of the People Act 1867, which greatly expanded the male franchise. In 1851, Harriet Taylor Mill had published 'Enfranchisement of women' in the *Westminster Review*, and at an election meeting in 1865 John Stuart Mill raised women's enfranchisement as a public political issue. In 1886, John Stuart Mill[62] presented a petition to parliament calling for the enfranchisement of women. The following year the Manchester Women's Suffrage Committee was formed, soon to be united in a national Committee based in London. When the Reform Bill was before parliament John Stuart Mill introduced an amendment – changing the word 'man' to 'person' and thereby entitling women to vote. The amendment was defeated.

A legal challenge to disenfranchisement came in *Chorlton v Lings*.[63] It was argued before the Court of Common Pleas that the Representation of the People Act 1867 had conferred on women a right to vote. The argument centred on the use of the word 'man' in the act. It was contended that Lord Brougham's Act[64] which stipulated that the word 'man' includes 'women' applied to an interpretation of the Representation Act. Chief Justice Bovill rejected such a view:

---

[61] Campaigning for homeless emigrants in Australia, Caroline Chisholm rescued thousands of homeless, penniless young girls from a life of subsistence in the bush or life in the brothels. The girls came from workhouses and orphanages in England, the ships' captains received bonuses for every women transported. In 1846, Chisholm founded the Family Colonisation Loan Society in England. By 1862, she and her husband had brought to Australia over 11,000 emigrants. Chisholm successfully persuaded the government of Victoria to provide grants to establish shelters for the emigrants.

[62] A member of parliament and radical reformer. See, *inter alia, Representative Government* (1865), 1958, Indianapolis: Bobbs-Merrill; See, also, *On Liberty* (1859), 1989, Cambridge: CUP, and *The Subjection of Women* (1869), 1989, Cambridge: CUP.

[63] [1868] LR IV 374.

[64] The Interpretation Act, 13 and 14 Vict c 21.

The conclusion at which I have arrived is, that the legislature used the word 'man' in the Act of 1867 in the same sense as 'male person' in the former Act; that this word was intentionally used, in order to designate expressly the male sex; and that it amounts to an express enactment and provision that every man, as distinguished from women, possessing the qualification, is to have the franchise. In that view, Lord Brougham's Act does not apply to the present case, and does not extend the meaning of the word 'man' so as to include women.[65]

Mr Justice Willis, Byles J and Keating J agreed. In accepting Bovill CJ's interpretation, Willis J turned to comment on the wider issue. In declaring himself opposed to any view that women were excluded from the franchise on the basis of 'fickleness of judgment and liability to influence' which would be quite inconsistent 'with one of the glories of our civilisation – the respect and honour in which women are held', Willis J declared that the prohibition against voting – and the prohibition against peeresses in the House of Lords – could be explained:

> ... out of respect to women, and a sense of decorum, and not from their want of intellect, or their being for any other reason unfit to take part in the government of the country, they have been excused from taking any share in this department of public affairs.[66]

In 1869, Mill published *The Subjection of Women*. The right to vote was but one campaign. Women were also seeking equal rights in education, in politics and in the medical profession. Millicent Garrett Fawcett[67] played a leading role in the struggle for women's equality:[68] her memorial in Westminster Abbey describes her as having 'won citizenship for women'. Her involvement in the suffrage movement became intense after the death of her husband in 1884. But while her life was primarily[69] devoted to the campaign for the vote, Millicent Garrett Fawcett neither joined in the more militant campaign led by the Pankhursts,[70] nor did she believe that the women's movement alone would achieve its objective: social change was needed before success would be achieved.

In 1897, the differing suffrage movements were to be united under the National Union of Women's Suffrage Societies (the NUWSS), led until 1919 by Millicent Garrett Fawcett. By 1913 the number of affiliated societies had

---

[65] [1868] LR IV 387.
[66] [1868] LR IV 392. For the feminist analysis of the North American *Persons* cases, see Chapter 1.
[67] 1847–1929. See Strachey, R, *Millicent Garrett Fawcett*, 1951, London: John Murray.
[68] With her husband Henry Fawcett, Millicent founded Newnham College, Cambridge, at which her daughter, Phillippa, was placed first in the mathematics tripos.
[69] Education, morals, employment and married women's right to own and manage property (finally achieved in 1882 with the Married Women's Property Act) were also within her campaigning objectives.
[70] On which see, further, below, pp 42–43.

reached 400. Under the banner of the Women's Union for Parliamentary Suffrage, the leadership of Emmeline,[71] Christabel[72] and Sylvia[73] (Emmeline's daughters) Pankhurst[74] injected new energy into the campaign and the age of militancy in support of the right to vote began. Millicent Garrett Fawcett was to remain staunchly opposed to violence in support of the campaign, and her attitude to the Pankhursts was ambivalent. Nor were the Pankhursts themselves united in their objectives: for Christabel and Emmeline militancy was a legitimate means in the pursuit of the right of middle-class women to vote; whereas for Sylvia the objective was the right of all women – working- and middle-class – to the vote. Sylvia Pankhurst also came to oppose the militancy of the campaign and in 1914 she founded the East London Federation of Suffragettes which included a programme for both socialism and pacifism.

The tide of public opinion started to turn in women's favour in 1909 when the authorities started to force feed hunger-striking suffragettes imprisoned as a result of their campaign. A Bill to give women the right to vote passed Second Reading in 1910 but was defeated by the Prime Minister, Asquith, acting in concert with Lloyd George, the Opposition Leader. The failure of a second Bill in 1911 sparked violent protest all over London: 217 women were arrested. A Reform Bill of 1913 met a similar fate, being defeated on a technicality. Its defeat met with swift reaction. Militant suffragists committed arson; threw bombs at churches and damaged golf courses. When an attempt was made to burn down Lloyd George's country house, Emmeline Pankhurst was arrested and charged with inciting to commit a felony, arrested, tried and found guilty. She was sentenced to three years' penal servitude.

Fearful of the consequences of imprisonment and hunger-strikes the government hurriedly passed the 'Cat and Mouse' Act,[75] which enabled the authorities to release hunger-striking prisoners who were in medical danger and re-arrest them on their physical recovery. In Mrs Pankhurst's case, she was released after only nine days in Holloway Prison, having immediately begun a hunger-strike. She was released for treatment. When she announced her intention to attend and address a rally, the police returned her to Holloway. After only five days she was again released.

The day after her second release was Derby Day. On that day, Emily Wilding Davidson threw herself under the hooves of the racing horses and was killed. Worldwide attention focused on the tragedy. Mrs Pankhurst was

---

[71] 1858–1928.
[72] Dame Christabel Pankhurst, 1880–1958. Christabel studied law at Manchester University and was a founder member of the Women's Social and Political Union in 1903.
[73] 1882–1960.
[74] 1880–1958.
[75] Prisoner's (Temporary Discharge for Ill-health) Act 1913.

prevented from attending her funeral procession as the police once again took her back to prison, where after only three days of a hunger-strike she was once again released only to return to prison for a fourth time for a short period before her life became endangered and she was again released. Shortly afterwards she left the country and travelled to America to raise money for the cause. On her arrival, however, she was detained at the request of the British Government. The storm of protest over her detention in America, and the political pressure put on the President by American women soon led to her release. On her return to England Mrs Pankhurst was once more detained: she was to endure a further eight attempts at forcing her to serve her sentence. In 1912, there had been 290 women suffrage prisoners under the Cat and Mouse Act; in the following year, 182. The public attention, and changing public mood resulted in 39,540 Friends of Women's Suffrage enrolling in support of the cause.

The persistence of the suffragettes combined with the involvement of women in industry during the First World War acted as catalysts for winning the right to vote. In 1916 an all-party conference on electoral reform was established under the chairmanship of the Speaker of the House of Commons. The Parliament (Qualification of Women) Act 1918 provided that women were eligible to stand for election to the House of Commons – although the right to vote was still denied to women under the age of 30.

The Representation of the People Act 1918 which implemented the conference's proposals, introduced a full franchise of all men in parliamentary elections and conferred the right to vote in Parliament on all women over the age of 30 who were either local government electors or the wives of local government electors. Full equality with men was delayed until 1928.

The franchise in the United States of America

In the United States, the campaign for women's votes may be traced to 1848 with a meeting in Seneca Falls, New York, which protested against women's political, economic and social inferiority. The outcome of the convention was the *Declaration of Sentiments*.[76] The early campaign for the vote was allied to, and confused by, the activists' abolitionist stance in relation to slavery. For abolitionists also the women's movement represented a problem: the fight for the abolition of slavery was radical and difficult on its own: to be complicated by the demand for women's rights might damage their own primary objective. Following the Civil War the Fourteenth Amendment to the Constitution was passed, declaring the equal protection of law to all male

---

[76] See Steele Commage, H (ed), *Documents of American History*, 1956, New York: Appleton-Century-Crofts, pp 315–36; Smith, TV, *The American Philosophy of Equality*, 1927, Chicago: Chicago UP, pp 327–31.

citizens. Disagreements over the feminist response to the Fourteenth Amendment led to the formation of two separate organisations: the National Woman Suffrage Association and the American Woman Suffrage Association,[77] which worked separately until their merger in 1890 into the National American Woman Suffrage Association.[78]

Susan B Anthony[79] and Elizabeth Cady Stanton were two of the leading feminists of their era. In 1868, following the Civil War, Susan B Anthony and Elizabeth Cady Stanton launched their own newspaper, *Revolution*. The paper's motto reflected Anthony's ambitious aims: 'Men, their rights and nothing more. Women, their rights, and nothing less.' In 1872, Anthony cast her vote and was put on trial. Together, Anthony and Cady Stanton wrote *The History of Woman Suffrage*.[80]

By 1890, women's rights had advanced considerably. Initially women were granted the right to vote in school elections.[81] Municipal suffrage was granted to women in Kansas in 1887 and in 1890 Wyoming entered the Union as the first State with full suffrage for women, to be followed by Colorado in 1893 and Utah and Idaho in 1896. Not until 1910 did any other State enfranchise women,[82] to be followed in 1911 by California, and in 1912 by Arizona, Kansas and Oregon. A limited right to vote in presidential elections was granted to women by Illinois in 1913. It was to be in 1919 that Congress passed a national amendment securing full voting equality for women.[83] The suffragist movement was further complicated by the issue of votes for black women in the South. While the abolition of slavery was inextricably linked with the movement for women's equality and the vote, following the Civil War, the position of blacks in society was increasingly marginalised in the woman's movement and formed the focus for disputes between suffragists, as did the question of the enfranchisement of immigrant women.

Resistance and opposition to women's suffrage proved strong, with the 'anti-suffragists' employing emotive language centring on the 'women and the home', or more accurately the 'women in the home'. Theologians employed the Scriptures in their attack; others adopted the argument that women were physically incapable of undertaking the duty of voting. Octavius B Frothingham argued that men were characterised by rationality, by judgment; whereas women were emotional, idealistic, sentimental,

---

[77] Led by Lucy Stone (1818–93).
[78] The first president of the NAWSA was Elizabeth Cady Stanton.
[79] 1820–1906.
[80] Stanton, A and Stanton, C, *The History of Woman Suffrage*, 1881, New York: Fowler & Wells; repr 1969, New York: Arno and New York Times.
[81] By 1890, 16 States had introduced school suffrage.
[82] Washington DC.
[83] Ratified in 1920 as the Nineteenth Amendment.

irrational.[84, 85] The 'difference' argument was also employed to oppose the franchise: women were needed in the home; bearing and rearing children. Having the vote implied civic responsibilities which would conflict with women's natural and proper duties in the home. The argument that women did not want the vote was also employed both by male and female anti-suffragists, an argument which when interpreted meant that white, middle-class women (who were deemed better off in the home) should not have the vote, and accordingly neither should any other woman. The argument that it was *unwomanly* was employed: why should a woman need the vote when their husband's could vote for them?

The 'equality/sameness/difference' debate was also employed on both sides of the argument. On the anti-suffragists' side, the argument about 'women's place' in the 'private sphere' of life – in the home. To counter the argument of the anti-suffragists that centuries of women's suppression rendered women *unfit* to vote proved difficult. The suffragists insisted that women were equal: that women represented 50 per cent of the population and had a legitimate right to participation in the democratic process.

EDUCATION FOR WOMEN

While Mary Wollstonecraft, Hariett Martineau and Josephine Butler campaigned for equality in education in England as part of their overall strategy for eliminating discrimination against women, Emily Davies[86] focused almost all her energies on women's education. In 1862 Emily Davies became editor of a new feminist newspaper, *The Englishwomen's Journal*. In 1865, she and other feminists formed an education committee which lobbied for the right of girls to sit preliminary entrance examinations for colleges which had previously only been open to boys. In 1873, Davies opened Girton College, Cambridge, the first undergraduate college for women, and became its first Mistress until 1875. She also campaigned successfully for women to be given degrees by London University in 1874.[87]

---

[84] The same arguments employed in the late 20th century to oppose further equality between men and women.

[85] Frothingham, OB, 'The real case of the "remonstrants" against woman suffrage' (1890) 11 The Arena 176, p 179.

[86] 1830–1921.

[87] Oxford first conferred degrees on women in 1920; Cambridge delayed conferring degrees on women until 1948.

Science and medicine

Historically, women have always practised the art of medicine. In ancient Egypt, in classical Greece and Rome and in the Middle Ages women were doctors. The medical school at Salerno near Naples, founded in the tenth century, had women students. In the sixteenth century women in England were allowed to enter the qualifying examinations for medicine. From around that time, however, until the mid nineteenth century women became excluded from medicine. In England, those practising medicine in the sixteenth and seventeenth centuries were liable to prosecution for witchcraft. In the other sciences a similar pattern can be found. In classical times women were free to study mathematics and philosophy, but again around the seventeenth century they were denied this right.

In England and the United States, the names of Elizabeth Blackwell[88] and Elizabeth Garrett Anderson[89] dominated the struggle for the right to practise medicine. Elizabeth Blackwell started her career as a headmistress in Kentucky in 1842. In 1844, she applied to medical schools in New York and Philadelphia, but was rejected on the basis of her sex. She was finally awarded her degree by a small medical school in Geneva, New York.[90] In 1853, Elizabeth Blackwell and two other women doctors, her sister Emily and Marie Zackrzewska, opened a dispensary and medical college for women in New York. In 1858, Blackwell returned to England, from where her family had emigrated when she was seven. For the rest of her career, Elizabeth Blackwell was Professor of Gynaecology at what is now the Royal Free Hospital.

Inspired by a lecture given by Dr Elizabeth Blackwell, Elizabeth Garrett Anderson was ultimately to become the first woman doctor in England, although she was forced to take her qualifying examinations in Paris. Having been rejected for university courses, Elizabeth Garrett Anderson studied medicine privately, although she pursued a midwifery course at the London Hospital. In 1865, the Society of Apothecaries granted her a qualification certificate and she then ran a dispensary for women. In 1870, she took her final medical examination. In 1872, Elizabeth Garrett Anderson opened the New Hospital, a hospital staffed entirely by women, for women.[91] In 1869, Sophia Jex-Blake and six others persuaded the University of Edinburgh to admit women to lectures in medicine. The University, however, reneged on its own regulations. When Sophia Jax-Blake and others took the matter to law, the University claimed that its own regulations were *ultra vires*. The judges agreed: the purpose of a university was the education of men.[92]

---

[88] 1821–1910.
[89] 1836–1917.
[90] Following her training, the college passed a resolution barring further women students.
[91] It later became the Elizabeth Garrett Anderson Hospital.
[92] *Jex-Blake v Edinburgh University Senatus* (1873) 11 M 784.

In the United States,[93] the proportion of women doctors has traditionally been lower than in other countries.[94] Women had always played an informal role in medicine – as midwives, as healers. The interesting historical question is, why did women find themselves denied entry to the emergent medical profession? The question is particularly interesting in relation to the United States of America, for while in Europe male university-trained physicians had long dominated the profession, in the United States around 1800 there were few such trained physicians: lay practitioners were the norm, specialists the exception, and women played an equal role in dispensing health care. In the early 1800s, however, the position appears to have changed. The increasing number of trained physicians distinguished themselves from the 'informal' medical profession (of lay practitioners, healers, nurses and midwives).

In the 1830s and 1840s, women reacted against the newly established male monopoly of medical practice by establishing the Popular Health Movement. Preventive measures formed a significant part of the movement. The Popular Health Movement was overtly feminist: demanding rights for women in general as well as the greater participation of women in the medical profession and the improvement in women's health. The Popular Health Movement later broke up into sectarian groups and lost its force. The male medical profession did not let its existence go unchallenged. In 1848 the American Medical Association was formed. Throughout the rest of the century the medical profession attacked lay practitioners, sectarian doctors and women medical practitioners. The attacks were overtly sexist and virulent: when women were eventually admitted to medical schools they faced the hurdles of male professors who would not discuss anatomy in front of women and of sexual harassment from male students. As women gradually succeeded in gaining entry into medical positions they distanced themselves from the Popular Health Movement and allied themselves with their new, male, colleagues. Class played its own role: those gaining entry were largely middle-class and those refused entry lower-class women.

Midwifery, traditionally practised by women denied entry to the 'profession', soon came under attack. In 1910, it is recorded that some 50 per cent of all babies were delivered by midwives, of whom a majority were black or working-class. With the emerging specialism of obstetrics and gynaecology under the control of the 'profession', midwifery as hitherto practised, became a threat to the profession. Midwifery was to become controlled by the profession. Throughout the early twentieth century State laws were passed to outlaw the practice of midwifery other than by an appropriately trained

---

[93] For a full analysis see Ehrenreich, B and English, D, 'Women and the rise of the American medical profession', in McElroy, W (ed), *Freedom, Feminism and the State*, 1982, USA: Cato Institute, Chapter XXIV, which is relied on for this introduction.

[94] In 1982, eg, in England, 24 per cent of doctors were women; in Russia, 75 per cent; whereas in the United States, only seven per cent of doctors were women.

member of the medical profession: one consequence of which was to deny medical care to poor and working-class women.

Thus excluded from the profession and their traditional role as midwives, the only remaining role for women was nursing. Florence Nightingale provided the example. Nursing schools in the United States started to be established after the Civil War. Recruitment was aimed at upper- and middle-class women, although when the reality of nursing (hard, heavy work) became known, colleges were forced to recruit from the 'lower classes', who were to be trained by those upper- and middle-class women who had preceded them. Nursing was stamped, both in England and the United States, with the mark of middle-class values: those of womanhood, motherhood, femininity, subservience and care. In contradistinction to this characterisation is that of the doctor: rational, objective, logical and professional.

No introductory overview of early feminist achievements would be complete without an appreciation of the pioneering work of Florence Nightingale: the 'Lady of the Lamp'.[95] Born into the upper-classes, Florence and her sister were groomed to become ladies of leisure. When she was 24 she was determined to pursue a career in nursing: an aspiration refused by her family. She initially studied privately, and subsequently continued in Germany. In 1853, she was appointed superintendent of the Institution for the Care of Sick Gentlewomen in Distressed Circumstances in Harley Street, London.

In 1854, however, she became aware of the situation of troops in the Crimea. A lack of adequate medical treatment was causing widespread death. At the Secretary of State for War's[96] request, Nightingale led a party of British nurses to the Crimea. For two years, Nightingale and a team of 38 nurses struggled with the organisation of supplies and the treatment of the sick, wounded and dying. She also organised a reading room, organised classes, schools and plays. In 1856, Florence Nightingale fell ill, and returned home to England. Concerned over the situation she had left behind, Nightingale pressed for a Royal Commission on barracks, military hospitals and the Army Medical Department, which was eventually established under the chairmanship of Sidney Herbert. For the next 50 years, Florence Nightingale was seriously ill, believed to be on the point of death. From her sickbed in 1860, she established a school for nurses at St Thomas's Hospital and raised £45,000 of public money to finance its cost. She also supervised nurses' training; worked on Poor Law reform; gathered statistics on childbirth and campaigned for ventilation and drainage. In 1907, Florence Nightingale became the first woman to be awarded the Order of Merit. It was Florence

---

[95] 1820–1910.
[96] Sidney Herbert.

Nightingale's example which inspired Henri Dunant to found the International Red Cross.[97]

The legal profession

In England, Canada and the United States, women were long denied entry to the legal profession. Two primary explanations suggest themselves. First, men had a personal interest in maintaining their privileged position. Secondly, women's exclusion was justified on the pretext of 'maintaining professional standards'. The first application from a woman to be enrolled as a solicitor in England was made in 1886, some seven years after Arabelia Mansfield had been admitted to legal practice in the United States. The application was rejected. In 1903, when Bertha Cave applied for admission to the Bar on behalf of herself and other law graduates, the Bar and the judges decided that the Bar should remain confined to men only. The first woman to be called to the Bar in England was Ivy Williams who succeeded in 1921. The first woman solicitor was Carrie Morrison who was admitted to practice in 1923. With the introduction of the female franchise, the Sex Disqualification Act of 1919 expressly stated the right of women to become barristers and solicitors. In that year, there were 20 women barristers. By 1955, there were 64, some 3.2 per cent. By 1976, the figure had reached 313, or 8.1 per cent and, in 1997 2,272, or 24 per cent. In 1995, of 63,628 practising solicitors in England and Wales, a mere 18,417, or 28.9 per cent, were women. In 1998, that figure has risen to 23,700, or nearly 33 per cent of the profession.

THE TWO WORLD WARS AND WOMEN'S EQUALITY

The First and Second World Wars[98] were to provide a major opportunity for women to participate in the public world previously almost exclusively occupied by men. With the outbreak of war in Europe in 1914, the suffrage movement found itself occupied with an altogether different challenge. Feminist strategists divided. On the one hand there were those women who saw in the war effort an opportunity for women to prove themselves worthy of the vote. On the other hand, there were feminists who adopted a pacifist stance, a difficult and personally dangerous position to adopt in the face of the threat to national freedom.

---

[97] Marie Curie, 1867–1934, was the first outstanding woman scientist, winning the Nobel Prize twice: once with her husband in physics, once alone in chemistry. Born in Warsaw, which at the time was occupied by Russia, Marie Curie studied at the Sorbonne in Paris. She was to become the first woman professor at the Sorbonne. She died in 1934 as a result of years of exposure to radium.

[98] See Rowbotham, S, *A Century of Women: The History of Women in Britain and the United States*, 1997, New York: Viking.

The contribution of women to the war effort, notwithstanding differences between suffragist activists, was seminal. Many upper- and middle-class women became nurses. Women not accepted by official organisations joined together on a voluntary basis. The Women's Land Army Service Corps, a voluntary organisation, became adopted officially and became the Women's Land Army. In 1917, the Women's Army Auxiliary Corps (WAAC) and the Women's Royal Naval Service (WRNS) were founded, to be followed by the Women's Royal Air Force in 1918. Women who had previously been employed in domestic service or as dressmakers joined the workforce. As the men left work for the services, the demand for female labour intensified, often in the face of strong opposition from male trade unions. But the demand for equality for women in the workplace grew: in 1918, women transport workers demanded equal pay – a demand which was not to be conceded.

In November 1918, peace was declared. With the return of the men from the war came the pressure for women to give up their employment in order to free the jobs for the men. But a fundamental shift in attitudes had occurred. No longer were women prepared to go back into domestic service: they had experienced the 'male' world, and demanded to remain included in it on an equal basis. The trades union movement became attractive to women: organisation was power. The Lord Chancellor established a Women's Advisory Committee. When the International Labour Organisation met for the first time in 1918, two women delegates were among the four delegates from Britain.

In the United States of America, there existed strong opposition against involvement in a European war. The conflict for women activists lay in the question of priority for the right to the vote and the need for peace. In 1917, the President[99] declared that those opposed to the war were disloyal citizens, and the Espionage Act introduced a new criminal offence of speaking or writing or organising against the war, and carried a possible prison sentence of 20 years and heavy fines.

In the post-war years of the 1920s in Britain, two principal strands of feminist thought emerged. On the one hand, the National Union of Societies for Equal Citizenship[100] (NUSEC) argued not for equal rights for women on the same basis as men, but on the basis of women's particular characteristics and needs. The Women's Co-operative Guild, which by 1930 had a membership of 66,566, also called for the recognition of women's differing needs, demanding better housing, health and maternity welfare services, libraries and municipal baths.

---

[99] Woodrow Wilson.
[100] Previously the National Union of Women's Suffrage Societies.

THE POSITION OF WOMEN IN CONTEMPORARY SOCIETY

The unlocking of the doors to the public world of work in Western societies has not resulted in equality within the world of work. Two factors dominate this unequal position: continuing discrimination against women in the workplace and in relation to promotion – covert if not overt – and the role of women as primary child carers.

A detailed study of patterns of work in four countries[101] – China, Japan, the United Kingdom and the United States of America – reveals not only a wealth of comparative statistical data, but also the extent to which work patterns are institutionalised and supported by State ideology. The data also indicates the extent to which the separation of the 'private sphere' (home and the family) from the 'public sphere' (work) has become institutionalised in Western capitalist industrialised societies. It was Max Weber who identified the necessity of the separation of the 'household' from the 'enterprise', in the interests of rational bureaucracy.[102] Stockman, Bonney and Xuewen state, in considering the analyses of Talcott Parsons, that there are two possible interpretations of the consequences of this separation in terms of the social roles of men and women. On the one hand, it can be argued that this separation fuels the evolution of the 'isolated nuclear family', which is functionally efficient for industrial capitalism, because it is mobile and also well adapted to fulfil 'socialisation functions'. Industrialisation and the growth of the nuclear family also, in Parsons' analysis, reinforces the division of labour within the family and the primary role of women as carers and the role of men as the primary earner.[103] The second interpretation concerns the rise in individuation and the recruitment of personnel on the basis of merit, and the correlative decline in the significance of race, ethnicity or gender. If this interpretation is adopted, it should follow that women enter the workplace on the basis of complete equality with men. The statistical data supports the former interpretation rather than the latter.

Participation in employment

Stockman, Bonney and Xuewen's comparative research reveals the extent to which political ideology affects the role of women in employment. In China, for example, with its emphasis on Chinese socialism, women's equality is a

---

[101] Stockman, N, Bonney, N and Xuewen, S, *Women's Work in East and West: The Dual Burden of Employment and Family Life*, 1995, London: UCL Press.
[102] Weber, M (1864–1920), *Economy and Society*, 1987, Berkeley: California: California UP. See, also, Parsons, T, *Societies: Evolutionary and Comparative Perspectives*, 1966, New Jersey: Prentice Hall.
[103] Parsons, T, Bales, J, Olds, M, Zelditch, P and Slater, E, *Family, Socialisation, and Interaction Process*, 1955, New York: Free Press.

central feature of government policy. The participation of women in the workforce is the highest of the four countries studied, the State provides extensive child care facilities and there is an extensive sharing of domestic roles between husband and wife. By contrast, in Japan, an economy characterised by the large corporation, life-long employment (of men) and corporate provision of housing (for men and their families), women who are employed by the large corporation are taken on under very different conditions from men: '[T]heir position is much more marginal, temporary and peripheral.'[104] Whereas women may be recruited as full time employees initially, women will be expected to leave work after either marriage or childbirth. If they re-enter employment, it will be as temporary workers or on a part time basis: '[A] woman's career is seen as being based in the home as a wife and mother.'[105]

Of the four countries studied, China reveals the least gender discrimination, followed by the United States of America, the United Kingdom and Japan. In the United Kingdom, 61 per cent of women under the age of 65 are employed, against 64 per cent in the United States of America.[106] The employment rates of women dip markedly in Japan and the United Kingdom, but less so in the United States, and hardly at all in China, during the primary childbearing years of 24 to 35.

Occupational differences

In terms of occupational differences between the United States and the United Kingdom, women are under-represented in production, transport and labouring. In both countries women are concentrated in services and clerical and related occupations. In 1990, an estimated 78 per cent of women were in clerical and related occupations in Britain:[107] in the United States this figure rises to between 80 and 90 per cent.[108] In the top two occupational groups – professional, technical-related and administrative and managerial, 32 per cent of American women are employed, whereas in the United Kingdom that figure is only 19 per cent.[109]

---

[104] *Op cit*, Stockman, Bonney and Xeuwen, fn 101, p 42.

[105] *Op cit*, Stockman, Bonney and Xeuwen, fn 101, p 42.

[106] *Op cit*, Stockman, Bonney and Xeuwen, fn 101, p 61, citing Blachflower, D and Oswald, A, 'International patterns of work', in Jowell, R, Witherspoon, S and Brook, L (eds), *British Social Attitudes: Special International Report*, 1989, Aldershot: Gower.

[107] British Labour Force Survey, 1992, OCPS.

[108] US Bureau of the Census, 1991.

[109] *Op cit*, Stockman, Bonney and Xeuwen, fn 101, p 69, citing Dale, A and Glover, J, *An Analysis of Women's Employment Patterns in the UK, France and the USA*, 1990, London Employment Department Group, Research Paper 75. See, also, Dex, S and Shaw, L, *British and American Women at Work*, 1986, London: Macmillan; Brinton, M, *Women and the Economic Miracle: Gender and Work in Postwar Japan*, 1993, Berkeley, California: California UP.

Part time work

Part time work for women, particularly in the child-rearing years, is a feature of Japanese, United States and United Kingdom employment practices, but does not feature largely in Chinese society. Each of the capitalist countries, but not the communist-socialist, thus retains the distinction between the gendered role of mothering and the traditional significance of the 'private' as the place in which children are reared. Stockton, Bonney and Xeuwen reveal that in China, women are entitled to up to two years of maternity leave, although in practice, in the sample studied, three-quarters of women took six months or less. On their return to work, Chinese women are entitled to resume their careers at the same seniority level. By contrast in Japan, as noted above, women are expected to leave employment for child-rearing purposes, and if they return to the workforce, it will be at a much lower level.

Women's pay

In Japan, women's annual income amounts to only 47.58 per cent of men's income. In Britain, women's weekly earnings in 1987 were 67 per cent of men's. Part time female workers earned just 57 per cent of men's income, whereas full time working women earned 74 per cent of men's income.[110] Full time women workers in the United States earn 70 per cent of male earnings.[111] In China, by contrast with Japan the United States and the United Kingdom, there is very little difference in rates of pay between men and women. In Britain, part time work is heavily concentrated among married women with young children. Women who continue in full time employment with young children are generally those in the higher occupational jobs. In 1989–91, 34 per cent of women with children under the age of five in the highest occupations (ie, professions, employer or managerial), remained in full time work, compared with only 13 per cent of all mothers with children under the age of five. Of unskilled manual women workers only two per cent remained in full time employment.

The British Central Statistical Office Report 1995[112]

One of the most fundamental changes in the United Kingdom labour market this century has been the increasing participation of women, particularly the extent to which they have taken up part time work.[113]

---

[110] *Op cit*, Stockton, Bonney and Xeuwen, fn 101, p 74.
[111] *Op cit*, Stockton, Bonney and Xeuwen, fn 101, p 74, citing US Bureau of Census 1991.
[112] Whitmarsh, A, *Social Focus on Women*, 1995, London: HMSO.
[113] *Ibid*, p 21.

In 1971, 44 per cent of women were 'economically active' (in either full time or part time employment); in 1994 53 per cent, and the figure projected for the year 2006 is 57 per cent. By contrast, between 1971 and 1994, the economic activity rate for men fell to 73 per cent, and is projected to fall to 70 per cent by the year 2006. Of mothers with children between the ages of five and 10, in 1994, 20 per cent were working full time, 44 per cent part time, six per cent were unemployed[114] and 30 per cent were 'inactive'. The number of women working part time in the United Kingdom between 1984 and 1994 rose by 19 per cent, whereas the increase in women's full time employment was only 12 per cent. In 1994, 45 per cent of economically active women worked part time, nearly twice as many men as women worked full time, while five times as many women as men worked part time.

Childcare looms large in the explanations for economic activity, full or part time, or inactivity, and a woman's economic activity is also affected by the number of children she has. Of women with three or more children, over 50 per cent were economically inactive in 1994, compared with less than one-third of women with one child. Moreover, where there is more than one child the mother is most likely to be working part time, if at all. The number of places in registered day nurseries in the United Kingdom in 1993 was over 120,000, compared with 1981 when there were less than 20,000. The number of total day places available for children under five in 1993 was close to one million.[115] Given the number of women who could potentially be in the workforce, and compared with the position in China, women's poverty and economic underactivity is most clearly explained by the failure of successive governments to invest in childcare facilities.

Women's earnings

Women remain lower paid than men in the United Kingdom according to the Government's statistics. In 1994, one-third of women earned £190 per week or less, compared with only 13 per cent of men. On the other hand, 75 per cent of men earned over £230 per week compared with only 50 per cent of women.

Occupational data

Clerical and secretarial remains the highest source of employment for women, with nearly 80 per cent of active women being in such employment. Personal and protective services is second, with just under 65 per cent, sales only

---

[114] In 1994, 885,000 women were unemployed.

[115] The Labour Government elected in 1997 is committed to greater childcare facilities, and to introducing a legal right to enable both mothers and fathers to take unpaid leave to care for children.

slightly lower. Under 50 per cent of women are in associated professional and technical employment, and 40 per cent in professional employment. Just over 30 per cent of women are managers and administrators; 20 per cent plant and machine operatives, and approximately 10 per cent are in craft and related occupations. Women outnumber men by four to one in the health sector and by two to one in the education sector. However, when it comes to seniority of employment position, the statistics reveal another picture.

In primary schools in England, Wales and Northern Ireland in 1991–92, women represented 81 per cent of all teachers, but only 57 per cent of head and deputy head teachers. In secondary schools, women represent 49 per cent of all teachers, but only 30 per cent are head and deputy head teachers. In the police force, where women have traditionally been under-represented, 13 per cent (or nearly 20,000) of police officers in the United Kingdom in 1994 were female. In 1994, of Chief Constables, Deputy Chief Constables and Assistant Chief Constables of approximately 42 police forces, only six were women. There were nine Chief Superintendents, 36 Superintendents, 70 Chief Inspectors, 285 Inspectors, 1,330 Sergeants and 18,245 Constables. Among the officers of the armed forces in the United Kingdom in 1995, seven per cent were women.

CHAPTER 3

PATRIARCHY

Aristotle, *The Politics*:[1]
For the male is more fitted to rule than the female, unless conditions are quite contrary to nature ...

Bacon, *Abridgement of the Law*:[2]
... the husband hath by law the power and dominion over the wife, and may beat her, but not in a violent or cruel manner.

Luce Irigaray, 'The bodily encounter with the mother':[3]
Their discourses, their values, their dreams and their desires have the force of law, everywhere and in all things. Everywhere and in all things, they define women's function and social role, and the sexual identity they are, or are not, to have.

While the theme of patriarchy runs throughout this book, it is useful to focus on the concept at this early stage.[4] Patriarchy and patriarchal theory, originating in ancient Greek thought, may be traced in English political theory at least to the seventeenth century which represented its high watermark. Notwithstanding its demise as a dominant political philosophy, however, patriarchy remains evident in both the public and private spheres of life and in the laws and legal institutions regulating society.

EXPLAINING PATRIARCHY

Patriarchy represents one of the most conceptually and analytically complex theoretical constructs and lies at the heart of traditional jurisprudence and the feminist critique. Not only is the concept difficult, but there exist also differing contemporary interpretations of it. Thus liberal feminists, cultural feminists, radical feminists, Marxist-socialist feminists, black feminists, lesbian feminists all have perceptions regarding patriarchy which while often overlapping, by no means converge into a coherent agreed definition. Thus the paradox exists:

---

1   Aristotle, *The Politics*, Sinclair, TA (trans), 1962, London: Penguin, Bk I xii, 1259a37.
2   1832.
3   Irigaray, L, 'The bodily encounter with the mother', in *Sexes et Parentés*, Macey, D (trans), 1993, New York: Columbia UP.
4   Patriarchy: a form of social organisation in which a male is the head of the family and descent, kinship, and title are traced through the male line; any society governed by such a system: *Collins English Dictionary*, 3rd edn, 1991, HarperCollins, p 1143.

patriarchy represents a core concept within feminist analyses of society and law, yet the content and meaning of that core concept remain contentious.

Theoretical explanations of the origins of patriarchy

Early political conceptions of patriarchy

In *Leviathan*, 1653, political philosopher Thomas Hobbes[5] laid to rest the confusion between adherence to the law of God and the law of man. The time of the 'Divine Right of Kings', in which the monarch claimed absolute power over and allegiance from his subjects on the basis that monarchical power was derived directly from God, had passed. In its place, Hobbes posited the Mortal God, the Leviathan, sovereign over all his subjects and to whom all subjects owed allegiance in return to the protection of the sovereign. In the turbulence of Hobbes' times, the Leviathan offered both security and social stability. Laws are but the commands of the sovereign to his subjects. The key to understanding sovereignty lies in the core concept of power – absolute power. In Wayne Morrison's assessment, 'Hobbes ushers in the modern subject-sovereign relationship and provides a new epistemological configuration and legitimacy for the power to command'.[6] That power, albeit gained through the consent of the governed, is patriarchal.

Hobbes appears ambivalent about the status of women. In *Elements of Law*, for example, Hobbes writes that 'the father or mother of the family is sovereign of the same'.[7] Elsewhere, it appears that only fathers have patriarchal right.[8] In *Leviathan*, Hobbes discusses the concept of equality. It is clear at this point that this equality – which stems from the ability of each individual to injure or kill another – includes women. The significance of the individual power to harm others is the basis of his political philosophy: in order to prevent harm and to ensure social stability, power must be conferred, through consent, to a sovereign: a Leviathan. In relation to children, the mother is 'sovereign'.[9] In Susan Moller Okin's analysis, this sovereignty later disappears from view, and Hobbes 'proceeds to present the family as a strictly and solely patriarchal institution'.[10]

---

[5] See Morrison, W, *Jurisprudence: From the Greeks to Post-modernism*, 1997, London: Cavendish Publishing, Chapter 4.

[6] *Ibid*, p 99.

[7] Hobbes, T, *De Corpore Politico*, Chapter IV, p 158, and see Sommerville, JP, *Thomas Hobbes: Political Ideas in Historical Context*, 1992, Basingstoke: Macmillan.

[8] For discussion of Hobbes' views, see Pateman, C, *The Sexual Contract*, 1988, London: Polity, Chapter 3; Moller Okin, S, *Women in Western Political Thought*, 1979, Ewing, New Jersey: Princeton UP, Chapter 9.

[9] Hobbes, T, *De Cive*, repr 1972, Garden City: Doubleday & Co, IX, 3.

[10] *Ibid*, Moller Okin, fn 8, p 198.

Patriarchy

Patriarchy was central to the work of Sir Robert Filmer writing in the seventeenth century,[11] and to John Locke who launched a devastating attack on Filmer's work.[12] As political theory, patriarchalism reflected the view of society being ruled by an absolute ruler, to whom all subjects were subservient. No individual was free: each was subordinate to a superior political force. Patriarchy explained all social relations: sovereign/subject, father/child, master/servant. Each has his or her assigned role, not predicated on choice but on some form of natural allocation of societal roles. The rationale for patriarchal power lay, for Filmer, in his interpretation of the scriptures, and the role assigned to Adam by God:

> By the appointment of God, as soon as Adam was created he was monarch of the world, though he had no subjects; ... Adam was a King from his creation ... Eve was subject to Adam before he sinned; the angels who are of a pure nature, are subject to God ...[13]

For Filmer, the idea of some form of social contract between the people and the sovereign was mythical.[14] Firmly opposed to the idea of social consent, and the notion that citizens somehow, somewhere, at some time, agree to be governed on certain contractual terms, Filmer mounted a fierce attack. If the consent of the people is required, who are these people? Do they include women and children? Are children to be included in the votes of their parents, as if they had 'tacitly consented'? Such an argument could not, in Filmer's view, be sustained with logic. Men were not born free at birth, as social contract theory insisted, rather men are born into a preordained subject status: for men subjection to the monarch, for women subjection to the monarch and her father and husband.

John Locke took issue with Filmer on a number of fronts. On the sovereignty accorded to Adam by Filmer, Locke took issue with Filmer's use of biblical sources,[15] arguing that the references provided no authority for the sovereignty of man alone. Locke, however, also remained ambivalent about women, seemingly accepting the 'natural' inferiority of women's social status, but always insisting that women could overcome their 'natural' disabilities.

It is with the *Second Treatise* that Locke develops his own distinctive theory of social relations rooted firmly in social contract theory. Men and women enter into a voluntary contract with each other:

---

[11] Filmer, R, *The Anarchy of a Limited or Mixed Monarchy*, 1648; *The Freeholder's Grand Inquest*, 1648; *Observations upon Aristotle, Touching Forms of Government*, 1652; *Patriarcha*, 1680. See Laslett, P (ed), *Sir Robert Filmer, Patriarcha and Other Political Works of Sir Robert Filmer*, 1949, Oxford: Basil Blackwell.

[12] Locke, J, *Two Treatises on Government* (1690), 1924, London: JM Dent.

[13] *Ibid*, Laslett, p 289.

[14] On social contract theory see, for further discussion, Chapter 6.

[15] Specifically, *Genesis*, 3:16.

> Conjugal Society is made by a voluntary Compact between Man and Woman: tho' it consist chiefly in such a Communion and Right in one another's Bodies, as is necessary to its chief End, Procreation; yet it draws with it mutual Support and Assistance, and a Communion of Interest too, as necessary not only to unite their Care, and Affection, but also necessary to their common Off-spring, who have a Right to be nourished and maintained by them, till they are able to provide for themselves.[16]

However, there remains within Locke's writing hints of patriarchy. Whereas husband and wife are equal, there will be occasions when a 'last Determination' must be made. That last Determination falls to the husband, by virtue of his greater 'ability and strength'. This power of decision arises in matters pertaining to jointly held properties and interests. In Locke's view, the husband's power leaves the wife:

> ... in the full and free possession of what by Contract is her Peculiar Right, and gives the Husband no more power over her Life, than she has over his. The *Power of the Husband* being so far from that of an absolute monarch that the *Wife* has, in many cases, a Liberty to *separate* from him; where natural Right or their Contract allows it, whether Customs or Laws of the Country they live in; and the Children upon such Separation fall to the Father or Mother's lot, as such contract does determine.[17]

In relation to civil society, man is originally born into a 'state of nature'. The transformation from a state of nature to civil society is brought about, through the consent of its members, in order to provide the rules necessary for the governance of all people. Locke's position on women within the political society remains obscure. On the one hand, Locke is clear as to women's natural equality. On the other hand, ultimate decision making power over matters of common interest is accorded to the husband. The question then arises as to whether women are accorded political equality alongside their husbands, or whether it is the husband who is deemed to be representative of the family in political life. Locke separates paternal right within the family from political right. By means of this separation, woman is excluded from the political sphere and confined, in the 'natural subordination' within the private sphere of the family.[18]

In the nineteenth century, John Stuart Mill was to consider the status of women in society. Mill regarded the relationship between the sexes as one characterised by the 'legal subordination of one sex to the other'.[19] In his view, this subordination of women by men, came about not by any conscious thought or experimentation with differing forms of social organisation, but rather through the unreflective acceptance of the status quo handed down

---

[16] *Op cit*, Locke, fn 12, Pt II, p 78.
[17] *Op cit*, Locke, fn 12, Pt II, p 82.
[18] See *op cit*, Pateman, fn 8, Chapter 4.
[19] Mill, JS, *The Subjection of Women* (1869), 1989, Cambridge: CUP, p 119.

through history. In the 'earliest twilight of human society' women were subjugated by men on the basis of their physical inferiority, and that state of subjection had simply continued and become translated into rules of law. With slavery abolished, the state of marriage, for Mill, remained the last vestige of slavery in society.

Lawful patriarchy within the family in earlier times

Women in the nineteenth century, governed by the doctrine of 'one flesh', found themselves tied to husbands whose every whim – violent or sexual – could be forced upon her, with no legal rights over her children whatsoever, thus tying her more firmly into a state of dependency in the condition of slavery.[20] This view is endorsed by Sir Henry Maine:

> I do not know how the operation and nature of the ancient Patria Potestas can be brought so vividly before the mind as by reflecting on the prerogatives attached to the husband by the pure English Common Law, and by recalling the rigorous consistency with which the view of a complete legal subjection on the part of the wife is carried by it ...[21]

The legal subjection included the right of the husband to sexual intercourse with his wife. Under the one flesh doctrine (and the flesh was his) enshrined in law, on marriage the wife impliedly consented to sexual intercourse 'on demand' (the converse position did not, of course, pertain). Until 1884, a wife refusing her husband's sexual demands could find herself imprisoned for such refusal, and the husband could apply for an order of restitution of conjugal rights against his wife. Moreover, until 1891, in order to enforce his rights, the husband was entitled to imprison his wife in the matrimonial home.

In earlier times, the English church courts had jurisdiction over matters of morals. The underlying rationale for such involvement in private morality, enforced predominantly against women, and most especially married women, lay in the need to preserve legitimate lines of succession to family property, and to uphold the authority and superiority of men. Up until 1746, adultery could be prosecuted as a misdemeanour. By 1670, if a woman was found to have committed adultery, the husband could pursue a claim against the seducer of his wife for criminal conversation: 'crim con'.[22] Criminal conversation was a common law adaptation of the law of trespass, and was tried in the King's Bench Division of the High Court. The wife played no role in the proceedings, and was unable either to testify on her own behalf or call witnesses: she, after all, had no legal personality. Trial was by jury. The award

---

[20] On women's former legal disabilities, see, further, Chapter 2.
[21] Maine, H, *Ancient Law*, 1972, London: JM Dent, pp 93–94.
[22] For a detailed history of this action, see Stone, L, *Road to Divorce: England 1530–1987*, 1992, Oxford: OUP, Chapter IX.

of damages was high: in 1790, a jury awarded, without deliberation, £700; in 1802, £5,000, and in 1815, after an hour's deliberation, an award of damages was reduced from £30,000 to £15,000. The action for crim con was abolished in 1857, following fierce debate, when the first Divorce Bill was passed. Objections to the action included the publication of court proceedings which caused English law to come into disrepute, especially in Europe, and no doubt a degree of public hilarity at the expense of the parties. The action was also deplored for its representation of women as mere property, injury to which could be recompensed by an action for damages. Further, Lawrence Stone argues, there was a sense of concern over the confusion between the 'external world of commerce and the marketplace with the private world of Victorian domesticity and love', two spheres which the public mind was coming increasingly to view as entirely separate.[23]

The introduction of judicial divorce in 1857 did not mark the end of the patriarchal tradition. Despite strong advocacy for equality in the law of divorce between men and women, Parliament introduced divorce on restrictive discriminatory terms. Whereas a husband could sue for divorce on the basis of his wife's adultery, a wife could only petition on the husband's adultery if this were accompanied by incest, bigamy, cruelty, involuntary desertion or rape or an unnatural offence.[24] With the action for crim con abolished, some means was deemed essential to allow husbands to recover damages from a seducer: the concept of the 'co-respondent' was introduced. The rationale for the availability of divorce on the ground of adultery *simpliciter* against the wife continued to lie in the fear that a wife might try to foist an illegitimate child on the husband, thus threatening the line of the legitimate succession of property.

A further battle raging at the time of the divorce reform was over a woman's right (or non-right) to own or manage her property on marriage. For wealthy women, the device of settlement could be used, whereby a wife kept control over her property during marriage through trustees. For the bulk of the population, however, no such protection was available. On marriage wives could neither own nor manage property. Moreover on separation a husband remained legally entitled to seize his wife's property (juristically, the property became his on marriage, and hence it follows that it was 'his' property). The Divorce Reform Act 1857 secured the right for separated or deserted wives to hold and manage their own property, but did not extend the same right to women living in marriage: that was not to be achieved until 1882.[25]

---

[23] *Op cit*, Stone, fn 22, p 291, citing Houghton, N, *The Victorian Frame of Mind*, 1957, New Haven: Yale UP, pp 348–93.
[24] Matrimonial Causes Act 1857, s 27.
[25] See the Married Women's Property Act 1882.

The availability of divorce, and the resort to divorce by women, was overshadowed by the number of women who applied for maintenance in the courts. In 1886, the Maintenance of Wives Act was passed, which provided that a magistrates' court had jurisdiction to award temporary order for maintenance for wives of deserted wives or victims of domestic violence. Stone records that in around 1900, some '10,700 wives applied on their own behalf' and 'another 4,000 or so applications were made on behalf of paupers by the Poor Law authorities'. At the same date, only 700 applications for divorce were made.[26]

It was in the Victorian era that English married women were first given the right to custody over their children. In relation to unmarried mothers, the law, since at least the time of Elizabeth I,[27] provided that children born outside marriage were under the sole control of their mothers: in relation to their natural fathers, such children were *fillius nulius*. Married women accordingly were discriminated against under the common law. A father's right to the physical possession of his child could only be lost if to enforce the right would lead to the child's moral or physical harm.[28] From 1660, if the father appointed a testamentary guardian, the guardian's rights superseded those of the mother which would otherwise have accrued on the death of her husband.[29] Talfourd's Act 1839 for the first time entitled a mother to claim custody of her children until they reached the age of seven and contact with them until the age of majority, provided that she had not been guilty of adultery. Mothers' rights were extended in 1873,[30] giving the courts jurisdiction to grant custody to a mother until the child reached the age of 16. The right of the father to defeat the mother's claim to custody by granting a testamentary guardian was abolished in 1886.[31] In 1925, the Guardianship of Infants Act provided that neither mother nor father had superior claims to their children before the courts. That Act also permitted mothers for the first time to appoint testamentary guardians. It was not to be before 1973 that the first statutory declaration was to be made as to the equality of mothers and fathers equal, separately exercisable rights.[32]

---

[26] *Op cit*, Stone, fn 22, p 386.
[27] Reigned 1558–1603.
[28] See *Re Andrews* (1873) LR 8 QB 153, p 158.
[29] Tenures Abolition Act 1660.
[30] Custody of Infants Act 1873.
[31] Guardianship of Infants Act 1886.
[32] Guardianship Act 1973, s 1.

CONTEMPORARY PATRIARCHAL MANIFESTATIONS

The 'public' sphere

Patriarchy operates in both the 'public' and the 'private' sphere of life.[33] In the public sphere, one of the most enduring historical exclusions of women lay in the denial of the right to vote.[34] By denying, through law, the right to vote, women were denied the opportunity to influence the political process and the content of legislation, remaining dependent upon men to represent their interests. With the formal right to equality in the electoral process secured, however, the patriarchal tradition remains evident in the public sphere of politics and employment.

Women remain under-represented in the vast majority of legislatures around the world. In the United Kingdom, the current membership of the House of Commons is 547 men and 112, or 17 per cent, women, the latter figure being the highest proportion of women in Parliament in history. The highest figure for participation in the legislative process comes from Norway, with approximately 40 per cent of women in the legislature. Popularly regarded as 'one of the best (man's) clubs in London', Parliament is not organised to suit the needs of women. The hours of work are a principal problem, with late night, and occasionally all night sittings which disadvantage women who also carry family responsibilities. The major political parties, up until the 1997 election, placed little emphasis on the selection of women parliamentary candidates, and it is more than probable that constituency selection committees, whose membership is predominantly male, would be cautious in selecting a woman, particularly one with young children.

The legislature is not the only institution to reflect an exclusionary position in relation to female membership.[35] As the data provided in Chapter 2 reveals, despite the formal equality of women in the employment sector, women continue to earn less than men, continue to have less chance of promotion than men, and remain under-represented in the higher echelons of the professions, management and industry. Many women who have broken through the 'glass ceiling' have done so largely by conforming to male expectations and forfeiting their private lives, and in particular children.

---

[33] On which distinction, see, further, Chapter 6.
[34] On which struggle, see, further, Chapter 2.
[35] A classic illustration of Victorian values is reflected in the fact that even Barbara Mills, the first female Director of Public Prosecutions in England, and a graduate and honorary fellow of her Oxford University college, has been denied full membership of the Oxford and Cambridge Club: see Figes, K, *Because of Her Sex*, 1995, London: Pan, p 49.

The 'private' sphere

The private sphere of life provides the backdrop for the public sphere: relations within the private sphere, and particularly the division of labour within the family, often if not invariably dictate the capacity of individuals to participate fully in the public world of government and employment.

The invisibility of women

Women's confinement to the 'private' – to the domestic world traditionally unregulated by law – ensured that women were largely invisible to the law. Women were the 'other sex', relegated to the control and sovereignty of the husband. Thus men were the subjects of law, women invisible. As seen above, English law has been slow to divest itself of this ideological stance. The invisibility of women masked the absence of women's rights. That the law only became alert to the problem of domestic violence in the 1970s attests to that invisibility.[36] Law's blindness to the private sphere explains the perpetuation of exploitation of and violence against women in the family. That which law does not explicitly proscribe infers implicit acceptance. The position of wives under English law with regard to marital sexual intercourse was determined by Sir Matthew Hale in *The History of the Pleas of the Crown*:[37]

> But the husband cannot be guilty of a rape committed by himself upon his lawful wife, for by their mutual matrimonial consent and contract the wife hath given herself up in this kind unto her husband which she cannot retract.[38]

The power of the husband to discipline his wife in marriage was propounded by Bacon writing in 1736: a husband might beat his wife, but not in a 'cruel or violent manner', and confine her in order to ensure her obedience.[39] While Sir William Blackstone, writing in the late eighteenth century, asserted that the practice of chastisement had died out in 'polite society', he accepted that 'the lower rank of people, who were always fond of the old common law, still claim and exert their ancient privilege'.[40]

---

36 See Pizzey, E, *Scream Quietly or the Neighbours Will Hear*, 1974, London: Penguin; Domestic Violence and Matrimonial Proceedings Act 1975, s 1; Domestic Proceedings and Magistrates' Courts Act 1978, s 16.

37 Hale, M (Sir), *The History of the Pleas of the Crown* (1736), 1971, London: London Professional Books.

38 *Ibid*, Vol 1, Chapter 58, p 629. For a literary example of the assertion of husbands' rights, see Galsworthy, J, *The Man of Property, (The Forsyte Chronicles, I)*, (1906), 1951, London: Penguin, pp 264–65: 'The morning after a certain night on which Soames at last asserted his rights and acted like a man, he breakfasted alone ... [i]n the cool judgment of right-thinking men, of men of the world, of such as he recollected often received praise in the Divorce Court, he had but done his best to sustain the sanctity of marriage, to prevent her [Irene] from abandoning her duty, possibly, ... from [adultery].'

39 Bacon, *Abridgement of the Law*, 1736, Tit baron and Feme (B).

40 Blackstone, Sir W, *Commentaries on the Laws of England 1765–69*, 1978, New York: Garland.

That in the United Kingdom, domestic violence did not come to the renewed attention[41] of the legislature until 1975,[42] and the criminalisation of rape within marriage did not come about before 1992,[43] attests to law's seminal blindness to social fact and its disregard for male dominance within the private world of the family.[44]

It is to this classification of the private and the public spheres of life – the former largely unregulated, the latter closely regulated – that feminist legal scholars have devoted much analysis and discourse. In feminism's now seminal phrase, 'the personal is political'. From a feminist perspective, so-called 'private' life cannot be isolated from society's attention: the refusal of society and law to recognise the realities of patriarchy have for too long rendered women vulnerable to abuse, manipulation and violence.

However, whilst the germ of this thesis is relatively easy to digest, closer analysis reveals many complexities, for the matter in hand is crucially related to liberal political philosophy and to continued (male) resistance to the realisation of the full equality of women. It must be conceded that conceptualisation of the 'public' and 'private' spheres of life is by no means lacking in difficulty, as is the extent to which law exerts its regulation. The classic illustration of the 'private sphere' is that of the family. Yet, nowadays, the State increasingly impacts upon the family via, *inter alia*, the regulation of marriage and divorce; the treatment of children; financial provision; domestic violence; social security entitlements. Nor is the 'public sphere' more easily or more accurately definable: if the 'public' sphere is that area of life which is regulated by law, as one conceptualisation insists, we may then be clear that matters such as employment, the provision of goods and services (including health and education), for example, fall clearly within the public sphere.

---

[41] See Power Cobbe, F, *Wife Torture in England*, 1878, which led to the Matrimonial Causes Act 1878, giving a criminal court the power to make a separation, maintenance and custody order in favour of a wife whose husband had been convicted of aggravated assault on his wife, if her future safety was in doubt.

[42] See the *Report of the Select Committee on Violence in Marriage*, HC 553, 1974–75. See, also, *op cit*, Pizzey, fn 36; Maidment, S, 'The law's response to marital violence in England and the USA' (1977) 26 ICLQ 403; Eekelaar, JM and Katz, SN, *Family Violence*, 1978, Toronto: Butterworths; Hoggett, B, Pearl, D, Cooke, E and Bates, P, *The Family, Law and Society: Cases and Materials*, 4th edn, 1996, London: Butterworths, Chapter 9.

[43] *R v R* [1992] 1 AC 599; *SW v United Kingdom; CR v United Kingdom* [1996] 1 FLR 434; [1996] Fam 275. See the Law Commission's response in *Rape Within Marriage*, Working Paper No 116, 1990, London: HMSO.

[44] On domestic violence, see, further, Chapter 11.

Extending the private sphere?

There is now a well documented movement in the West, and particularly in the United Kingdom, towards 'privatisation' of the ownership and management of public service provision.[45]

Furthermore, the privatisation movement may be viewed as extending to previously regulated areas of the 'private' which have formerly been regulated by law. If one takes by way of example the law relating to divorce, financial provision and property settlements on divorce, up until the present time these have been largely regulated by the Matrimonial Causes Act 1973, which provides a detailed scheme of the facts sufficient to evidence the breakdown of marriage, and an equally detailed statutory scheme for the settlement of disputes/claims over ancillary matters relating to financial provision and matrimonial property. It is true that the law allows – even encourages – parties to a marriage to reach agreements over such matters which can then be incorporated into an order[46] endorsed by the court. Thus, increasingly, parties to a marriage are seen to be 'bargaining in the shadow of the law'. In the 1990s, however, the Government has been seeking to roll back the frontiers of State regulation of divorce and its implications. Privatisation is again the key word: the facts evidencing the breakdown of marriage are to be removed from the statute book. From 1999 in England, divorce will become available at the instigation of either party following the filing of a declaration that the marriage has irretrievably broken down, followed by a substantial period of reflection during which agreements must be reached, with the assistance of some form of mediation, as to the arrangements for any children of the marriage and matters pertaining to financial provision and property distribution.[47] While in practice the current law has, in the view of the Law Commission, proved 'misleading, discriminatory and unjust',[48] the privatisation of divorce under the reformed law may prove equally disadvantageous for women seeking to reach fair agreements about finance, property and children following divorce unless the mediation process provides the requisite protection for the economically weaker party.[49]

---

[45] See, eg, the privatisation policy of the Conservative Government, 1979–96, during which British Gas, British Rail, the British Nuclear Industry, British Telecom have all been privatised.

[46] A 'consent order'.

[47] Family Law Act 1996.

[48] Law Commission, *Facing the Future: A Discussion Paper on the Ground for Divorce*, Law Com No 170, 1998, London: HMSO; Law Commission, *Family Law: The Ground for Divorce*, Law Com No 192, 1990, London: HMSO.

[49] This fear is borne out by evidence from Australia and New Zealand. See Neave, M, 'Private ordering in family law – will women benefit?', in Thornton, M (ed), *Public and Private: Feminist Legal Debates*, Melbourne: OUP, p 144.

A similar philosophy may be found in the law relating to children. Until the Children Act 1989 was brought into force, the guiding principle was that where parents separated, it was a matter for the courts to determine – utilising the concept of the best interests of the child – the future arrangements regarding children.[50] Under public law provisions, the grounds on which local authorities could intervene to protect children from poor parenting (whether evidenced by neglect, ill-treatment or abuse) were stringently defined by statute and the courts.[51] The policy of local authorities was geared primarily to the protection of the child and their powers both sweeping and severe. Under the Children Act 1989, however, the protection policy has given way to a policy which attempts to promote the idea of a partnership between local authority social services departments and the parents of children, whereby local authorities may provide advice and assistance, and if necessary voluntary accommodation for children in need.[52] Where, however, a local authority wishes to protect a child through taking it into non-voluntary care, and under the old law there existed numerous grounds on which this could be effected against the parents' wishes, there exists nowadays a single criterion on which children may be removed from their parents: that of avoidable 'significant harm' attributable to the parents' care.[53]

In relation to both the private and public law relating to children, where matters come before a court of law, the court is directed both to give paramountcy to the welfare of the child,[54] but also not to make any court order unless so to do would make a significant contribution to the child's welfare.[55] That there is a potential for a conflict between these two guiding principles is evident. It is not intended here to pursue a detailed analysis of family law, but rather to demonstrate that, at differing times, employing differing philosophies, the 'private' area of life may be both significantly regulated and then deregulated according to prevailing political philosophy.

Moreover, it is not necessarily the case that regulation or deregulation is uniform in respect of the private area of life. Law may regulate by deliberate statutory or common law control, but it may equally be regulated by *ignoring* certain aspects of private life. An illustration of such 'non-control' may be seen in relation to homosexuality. The law is clear, for example, that the only persons eligible to marry under English law are respectively male and female.

---

[50] See, eg, Guardianship of Minors Act 1971; Guardianship Act 1973; Matrimonial Causes Act 1973; Domestic Proceedings and Magistrates' Courts Act 1978.

[51] See, eg, the Custody of Children Act 1891; Children and Young Persons Acts 1933 and 1963; Children and Young Persons Act 1969; Children Act 1975.

[52] See Pt II and Sched II of the Act.

[53] See the Children Act 1989, s 31; see, also, for the House of Lords' interpretation of this section, *Re M (A Minor) (Care order: threshold conditions)* [1994] 2 AC 424; [1994] 2 FLR 577.

[54] Children Act 1989, s 1.

[55] Children Act 1989, s 1(5).

Consistently, the law has refused to recognise the validity of a purported marriage between persons of the same sex, and furthermore, even where one of the parties has undergone a sex change operation, the law will not recognise – for the purposes of the law relating to marriage – that a person's gender has been changed and may be recognised.[56]

By refusing to recognise a person's individual human right to marry according to the law,[57] that individual is rendered non-existent, an 'outsider', a non-person in the eyes of the law. Even the law's refusal to recognise the existence of certain categories of person is inconsistent. As Katherine O'Donovan has argued,[58] male homosexuality is regulated by law, whereas female lesbianism is unregulated, and through regulation homosexuality is defined by concepts of 'circumscription of areas of privacy' whereas female lesbianism may be categorised as 'invisible' to the law.[59]

Abortion law also represents an area which straddles the public and private. Whereas, *par excellence*, the legal right to abortion should be viewed as a matter for a woman's determination alone, the cultural and religious sensitivities towards abortion intrude. In the United Kingdom, the Abortion Act 1967[60] provides that an abortion is available on medical (psychological and physical) and social grounds for a woman up to 22 weeks of pregnancy, upon the certification of two doctors.[61] Thus, the availability of abortion – dependent upon medical approval – confers not an absolute right but rather a conditional claim. In the Republic of Ireland, with the close nexus between Church and State, abortion remains unavailable. In the United States of America, the abortion issue has become one of fierce constitutional and feminist debate. From a feminist standpoint, the mother's 'right' to control her own body is circumscribed by external – public – factors represented by the interest of the State and society and the interests of the genetic or social father of the foetus.

Despite conceptual difficulties, however, the notions of the public and the private retain a central importance to feminist legal theory, an importance which transcends analysis of purely domestic law and may been seen also in relation to international law. Hilary Charlesworth, for example, has argued that the public/private dichotomy explains the differing treatment under

---

[56] See *Corbett v Corbett* [1971] P 83; *Rees v United Kingdom* [1987] 2 FLR 111; *Cossey v United Kingdom* [1991] 2 FLR 492.

[57] See the European Convention on Human Rights and Fundamental Freedoms, Art 12.

[58] See O'Donovan, K, *Sexual Divisions in Law*, 1985, London: Weidenfeld and Nicolson, especially Chapter 1.

[59] *Ibid*, O'Donovan, p 7. See also, Mason, G, '(Out)Laws: acts of proscription in the sexual order', in Thornton, *op cit*, fn 49.

[60] As amended by the Human Fertilisation and Embryology Act 1990.

[61] Abortion Act 1967, s 1(1)(a), as amended by the Human Fertilisation and Embryology Act 1990.

international law of differing crimes.[62] Thus genocide, torture, violence in armed conflict may all attract sanctions. However, international law has been slow and cautious in its approach to the specific problems which women suffer in wartime: in particular rape by members of armed forces. International law has also proven inept in changing cultural practices which particularly affect women. Whether the practice be that of the footbinding of women, or Hindu suttee – the burning of the widow on the funeral pyre of the husband – or that of the circumcision of young girls and women, international law has shown a willingness to consign such practices to the private sphere which is 'not the law's business'.

INEQUALITY IN THE PUBLIC AND PRIVATE SPHERES

The struggle for the enfranchisement of women has been discussed in Chapter 2. As noted there, the right to vote is the hallmark of citizenship, of full participation in the *polis*. However, whilst the vote for women was finally won across the Western world, that right did not automatically confer full and equal rights upon women in other spheres of life. The legal and medical professions represented two of the most, but certainly not the only, intractable bodies which opposed women's entry. As Kate Millett has written:

> [O]ur society, like all other historical civilisations, is a patriarchy. The fact is evident at once if one recalls that the military, industry, technology, universities, science, political office, and finance – in short, every avenue of power within the society including the coercive force of the police, is entirely within male hands.[63]

The significance of patriarchal attitudes within both the public and private spheres has a resonance far greater than simply the statistical representation of women in differing walks of life. The historical fact of gendered inequality, absorbed into law, explains the phenomenon of hierarchy within law – man as the subject of law, women the 'other'. While the law speaks in gender-neutral language, deconstructing the language of law reveals that the primary subject of law is male.[64] Man is the referent by which woman is judged. It is by the imposition of male standards that a woman is constructed. In the public sphere of paid employment, man is the paradigmatic subject of the law. Manifestations abound: for women to succeed, they must succeed by male standards and on male terms; sexual harassment in all sectors of employment remains largely unabated, notwithstanding its legal proscription; in the

---

[62] Charlesworth, H, Chinkin, C and Wright, S, 'Feminist approaches to international law' (1911) 85 AJIL 613. (See *Sourcebook*, p 537.)
[63] Millett, K, *Sexual Politics* (1972), 1977, London: Virago, p 25.
[64] See, further, Chapter 1 on feminist legal methods.

United Kingdom, women but not men are entitled to maternity leave, thus perpetuating the notion that women alone should bear the practical responsibility of nurturing and the inevitable consequence of career disruption and the problem of re-entry into employment at the same level. Women's work in the private sector has profound implications for her work in the public sphere. Women continue to bear the brunt of domestic and childcare responsibilities, irrespective of their role in paid employment. The female paid employee does not leave work in the public sphere for relaxation in the private sphere. For here too she toils. Of the four societies studied by Stockton, Bonney and Xuewen,[65] only in China do women participate on equal terms in the public sphere of work and enjoy a significant sharing of responsibilities in the private sphere of the family.[66] By contrast in Japan, the United States and the United Kingdom, women, irrespective of their employment status, continue to undertake the role of primary domestic worker. It is this responsibility which contributes so significantly to women's low employment status and the predominance of women in part time employment, and the designation of so many low status jobs as 'women's work'.

The Subject of law: woman as 'Other'

It is to Simone de Beauvoir[67] that credit is due for her perceptions about women as 'Other':

> Now, what peculiarly signalises the situation of woman is that she – a free and autonomous being like all human creatures – nevertheless finds herself living in a world where men compel her to assume the status of the Other.[68]
>
> History has shown us that men have always kept in their hands all concrete powers; since the earliest days of the patriarchate they have thought best to keep woman in a state of dependence; their codes of law have been set up against her; and thus she has been definitely established as the Other.[69]

In the linguistic tradition of binary opposites,[70] subject/object, self/other, male/female, public/private, power/powerlessness, dominance/subordination etc the former half of the pair is the dominant, the latter half the subordinate. The self of law is the male self. The status of 'manhood', according to Hegel, was acquired by 'the stress of thought and much technical

---

[65] The United States of America, United Kingdom, Japan and China. The research is discussed in Chapter 2.

[66] Stockton, N, Bonney, N and Xuewen, S, *Women's Work in East and West*, 1995, London: UCL Press.

[67] See de Beauvoir, S, *The Second Sex* (1949), Parshley, H (ed and trans), 1989, London: Picador.

[68] *Ibid*, p 29.

[69] *Ibid*, Part III, Chapter 1, p 171.

[70] See on this, further, Chapter 9.

exertion'.[71] That male selfhood, manhood, required clear delineation from woman. The male is depicted universally as powerful, rational, logical, reasonable and non-affective (in public). The universal depiction of woman, on the other hand, is as emotional, irrational, lacking reason and powerless. Thus woman's construction, as the Other, and against the male standard, defines what men are not. Woman is thus, in Luce Irigaray's analysis,[72] a man's mirror, a mirror which in the words of Ngaire Naffine, 'reflects him back whole, as a clearly defined image'.[73]

Where the legislature acts ostensibly to eliminate through law those practices which discriminate against women, or which disable women – physically, emotionally or psychologically – the ironic consequence is that the law is framed either in male language, or cast in terms which ignore the effect of such practices on women by introducing legal standards which deny women's subjectivities. Three examples of this phenomenon will be considered here. The first is the law relating to physical violence against women and the treatment of women by the legal system who respond with violence to the infliction of violence upon them; the second the law relating to sexual harassment; the third the law relating to pornography. While each of these examples are discussed more fully elsewhere in this work, their relevance to the issue of patriarchy and the public/private debate demands introductory coverage at this point.

Physical violence against women

Prior to the introduction of specific domestic violence legislation, English criminal law provided (and of course continues to provide) a range of charges regulating violent behaviour: ranging from assault and battery through to rape, manslaughter and murder. It is the law relating to domestic violence and rape which is particularly revealing of law's exclusion of women's subjectivities.

Domestic violence – statistically most frequently inflicted by a man on a women – may be represented as the successor to, or perpetuation of, the formerly socially accepted right of men to control their wives; rape as the manifestation of male power over women. As a phenomenon, domestic violence is inherently and inseparably connected to male power and female powerlessness; male dominance and female subordination.

Criminologists and psychologists seek rational explanations for the phenomenon regarded as one of the most widespread and under-reported crimes throughout the world.[74] Thus, social deprivation, economic

---

[71] Hegel, G, *Philosophy of Right*, Knox, T (trans), 1952, Oxford: OUP, p 33.
[72] See Irigaray, L, *Speculum of the Other Woman*, Gill, G (trans), 1985, New York: Cornell UP.
[73] Naffine, N, 'Sexing the subject (of law)', in Thornton, *op cit*, fn 49, p 36.
[74] See the United Nations Reports, *The World's Women 1970–90*, 1991, London: HMSO; *The World's Women 1995: Trends and Statistics*, 1995, London: HMSO.

depression, personality disorders, experientially learned violence, are offered to explain – and thus partially to exclude – the perpetrator, as if somehow circumstances or factors external to the violent man reduce his liability for the violent acts.

To cast around for such near-justificatory explanations, from a feminist perspective, is to miss – not necessarily deliberately, but almost certainly subconsciously – the central explanatory feature of domestic violence: male control and its maintenance.[75] That other factors play a part in explaining such violence is undeniable, but as Dobash and Dobash have argued, alone they have insufficient explanatory power.[76]

From this perspective, domestic violence, perpetuated in the private sphere of life, the home, is a prime manifestation of patriarchal authority. The gender inequality of the public world becomes reinforced in the 'private' world of the family. In addition to controlling women through repeated physical assertions of power, violence against women has the effect of silencing women and thereby reinforcing, through women's silence, male authority. Catharine MacKinnon's perceptive words are particularly apt within this context:

> ... when you are powerless, you don't just speak differently. A lot, you don't speak. Your speech is not just differently articulated, it is silenced. Eliminated, gone.[77]

As Martha Mahoney reveals through her research into the experience of battered women,[78] the most dangerous time for a victim of violence is when she seeks to leave the perpetrator of that violence. When a man's power and identity and self-esteem is dependent upon his authority over his partner, expressed through violence, the threat to leave is a direct challenge to his authority over her.[79]

---

[75] See, *inter alia*, Dobash, R and Dobash, R, *Women, Violence and Social Change*, 1992, London: Routledge and Kegan Paul; Edwards, S, *Sex and Gender in the Legal Process*, 1996, London: Blackstone; Freeman, M, 'Violence against women: does the legal system provide solutions or itself constitute the problem?' (1980) 7 British JL Soc 215; Pahl, J (ed), *Private Violence and Public Policy. The Needs of Battered Women and the Response of the Public Services*, 1985, London: Routledge and Kegal Paul.

[76] Dobash, R and Dobash, R, *Violence Against Wives: A Case Against the Patriarchy*, 1979, New York: Free Press.

[77] MacKinnon, C, *Feminism Unmodified: Discourses on Life and Law*, 1987, Cambridge, Mass: Harvard UP, p 39.

[78] Mahoney, M, 'Legal images of battered women: redefining the issue of separation' (1991) 90 Michigan L Rev 1.

[79] Statistical evidence from Australia and the United States of America supports this interpretation: in Australia, nearly half the female victims of spousal murder were either separated or in the process of separating at the time of their deaths. In the USA, violence against women occurred in 36–60% of divorcing spouses. See Wallace, A, *Homicide: the Social Reality*, 1986, Sydney: NSW Bureau of Crime Statistics and Research; *ibid*, Mahoney, both cited in Astor, H, *The Weight of Silence: Talking About Violence in Family Mediation*, in Thornton, *op cit*, fn 49, p 179.

Domestic violence also, however, reveals the limitations and deficiencies of the liberal insistence on separate public and private domains. Domestic violence is a matter for public concern, and attempted control, however inadequate, by the State.

In the case of rape, the same considerations apply: rape concerns control and the maintenance of patriarchal power. In Catharine MacKinnon's view, '[w]omen's sexuality is, socially, a thing to be stolen, sold, bought, bartered, or exchanged by others'.[80] For the victim of rape, the legal process itself contributes to the psychological pain. While the rapist is on trial for his actions, the requirements of *mens rea*, the guilty intent, require proof of the victim's lack of consent. Too often, almost inevitably and invariably, this places the woman's reaction to the attempted rape, and her sexual history, especially in relation to the defendant, on trial.[81] Thus the woman's sexuality is on trial, not the man's, and a finding of guilt is dependent upon the court's finding that the woman is 'innocent' enough in her private life to refute the defence's claim that her private life negates her credibility as a witness.

Sexual harassment

> Sexual harassment, the legal claim, is a demand that State authority stand behind women's refusal of sexual access in certain situations that previously were a masculine prerogative.[82]

If the world of work is classified as existing in the public (regulated) sphere, and sexuality classified as existing in the private (unregulated) sphere according to traditional liberal thought, sexual harassment presents complexities both for the role of law and for classical liberal theory. Employment law has long been characterised by the male subject of law. The admission of women to the male world of work, albeit in a selective and often discriminatory manner, introduces the possibility, and reality, of the sexual harassment of women, a manifestation of patriarchal attitudes exhibited in the public world of employment.

Sexual harassment in employment is both patriarchal and hierarchical. Patriarchal in that it manifests traditional male views as to what women either (a) deserve, or (b) expect; hierarchical in that it is so often inflicted on women in junior positions to men. As Helena Kennedy QC has commented, '[T]he combination of sex and power is a particularly destructive one'.[83]

---

[80] MacKinnon, C, 'Rape: on coercion and consent', in MacKinnon, *op cit*, fn 77, p 172.
[81] See Temkin, J, *Rape and the Legal Process*, 1987, London: Sweet & Maxwell. See, further, Chapter 11.
[82] MacKinnon, C, 'Sexual harassment: its first decade in court', in MacKinnon, *op cit*, fn 77, p 103. See, also, MacKinnon's earlier work, *Sexual Harassment of Working Women*, 1979, New Haven: Yale UP.
[83] Kennedy, H, *Eve Was Framed*, 1993, London: Vintage.

'Discovered' as a phenomenon in the 1970s, the law has reacted with relative pace to provide remedies. From a feminist perspective, sexual harassment replicates many of the problems faced by victims of race: the embarrassment and shame of reverbalising, and hence reliving, the experience in a court of law; the possibility of repercussions from the perpetrator; the possibility of being disbelieved and the correlative difficulties entailed in convincing a court of law that the plaintiff's demeanour, conduct or words did not actively encourage the conduct complained of.

From a feminist theoretical perspective, sexual harassment may be subsumed within both the 'gender difference' approach or the 'dominance' theory of Catharine MacKinnon. The law has chosen to categorise sexual harassment as a species of sexual discrimination.[84]

The law relating to sexual harassment reinforces feminist arguments which counter the liberal thesis of the public and private spheres of life. Sexuality is defined as being within the domain of the private: when sexuality in the form of sexual harassment enters into the workplace, the private has entered the public – and is regulated by law. Only where the law limits actions of sexual harassment, for example, by providing that the law does not extend to small businesses (but why should it not?), can the liberal thesis be sustained.

Pornography

The liberal thesis of the public and private also breaks down in relation to the legal regulation of pornography. Conversely, patriarchy does not. Pornographic representations of women are manufactured by the pornography industry for (mainly but not exclusively) male private consumption. The law defines what pornography is, and controls the distribution and sale of pornography. Thus consumption of pornography in the private sphere, produced in the public sphere, is controlled by law. As will be seen in Chapter 12, the legal response to the phenomenon of pornography has been ambivalent. In the United States of America, regulation of pornography comes into direct conflict with the First Amendment to the Constitution: the right to free speech. The definition of pornography judicially adopted in the United States in 1973 became whether:

> ... the average person, applying contemporary community standards, would find that, taken as a whole, appeals to the prurient interest; that which depicts

---

[84] In the United Kingdom, the Sex Discrimination Act 1975 outlaws direct and indirect discrimination on the basis of sex. In Australia the Sex Discrimination and Other Legislation Amendment Act 1992 (Cwlth) is more explicit: defining sexual harassment as 'an unwelcome sexual advance and the target of that behaviour reasonably believed that, if the advance was rejected, employment disadvantage would follow'. In the United States of America, sexual harassment claims fall under Title VII of the Civil Rights Act 1964, which prohibits discrimination based on sex.

and describes in a patently offensive way ... sexual conduct as defined by the applicable State law; and that which, taken as a whole, lacks serious literary, artistic, political or scientific value.[85]

Legislation dealing with pornography casts the terms of regulation not on the basis of violence or discrimination against women, but in terms of obscenity and pornography's capacity to deprave and corrupt the consumer – the approach adopted under Australian, English and United States' law. Pornography has thus been defined as an issue of morality, not an issue of discrimination against women, or incitement to sexual hatred.

From a radical feminist position,[86] pornography is a patriarchal manifestation, a political issue centrally concerned with women's status in society. From this perspective, pornography has little to do with free speech, as protected under the American Constitution, and everything to do with discrimination and violence against women. Pornography, in this view, represents male power over women, and the power of male pornography producers to perpetuate sexual inequality and discrimination through the constant representations of women violated and oppressed: as an object for the sexual use of men. Pornography is thus beyond all else, a manifestation of patriarchal power.

PATRIARCHY AND ESSENTIALISM

Given the history of dominant Western feminist theory, it is not white middle-class women who are different from other women, but all other women who are different from them.[87]

The issue of essentialism is discussed more fully in Part III. Nevertheless, the question which needs to be addressed within the context of patriarchy and the public and private spheres of life, is the extent to which differing women experience patriarchy in differing forms. Race, class and non-heterosexuality all impact on women's experience of patriarchy. Moreover, nationality, religious and cultural mores each impose their own forms of domination.

Patricia Williams' writing reveals much about patriarchy from the perspective of an American woman of colour. In *The Alchemy of Race and Rights*,[88] for example, Patricia Williams discusses the importance of legal

---

[85] *Miller v California* 413 US 15, 24 (1973).
[86] See Dworkin, A, *Pornography: Men Possessing Women,* 1981, London: The Women's Press; MacKinnon, C, 'Francis Biddle's sister', in MacKinnon, *op cit,* fn 77; see, also, MacKinnon, C, *Only Words,* 1994, London: HarperCollins.
[87] Spelman, E, *Inessential Woman: Problems of Exclusion in Feminist Thought,* 1990, London: The Women's Press, p 162.
[88] Williams, P, 'The pain of word bondage', in *The Alchemy of Race and Rights,* 1991, Cambridge, Mass: Harvard UP.

rights for women of colour compared with the relative lack of legal formality which attended her white, male colleague's negotiation of a contract.[89] For Williams, with the lack of trust with which she perceived herself to be treated by the white landlord, the formality of the legal contract provided her with the security she needed, and security for the white landlord who, in the absence of the contract defining his rights and her liabilities, she felt, would not have been able to reach an agreement. The history and legacy of slavery and racial segregation also imposes its own burden on women of colour in the United States. Not only oppressed by patriarchal society, but also oppressed by racism from whites (including white women), the extent to which patriarchy may be argued to be the dominant form of oppression becomes unclear. When the issue of class is joined to sexism and racism, there appears to be a multiplicity of oppressive forces which is almost impossible to unravel.

With the wave of immigration into the United Kingdom in the 1960s, came different illustrations of women's unequal status in relation to men. Differing family forms exhibited among differing cultural groups also poses questions for the argued centrality of patriarchy as a form of women's oppression. The traditional separation of society into the world of the public and the world of the private, the family being the principal institution of the private sphere becomes more complex when differing contemporary family forms are considered.

The Judicial Studies Board's *Handbook on Ethnic Minority Issues*,[90] recognises the diversity of family forms. Its data reveals that the size of household in both Indian and Pakistani/Bangladeshi households average 3.8 and 4.8 persons respectively as compared with 'white' households the mean size of which is 2.5, whereas 'West Indian' households are almost identical to 'white' households, with a mean size of 2.6. Forty-one per cent of Pakistani/Bangladeshi households contain six or more persons, compared with only two per cent of white families.[91] The extended family is far more prevalent within Asian and African family systems than in the conventional British family. There is thus a more extensive support system within Asian and African families than in British families. Furthermore, there is evidence which reveals that among Afro-Caribbean immigrants, there is a far higher proportion of women as sole head of the household than is the case with 'British' households, even bearing in mind the high incidence of divorce in Britain. When speaking of 'the family' and 'family relationships', therefore, it is important to bear in mind the differing family forms. It cannot merely be

---

[89] See *op cit*, Williams, fn 88.
[90] 1994, Chapter 6.
[91] On the other hand, 60 per cent of Pakistani/Bangladeshi families and 84 per cent of Indian families are between one and five persons, the range that accounts for almost all 'white' families.

assumed that a woman is oppressed within the traditional family, structured on the lines of the nuclear family: one male, one female and two children.

Arranged marriages among the Asian population in Britain also raise issues for patriarchy. In *Singh v Singh*,[92] the orthodox Sikh petitioner in a suit for nullity of marriage had, at the age of 17, been through a ceremony of marriage to a 21 year old Sikh man whom she had never previously met. When she met her husband, she refused to live with him or to go through the religious ceremony as required by her culture. The Court of Appeal refused to grant her a decree of nullity, based on two grounds, namely duress (from her parents) and incapacity to consummate due to invincible repugnance, holding that her dislike for her husband did not amount to a psychological or sexual aversion on her part sufficient to establish incapacity to marriage.[93] By way of contrast, in *Hirani v Hirani*,[94] the Court of Appeal, on similar facts, granted a decree of nullity to the petitioning wife, a Hindu, on the basis that a case for duress was made out by reason of her parents threatening to throw her out of the family home should she refuse to go through with the marriage. The experiences of these petitioners reveals that the oppressive forces came not just from the patriarchal tradition, but also from the oppressive forces of religion and culture.

It has been claimed that first and second wave feminism ignored lesbian experience. From the perspective of lesbian feminists, the issue of patriarchy, especially within the private sphere of life, has little resonance: the experiential reality of lesbians is, for lesbian feminist Patricia Cain, one of non-subordination. She also views heterosexuality as playing a part in the maintenance of patriarchy[95] Whether the approach is cultural feminism or radical feminism, or Marxist-socialist feminism, no theory takes into account the reality of lesbian experience, or the significance of lesbian experience for feminist theory. Only with postmodernism does feminism start to be inclusive, to listen to the voices of lesbian feminists. And what lesbian feminists have to say on private patriarchy is relevant: as Cain asserts, while some lesbian relationships may, in terms of hierarchy, emulate heterosexual couples, for many they do not: lesbians live, for the most part, in private lives which are non-patriarchal. They cannot, in the public sphere, but be subjected to the same patriarchal manifestations as heterosexual women, coupled perhaps, with stigmatisation and discrimination because of their non-heterosexual gender.

---

[92] [1971] P 226; [1971] 2 All ER 828; [1971] 2 WLR 963; 115 SJ 205.
[93] See, conversely, *Kaur v Singh* [1972] 1 All ER 292, in which a decree of nullity was granted to the wife when following an arranged marriage the husband refused to arrange the requisite religious ceremony and was held, by analogy, thereby to have refused to consummate the marriage.
[94] [1982] 4 FLR 232.
[95] Cain, P, 'Feminist jurisprudence: grounding the theories' (1989) Women's LJ 191.

CONCLUSION

While patriarchy as the dominant political philosophy had 'had its day' by the end of the seventeenth century, the concept remains alive within society and law in both the public and private spheres of life, to the continuing detriment of women's equality. The task for feminist jurisprudence is to continue the research and debate to reveal the full extent of remaining patriarchalism and to press for legal and social change. While the majority of formal legal inequalities have been removed, at least in Western liberal democracies, institutional structures and practices continue to reveal both discriminatory and exclusionary treatment of women. Formal legal equality under employment law cannot alone achieve substantive equality for women in the public sphere unless and until women's traditional childcare and domestic unpaid work changes. As has been seen in Chapter 2, research conducted into women's employment patterns in China, Japan, the United Kingdom and the United States of America reveal that in China alone a woman's career path is only mildly affected by childbirth and childcare, with women able to return to their employment, supported by State and other institutional childcare facilities, at the same level at which her career was temporarily interrupted.[96] Women will only achieve substantive equality with men when the last vestiges of male patriarchal sexual attitudes are displaced – both within the public and the private sphere. Notwithstanding that, the concept of patriarchy must be understood within the diversity of women's lives, and against the multifarious factors which affect different women in different ways.

---

[96] *Op cit*, Stockton, N, Bonney, N and Xuewen, S, fn 66.

PART II

CONVENTIONAL JURISPRUDENCE AND FEMINIST CRITIQUE

CHAPTER 4

CONVENTIONAL JURISPRUDENCE AND FEMINIST CRITIQUE: I

ANCIENT GREEK POLITICAL THOUGHT AND NATURAL LAW THEORY

INTRODUCTION

Throughout the centuries, from Ancient Greece to the current time, theorists have been analysing the structure of society and the system of legal rules which is part reflective, in part constitutive and in part supportive of the social structure. Irrespective of approach, or time, political and legal theorists have portrayed the individual subject of law in one of two ways. On the one hand, the legal subject is portrayed as a genderless individual. On the other hand, women have – where they have been considered at all – been portrayed as in some sense different (from men) and generally in an inferior social and legal position to men. Women, accordingly, have either been ignored or assumed to be inferior. It is with feminist scholarship, identifiable in its infancy in the time of Mary Wollstonecraft's writings in the eighteenth century,[1] and approaching maturity towards the end of the twentieth century, that the traditional assumptions about society and law have been challenged. Whether Ancient Greek theory, natural law, positivist analysis of law, liberalism, utilitarianism, social contract theory or the Marxist analysis of law is considered, from a feminist standpoint women are either *invisible,* or *excluded,* or *relegated to a position of social and political inferiority.* In this chapter, ancient Greek thought and natural law theory are considered.

THE GREEK PHILOSOPHERS

The writings of Plato[2] and Aristotle[3] have been characterised as displaying a deep misogyny.[4] The position is rather more complex than that, however, and

---

[1] See Wollstonecraft, M, *Vindication of the Rights of Women* (1792), 1967, New York: WW Norton.
[2] c 427–347 BC.
[3] 384–322 BC.
[4] See, eg, Moller Okin, S, *Women in Western Political Thought,* 1979, Ewing, New Jersey: Princeton UP. (See *Sourcebook,* pp 286–300.)

there exist contradictions and complexities within the writing. While misogyny shines through from much of their writings, there is also an ambiguity about women's positions in society.

Reason in Greek philosophy

Plato and Aristotle both distinguish form and matter. Form corresponds with the rational mind: with Reason; matter is non-rational, it is the object of rational thought and knowledge. In the *Timaeus*,[5] Plato writes that mind, which participates in the cosmic Reason which infuses the world, is distinctive from opinion:

> But we must affirm them to be distinct, for they have a distinct origin and are of a different nature; the one is implanted in us by instruction, the other by persuasion; the one is always accompanied by true reason, the other is without reason; the one cannot be overcome by persuasion, but the other can; and lastly, every man may be said to share in true opinion, but mind is the attribute of the gods but of very few men.[6]

Reason is an attribute of the soul, and on death the soul frees itself from the earthly body: the soul thus rules over, dominates, the body:

> So it appears that when death comes to a man, the mortal part of him dies, but the immortal part retires at the approach of death and escapes unharmed and indestructible.[7]

In Genevieve Lloyd's analysis, this early separation of rationality and form, and the relation of dominance and inferiority between them 'has been highly influential in the formation of our contemporary ways of thinking about knowledge'.[8] It establishes the binary mode of thought – the rational and irrational – the superior and inferior – which infuses all later constructions of knowledge, and represents the early distinction between the rationality (and superiority) of man and the irrationality (and inferiority) of women.

Plato

In *The Republic*,[9] Plato sets out his vision of an ideal State. Speaking through the mouth of Socrates,[10] in debate with Glaucon, the subject of the appropriate

---

[5] The *Timaeus* is Plato's account of the creation of the universe. It explains the manner in which the universe can be understood by the rational mind.

[6] Plato, *Timaeus*, Jowett, B (trans), in Hamilton, E and Cairns, H (eds), *Plato: The Collected Dialogues*, 1963, Ewing, New Jersey: Princeton UP, p 1151, 51e.

[7] Plato, *Phaedo*, in Hamilton and Cairns, *ibid*, pp 40, 106e.

[8] Lloyd, G, *The Man of Reason: 'Male' and 'Female' in Western Philosophy*, 1984, London: Methuen, p 7.

[9] Plato, *The Republic*, Lee, D (trans), 2nd edn, 1974, London: Penguin.

[10] 470?–399 BC.

role of women and the family is discussed. The starting point for discussion is equality between men and women, with women being trained 'physically and mentally' in the same manner. It is recognised, however, that women and men have different natures and that accordingly it is difficult to argue that they should fulfil the same functions. In Socrates' view, the only relevant difference between man and women is that the 'female bears and the male begets',[11] a difference which is not regarded *per se* as a determinative women's role. The 'best' women are to be treated as Guardians[12] and follow common occupations with men. The appropriate role of women is determined, not by biological characteristics, but by abilities: thus some women will be fitted to be physicians on the basis of equality with men.

As if this were not radical enough at the time, Plato goes on to consider the family and concludes that the private family presents an obstacle to the best service of the State, which requires both the production of the best children possible and the abolition of romantic ties between men and women. The Rulers must identify the couples whom they want to mate, and the children will be reared in State nurseries. Women Guardians have become the bearers of children for the State: the private family is abolished and women and children are owned in common. Woman's position, freed from the demands of domesticity, Plato tells us, through Socrates, is one of equality in which she is fitted to do all the tasks in society. The fact that the 'female bears and the male begets' is not a relevant difference for the purposes of assigning differing social roles. Men as well as women are fitted for childcare.[13]

'The three values on which both his ideal and his second-best cities are based are, rather [than happiness], harmony, efficiency and moral goodness.'[14, 15] Man's acquisitive nature, reflected in private property, is potentially damaging to the harmony, *eudaemonia*, of the city. The abolition of private property could only enhance harmony within the city. For Plato, the purpose of government is to ensure the harmony and well being of its citizens.[16] Plato, for example, in *The Republic* writes that women are twice as evil as men, and yet in both *The Republic* and the later *Laws*, considers that the physical differences between men and women had no greater significance than the biological fact that women bear children and men beget them. Aside

---

11 *Op cit*, Plato, fn 9, Bk V, 454e.
12 The ruling class.
13 *Op cit*, Plato, fn 9, 460b.
14 See *op cit*, Moller Okin, fn 4, Chapters 1 and 2. See, also, Lyndon Shanley, M and Patemen, C (eds), *Feminist Interpretations and Political Theory*, 1991, London: Polity.
15 Moller Okin, S, 'Philosopher Queens and private wives', in Moller Okin, *op cit*, fn 4, p 28.
16 Note that Plato throughout his writing, distinguishes between the 'ideal city' and the 'second-best city'. The highest stratum in society is that of the Guardian class, who alone has the capacity to rule.

from this child-bearing function, females – if properly educated and trained alongside males – should participate fully in civic and military life: '... women should in fact, so far as possible, take part in all the same occupations as men, both in peace within the city and on campaign in war, acting as Guardians and hunting with the men like hounds ...'[17] This equality, however, was to be confined to the Guardian class, the elite in society who alone had the power to rule. For other classes, the position of women remained unequal. The class distinction applied also to Plato's radical views on the abolition of both private property and the family which he advocated in order to avoid the evils of self-interest which he perceived to stem from the ownership of property. Accordingly, all property – of which women were a subclass – was to be owned in common. The establishing of private families was viewed as antithetical to civic harmony, encouraging selfishness and greed. With the communalisation of the property of Guardians in the 'ideal city' comes the communalisation of women: the private sphere is thereby abolished in Plato's writing on the ideal city.[18] With the abolition of the family among the Guardian class, women and men were to mate in order to produce children of the highest quality who would be fit to rule. Woman was thus both equal to and yet owned by men. Women as 'property' enters into political thought with Plato. With the private family abolished, women of the highest class were freed for service alongside men. While the nature and physical characteristics of men and women differ,[19] men and women of the Guardian class are equal in terms of employment: only relevant characteristics play a role in the assignment of appropriate tasks.

For women of the lower classes marriage was to remain in place and the traditional domestic role of women preserved: in the private sphere. The woman, however, here is not in any sense equal to her husband, but a subordinate. The husband has all the powers that her father had, plus the right to sexual intercourse on demand. Should her husband die, the wife returned to the custody of her father, whose power over her destiny was absolute. Here woman is most clearly identified as property: a 'thing' to be kept or given away. Women were not eligible to own property, being regarded by law as lacking legal capacity in the same manner as children.

A sophisticated interpretation of Plato's concept of woman is offered by French feminist psychoanalyst and philosopher Luce Irigaray. Among Irigaray's voluminous writings is her interpretation of classical myths. Here her deconstruction of Plato's myth of the cavern[20] is discussed in order to reveal Plato's attitude to women. In the Myth, Plato describes men dwelling in

---

[17] *Op cit*, Plato, fn 9, Bk V, 466d.
[18] On the 'public' and 'private' spheres of life see further Chapters 3, 5 and 7.
[19] Woman's role in part being procreation and her lesser physical strength being acknowledged.
[20] *Op cit*, Plato, fn 9, Bk VII.

a 'sort of subterranean cavern with a long entrance open to the light on its entire width'.[21] The men are shackled and their heads fettered so that they can neither move their arms or legs nor turn their heads. Behind and higher up from the prisoners is a fire burning. Between the fire and the prisoners, a 'road' has been built, from which exhibitors produce puppet shows. An opaque screen separates the prisoners and others in the cave. In addition to the puppets there are men carrying implements, and human images and animal images. All that the prisoners can see is the shadows of the reflections of the puppets, implements and human and animal images: this constitutes their 'real' world; their reality. The prisoners are then released and forced to leave the cavern, up the ascent which is 'rough and steep', and into the sunlight.[22] At first their eyes would be blinded by the sun and unable to see, only later would they adjust and be able to see the sun, not in reflections or phantasms, 'but in and by itself in its own place'. In Irigaray's interpretation, as the men emerge from the 'reality' of the cavern and enter into the world of Ideas, the images of the cavern start to fade and disappear, they are leaving the womb, leaving the mother's body behind as they enter into the world of Ideas.[23]

The cavern – with its shadows and reflections – is a reflection of the outside world, a reflection which becomes blurred and more distant in the ascent to the real world and to the world of Ideas. The cavern/womb is left behind. The cavern and the world of Ideas are imaginary mothers and fathers. In leaving the cavern, the mother is abandoned. In the world of Ideas, the physical origins of the prisoners are disconnected. As Margaret Whitford writes:

> The Platonic myth stages a primal scene in which Plato gradually manages to turn his back, like the pupil/prisoner, on the role of Mother altogether. From Irigaray's point of view, the consequences of this are not only philosophical but also social ...[24]

Thus the world of Ideas is the world of the father, the patriarchal world, from which the mother, the physical, the world of shadows in the cavern, is excluded. Women in Platonic philosophy, then, despite Plato's ostensible granting of equality to the highest class of women, are 'shadow' or 'fake' men. Philosophy is the male domain, women who have been 'downgraded' into the material world, are excluded.

---

21 *Op cit*, Plato, fn 9, 514b.
22 *Op cit*, Plato, fn 9, 515d, 515e, 516a.
23 For in-depth analysis, see Whitford, W, *Luce Irigaray: Philosophy in the Feminine*, 1991, London: Routledge, pp 105–13.
24 *Ibid*, Whitford, p 110.

Aristotle

Like his predecessor Plato, Aristotle sought to analyse the 'ideal State' and 'ideal' constitution. In *The Politics*,[25] Aristotle claims that the State is a natural entity: human beings are human beings because they are political. There are a number of fundamental assumptions made by Aristotle, who, unlike, Plato is not seeking to change the world, but rather to explain the world as it exists. By comparison, Aristotle is an arch conservative. First the State is natural: 'man is born for citizenship'.[26] Secondly, happiness is the highest virtue and goal in life: what amounts to happiness, is defined by considering the characteristic functions of man.[27] Thirdly, men are naturally superior to women and slaves and children. Disassociating himself from Plato's call for the abolition of the private family and the ownership 'in common' of women and children, Aristotle reinstates the private family as the natural, and best, unit for the preservation of the State. Within that family unit, Aristotle makes it abundantly clear that it is the husband who is master of the household, for he is by nature 'more fitted to rule than the female ...'.[28]

Aristotle's views about women are complicated by his considerations of class. Slavery, for Aristotle, was a natural state. Equally natural is that the husband should be master of the slaves. Slaves could be either male or female. However, in his treatment of women and slaves, a distinction between the two enters the picture. A free woman is different from a slave woman. Neither women nor slaves participate in the *polis*, but in the private sphere of life each has a different role to play. Wives bear children who will become citizens, and act as companions to their husbands; slaves do the menial work in the household. What distinguishes the free individual (whether male or female) from the slave (whether male or female) is, in Elizabeth Spelman's analysis,[29] a combination of biological and psychological characteristics. Thus a free female (or woman) is characterised as having a female body and a deliberative capacity without authority; a female slave has a female body but no deliberative capacity; a male citizen has a male body and deliberative capacity with authority and a male slave has a male body and no deliberative capacity. These distinctions become important when considering just who it is that Aristotle is considering when he speaks of 'women', for it becomes clear that he is speaking only of a particular class of women: the free woman, and that 'slave women' are excluded.

---

[25] Aristotle, *The Politics*, Sinclair, TA (trans), 1962, London: Penguin.
[26] Aristotle, *The Nicomachean Ethics*, I.7 1097a34 (c 372–382 BC), Ross, D (trans), 1925, Oxford: OUP, p 12.
[27] Ibid, *The Nicomachean Ethics*, 1097a15.
[28] Ibid, *The Politics*, Bk I, xii, 1259a37.
[29] See Spelman, E, *Inessential Woman,: Problems of Exclusion in Feminist Thought*, 1990, London: The Woman's Press, Chapter 2.

Aristotle[30] rejected Plato's 'extreme unity' in relation to property, including women. In *The Politics* Aristotle argues that private property should remain the favoured arrangement, and that in relation to the family the husband and father has absolute power. Slaves, a class of people whose inferior status is a natural condition, are distinguishable from females, not only in their status but also in their roles. The slave's primary function is to serve his or her master; the female's primary natural function is reproduction and the maintenance of the family home. The function ascribed to females determines the extent of their rationality, which is inferior to that of a man's: '... [T]he slave is entirely without the faculty of deliberation; the female indeed possesses it, but in a form which remains inconclusive; and if children also possess it, it is only in an immature form.'[31]

NATURAL LAW THOUGHT

It is impossible to provide more than a mere sketch of the rich history of natural law in Western philosophy and political thought and the legacy it leaves to modern constitutions. Nevertheless, a basic understanding of its nature and evolution is instructive for it reveals the manner in which the requirements of good law – morally worthwhile law – have been stipulated over centuries. The question for feminist jurisprudence is whether the traditional conceptions of natural law thought are able to encompass the demands of women for equal respect.

Natural law in ancient Greece and Rome

Aristotle[32] stated that 'the rule of law is preferable to that of any individual'. The appeal to law as a control over naked power has been apparent throughout history. At a philosophical level the natural law tradition – whether theological or secular – instructs that the power of man is not absolute, but is rather controlled and limited by the requirements of a higher law. To the ancient Greeks man was under the governance of the laws of nature – the natural forces which controlled the universe: although this view is more closely aligned to the 'law of nature' than 'natural law' as it came to be understood in later times. However, from the time of Socrates, Plato[33] and

---

[30] *Op cit*, Moller Okin, fn 14, Chapter 4; Saxonhouse, A, 'Aristotle: defective males, hierarchy and the limits of politics', in Lyndon Shanley, M and Pateman, C (eds), *Feminist Interpretations and Political Theory*, 1988, London: Polity.
[31] *Op cit*, Aristotle, fn 25, Vol I, 1260a.
[32] *Op cit*, Aristotle, fn 25, Vol III, p 16.
[33] 427–347 BC.

Aristotle[34] the quest for virtue – or goodness or justice under the law – has been a recurrent theme.

An early – and famous – formulation of the dictates of natural law was offered by Cicero:[35]

> True law is right reason in agreement with Nature; it is of universal application, unchanging and everlasting; it summons to duty by its commands, and averts from wrong-doing by its prohibitions. And it does not lay its commands or prohibitions upon good men in vain, though neither have any effect on the wicked. It is a sin to try to alter this law, nor is it allowable to attempt to repeal any part of it, and it is impossible to abolish it entirely. We cannot be freed from its obligations by Senate or People, and we need not look outside ourselves for an expounder or interpreter of it. And there will not be different laws at Rome and at Athens, or different laws now and in the future, but one eternal and unchangeable law will be valid for all nations and for all times, and there will be one master and one ruler, that is, God, over us all, for He is the author of this law, its promulgator, and its enforcing judge.[36]

It is from ancient Greek philosophy that natural law enters into Roman law. From the *Corpus Iuris Civilis*[37] is derived *ius civilis*, *ius gentium* and *ius naturale*. *Ius civilis* denotes the law of the State; *ius gentium* the law of nations; and *ius naturale* 'a law which expresses a higher and more permanent standard. It is the law of nature (*ius naturale*), which corresponds to "that which is always good and equitable"'.[38]

Natural law theory, whether theological or secular, is predicated upon an interpretation of a higher law, to which human law is subject for its authority. Theological natural law,[39] concerns the interpretation of God's will as interpreted through the scriptures. There exists, as with texts emanating from Ancient Greece, a deep ambivalence concerning the role of women in the scriptures.

Christian natural law thought

Whether natural law, as interpreted by male philosophers, includes women in its lofty ideals is questionable. Feminist analysis of the Scriptures suggests that the position of women was rooted in inequality. St Paul, citing Genesis 2, states that while 'man is the image and glory of God', the 'woman is the glory

---

[34] 384–322 BC.
[35] 106–43 BC.
[36] Cicero, *De Republica*, III, xxii, 33, cited by d'Entrèves, AP, *Natural Law*, 2nd edn, 1970, London: Hutchinson, p 25.
[37] AD 534.
[38] *Ibid*, d'Entrèves, fn 36, p 24.
[39] *Ibid*; d'Entrèves, fn 36; Finnis, JM, *Natural Law and Natural Rights*, 1980, Oxford: Clarendon.

of man'; '... the man was not created for the woman's sake, but the woman for the sake of the man'.[40] The first and most obvious inequality lies in the gendered identity of God. As Elaine Pagels has written:

> ... while it is true that Catholics revere Mary as the mother of Jesus, she cannot be identified as divine in her own right: if she is 'mother of God', she is not 'God the Mother' on an equal footing with 'God the Father'.[41]

Moreover, Pagels argues that diverse Jewish and Christian Gnostic works, which are characterised by heterodoxy, rather than orthodoxy, 'abound in feminine symbolism that is applied, in particular, to God'. The fate of these Gnostic scriptures was, however, to be condemned as 'heretical' by around AD 200. Theologian Mary Daly has also analysed aspects of early Christianity. In her analysis of the myth of the Fall of Adam and Eve, Daly writes that Eve is characterised as the evil temptress, and that this characterisation:

> ... has affected doctrines and laws that concern women's status in society and it has contributed to the mind-set of those who continue to grind out biased, male-centred ethical theory ...[42]

It is with Augustine[43] that the debate concerning equality between men and women renews. In Genevieve Lloyd's analysis, Augustine opposed the now established acceptance of women's inferiority by virtue of her 'lesser rationality'.[44] While woman was spiritually equal, she was nonetheless unequal, and subordinate, to man in human nature, by virtue of 'the sex of her body'.[45] Woman is cast in the role of 'help-mate' to the man. Woman is equal to man in so far as she has been made in God's image, but in respect of her help-mate role she is not in God's image. This reconceptualisation of woman as different from man only in respect of her physical difference, while ostensibly granting women equal rationality in all other respects, is, Lloyd argues, a perpetuation of the alignment 'of maleness with superiority, femaleness with inferiority', despite Augustine's declared position that men and women are spiritually equal.

The Scriptures and Gospels provided the basis for Christian natural law thought which developed in the Middle Ages. Natural law was perceived as God-given, communicated to man by Revelation, and remaining absolutely binding upon man and unchanging in its content. As a result, the dictates of

---

[40] 1 Cor 11: 7–9.

[41] Pagels, EH, 'What became of God the mother? Conflicting images of God in early Christianity', in Abel, E and Abel, EK (eds), *The Signs Reader: Women, Gender and Scholarship*, 1978, Chicago: Chicago UP. (See *Sourcebook*, p 44.)

[42] Daly, M, *Beyond God the Father: Toward a Philosophy of Women's Liberation*, 1973, London: The Women's Press, p 44. (See *Sourcebook*, p 47.)

[43] AD 354–430.

[44] See *op cit*, Lloyd, fn 8, Chapter 2, on Philo who, writing in the first century AD, adopted Greek philosophical models in his interpretation of Jewish scriptures.

[45] Augustine, *Confessions*, XIII, Chapter 32, cited in Lloyd, *op cit*, fn 8, p 29.

natural law take precedence over man-made laws. If the demands of the State conflict with the laws of God, the obligation to God must prevail. Undoubtedly the most powerful writing of the Middle Ages comes from St Thomas Aquinas:[46]

> This rational guidance of created things on the part of God ... we can call the Eternal Law. But, of all others, rational creatures are subject to divine Providence in a very special way; being themselves made participators in Providence itself, in that they control their own actions and the actions of others. So they have a share in the divine reason itself, deriving therefrom a natural inclination to such actions and ends as are fitting. This participation in the Eternal law by rational creatures is called Natural Law.[47]

The soul, for Aquinas, has a unity, comprising intellect, will and understanding. The senses are not part of the soul, but rather part of the soul in the body. However, when it comes to equality under God, while there is no distinction between men and women in the primary sense, in a secondary sense women are placed in a position of inferiority:

> ... for man is the beginning and end of woman; as God is the beginning and end of every creature.[48]

Natural law and positive law[49]

The ancient concepts of natural law thus concern an evaluation of the validity of human law against some higher source of authority, whether theological or secular, which is both eternal and universal. The demands of natural law challenge the law of human rulers – demanding that law conform to higher principles. One such principle is the respect for individual rights and freedoms, and it may therefore be argued that the protection of human rights is a natural law concept. It should not be assumed, however, that the assertions that the rights of man derive from natural law has been completely or unequivocally accepted.

In the nineteenth century, for example, the rise of nationalism in the West challenged doctrines of natural law. The same century also witnessed the rise in *positivism* – the legal-theoretical schools of thought concerned solely to identify and define the concept of valid human law.[50] These two developments – nationalism and positivism – shifted the focus of attention

---

[46] 1225–74.
[47] Aquinas, T, *Summa Theologica*, 1a 2ae, Q 91, Arts 1 and 2, cited in d'Entrèves, *op cit*, fn 36, p 43.
[48] *Ibid*, Aquinas, I, Q 76, Art 4, Vol IV, pp 39–43, cited *op cit*, Lloyd, fn 8, p 35.
[49] See *op cit* Finnis, fn 39; Hart, HLA, *The Concept of Law*, 1961, Oxford: OUP.
[50] See, further, Chapter 5.

away from individual rights towards an analysis of State power. By way of illustration, Hegel's *Philosophy of Right*[51] portrayed the picture of the State as absolutely sovereign, its form and content being determined by history, but its existence and power being unrestricted by any form of natural law.

While natural law, as a dominant philosophical tradition, largely faded from the jurisprudential imagination with the challenge of positivism, natural law remains a constant and recurrent theme in jurisprudence. The Second World War, and in particular Nazi Germany, with all its revelations of the cruelty of the human spirit, and failure to respect individuals who belonged to different, non-Aryan, races, revealed the limitations of many things, not least of all the consequences of the powerful State.[52] The interest in natural law was revived by the German scholar Gustav Radbruch, which sparked the influential debate between Professors Lon Fuller[53] and HLA Hart.[54] Natural law has not lost its power: natural law underpins the law relating to human rights, with its insistence on fundamental rights which inhere in individuals,[55] and resonate through the fundamental principles of international law. Where natural law reveals its limitations, from the perspective of women, is in its failure to articulate clearly the right to freedom from discrimination on the basis of gender, race and class. To proclaim the fundamental 'rights of man', which challenge State power and demand protection under the rule of law, is little more than rhetoric when the specifities of gender, race and class inequalities are brought into the debate. For this reason, natural law has attracted little feminist debate, other than within the field of feminist theology.[56]

The rise of positivism, and its implications in legal theoretical terms, is considered in the next chapter.

---

[51] 1821.
[52] On the Holocaust, see, further, Chapter 6 and references therein.
[53] Professor of Law, University of Harvard. See Fuller, L, 'Positivism and fidelity to law – a reply to Professor Hart' (1958) 71 Harv L Rev 630.
[54] Professor of Jurisprudence, University of Oxford. See Hart, HLA, 'Positivism and the separation of law and morals' (1958) 71 Harv L Rev 593.
[55] For contemporary analysis of natural law theory, see *op cit*, d'Entreves, fn 36; *op cit*, Finnis, fn 39.
[56] *Op cit*, Daly, fn 42; Daly, M, *Gyn/Ecology: the Metaethics of Radical Feminism*, 1979, London: The Woman's Press.

CHAPTER 5

CONVENTIONAL JURISPRUDENCE AND FEMINIST CRITIQUE: II

POSITIVE LAW AND SOCIAL CONTRACT THEORY

THE ORIGINS OF POSITIVISM: THE AGE OF MODERNITY

Cogito ergo sum. The age of modernity and modern thought begins with French philosopher René Descartes.[1] Descartes, in his philosophical quest for truth and knowledge, argued that, in the search for truth, everything – including one's own existence – must be doubted. This is the philosophical practice labelled the 'Cartesian doubt'. The doubt as to his own existence ended with *cogito ergo sum:* I think therefore I am. His own existence was verified by his capacity to think: thus to state 'I exist', is proof of that existence. Freed from the Cartesian doubt of his own existence Descartes proceeded to inquire what kind of 'thing', or 'substance' he was – what was his *essence?*

Thus began the age of modernity, which was celebrated in the eighteenth century Enlightenment, and has held the philosophical imagination until the late twentieth century. The concepts central to Enlightenment thought are those of rationality and individual autonomy. Rejecting the theories of natural explanations for physical and human reality, across the sphere of human thought, reason and rationality dominated. From this period stem the 'grand' theories of thought and language, whether in philosophy,[2] politics, science[3] or the arts. The Enlightenment of the eighteenth century represented a reaction against explanations of Being vested in religion, superstition and mythology. The Enlightenment project centred on rationality and objectivity – the intellectual search for truth and knowledge unshackled by the subjectivity and irrationality of faith. Science and scientific knowledge became the successors to former irrationalities as the validating criterion for truth. In 'Berlinische Monatsschrift', philosopher Immanuel Kant[4] was to write that '[I]f it is now asked whether we live at present in an Enlightened age, the answer is: No, but

---

[1] 1596–1650.
[2] See Kant, I (1724–1804), 'Berlinische Monatsschrift', in Reiss, H (ed), *Kant's Political Writings*, 1977, Cambridge: CUP, p 54.
[3] On Sir Isaac Newton (1643–1727), see Cohen, I, *The Newtonian Revolution*, 1980, Cambridge: CUP.
[4] 1724–1804.

we do live in an age of Enlightenment', and that '[S]apere aude, have the courage to know: this is the motto of Enlightenment'.[5] The Enlightenment was neither an event, nor a project capable of completion: rather it represented a process of thought, of knowledge, which continues to exert its influence in current times. Immanuel Kant, John Locke, Jean-Jacques Rousseau, Charles-Louis de Secondat Montesquieu, Sir Isaac Newton, Francois-Marie Arouet Voltaire represent but a few of the prominent Enlightenment thinkers.[6]

In the political arena, the differing conceptions of the social contract – the contract between the rulers and the ruled – expressed by Thomas Hobbes,[7] John Locke[8] and Jean-Jacques Rousseau,[9] emerged in the Enlightenment period and continue to influence contemporary political thought.

LIBERALISM

Liberal theory represents the underlying political theory behind much contemporary Western legal theory, including modern positivist theory and social contract theory. Liberalism, variously defined, comprises three principal notions: rationality, the maximisation of individual liberty, and the control of governmental power through law. In stressing the primacy of individual liberty, liberal theory assumes that individuals in society are gender-, race-, class- and age-neutral. That is to say, each individual is assumed to share the same characteristics, and to be equally equal for the purposes of theorising, having equal capacities to reason. However, when liberalism is translated into practice, it is immediately apparent that society cannot be viewed in this fashion. The empirical evidence against the existence of true equality condemns liberalism. Society is sexist, racist, and ageist and is divided by social class in a manner which confounds classification even along the lines of sex, race and age. Liberalism nevertheless continues to represent the dominant legal and philosophical influence in Western industrial society.

Liberalism emerged as a product of the changing economic circumstances. The demise of feudalism and the rise of capitalism gave rise to new demands for equality. In England, the conflict between feudalism and capitalism may be traced to the mid seventeenth century with the Civil War and the period of Republican rule under Oliver Cromwell, from 1653 to 1658. The restoration of the monarchy under Charles II in 1660 led to expansions in the fields of

---

[5] *Op cit*, Reiss, fn 2, pp 54–60.
[6] 1724–1804, 1637–1704, 1712–78, 1689–1755, 1642–1727, 1694–1778 respectively.
[7] See Hobbes, T, *The Leviathan* (1651), Tuck, R (ed), 1991, Cambridge: CUP. (See *Sourcebook*, pp 316–17.)
[8] See Locke, J, *Two Treatises on Government* (1690), 1924, New York: JM Dent; Rousseau, J-J, *The Social Contract* (1762), 1913, New York: JM Dent.
[9] *Ibid*, Rousseau.

commerce, science and the development of the Navy, although the King's Roman Catholic sympathies were to cause civil unrest. The increasing conflict between Parliament and the Crown was finally to be settled in 1688 with the Scottish Petition of Right and the English Bill of Rights. The dawning of the Age of Enlightenment sowed the seeds of liberalism.

Liberal philosophy, arising out of Enlightenment thought, is grounded in the individuality of the rational person. The early liberal theorist John Locke advocated limited government under a contract between government and people which, if breached by government, legitimated the withdrawal of the contract by the people. The autonomy and freedom of the person became a central focus of liberal thought. It was man's capacity to reason which set man aside from the animal kingdom.

The concept of rationality, however, carried with it certain assumptions. One was the distinction drawn between body and mind, and the association of the body with nature and mind with culture – a distinction which has dogged feminist theory to the current day. Manifestations of the alliance between body/nature and mind/culture came early: for Aristotle 'woman has a deliberative faculty but it is without authority',[10] and accordingly 'the male is by nature superior and the female inferior; the one rules and the other is ruled'.[11] David Hume,[12] Jean-Jacques Rousseau,[13] Immanuel Kant[14] and Georg Wilhelm Friedrich Hegel[15] all questioned woman's rationality. For Hegel, for example, woman was more attuned to nature than culture:

> The difference in the physical characteristics of the two sexes has a rational basis and consequently acquires an intellectual and ethical significance. This significance is determined by the difference into which the ethical substantiality, as the concept, internally sunders itself in order that its vitality may become a concrete unity consequent upon this difference.[16]

Furthermore:

> The difference between men and women is like that between animals and plants. Men correspond to animals, while women correspond to plants because their development is more placid and the principle that underlies it is the rather vague unity of feeling. When women hold the helm of government, the

---

[10] Aristotle, *The Politics*, Sinclair, TA (trans), 1962, London: Penguin, 1 13. 1260 a13.
[11] *Ibid*, 15. 1254 b 13–14.
[12] 1711–76. See Hume, D, *A Treatise of Human Nature* (1740), 1938, Cambridge: CUP; *An Enquiry Concerning the Principles of Morals* (1751), Selby Bigge, LA (ed), 3rd edn, rev Nidditch, PH, 1902, Oxford: Clarendon; *History of England* (1778), 1983, Indianapolis: Library Classics.
[13] 1712–78; see *op cit*, Rousseau, fn 8.
[14] 1724–1804. See Kant, I, *Critique of Pure Reason* (1781), Kemp-Smith, N (trans), 1965, New York: St Martins; *Critique of Practical Reason* (1788), White Beck, L (trans), 1949, Chicago: Chicago UP.
[15] 1770–1831. See Hegel, G, *The Phenomenology of Spirit* (1807), Miller, AV (trans), 1977, New York: OUP; *Science of Logic* (1812–16), Miller, AV (trans), 1969, London: Allen & Unwin.
[16] Hegel, G, *Philosophy of Right* (1821), Knox, T (trans), 1952, Oxford: OUP, para 165, p 144.

State is at once in jeopardy, because women regulate their actions not by the demands of universality but by arbitrary inclinations and opinions.[17]

The debate about gender was rife in the Enlightenment period of the late seventeenth and early eighteenth centuries. As reason and rationality replaced superstition and irrational belief, the mind took priority over nature. Enlightenment thought centred on human capacity for universal reason. But if rationality was universal, and all human beings equal, how could the position of women – with their differing physical attributes – be explained? For Jean-Jacques Rousseau, the answer was clear: woman's role was determined by biology:

> The male is male only at certain moments; the female is female her whole life ... everything constantly recalls her sex to her, and to fulfil its functions, an appropriate physical constitution is necessary to her ... she needs a soft sedentary life to suckle her babies. How much care and tenderness does she need to hold her family together! ... The rigid strictness of the duties owed by the sexes is not and cannot be the same.[18]

This emphasis on woman's maternal function reinforced the idea that women occupy the private sphere of life, the home, and that they lack the rationality for participation in the public sphere of the economy and politics. It also perpetuated the dualism between mind and body, between culture – rationality of the mind – and nature – women's reproductive bodies, the emphasis on which was encouraged by emergent medical and scientific knowledge. Related to this were perceptions about the importance of women's role as carers and nurturers, imbued with femininity, and entrusted with the task of ensuring a climate of private morality. Not all Enlightenment thinkers, however, shared Rousseau's view of women and her appropriate role in the domestic sphere pursuing maternal functions. For Enlightenment thinkers such as Voltaire and Montesquieu, women were capable of equality with men, and should not be regarded as being under the authority of the husband and represented as capable only of maternal functions.

It was, however, against writings such as those of Rousseau against which Mary Wollestonecraft argued. In her seminal *Vindication of the Rights of Women*,[19] Mary Wollestonecraft was to equate, as was John Stuart Mill in the nineteenth century, the lack of rights for women to the denial of rights to slaves. Male enlightenment thought which generated a different 'virtue' for women and men, was contradictory:

---

[17] *Op cit*, Hegel, fn 16, para 166, p 264.
[18] Rousseau, J-J, *Emile* (1762), Bloom, A (trans), 1991, Harmondsworth: Penguin, p 450.
[19] Wollestonecraft, M, *Vindication of the Rights of Women* (1792), 1967, New York: WW Norton.

If women are by nature inferior to men, their virtues must be the same in quality, if not in degree, or virtue is a relative idea ... virtue has only one eternal standard.[20]

But the issue was not put to rest: in the much later work of Austrian psychiatrist and founder of psychoanalysis Sigmund Freud,[21] woman are said to 'have little sense of justice', and 'their social interests are weaker than those of men, and that their capacity for the sublimation of their instincts is less'.[22] Thus, the issue of women's rationality has lain at the heart of masculine political and psychoanalytic theory from time immemorial. It is the claim to equality as equal, rational persons which women demand, and, within the context of liberalism, liberal feminism[23] seeks to achieve.

The rise of legal positivism

In the United Kingdom, the Scottish philosopher David Hume laid the foundations for positivism.[24] Positivism, in its many forms, concerns the endeavour of isolating the law laid down by human superior (the sovereign power) to human inferior (the subject).[25] In essence, Hume's thesis was that, in logic, it is not possible to derive a statement of fact (an *existential statement*) – from a statement of what ought to be (a *normative statement*). On this reasoning only by keeping separate statements of fact and statements of 'ought' – or moral statements – can there be a true understanding of reality, and law. The implication of such a distinction for law and legal theory is that no moral statement as to what 'ought to be' can be inferred from a purely factual statement. This essential logical separation of the factual from the normative underlies the positivist endeavour: the attempt to provide a coherent logical structure of legal rules, and legal rules alone unaffected by morality. For the positivist, whatever is enacted according to the accepted constitutional procedure employed within the State is valid law and entails an absolute obligation of obedience. As such there can be no claim to 'freedoms' or 'human rights' which are capable of overriding the positive law. According to positivist theories of law, while in a perfect world the positive law may – and ideally should – conform to moral precepts, should it fail so to do, according to positivist theories of law, the individual is powerless to confront the law.

---

[20] *Op cit*, Wollestonecraft, fn 19, p 108.
[21] 1856–1939.
[22] See Freud, S, 'Femininity', in *New Introductory Lectures on Psychoanalysis,* 1933, London: WW Norton, p 184.
[23] See, further, Chapter 7.
[24] See *op cit, An Enquiry Concerning the Principles of Morals,* fn 12.
[25] See, eg, Austin, J, *The Province of Jurisprudence Determined* (1832), 1954, London: Weidenfeld and Nicholson; and Hart, HLA, *The Concept of Law,* 1961, Oxford: OUP, Chapters I–IV.

The nineteenth century rise in positivism represented both an attack on the claims of natural law over and above that of man-made law and an attempt to analyse scientifically the law as it exists in fact. The doctrine of natural law for which so much had been claimed in relation to human rights and freedoms was placed on the defensive.[26]

The elements of positivist thought

Positivist jurisprudence is most closely associated with the nineteenth century jurist John Austin,[27] and his twentieth century successors Hans Kelsen[28] and HLA Hart.[29, 30] It is not intended here to introduce in any detail the theories of these analysts, but rather to consider the central elements of a positivist analysis of law, and the manner in which that analysis precludes considerations which are fundamental to women's equality.

In severing legal theory from natural law thought, positivists claim that laws and legal systems must be understood as purely human phenomena: the

---

[26] The protection of rights based on natural law was further damaged by the utilitarians, whose philosophy underpins early positivist thought. Thomas Hobbes, Jeremy Bentham and John Austin all subscribed to the tenets of utilitarianism: the principle that an action (or law) is ethical if it conformed to the principle of creating the greatest happiness for the greatest number of people in society. Having rejected natural law as providing the lodestar for enactment of positive law, the utilitarians adopted the principle of *utility*. By *utility* is meant that the proper guidance in the formation of laws is the overall effect of a legislative proposal on society as a whole. A proposal for legislation will be in conformity with the doctrine of utility if it increases the sum of happiness in society overall. The leading exponent of the utilitarian school was Jeremy Bentham whose *Principles of Morals and Legislation* was to exert enduring influence. Bentham dismissed the idea of natural law and natural rights: natural rights were 'nonsense' – and worse – 'nonsense on stilts'. Essentially, the doctrine of utility requires that the benefits and burdens of legislative proposals should be calculated, using a form of 'felicific calculus', to determine whether the net effect of legislation will increase the 'sum of happiness' in society overall. If the benefit to society *as a whole* will benefit then legislation is justified and desirable. The most blatant and obvious flaw in this notion is that it ignores the position of the individual in society – treating the individual as merely a part of the whole, and not as an individual being with his or her characteristics, needs or desires. The potential for the use of the 'felicific calculus' is to undermine the individual. Accordingly, harsh treatment of an individual or a group of persons may be justified simply because that treatment will benefit society overall. There is nothing here of evaluating legislative proposals according to their moral worth – all is reduced to a calculation of efficiency and the benefit for society at large. See *op cit*, Hobbes, fn 7; Bentham, J, *A Fragment on Government* (1776), 1948, Oxford: Basil Blackwell; *Introduction to the Principles of Morals and Legislation* (1789), Burns, JH and Hart, HLA (eds), 1977, London: Athlone; *op cit*, Austin, fn 25.

[27] *Op cit*, Austin, fn 25.

[28] See Kelsen, H, *The General Theory of Law and State*, 1961, New York: Russell; *The Pure Theory of Law*, 1967, Berkeley: California UP.

[29] See Hart, HLA, 'Positivism and the separation of morals' (1958) 71 Harv L Rev 593, and *op cit*, Hart, fn 25.

[30] See, on Austin, Kelsen and Hart, Freeman, M, *Lloyd's Introduction to Jurisprudence* (1994) 6th edn, London: Sweet & Maxwell, Chapters 5 and 6.

'positing' of law by a sovereign body for the guidance of human conduct within society. Law is viewed as an autonomous, discrete, scientific domain of enquiry divorced from both naturalistic perceptions of morality, and from sociological explanations of the origins, nature and effects of law in society. For liberal positivist HLA Hart, positivism has five principal characteristics. First, law emanates from a determinate (human) sovereign power. Secondly, there is no necessary and/or inevitable connection between law and morality. Law may be criticised from perceptions of morality, and morality underlies the law and legal system, but from a scientific theoretical perspective, law must be theorised as an autonomous entity. To argue that immoral laws are invalid, is to confuse law and morality and to deny both the potential of a positivist analysis of law and undermine the role of morality as a means for subjecting law to critique. Thirdly, a positivist analysis of law takes care not to confuse an analysis of law with law's sociological origins or effects: it is with the analysis of law 'as it exists' that positivism is concerned. Fourthly, law being a rational, autonomous order, it is legal rules, and legal rules alone, which determined the outcome of legal cases. A positivist analysis insists that it is legal rules, not policy considerations, nor moral or equitable principles which explain the working of the legal order. Finally, laws alone – unlike moral precepts and principles and social policy – can be identified according to the predetermined criterion of validity.[31] In Hart's theory, legal rules are supplemented by equitable principles which operate in the judge's discretion: being non-legal, these principles remain outside the self-embracing structure of rules.

Positive law theory has little concern with the effect of law upon the individual, but is concerned with the necessary conditions which must exist in order for law to be identifiable with a coherent structure and be generally effective in the regulation of society. Professor Hart – now a classic liberal positivist theorist – does insist that law should contain a 'minimum content of natural law', however this insistence is centred on a supposedly gender-neutral person and nowhere does Hart consider the problems of gender or class. Hart's theory is cast in male language. The traditional justification would no doubt be forthcoming: that for the purposes of interpretation and understanding the word 'man' includes 'woman'. This, however, is not enough. For a wide ranging liberal theory of law totally to ignore the differences and similarities between men and women is to deny a vast and important perspective. In *The Concept of Law*,[32] Hart considers the minimum content of natural law within positivist theory. The requirements, which are

---

31 Variously expressed: by Austin as the illimitable, indivisible, sovereign; by Kelsen as the 'Basic Norm' and by Hart as the 'ultimate rule of recognition'. A legal rule is valid provided that it conforms to the requirements of the ultimate rule: traditionally identified within the United Kingdom as 'what the Queen in Parliament enacts is law'.

32 *Op cit*, Hart, fn 25, Chapter IX.

not specified in any detail, are dictated by 'man's nature'. 'Man' is perceived to have varying degrees of intelligence, limited altruism, varying physical strength. Moreover, the world is one characterised by limited resources. Accordingly, for law to serve its constituents, it must contain rules which protect the vulnerable against the strong, provide for some approximate equality and provide against exploitation and greed by the strongest in society. This is sound common sense, and indeed Hart acknowledges that his perceptions about human (male?) nature are mere truisms. However, even his 'truisms' are suspect from a feminist perspective, for notwithstanding Hart's perceptiveness concerning human nature, and the need for law to recognise differing human attributes, by focusing on human nature in a non-gendered manner Hart blind's himself to the possibility that there exists within society a *traditional and systematic* practice of discrimination against women which has not been addressed. The traditional discriminations experienced by women – whether in the public field of employment or in the private sphere of the family – demand recognition, especially within Hart's liberal theory which he claims to be a 'sociological' approach. To recognise, for example, as Hart does, 'human vulnerability', without a recognition of the manner in which vulnerabilities differ according to gender (and race and class) is to ignore too much about the reality of gender-structured society.

This last point raises the general objection to positivist theory from a feminist perspective, whether the theory be that of Austin, Kelsen or Hart. Positivist theory has its rationale in the separation of law from other social systems of organisation and control in order to achieve an explanation of law's structural clarity and autonomy. In the course of achieving this goal, however, the reality of society gets 'lost'. From a legal feminist perspective, this blindness to the reality of society which is inherent and essential to the positivist enquiry and theory, ignores that which is central to the feminist quest: the search for explanations as to law's gendered nature and the achievement of equality. From a feminist legal-sociological perspective, to theorise about law's autonomy and neutrality is to reason from false assumptions. Law is not autonomous. Law is not gender neutral. Law is predicated on power – power associated with class and gender. Positivism is thus blinkered theorising: the attempt to theorise law as an enclosed, autonomous, self-validating order in which the legal subject is manifested only in the assumption of disembodied individuality and rationality, with the consequence that the concepts of substantive law are imbued with the same assumptions.

Positivist theory, with its insistence upon autonomy, moral neutrality and rationality masks the reality of law from a feminist perspective, and offers little towards an understanding of the manner in which law supports the economic base, which of itself determines the position of women and class within society, or of law's patriarchy in terms of its exclusion of women from the public sphere, or discriminatory admission to the public sphere, or the confinement of women within the private sphere of life in conditions of economic dependency, either on a male partner, or the State.

Moreover, the picture painted by positivist theory is based on a false premise: that of the rationality of law. In common law jurisdictions the projection of law's rationality is enhanced and supported by the doctrine of precedent. In Ronald Dworkin's analysis, law unfolds like the chain novel: each chapter being constrained by what has gone before yet the whole novel exhibiting an innate coherence.[33] This comforting portrait of the law disguises law's reality: law is undeniably rational in some of its manifestations, yet in others displays little rationality and certainty. In addition, many patriarchal assumptions are displayed in the operation of law.[34] To return to already introduced aspects of law, from a feminist perspective, the English law relating to provocation which precludes the notion that women and men respond to violence in differing ways, ignores women's experience. The English law relating to financial provision and property on divorce is not predicated on consistency and the doctrine of precedent, but on the achievement of fairness between the parties. The legal system in cases of rape and sexual violence itself is damaging to the victim of the violence: forcing a detailed examination of the victim's behaviour and, in some instances, past sexual history in order to ascertain the credibility of the victim's evidence. Law's regulation of pornography, from a feminist perspective, lacks the rationality law proclaims for itself. Framing pornography law in the language of obscenity, and concentrating on whether or not pornographic representations are likely 'to deprave and corrupt', or other similar formulations, misses a core feature of pornography. As Andrea Dworkin and Catharine MacKinnon have so forcibly argued, the harm of pornography lies in its symbolic and actual denigration of women, reinforcing stereotypical images of women as sexual objects, thereby demeaning women and enhancing discrimination against women.

Positivist theory has not been subjected to great feminist analysis, perhaps on the basis that it is 'too antediluvian to merit explicit attention'.[35] Nevertheless, positivism exemplifies the extent to which modernist thought adopts the assumption that men and women are both subjects of law, that law is rational, coherent and all-embracing, and that law is applied neutrally as between State and citizen and as between citizen to citizen. That this is a fundamental fallacy is revealed in feminist reasoning about law, which is critically concerned not with the traditional positivist claims to law's autonomy and rationality as a closed intellectual domain, but with an analysis

---

[33] See, further, below.
[34] See, in particular, Smart, C, *Feminism and the Power of Law*, 1989, London: Routledge and Kegan Paul.
[35] The phrase is Professor Nicola Lacey's. See Lacey, N, 'Closure and critique in feminist jurisprudence', in Norrie, A (ed), *Closure or Critique: New Directions in Legal Theory*, 1993, Edinburgh: Edinburgh UP, p 196.

of, variously, law's blindness to gender and the deleterious, discriminatory effects of this blindness; the liberal dichotomy between the public and private spheres of life which underpin modern positivist analysis; the relevance of gender, race and class to legal analysis and the need to make heard the distinctive voices of woman in all her manifestations, and to effect change in the legal order in order to realise women's equality under the law.

Pre-eminent liberal legal philosopher Ronald Dworkin attacks positivist analyses of law which posit rules at the heart of the explanation of law. Dworkin explicates the role of principles in law, and the manner in which principles, rather than rules, may in 'hard cases' determine the outcome of a particular case. Principles do not operate in the same manner as legal rules: they have, as Dworkin explains, a 'different weight and dimension' than legal rules; they apply or do not apply according to their relevance to the particular case – there is nothing automatic or invariable about their application. If, then, principles are to be included within a positivist explanation of law, how can this be achieved? Dworkin argues that they cannot be so included. Not only are they qualitatively different and not automatically applicable, but principles are incapable of being encompassed under the ultimate rule of recognition (in the United Kingdom, that the Queen in Parliament ought to be obeyed), since the rule of recognition is the criterion for the validity of concrete, specific legal rules.

Significantly, Dworkin argues against Hart on the matter of judicial discretion.[36] Hart is emphatic that judges have an area of discretion, in which principles play their role. Dworkin by contrast argues that in every significant (or 'hard') case, there will be only one right answer and that it is the task of the judiciary to tease out this right answer by following the evolutionary nature of legal development and reaching a decision in the instant case which 'fits' with constitutional precedent.[37] In *Taking Rights Seriously*,[38] in which Dworkin takes positivism in general, and HLA Hart's version of positivism in particular, to task, Dworkin argues that it is rights, underpinned by principles, not discretion which determine the outcome of difficult cases. In each difficult case, for which no precedent exists, judges employ not discretion to determine the outcome, but the existing principles within the legal system. These equitable principles – such as 'no man shall profit from his own wrong' – underlie rights. Principles, Dworkin insists, have a 'different dimension and weight' than do legal rules: their application will depend upon the facts of the instant case, and principles will be employed not in a routine 'all-or-nothing' fashion, but according to their appropriateness. Thus, Dworkin argues, positivism is deficient in its inability to accommodate within its formal and

---

[36] Dworkin, R, *Taking Rights Seriously*, 1977, London: Duckworth.
[37] See Dworkin, R, *Law's Empire*, 1986, London: Fontana.
[38] *Ibid*, Dworkin, 1977.

formalistic structure the concept of principles, and in its reliance on judicial discretion.

Dworkin's primary focus is on rights which are underpinned by the principles within the legal system, rather than with formal rules analysed from a positivistic perspective. Principles represent:

> ... a standard that is to be observed, not because it will advance or secure an economic, political, or social situation deemed desirable, but because it is a requirement of justice or fairness or some other dimension of morality.[39]

Principles thus underpin rights, and the judge must be sensitive to and enforce the rights of the parties. From this perspective, the task of the judge is not the mechanical application of legal rules, but rather an interpretative exercise grounded in the rights of the parties. The denial of judicial discretion in Dworkin's analysis, allied to the concept of rights, results in there always being a 'right answer' in hard cases. Judges, adhering to the doctrine of precedent which gives a 'gravitational force' to his decision and which negates the idea of discretion, seek to develop the law in the manner best fitted to the underlying constitutional, moral and political framework of society. Thus, rather than a strict analysis of the components of the legal system, which for positivists are the legal rules, Dworkin develops a theory of adjudication. Dworkin's jurisprudence, in its critique of positivism and Hart's *Concept of Law*, breaks the mould of the positivistic/naturalistic opposition.

It is with *Law's Empire*,[40] however, that Dworkin's own distinctive brand of jurisprudence develops most fully.[41] Dworkin seeks to explain law's role by excavating 'its foundations in a more general politics of integrity, community, and fraternity'.[42] In *Law's Empire*, Dworkin once again summons up his ideal judge, Hercules. Hercules, is the embodiment of the judicial tradition imbued with the maturity and wisdom which enables him to find the 'right answer' to 'hard cases'. The law unfolds, under Hercules' charge, like a novel. With the novel, even if there are several authors, the plot must have cogency and coherence. Each participant author, accordingly, must interpret preceding chapters in such a manner as to advance the requisite coherence in the story overall. Hercules does this in judicial interpretation and evolution of the law, in the same manner as the authors of the joint novel.

The community, which Hercules serves as a judge of the Supreme Court, interpreting the written Constitution, is the 'fraternal' (*sic*) community, committed to commonly held principles and beliefs, and instilling in its members, an obligation to obey:

---

[39] *Op cit*, Dworkin, 1977, fn 36, p 22.
[40] *Op cit*, Dworkin, 1977, fn 37, p 22.
[41] It is in *Taking Rights Seriously*, 1977, that the distinction between principles and policies, the problem of 'hard cases' and Hercules are introduced.
[42] *Op cit*, Dworkin, 1986, fn 37, viii.

> ... each accepts political integrity as a distinct political ideal and treats the general acceptance of that ideal, even among people who otherwise disagree about political morality, as constitutive of political community.[43]

Integrity as a political ideal comes about 'when we make some demand of the State or community taken to be a moral agent'.[44] Provided that the individual has the opportunity to 'have his/her say', to argue for or against a particular proposition in political debate and before the courts of law, the obligation to obey exists where the majority in society agree with a particular proposition. Judges articulate the prevailing moral standards in their legal judgments: these judgments 'are themselves acts of the community personified'.[45] There is thus a high degree of consensus in Dworkin's political community, the conditions for which, in Dworkin's view, both the United States of America and the United Kingdom[46] satisfy.[47] Moreover, as Allan C Hutchinson points out, Dworkin's assumption of 'fraternal community', 'a moral agency of principled proportions', is at odds with reality, for '... where others see despair and isolation in American political and social life, Dworkin sees an enviable community of personal contentment and social solidarity'.[48]

There are further contradictions in Dworkin's arguments. The appearance of Hercules as the superhuman adjudicator of competing arguments in hard cases, striving to present law in its 'best light' and consistent with previous decisions, yet departing from them when changed circumstances dictate, is arguably marred by two factors. The first is the extent to which Hercules follows majoritarian opinion. From a feminist perspective, the opinion of the majority is precisely what underpins the sexism and inequality which women have traditionally suffered and continue to experience, despite the many formal legal reforms. The second difficulty lies in Dworkin's assertion that judges do not have discretion, and that there is one inexorably right answer to hard cases. In his analysis of *Brown v Board of Education*[49] and *Regents of the University of California v Bakke*,[50] Dworkin considers the many differing approaches which Hercules might take, and the justification for the preference of one over another: in so doing, Dworkin reveals that, contrary to his claim that judges do not have discretion, Hercules makes choices. If Hercules makes choices, and in part those choices are informed by public opinion in order to

---

[43] *Op cit*, Dworkin, 1977, fn 36, p 211.
[44] *Op cit*, Dworkin, 1977, fn 36, p 166.
[45] *Op cit*, Dworkin, 1977, fn 36, p 148.
[46] And presumably Australia and Canada and other liberal democracies.
[47] For a critique of Dworkin's conception of community and his assumption of its 'fit' with Western liberal democracies, see Hunt, A, 'Law's empire or legal imperialism?', in *Reading Dworkin Critically*, 1992, Oxford: Berg.
[48] Hutchinson, A, 'The law emperor?', in *Reading Dworkin Critically, ibid*, p 60.
[49] 349 US 294 (1955).
[50] 438 US 265 (1978).

reach a decision favourable to the community, what prospect is there for feminist claims, claims which seek to remedy and overturn deeply embedded socio-cultural and legal discriminations? Paradoxically, while conceding that judges 'make choices', in order to fulfil their interpretative quest and to 'portray law in its best light', Dworkin continues to deny judicial discretion: the judge is not exercising discretion but judgment, constrained by the gravitational force of precedent and communitarian integrity. The distinction between discretion, judgment and choice is exceedingly fine.

There are a number of further problems with Dworkin's jurisprudence from a feminist perspective. One issue which causes difficulties for feminist scholars is whether Hercules is overtly male, as his name suggests, or whether he is capable of gender-neutrality in his interpretation of the law. The answer to this would appear to be negative. Notwithstanding Dworkin's insistence that Hercules is fictional – 'a lawyer of superhuman skill, learning, patience and acumen'[51] – the highest courts of law have not proven in practice, as feminist scholarship has revealed, to be the champions of women's rights. Women's traditional exclusion from law, legal system and *polis*, the failure of law to reflect women's identities or subjectivities in its construction of, for example, the law of provocation, or more generally law's insistence on the male Enlightenment values of reasonableness, rationality and objectivity, reflect women's exclusions. Nor has Hercules improved the position of women under the law. Such equality as has been won has been won by women through exposing the maleness of law, and pressing for women's recognition not just by law, but in law. A cursory reflection on the law relating to abortion[52] and pornography,[53] particularly as interpreted under the US Constitution, support this view. In relation to abortion, the seminal case of *Roe v Wade*[54] established women's constitutional right, under the doctrine of privacy, to abortion within the first trimester of pregnancy. As will be seen later, subsequent jurisprudence of the Supreme Court has rendered that 'right' flimsy and contingent. In relation to the protection of women from pornography, conceptualising pornography as 'speech' or 'expression', rather than harm to women and women's equality, has ensured that the Constitution of the United States protects male pornographers and consumers, not pornography's victims – primarily women. On the other side of the coin, law's acceptance that sexual harassment is a form of unlawful sexual discrimination; the elimination of a husband's immunity from the law of rape in marriage; rules providing for gender equality in employment and so on all suggest that in many areas the judges are sensitive to gender issues. The

---

[51] *Op cit*, Dworkin, 1977, fn 36, p 105.
[52] On which see Chapter 10.
[53] See, further, Chapter 12.
[54] 410 US 113 (1973).

problem is that judges are not consistent and do not construe gender-equality uniformly. There is thus sufficient evidence to conclude that, from women's perspective, the law is at least ambivalent and inconsistent in its protection of women's status and rights.[55] Thus Dworkin's theory of adjudication, which while intuitively plausible – in the absence of empirical sociological evidence – fails to convince. Dworkin himself has criticised the Critical Legal Studies movement,[56] the essence of which is the unravelling of law's inconsistencies, while accepting in part the challenge which Critical Legal Studies poses for liberal theory. At root, however, Dworkin is deeply sceptical about the aims of some Critical Legal scholars, who in his view, want to 'show law in its worst rather than its best light', and to mystify law 'in service of undisclosed political goals'.[57]

Furthermore, Dworkin's political 'fraternity', and his theory of adjudication, assumes too much about human nature to provide reassurance as to the role of law in society. Dworkin fails to address issues of power, race, gender and class. The same assumptions which are made by positivists are made by Dworkin. Thus, while Dworkin tries to break the stranglehold of positivism without falling into the arms of natural law theory, his own theory of adjudication reflects the same shortcomings: that of idealism and utopianism.

Moreover, the 'chain novel' imagery of law propounded by Ronald Dworkin[58] ignores the differing modes of moral reasoning and approaches to decision making which Carol Gilligan's controversial research has revealed.[59] As feminist lawyer Nicola Lacey has pointed out, positivism and the associated ideal of the liberal rule of law, with its insistence on formality and rationality, effectively denies the differing modes of moral reasoning; ignores the fact that an ethic of care, and human inter-connectedness plays a role in women's reasoning and, it must follow, women's legal reasoning, as much as hierarchy and rationality.[60] The reality of differing modes of reasoning requires recognition in legal theory. The success of the American Realist school in the 1920s and 1930s, and its contemporary successor, Critical Legal Studies, discussed in Chapter 6, is in part due to the unmasking of law's lack of rationality and coherence.

---

[55] On law's ambivalence in family law, see Smart, C, *The Ties That Bind; Law, Marriage and the Reproduction of Patriarchal Relations*, 1984, London: Routledge and Kegan Paul; see, also, Smart, C, *Law, Crime and Sexuality: Essays in Feminism*, 1995, London: Sage.

[56] On which see, further, Chapter 9.

[57] *Op cit*, Dworkin, 1986, fn 37, p 275.

[58] *Op cit*, Dworkin, 1986, fn 37.

[59] See Gilligan, C, *In A Different Voice: Psychological Theory and Women's Development*, 1982, Cambridge, Mass: Harvard UP; and see, further, Chapter 7.

[60] See Lacey, N, *Feminism and the Tenets of Conventional Legal Theory*, 1996 (see *Sourcebook*, p 309); see, also, Lacey, N, 'Feminist legal theory: beyond neutrality' [1995] CLP 1.

Conventional Jurisprudence and Feminist Critique: II

One further aspect of Dworkin's theory which has fallen to feminist analysis is Dworkin's concept of obligation to the community. In Chapter 6, Dworkin analyses the foundational concept of integrity as political virtue. Integrity insists, Dworkin asserts, 'that each citizen must accept demands on him' and may 'make demands of others'.[61] Integrity is intimately bound up with the moral authority of law. Each person in the community has 'associative responsibilities', to be determined by critical interpretation, in light of the requirements of justice. The analysis is developed through the concept of the 'dutiful daughter'. Dworkin asks: '[D]oes a daughter have an obligation to defer to her father's wishes in cultures that give parents power to choose spouses for daughters but not sons?'[62] Dworkin accepts that if the community holds the view that daughters are less equal than sons, then this is not a true community (a community of integrity). If, however, gender equality is accepted, but a culture believes that women need paternalistic protection, there exists a 'genuine conflict' in terms of moral, and associative, obligation. The daughter has a responsibility to defer to parental choice, but this responsibility may be overridden by claims to individual freedom and autonomy. How is the conflict to be resolved? Dworkin's solution reveals his lack of concern with the daughter's dilemma, and her lack of rights:

> ... a daughter who marries against her father's wishes, in this version of the story, has something to regret. She owes him at least an accounting, and perhaps an apology, and should in other ways strive to continue her standing as a member of the community she otherwise has a duty to honour.[63]

In Allan C Hutchinson's analysis, this response represents a 'powerful and destructive dynamic at work', and represents the 'oppression of women masquerading as honour'.[64] The critique is elaborated by Valerie Kerruish and Alan Hunt who detect conservatism in Dworkin's analysis of the obligation imposed on the 'dutiful daughter'. This conservatism is manifested at two levels. In the first place, the authors argue that Dworkin is imposing the duty to resolve the conflict between individual autonomy and community duty upon the person who has been wronged. In the second place, and at a deeper level, conservatism is apparent in Dworkin's insistence that the daughter – whose rights are being sacrificed in the name of community – accept the 'normative power embedded in the discriminatory rule', notwithstanding the presumption that Dworkin himself 'does not approve of

---

[61] *Op cit*, Dworkin, 1986, fn 37, p 189.
[62] *Op cit*, Dworkin, 1986, fn 37, p 204.
[63] *Op cit, Reading Dworkin Critically*, fn 47, p 205.
[64] *Op cit, Reading Dworkin Critically*, fn 47, p 63.

the practice',[65] and notwithstanding Dworkin's otherwise deep commitment to the liberal conception of equality.[66]

Finally, Dworkin's evolving, subtle, and sometimes contradictory, jurisprudence falls into the trap of reifying law. While positing law in the political community, Dworkin demands that it is law, rather than politics, which regulates society. Law's 'empire' is just that: the single most powerful edifice in society. Standing Marxist theory on its head, law is the infrastructure, all else, economics, politics, ideology, religion, are superstructural. As Alan Hunt has written:

> His failure [to change the landscape of legal theory] is precisely the refusal to confront the inescapably political dimension of law or to acknowledge that law is politics in a special and distinctive form.[67]

SOCIAL CONTRACT THEORY

Thomas Hobbes, John-Jacques Rousseau, John Locke and John Rawls all present variants of social contract theory. For Thomas Hobbes, men come together in civil society and contract with the sovereign for the greater security of society as a whole.[68] The individual's rights are limited by that contract, although the sovereign holds individual rights on trust and cannot force the individual to harm himself. The central depressive thrust of Hobbes' writing is encapsulated in the idea that in a state of nature man would be at constant war with other men; that life would be 'nasty, brutish and short'. By contrast, John Locke's social contract theory[69] places heavy emphasis on the individual rights of man, rights which cannot be contracted away to the State.

The most comprehensive contemporary liberal social contract theory is offered by John Rawls. In *A Theory of Justice*,[70] Rawls considers the fundamental principles which individuals, stripped of self-knowledge (behind a 'veil of ignorance') would choose for the just ordering of society. Knowing nothing of one's own abilities and position in society, but having a general knowledge of economic systems and human psychology, individuals behind the veil of ignorance would proceed cautiously and would base their reasoning on the possibility that once the veil of ignorance is lifted, they might

---

[65] Kerruish and Hunt, in Hunt, *op cit*, fn 47, pp 209, 211.
[66] The liberal conception of equality is described by Dworkin as 'the nerve of liberalism': see Dworkin, R, 'Liberalism', in *A Matter of Principle*, 1986, Oxford: OUP, pp 181, 183.
[67] *Op cit*, Hunt, fn 47, p 41.
[68] *Op cit*, Hobbes, fn 7.
[69] *Op cit*, Locke, fn 8.
[70] Rawls, J, *A Theory of Justice*, 1972, Oxford: OUP.

end up in the 'worst off' position in society. Accordingly, the principles chosen would be directed to ensuring that the 'worst off' in society were in the best possible position given alternative outcomes of decision making.

The resultant principles which would emerge would be, first, that priority is to be given to liberty without which no individual can achieve his life plan. Secondly, inequalities in the distribution of wealth in society are justifiable only in so far as the achievement of greater wealth on the part of the most talented would compensate the 'worst off' in society. Finally, there is to be equality of opportunity in terms of access to political and economic life.

John Rawls' *A Theory of Justice* was published to much critical acclaim. Hailed as the most comprehensive contemporary exposition of the social contract, Rawls elaborates on the ideas of earlier writers such as Locke, Paine and Rousseau. The result is a painstakingly worked and reworked calculation of the criteria for a 'nearly just society'. The formula to which Rawls works is to hypothesise about placing representative people from differing walks of life in a society behind a 'veil of ignorance'. This veil prevents individuals from knowing their personal characteristics, including *inter alia* their intelligence, wealth, class or position in society. Only by stripping people of their individuality does Rawls consider that the principles on which society should be based – and hence laws – can be reached. Rawls does not envisage that everyone in a society at any point in time will go behind this 'veil of ignorance'. Rather, the original position (under the veil of ignorance) is a mental construct to be used for the determination of rational principles for the ordering of society. The original position is not 'a general assembly' of all persons living at one point in time, nor is it 'a gathering of all actual or possible persons'.[71]

Rather than an assembly of all persons, those in the original position are viewed as being 'representatives' of a class of persons: the representative being the 'head of the family'.

Knowledge and ignorance behind the 'veil of ignorance'

In order to maximise the rationality and disinterestedness in decision making about society and laws, Rawls denies the representatives behind the veil of ignorance certain knowledge. Such persons do not know their 'class position', nor 'their intelligence, strength or the like', nor whether he or she is an optimist or pessimist; have no idea of their own 'rational life plan' and have no knowledge of their own 'conception of the good'. Neither does the representative know the particular facts about his or her own society; its stage of development or politics, and his or her place within that society. The

---

[71] *Op cit*, Rawls, fn 70, p 139.

disembodied, ungendered representative person does, however, know the general facts of human society, including knowledge of politics, economics and psychology.[72]

By denying parties any particular knowledge of their personal situation, Rawls considers that the parties will be unable to bargain to reach decisions about justice from a self-interested position. Rather, parties – who will have a general desire to achieve their 'life plan' and to participate as fully as possible in the good of society – will adopt an attitude to decision making which, should they end up as less advantaged than others, will protect their position as far as possible. The parties behind the veil of ignorance are vaguely pessimistic about their own end position, and as a result will always gear their decisions towards the 'worst off' position in society.

The principles of justice

The principles which would be chosen by this representative congress of people will prioritise liberty over equality: each will have an equal right to the 'most extensive basic liberty compatible with a similar liberty for others'. Liberty may only be restricted in the interests of achieving greater liberty for all, and restrictions on liberty must be both acceptable to those whose liberty is being restricted, and consistent with the overall maximisation of liberty in society. The second principle of justice is that social and economic differences are to be distributed so that they are to everyone's advantage on the principle of equal access for all. Where there is an inequality in the distribution of primary social goods (liberty, opportunity, income and wealth), those inequalities may be justified on the basis that for every gain of those who find themselves the best advantages, the 'worst off' in society will also benefit from that person's advantage. The principles are ordered lexically – that is to say the first principle is 'prior to the second'[73] – and accordingly no departure from the first principle is justified by any greater social or economic advantages which might flow from such a departure.

From a feminist perspective a number of large questions loom out of Rawls' conception of the criteria for selecting principles of justice in society, and *A Theory of Justice* has been submitted to feminist scrutiny.[74] Amongst other matters, the question of the gender of Rawls' 'representative persons'

---

[72] *Op cit*, fn 70, p 137.
[73] *Op cit*, fn 70, p 61.
[74] Matsuda, M, 'Liberal jurisprudence and abstracted visions of human nature: a feminist critique of Rawls' *A Theory of Justice*' (1986) 16 New Mexico L Rev 613 (see *Sourcebook*, pp 325–27); Moller Okin, S, *Women in Western Political Thought*, 1979, Ewing, New Jersey: Princeton UP; 'Justice and gender' (1987) 16 Philosophy and Public Affairs 42; Kearns, D, 'A theory of justice – and love: Rawls on the family', in Simms, M (ed), *Australian Women and the Political System*, 1984, Melbourne: Longman.

arises. The 'representative person', the 'head of the household' at least implies that the representative person is gendered male. However, even if he is not, there is the suspicion that the representative is none other than the philosopher himself, and that the principles of justice adopted are those to which the philosopher himself adheres. Also central to the analysis is Rawls' attitude to the reality of equality in a just society. Rawls' methodology is subject to scrutiny by Mari J Matsuda[75] who argues, *inter alia*, that Rawls' abstractions are unhelpful:[76]

> To argue at the level of abstraction proves nothing and clouds our vision. What we really need to do is to move forward through Rawls' veil of ignorance, losing knowledge of existing abstractions. We need to return to concrete realities, to look at our world, rethink possibilities, and fight it out on this side of the veil, however indelicate that may be. By ignoring alternative visions of human nature, and by limiting the sphere of the possible, Rawls creates a gridlock in which escape from liberalism is impossible, and dreams of the seashore futile ...[77]

Susan Moller Okin in *Justice, Gender and the Family*[78] argues that Rawls has paid little or no attention to justice within the family, thus perpetuating the public/private distinction in terms of the justice constituency. Notwithstanding this failing, Moller Okin finds that Rawls' *A Theory of Justice* has potential from a feminist perspective. By applying Rawls' original position behind the veil of ignorance, the author argues that it is possible to reach decisions about a just society. A key point of justice within the family would be, for Moller Okin, the jointly shared responsibility for childcare. This would have an impact on the workplace, requiring employers to grant equal rights to time off for parenting, and flexible working hours in order to facilitate the demands made by children. Schools, too, would be implicated, and should ensure that children 'become fully aware of the politics of gender', in order that the traditional stereotyping of men's and women's attributes be overcome. The 'disappearance' of gender from the family and workplace, the socialisation of children within genderless families and schools, would result in a society which would exhibit true justice.[79]

For Carole Pateman, Rawls' thesis, resting on the primary construct of the original position, represents such an 'logical abstraction of such rigour that nothing happens there'.[80] As noted above, it is this abstraction that has also

---

75 At the time of writing, Assistant Professor of Law, University of Hawaii.
76 *Op cit*, Matsuda, fn 74.
77 *Op cit*, Matsuda, fn 74, p 624.
78 Moller Okin, S, *Justice, Gender and the Family*, 1989, New York: Basic Books.
79 For a critique of Susan Moller Okin's work on Rawlsian theory, see Lacey, N, 'Theories of justice and the welfare state' (1992) 1 Social and Legal Studies 323.
80 See Pateman, C, *The Sexual Contract*, 1988, London: Polity, p 43.

been criticised by Mari Matsuda.[81] In her view, Rawls' notion that self-interested individuals come together for the advantages which flow to the individual from collaboration and co-operation over-emphasises acquisitiveness, greed and self-interest. Rawls' individuals are excessively individualistic, and in their desire for the pursuit of their rational life plans and the maximum possible share in life's primary goods, ignore the possibilities of alternative modes of social life in which 'humour, modesty, conversation, spontaneity, laziness and enjoying the talents and differences of others also feels good'. What is called for is an abandonment of the abstracted original position, and decision making in the real world.

More fundamentally, for Carole Pateman, all social contract theory, in its insistence on spheres of individual liberty and individual rights, obscures the issue of gender, 'the original contract is a sexual-social pact, but the story of the sexual contract has been repressed'.[82] It is the sexual contract which explains the creation of a patriarchal social order which manifests itself in both the public and the private spheres of life. Through the distinction drawn by liberalism of life into two spheres, and theoretical emphasis being placed on the public, political, sphere, social contract theory leaves out, ignores, the patriarchal order. Those aspects of life – marriage, the home and family – are implicitly deemed by classic social contract theory to be unimportant to civic freedoms and rights enjoyed in the public sphere. Thus:

> Sexual difference is political difference; sexual difference is the difference between freedom and subjection. Women are not party to the original contract through which men transform their natural freedom into the security of civil freedom. Women are the subjects of the contract. The (sexual) contract is the vehicle through which men transform their natural right over women into the security of civil patriarchal right.[83]

The sexual contract is the original contract and lays the foundation, and the fundamental terms, for the social contract. It is the sexual contract which determines women's role as the nurturer and domestic worker. With the terms of the social – fraternal – contract in place, and the world divided into those areas of freedom and rights, the public sphere, and the areas free from legal regulation, the private sphere, the woman's role becomes affirmed as subordinate. Throughout her wide ranging scholarly study, Carole Pateman reveals, in relation to domestic labour, labour in the marketplace, classical social contract, Marxist and capitalist theory, the significance of this the original form of contractual relations: the sexual contract which underpins society. The social contract then is one between male citizens, between fathers

---

[81] *Op cit*, Matsuda, fn 74.
[82] *Op cit*, Pateman, fn 80, p 1.
[83] *Op cit*, Pateman, fn 80, p 6.

and brothers, to the exclusion of women. Women can enter into the contract only 'as men', on male terms, not as women.

The communitarian critique of liberalism

Liberal theory in general, and Rawls' *A Theory of Justice* in particular, also attracts critique from the point of view of those who reject the primacy of the individual as atomistic being and stress the individual as in relation with others: the communitarian critique. In part, the communitarian approach insists that the individual can have no identity or rights other than within the connections and relations created within the political community. Rawls' portrayal of the genderless individual imbued with the rationality to determine the principles of justice behind the 'veil of ignorance', and to develop his or her own rational life plan, is, from a communitarian perspective, a false conception for the individual cannot exist without society and community: justice, rights and rationality are only meaningful within the community.[84] Moreover, the individual subject is constituted by the community: the web of social relations into which the individual is born, and through which the subject individual moves throughout her life. The critique is also advanced by Drucilla Cornell who argues that the construction of the atomised individual effectively represents a denial of women through its implicit denial of the relational bonds between mother and child.[85, 86]

Communitarian philosophy stands opposed to liberalism's insistence on the primacy of the individual and stresses human interconnectedness. Rather than viewing individuals are imbued with individuality and autonomy, communitarianism in its many guises, insists that the individual is constructed through her interrelatedness within the community and

---

[84] See Sandel, M, *Liberalism and the Limits of Justice*, 1982, Cambridge: CUP; Taylor, C, *Philosophical Papers*, Vol 2, 1985, Cambridge: CUP; MacIntyre, A, *After Virtue: A Study in Moral Theory*, 2nd edn, 1984, London: Duckworth; *Whose Justice, Which Rationality?*, 1988, London: Duckworth; Gewirth, A, 'Rights and virtues' (1988) 38 Review of Metaphysics. See also John Rawls' response to the communitarian critique: 'Justice as fairness: political not metaphysical' (1985) 14 Philosophy and Public Affairs 3; 'Kantian constructivism in moral theory' (1985) Journal of Philosophy 77; 'The idea of an overlapping consensus' (1987) 7 OJLS 1; 'The priority of the right and ideas of the good' (1988) 17 Philosophy and Public Affairs 251; *Politician Liberalism*, 1993, New York: Columbia UP.

[85] Cornell, D, 'Beyond tragedy and complacency' (1987) 81 Northwestern University L Rev 693; 'The doubly prized world: myth, allegory and the feminine' (1990) 75 Cornell L Rev 644.

[86] For a detailed feminist critique of communitarianism, see Frazer, E and Lacey, N, *The Politics of Community: A Feminist Critique of the Liberal-Communitarian Debate*, 1993, Hemel Hempstead: Harvester.

emphasises societal values rather than individuality.[87] The values of communitarianism, connectedness and interdependency, are both relevant to feminist theory and practice. As seen in Chapter 1, feminism's consciousness raising techniques are situated within the concrete experiences of women, often within localities. Moreover the shared identities of women within their own location, be that cultural, racial, or through social stratification, has been an enabling, facilitating, characteristic for the development of theory.

However, while communitarian political philosophy shifts the libertarian focus on individuality, rationality and autonomy towards an understanding of the interconnectedness of society and the manner in which that interconnectedness constructs the individual subject, and emphasises societal interdependence, communitarian philosophy ignores both gender and power relations. Moreover, communitarian philosophy in denying individuality and autonomy of legal and social subjects, ignores the differences between people: subjectivities become 'shared', 'mutually sympathetic, understanding one another as they understand themselves'.[88] This 'shared subjectivity', in Iris Young's analysis, is not only impossible[89] but politically undesirable in so far as the striving for community – through the identification with similar others – makes co-existence with groups having different characteristics more, not less, difficult. In Young's view, the ideal of community 'is similar to the desire for identification that underlies racial and ethnic chauvinism'.[90] Accordingly, in denying difference and emphasising shared identities, communitarianism ignores the problems entailed in forging theoretical and practical objectives within feminism which, under the conditions of postmodernity,[91] demand the recognition of women's differing subjectivities, socially constructed through identification on racial and gender-orientated lines. Feminist scholarship in recent years has been keenly attuned to the differences between women, and the need for 'the implementation of a principled call for heterogeneity'.[92]

---

[87] See, for analysis, references cited at fn 85, and Taylor, C, *Sources of the Self*, 1990, Cambridge: CUP; Mulhall, S and Smith, A, *Liberals and Communitarian*, 2nd edn, 1995, Oxford: Basil Blackwell; Kymlicka, W, *Liberalism, Community and Culture*, 1989, Oxford: OUP; Cotterrell, RBM, *Law's Community*, 1995, Oxford: Clarendon.

[88] Young, I, 'The ideal of community and the politics of difference' (1986) 12 Social Theory and Practice 1, p 10.

[89] Given that, according to psychoanalytic theory, the subject cannot 'know' itself, let alone others, and that subjectivity, as Julia Kristeva analyses the concept, is always a 'process in being', 'heterogeneous, decentred', never fixed in meaning, but always fluid.

[90] *Ibid*, Young, p 12.

[91] On which see Chapter 9.

[92] *Ibid*, Young, p 13.

THE FAILURES OF TRADITIONAL JURISPRUDENCE

It may be seen from the above, necessarily brief and introductory outlines, that, in differing ways, traditional, male jurisprudence has been concerned with identifying the *characteristics* of valid law, not with the *effect of law* on the individuals it serves. It may be countered that natural law thought with its concern for the morality of law and the central notion of equality of all before the law – the concept of the rule of law – does entail an appreciation of the effects of law. This, however, from a feminist – and indeed a socialist, Marxist or more general classist or minority approach – is lamentably inadequate. Aristotelian equality – the principle of treating like alike and treating different cases differently – tells us little of the relevant criteria by which 'sameness' or 'difference' should be evaluated. Formal equality fails in other respects. To treat all equally gives no guarantee that all shall benefit: indeed all may suffer as a result of equal treatment.

It would not be too sweeping a conclusion to argue that women have been denied recognition in male jurisprudence. The only manner in which it is tenable to argue the converse, is to argue that women are 'men'. Laws, legal systems and conventional jurisprudence, in its many guises, have failed women – have either excluded women from law's domain, or required that woman enters the domain on male, patriarchal terms. The extent to which feminist analysis and scholarship has provided alternative, inclusionary, visions is considered in Part III.

PART III

SCHOOLS OF FEMINIST JURISPRUDENTIAL THOUGHT

CHAPTER 6

SCHOOLS OF FEMINIST JURISPRUDENTIAL THOUGHT: I

LIBERALISM AND MARXISM

INTRODUCTION

The liberal tradition in Western democracy[1]

As seen in Chapter 5, liberalism has long been the dominant political ethos in Western democratic society and hence in law. The key concepts of liberal thought are rationality, individuality, equality, liberty from interference from others or the State unless justified, the availability of legal rights, and the protection of the private sphere of life which is conventionally deemed to be 'not the State's interest'. The powers of the State must thus be constrained under the rule of law.

First and foremost, liberalism emphasises the priority of the freedom of the individual and his or her freedom from undue political, legal and economic restraint. Liberty is thus at the heart of the liberal tradition. Liberalism insists on the demarcation of the 'public' and 'private' spheres of life: whereas State regulation of the public sphere – the world of employment, commerce, politics and participation in the democratic process – is justified in the public interest, the private sphere is that realm of privacy within which individuals should be able to retreat from the pressures of the public world, and to live according to their own dictates, unrestrained by law and the State, other than for the protection of others. Correlated with the priority of liberty are perceptions about the individual's autonomy and rationality which enables individuals to pursue their own 'rational life plan'[2] without undue interference or restriction. Rationality requires that equal respect be given to each citizen in the pursuit of their personal legitimate goals in life. Equality between persons is also critical to the realisation of a liberal democratic State: no individual or group of individuals should be privileged in a manner which delimits the equality and freedom of others. Central also to liberalism is the concept of enforceable

---

[1] See, *inter alia*, Arblaster, A, *The Rise and Decline of Western Liberalism*, 1994, Oxford: Basil Blackwell; Laski, H, *The Rise of European Liberalism*, 1936, London: Allen & Unwin. For a feminist appraisal of liberalism, see Jaggar, A, *Feminist Politics and Human Nature*, 1983, New Jersey: Rowman and Littlefield.

[2] The phrase is that of John Rawls. See Rawls, J, *A Theory of Justice*, 1972, Oxford: OUP.

individual rights which may be called upon to enforce restrictions on State intrusion into a person's legitimate sphere of liberty.

Subsumed within these introductory remarks lie several difficult issues. First, if each individual as citizen is to enjoy maximum freedom, it is necessary that some restraints be placed on conduct in order to protect the freedoms and rights of others. Accordingly, it is false to speak of total freedom; rather what must be sought is maximum individual freedom consistent with the freedom of others. Secondly, it must be asked whether the State is justified – on the basis of protection of others – in interfering in all aspects of life, or whether the justification only relates to the public sphere of life. Entailed in this last point is the question of whether in fact there can be boundaries drawn around 'spheres of life' – the public and the private – in order to determine the legitimacy of State regulation.

One of the clearest expositions of liberal legal philosophy comes from the nineteenth century political philosopher, John Stuart Mill.[3] In 1859, John Stuart Mill's *On Liberty* was published. The essence of Mill's thought is encapsulated within the following paragraph:

> The object of this Essay is to assert one very simple principle, as entitled to govern absolutely the dealings of society with the individual in the way of compulsion and control, whether the means used be physical force in the form of legal penalties, or the moral coercion of public opinion. That principle is, that the sole end for which mankind are warranted, individually or collectively, in interfering with the liberty of action of any of their number, is self-protection. That the only purpose for which power can be rightfully exercised over any member of a civilised community, against his will, is to prevent harm to others. His own good, either physical or moral, is not a sufficient warrant.[4]

Mill thus emphasises the liberty of the citizen in which the State has no right to interfere unless justified in so doing for the protection of other members of society. The individual is free – subject to necessary restraints predicated upon the principle of the protection of others – to pursue his or her own goals in life, to live his or her own lifestyle however morally worthy or unworthy that may appear in the eyes of others. On this basis, each individual's preferences and predilections should be accorded equal respect by the law, and the individual should be accorded the maximum sphere of freedom to pursue his or her own chosen destiny and satisfy his or her own personal wants. If 'society' abhors an individual's lifestyle, it may attempt to educate the individual into reforming, but it may not – subject to the harm to others principle – seek through the means of law to control that person's conduct. Liberal philosophy places the individual centrestage. No individual may be sacrificed for the

---

[3] 1806–73.
[4] Mill, JS, *On Liberty* (1859), 1989, Cambridge: CUP, p 13.

community at large. Society – howsoever defined – is not, from this perspective, an entity whose interests, however legitimate, may override the supremacy of the autonomous individual.[5] Law's role, therefore, is one of providing the societal framework which accords to the citizen the maximum area of freedom which is consonant with the freedom of others. The structure demarcates an area of privacy – a private sphere – into which the State has to justify any intrusion.

The public and private spheres in liberal philosophy

> 'Public' may be used to denote State activity, the values of the marketplace, work, the male domain or that sphere of activity which is regulated by law. 'Private' may denote civil society, the values of family, intimacy, the personal life, home, women's domain or behaviour unregulated by law.[6]

The public/private distinction derives from ancient Greek thought which drew a distinction between the *polis*, the public sphere and the *oikis*, the private; the public world is that of male governance, the private is that of the home occupied by women and children.[7] By the seventeenth century the concept of the public and private spheres had been formulated as determinative of the appropriate sphere for both legal regulation (the public sphere) and the freedom from legal regulation (the private sphere). Thus, the family became largely invisible to law: a haven of legal liberty.

As will be seen, there remain difficulties in any attempt to rigorously distinguish between the two spheres, and there is much evidence for the conclusion that law, far from leaving the private sphere unregulated, plays a significant role in regulating the private and that the notion of a private sphere of freedom from law is largely mythical.

A central tenet of Western liberalism endorses this divide by insisting that there exists an area of personal individual privacy which is 'not the law's business'.[8] A similar idea is expressed in the time-worn expression that 'an English*man's* home is his castle' into which no one, without lawful authority, may intrude into an individual's personal space.[9] As seen above, the nineteenth century liberal philosopher and feminist activist John Stuart Mill was also to insist on a sphere of personal privacy into which the State must

---

[5] See, for a contrasting view, Devlin, P, *The Enforcement of Morals*, 1965, Oxford: OUP.

[6] O'Donovan, K, *Sexual Divisions in Law*, 1985, London: Weidenfeld and Nicolson, p 3. (See *Sourcebook*, pp 146–59.)

[7] See Arendt, H, *The Human Condition*, 1958, Chicago: Chicago UP; cf Swanson, J, *The Public and the Private in Aristotle's Political Philosophy*, 1992, New York: Cornell UP.

[8] See, eg, *op cit*, Mill, fn 4; *The Report of the Committee on Homosexual Offences and Prostitution*, Cmnd 247, 1957, London: HMSO, but cf *ibid*, Devlin, fn 5.

[9] See, eg, *Semayne's* Case (1605) 5 Co Pres 91a; 77 ER 194.

not intrude if individual freedom and rationality are to be respected. Accordingly, while law may intervene to prevent one individual's conduct from causing harm to another, law may not, without that justification, otherwise intrude on individual liberty. To reiterate, at the heart of liberal theory lie concepts of limited State power, individualism, rationality and privacy.

Women, traditionally, have been denied full and effective participation in society. Much of the discrimination so effectively perpetuated until this century (although not all discriminatory laws and practices have yet been removed) is explained through the conceptual separation of the public and private spheres of life. When the demarcation of the 'private' sphere is allied to patriarchal attitudes which insist on male superiority over women there exists a potent and potentially dangerous scenario from the perspective of women.

Liberal feminists accept the merits and strengths of liberal ideology but seek to unmask and rectify the inequalities which liberalism – through its implicit insistence that all individuals are equally equal – disguises. The task, from this perspective, is to act within the dominant ideology and seek to eliminate gender-based discrimination – to achieve true equality for women in all walks of life – without challenging the ideology itself and while remaining faithful to the liberal ideal of equality and autonomy. What liberal feminists, from Mary Wollstonecraft onwards, have sought to achieve is the elimination of practices and laws which effectively deny women access to the 'public sphere' of life and relegate women to the 'private sphere' of the home and family. By historically and traditionally excluding women from civic life, men not only seized for themselves the highground of policy and law making, but also subordinated and silenced women, denying women a voice in public affairs. Liberalism's biggest fraud lies in its assumptions that men and women are equal, when in fact it is all too apparent that traditionally the only voices being heard and given effect were male voices. Nowhere is this phenomenon more apparent, even nowadays, than in the legal system.[10] The feminist liberal movement has not been confined merely to achieving legal reforms such as the right to the franchise, the right to equal education, the right to own property, the right to admission to the professions and all other forms of employment, the right to equal pay and conditions of work, but has extended across all aspects of life.

In relation to the liberal respect for the private sphere of life, liberal feminists have analysed the position of women within the family, the rights of women to protection from sexual and other domestic violence, the rights of women in relation to that most private sphere of life: the control over reproduction, which demands that women be given access to and control over

---

[10] See, further, Chapter 11.

issues such as contraception, abortion and childbirth. Liberal feminism also, in seeking true equality and choice for women to exercise their own rationality and pursue their own life plan, examines the economic effects of domesticity on women's economic capacity in the public sphere of remunerated employment. Undeniably, women are free to choose to devote their lives to their children and family, but all too often – as social surveys and statistics continue to reveal – the responsibilities of the private sphere result in women being employed in part time, low paid jobs with little job security.[11] For those women who choose to pursue their own career, the stark choice must often be made as to whether to attempt to combine this career with domestic responsibilities, or to postpone the question of personal fulfilment through family life until their careers are well established – with the attendant risks of finding fulfilment in the public sphere at the expense of the private sphere.

Equality of opportunity is thus also inextricably linked to the meaning of substantive, rather than purely formal, equality. Discrimination in employment and other aspects of life, and the removal of such discrimination, has been a central focus of liberal feminism. Gender, the social construction of biological sex, should be irrelevant to issues such as the right to participate in spheres of employment, other than where physical attributes render women unable to fulfil the responsibilities entailed in that employment. Thus, whereas it may be justifiable for an employer who requires a worker to be able to lift 200 pound weights to employ a man rather than a woman, should a particular woman be able to satisfy the requirements of weight lifting, there is no legitimate cause for her exclusion from employment. Where the activity in question does not relate to physical strength, however, there should be no barrier placed in women's path to entry to that employment. Thus, for liberal feminism, gender is an issue which should be viewed, as it was in Plato's *The Republic*[12] as a concept which has little, if any, relevance to women's status in the public sphere, save where legitimate justifications can be adduced to support discriminatory practices. For the most part, women have the capacity, physical and intellectual, to operate in the public sphere under the same terms of reference as men. The conventional, Victorian, imagery of women as 'too feminine' for particular professions also continues to resonate in contemporary society and has resulted in women's long exclusion from such professions in which gender should make no difference. The early struggles for the right to vote, the right to full education and entry into universities and the professions bear witness to the representation of women, by men, as 'feminine', 'weak' and 'in need of protection' from the brute (male) realities of the public sphere. Conceptions of women as more rightly confined within the private sphere supported the resistance to women's demands for equality. In contemporary society, echoes of Victorian values continue to be 'heard' in the

---

[11] See, further, Chapter 2.
[12] On which see Chapter 4, but note the ambivalence in Plato's theory.

conceptualisation and reality of women as most appropriately employed within subordinate positions. Accordingly, as seen in Chapter 2, women are disproportionately represented within the fields of nursing, in childcare, in clerical work and in support positions within the professions. Further, women remain either excluded from or relegated to roles defined by male leaders in areas of employment.

The dilemma which liberal legal feminists face, it may be argued, is the too ready acceptance of the intrinsic and superficially attractive tenets of the liberal tradition. Liberalism's very tenacity as a philosophical and political foundation for Western society and law confirms its attraction, and it is tempting to accept that if only the formal, substantive inequalities from which women have suffered, and continue to suffer are eradicated through law, liberalism's empire will continue, a little tarnished but fundamentally unimpaired.[13]

By working within the framework, rather than challenging the underlying political philosophy, liberal legal feminism has achieved much by unearthing the inequalities and pressing successfully for legal change. The project will continue as scholars continue to research into and press for reform of discriminatory laws. The illustrations noted above underline the magnitude of the task which has both been undertaken and remains to be undertaken.

Liberal feminism argues that women, despite their physical differences, are equally capable of functioning in the public sphere, provided that the structured inequality in law and society can be removed. Thus, women are or could be 'just like men' and therefore accorded equality on that basis. This reflects the approach of liberal feminists who do not attack the law or legal system as inherently and unfailingly sexist, but rather view the law as having evolved in a manner which reflects the reality of social life and has been constructed according to male norms. If these norms could be deconstructed and a reconstruction effected which would include rather than exclude women, the law would be essentially fair.

As noted above, much significant reform has been achieved through use of this softly-softly approach: reforms in family law and employment law in the United Kingdom provide a wealth of examples of the strides made towards formal equality within the family and the workplace. For example, on equal parental responsibility for children, see the evolution from the father's automatic right to 'custody' of his children[14] through to the Children Act 1989 which makes explicit the equal rights and responsibilities of parents of legitimate (but not illegitimate) children. In relation to employment, see the Equal Pay Act 1970, Sex Discrimination Act 1975, and the significant gains

---

[13] Communitarian philosophy stands opposed to liberalism's insistence on the primacy of the individual and stresses human interconnectedness: see, further, Chapter 5.

[14] *Re Agar-Ellis* (1883) 24 Ch D 317.

made by women under Article 119 of the Treaty of Rome 1957 (founding the European Economic Community, now the European Community and Union). The social reality of women's position remains, however, rather different from that portrayed by formal legal equality.

There exists a fundamental difficulty with the 'liberal State'. With its emphasis on individual freedom, rights and equality, liberalism masks the gendered nature of society, the State and law. Achieving formal equality for women through the dismantling of existing inequalities before the law cannot, without more, achieve substantive equality. A number of issues are entailed here. First, for the most part the law is cast in gender-neutral terms, thus creating the liberal illusion that the law is blind to gender.[15] That this is not an accurate reflection of law's reality is demonstrated through analyses of the manner in which the law is applied in particular circumstances which have an adverse consequence for women, but not men, simply because 'man', not woman, is the referent – the Subject – of law.

The feminist critique of liberalism

A sceptical reaction to legal liberalism may lead to a different conclusion from that which suggests that the achievement of formal legal equality is an adequate good. In Chapter 2, the movement from culture to law was considered, and it was seen there, the many and various ways in which women have traditionally been treated as nurturers and carers of children, as subordinate to, and as possessions of, their husbands and other male kinfolk. It is not necessary, as was seen, to look to once physically and culturally remote societies to find such attitudes. It may be recalled, for example, that under English law, women were denied the right to own and manage personal property until 1882;[16] were accorded equal rights and duties in relation to their children under statute only in 1973;[17] were denied equality in access to divorce until after the Second World War; that until 1970 English husbands could recover damages from a man proven to have committed adultery with his wife, although no equivalent remedy was available to an aggrieved wife;[18] that English women were denied a remedy for rape within marriage, on the basis of implied consent through marriage to sexual access by their husbands irrespective of their own feelings, until 1991;[19] that in England women may be prosecuted for the murder of their violent husbands

---

[15] There are, of course, obvious exceptions to this, particularly in relation to abortion rights and other gender-specific medical issues.
[16] Married Women's Property Act 1882.
[17] Guardianship Act 1973.
[18] Law Reform (Miscellaneous Provisions) Act 1970.
[19] *R v R* [1992] 1 AC 599.

and until recently denied the right to a special defence of delayed provocation because the criminal law recognises only a defence of immediate provocation which is appropriate only to men.[20] Such examples illustrate the intractable nature of sexism and patriarchy in society and law.

The public and private spheres of life

As the quotation from Katherine O'Donovan's *Sexual Divisions in Law*[21] cited above makes clear, the public sphere of life is that of politics, law and employment in the marketplace, whereas the private sphere is that domain into which the individual retreats from the pressures of the world and in which the individual is sovereign and unregulated by the law. Neither concept is, however, as simple and straightforward as this brief introduction suggests.

As O'Donovan's analysis makes clear, the private sphere is rather more regulated than liberal theory would imply. Liberalism's insistence on the division is thus more ideological than real. As will be seen below, the law does for example regulate the private sphere particularly in relation to domestic violence, the protection of children from abuse and through controlling the terms on which a marital relationship may be entered into and terminated.[22] The law also controls that most private sphere of life: sexuality. Thus laws regulate the age of consent to both heterosexual and homosexual activity; laws regulate the availability of contraception and abortion advice and treatment. Law and medical practice control the management of pregnancy and childbirth.[23] Law also regulates permissible sexual activity between adults.[24] The 'private sphere' is also affected by fiscal controls imposed by the State through taxation and social welfare benefits, and more broadly through management of the economy which determines employment opportunities and conditions of employment. Thus it is arguable that the private-public distinction, which is so central to liberal theory, is itself fundamentally flawed. Further, the conceptual divide between the public and private masks and ignores the economic role of women within the family and home. As Katherine O'Donovan perceptively notes, even where law does not regulate

---

[20] *R v Ahluwalia* [1992] 4 All ER 889; *R v Thornton* [1992] 1 All ER 306. For discussion of the law's reaction to battered woman syndrome and its role, see, further, Chapter 11.

[21] *Op cit*, O'Donovan, fn 6.

[22] Although as O'Donovan states, Anglo-American law does not seek to regulate the marital relationship during its subsistence to the extent which civil law systems of continental Europe do through the provision of detailed family codes stipulating respective mutual rights, duties and responsibilities in marriage.

[23] See, further, Chapter 10.

[24] See *R v Brown* [1994] 1 AC 212, in which the House of Lords ruled that adults may not consent to assault in sexual activity.

an aspect of private life, that very non-regulation has meaning. As O'Donovan states:

> Not legislating contains a value judgment just as legislating does. Law cannot be neutral; non-intervention is as potent an ideology as regulation.[25]

As will be seen later, the ascription to women of a subordinate status to that of her husband, and her traditional familial (private) role, lends itself to a non-recognition of conditions of inequality and violence within the home. Law's blindness to the 'private' – conscious or unconscious – for too long left women in a position whereby they were unprotected from rape by their husbands; unprotected also from violence within the home,[26] and having unequal economic bargaining power, at the mercy of their economically active husband's financial generosity or otherwise, thus perpetuating notions of inequality and lack of worth. It is for reasons such as these that the statement that 'the personal is political' has become a central feminist perception.

Women's unpaid domestic labour in relation to child-bearing, caring and nurturing, represents the private unrecognised economy of most women's lives, and often determines the extent to which women can enter the marketplace of paid employment, and the terms on which they do so.[27] That this contribution is largely ignored by the State[28] ensures women's continuing dual role and unequal participation in the private sphere, while at the same time facilitating male participation through freeing the man from domestic responsibility. Women's child-bearing, caring and domestic role plays a central analysis in feminist theory, whether approached from a liberal, cultural or Marxist-socialist perspective.

Liberal feminism's quest for women's entry into the public sphere on the basis of equality with men is also not as unproblematic as it might at first sight appear, as O'Donovan's analysis reveals. First, there remains the problem of legal paternalism: the attitude of the State towards women's 'nature' and women's appropriate 'role'. Secondly, there remains the difficulty of securing substantive as opposed to formal equality in the marketplace. While these problems are recurrent themes throughout this book, brief illustrations at this point are necessary to elucidate the difficulties in the 'public/private' dichotomy.

In relation to 'women's nature and role', the traditional image of woman as mother and woman as carer comes to the fore. Historically, as discussed below, this reveals itself in the many legal disabilities from which women suffered. Conceptually and linguistically, the binary oppositions of

---

[25] *Op cit*, O'Donovan, fn 6, p 184.
[26] See, further, Chapter 11.
[27] On disparities in employment, see, further, Chapter 2.
[28] Contributions to the family are recognised under English law relating to financial provision on divorce: see the Matrimonial Causes Act 1973, s 25(2).

male/female, culture/nature, public/private and so on, are applied to the perceptions of woman as inferior, irrational, subordinate. From ancient Greece through to current times, these images are renewed and reaffirmed by the law and legal system. In earlier times, the concept of 'one flesh' on marriage, with the woman 'under the protection' of her husband and accordingly unable to own and manage her own property represented a clear expression of law's paternalism. Katherine O'Donovan discusses, in this regard, the English protective employment legislation which regulated the hours of female factory workers[29] and prohibited the employment of women in mining.[30] Ostensibly 'protective', the legislation had the effect of removing from women free choice and full autonomy of decision making in relation to employment. The seminal United States case of *Sears v Equal Employment Opportunities Commission*[31] reveals most starkly the dangers of law considering women's 'special nature'. In *Sears v EEOC*, the Equal Employment Opportunities Commission (EEOC) argued that Sears Roebuck & Co were discriminating against women. Two women employment experts submitted evidence. One of these supported the EEOC, while the other supported the company. At the heart of the matter lay women's suitability to succeed in the competitive world of insurance sales. The outcome of the case, which turned on an analysis of women's 'nature and role', was that the company had not discriminated against women: as Catharine MacKinnon expresses it, 'the argument on women's differences won, and women lost'. It is precisely because 'women's nature' can be manipulated in this manner, to argue both for and against equality, that cultural feminism which valorises women's special characteristics[32] is regarded with so much suspicion by other feminist scholars.

With regard to formal as opposed to substantive equality in the public sphere, O'Donovan analyses the shortcomings of law's attempts to provide equal opportunities for women, and questions the efficacy of sex discrimination legislation as currently formulated and applied. While the concept of equality has formally been ascribed to by the State,[33] the manner in which that ascription has been incorporated into law is fraught with

---

[29] Factories Act 1961.
[30] Mines Regulation Act 1842; Ten Hours Act 1844. The struggle for women to be admitted to the armed forces on the basis of full equality with men, and free from sexual harassment in that employment, remains a contemporary illustration of this discriminatory phenomenon.
[31] 628 F Supp 1264 (ND Ill, 1986), affirmed 839 F 2d 302 (7th Cir 1988). On this case see MacKinnon, C, *Toward a Feminist Theory of State*, 1989, Cambridge, Mass: Harvard UP, p 223, and references cited therein.
[32] See Chapter 8.
[33] See the English Equal Pay Act 1970 and Sex Discrimination Act 1975 and Equal Pay Directives of the European Communities issued under the Treaty of Rome, Art 119, which stipulates the requirements of equal pay.

difficulties.[34] Discrimination on the basis of sex is prohibited in the public sphere, and that discrimination may be either direct or indirect. For a complaint to be adjudicated it is necessary for the victim of discrimination to begin and pursue an action in law. This individualisation of the pursuit of formal equality thus leaves untouched the structured nature of gender-based discrimination within the public sphere as a whole. The creation of individualistic remedies while of some utility, does not create wide-scale structural and attitudinal change. Furthermore, as O'Donovan argues, liberalism is 'committed to creating similarities between women and men where possible and to minimising the differences between them'. The effect of this strategy is to 'lead[s] to assimilation of women to men in the public world and to a denial of needs and responsibilities arising from the private'.[35] Thus, women – in order to achieve formal equality – must enter the marketplace *as if* they are men: man is the standard for woman to achieve; man is the referent against which her inequality is to be judged. This position ignores both women's differing physique and physiology, and women's dual role as worker in the public and private spheres. To demand that women demonstrate that their abilities and capabilities are identical to men's is to privilege men over women; to make man the superior standard which must be reached before entry into the public sphere can be justified, without any consideration of the reality of most women's lives.

However, while feminists have successfully unravelled the paradoxes and illusions about the liberal State's insistence on a sphere of privacy into which law will not and should not intrude, and highlighted the dangers of this supposed neutrality of the State from a woman's perspective, it does not necessarily follow that there should be a total abandonment of the notion of some sphere of privacy in private life. What is required is not a police State in which every vulnerable person is protected, but rather appropriate remedies for those who suffer in the private sphere, together with the aspiration to and achievement of conditions of real gender equality in which the manifestations of patriarchal power would be absent. Changes to the status quo of women's equality therefore need to be undertaken not purely by law, which has limited efficacy, but primarily through cultural and political change. Feminist analysis and action has achieved much in relation to women's equality, and remains the foremost vehicle through which future changes may be achieved.

Such a conclusion, however, does not end the debate about the appropriate role of law within the private sphere. In Katherine O'Donovan's analysis, the absence of rights during the subsistence of marriage in English law,[36] represents a lost opportunity. Civil family codes, in specifying rights

---

[34] See *op cit*, O'Donovan, fn 6, Chapters 3 and 7.
[35] *Op cit*, O'Donovan, fn 6, p 174.
[36] Under English law, rights are established on the granting of a decree of nullity or divorce under the Matrimonial Causes Act 1973 (from 1999, the Family Law Act 1996) and not during marriage.

and duties within marriage, as opposed to on divorce, can, in laying down general principles, 'influence attitudes and behaviour. By expressing in its content general community beliefs concerning interpersonal justice it exhorts spouses to behave with justice towards one another'.[37] Katherine O'Donovan recognises, however, that there are difficulties with such an approach. Not only is there the liberal objection to regulating the 'private' sphere of life, and the problems inherent in effective enforcement of such law, but such extended regulation would also require an acceptance of the liberal State and its law as just. As O'Donovan asks, '... what is the nature of the State in feminist theory? Is it protector or oppressor?'.[38] At source, the issue of increased regulation or deregulation of private family life, lies in the liberal distinction between the private and the public. Unsettle the certainties of this false dichotomy, and the rational basis for law's intervention or non-intervention is undermined.

The question of the nature of the State is directly addressed by radical feminist Catharine MacKinnon. From a radical feminist perspective,[39] there exist further difficulties with the liberal State. Liberalism continues to suggest that equality for women is attainable, if only the obstacles to full participation in public life are removed. Equality for women, from a liberal perspective, is 'just around the corner'. However, what liberalism consciously or unconsciously conceals is the concept of *power* in society. If Catharine MacKinnon's analysis is considered in relation to the supposed public/private dichotomy, the idea of power and power relations can be more readily understood. In brief, it is MacKinnon's thesis that the liberal State is profoundly male and exclusionary of women. In MacKinnon's analysis, liberalism masks the reality of gender relations, which are political relations demarcated by power and powerlessness. An analysis of the State is a prerequisite for understanding the relative powerlessness of women. As MacKinnon asks, '[W]hat, in gender terms, are the State's norms of accountability, sources of power, real constituency?'. Further, '[I]s the State to some degree autonomous of the interests of men or an integral expression of them?'.[40] In the absence of a feminist understanding of the gendered nature and character of State power, MacKinnon argues that women can only accept and use State power (in the form of law) in order to improve women's formal position while at the same time leaving 'unchecked power in society to men'. Rationality, that central tenet of liberal philosophy, legitimates the State by implying that the State is objective; that the State merely reflects the 'way things are'. Thus law, for MacKinnon, with its objectivity and rationality, is a means whereby the status quo of male power and female powerlessness is

---

[37] *Op cit*, O'Donovan, fn 6, p 182.
[38] *Op cit*, O'Donovan, fn 6, p 184.
[39] On which see Chapter 8.
[40] *Op cit*, MacKinnon, fn 31, p 161.

reinforced, whilst at the same time maintaining the myth of its own neutrality and gender-blindness. Only when gender is understood to be a 'means of social stratification', rather than an ostensibly neutral, rational arbiter between equal conflicting interests, will the position of women be understood and improved. The law of sex discrimination, in MacKinnon's analysis, masks the reality of power. Whether the 'sameness' approach is adopted in law: that is to say that a woman qualifies for a particular position because she can demonstrate the same capabilities as a man, or whether the 'difference' approach: that which treats women as different from and deserving of different treatment from men, is adopted, the standard referent remains that of man. As MacKinnon writes:

> The philosophy underlying the sameness/difference approach applies liberalism to women. Sex is a natural difference, a division, a distinction, beneath which lies a stratum of human commonality, sameness. The moral thrust of the sameness branch of the doctrine conforms normative rules to empirical reality by granting women access to what men have: to the extent women are no different from men, women deserve what men have. The difference branch, which is generally regarded as patronising and unprincipled but necessary to avoid absurdity, exists to value or compensate women for what they are or have become distinctively as women – by which is meant, unlike men; or to leave women as 'different' as equality law finds them.[41]

For MacKinnon, only by understanding women's 'sameness' or 'difference' from men in terms of power and powerlessness, dominance and subordination, can the sterile debate about gender relevance be escaped from, and a cogent explanation provided as to power disparity. From this perspective sex discrimination law, in its reliance on the male referent elevates the male to a superior position. But, MacKinnon argues:

> [W]hat sex equality law fails to notice is that men's differences from women are equal to women's differences from men. Yet the sexes are not equally situated in society with respect to their relative differences. Hierarchy of power produces real as well as fantasised differences, differences that are also inequalities. The differences are equal. The inequalities, rather obviously, are not.[42]

Paradoxically, therefore, sex discrimination law, in refusing to recognise the cultural and social inequalities between men and women, fails to recognise that it is always *women* who are unequal to *men:* and never the reverse. Liberalism's claim to rationality and neutrality is thus unmasked as reflecting not gender-equality, but gender inequality.

Superficially, liberalism appears benevolent, egalitarian and protective of the rights and freedoms of citizens. Scratch beneath the veneer of liberalism's

---

[41] *Op cit,* MacKinnon, fn 31, p 220.
[42] *Op cit,* MacKinnon, fn 31, pp 224–25.

political ideology, from a feminist perspective, however, and unmasked are a number of fundamental difficulties and deficiencies. In short, liberalism ignores the realities of individual characteristics and ignores gender differences. Thus the subject of law, under classical liberal thought, while ostensibly gender-neutral, is male, and if women are to be subjects under the law, women must 'become male' – adopt the male standard. In social and legal relations, individuals are also affected by race, class, gender-orientation and age. Individuals are not raceless, classless, genderless or ageless. To portray as the subject of law a stereotypical anonymous, genderless, etc individual is to mislead. Beneath liberalisms' high sounding tenets and aspirations there have lurked a range of discriminatory practices and laws which it has been the task of feminists to redress.

In Robin West's[43] analysis, liberal feminism fails to attend adequately to the gendered nature of the legal system.[44] Too often the injuries women suffer are simply ignored, unrecognised or trivialised by the legal system which, focusing on autonomy and rationality, fails to take account of the reality of women's lives, and especially their reproductive role. Further, the stress on individuality and autonomy, in West's analysis, ignores the extent to which women value intimacy and connection with others, rather than individualism and isolation. Working within the sphere of cultural feminism, West calls for the recognition of woman's difference rooted in women's biological role, and the difference that difference makes. Robin West's theory, however, suffers from the criticism that the author is identifying woman's nature with her biology, and thereby perpetuating the very stereotypes which feminism seeks to deconstruct. In Robin West's analysis, feminist jurisprudence must 'bring about' the recognition by the legal system of the variety of harms suffered by 'all forms of being'.[45]

On the other hand, for radical feminist, Catharine MacKinnon, the issue in question is not woman's difference from man, or woman's sameness as man, but rather unravelling the question of power over and domination of women by men. Society, and law, is male: '[T]he State is male jurisprudentially, meaning that it adopts the standpoint of male power on the relation between law and society.'[46] Marxist-socialist feminism, alternatively, focuses less on gender *per se* than on the manner in which the class structure configures the social situation of both men and women.

---

[43] Professor of Law, University of Maryland.

[44] See West, R, 'The difference in women's hedonic lives: a phenomenological critique of feminist legal theory' (1987) 3 Wisconsin Women's LJ; 'Jurisprudence and gender' (1988) 55 Chicago UL Rev 1; *Narrative, Authority and Law*, 1993, Michigan: Michigan UP.

[45] Robin West also calls for masculine jurisprudence to become 'humanist jurisprudence'. See *ibid*, West, p 72. (See *Sourcebook*, pp 227–43.)

[46] *Op cit*, MacKinnon, fn 31, p 163.

MARXIST-SOCIALIST FEMINISM

Notwithstanding the failure and demise of Marxist politics, Marxism – in its many guises – remains as a powerful intellectual challenge to liberal philosophy. Marxism[47] has long been a site of special research interest for feminist scholars. The thought of Karl Marx[48] and Friedrich Engels[49] concerning the structure and evolution of society and the fundamental importance of the economic base – historical materialism – as the determinant of social relations and class structures in society, and the ideological function of law in supporting the economic base, represented a startling philosophical challenge to all political and legal thinkers. For jurists trained in classical Western political thought, Marx offered a powerful critique, for an essential feature of all Marxist thought is that law – far from being the central feature of society – is but a reflection of, and supporter of, the economic base, the infrastructure. Law is thus part of the 'superstructure': a part of those features of society – religion, politics and philosophy, which are secondary – in terms of the unfolding of society – to the economic base. As a result Marxists are not primarily interested in law, but rather in demonstrating the unfolding of society in a manner analogous to Hegel's dialectical, and natural, process. For Marx, the dialectical process is that of the material – or economic – base. Society evolves through differing stages, essentially from feudalism, to capitalism, to socialism and finally to communism. Only in the final stage of communism will the individual attain both equality and freedom.

The citizen's place in society is determined by the relations of production. In the capitalist phase, the owners of the means of production compel men by necessity to enter unequal contracts of employment where terms and conditions of work are set by the owner, and wherein the worker receives less than the full market value of his labour. It is thus private property and its ownership which subordinates the workers.

Marxism challenges the neutrality of law, and its self-proclaimed rational objectivity. From a Marxist perspective, the role of law is not to provide a minimal framework of law within which individual subjects of law are free to pursue their own goals. Nor is law primarily a source of protection for the individual against the power of the State. Rather law plays an ideological and political role which is far removed from neutrality and objectivity. From the Marxist perspective, liberalism's preoccupation with law, and with the rule of law, represents a fetishism which requires deconstruction, and a reconceptualisation of the role of law as an instrument of power for the

---

[47] See Collins, H, *Marxism and Law*, 1982, Oxford: Clarendon (see *Sourcebook*, pp 329–31); Hunt, A, *The Sociological Movement in Law*, 1978, London: Macmillan.
[48] 1818–83.
[49] 1820–95.

control of, and maintenance of, the power of the elite over the proletariat. Nor is law as central as liberal capitalist societies assume. The conditions in society, and the position of the individual, from a Marxist standpoint, is determined not by law, but by the economic base in society.

Marxist theory[50] is premised on the view that societal – political and economic – evolution occurs in a cyclical manner: from feudalism to capitalism to socialism and ultimately to communism which represents the condition of the purest freedom of the individual. Marxism is thus concerned with the meaning of history.[51] Historical materialism[52] is concerned with the scientific study of the conditions under which social transformations occur. Central to an understanding of this evolutionary process is the material (economic) base and its ownership. Two factors dominate the circumstances in which individuals find themselves: the *relations of production*, the means by which individual needs are satisfied; the *forces of production* (the available natural resources and technological skills). This material base represents the infrastructure of society. All else – culture, ideology, laws, religion, politics – will be dependent upon the relations of production and are superstructural – that is to say they arise out of the material base, the infrastructure.

The violent overthrow of feudalism, both freed 'serfs' from the master to whom they were tenured, and freed the master's land for use as capital.[53] The nineteenth century industrial revolution consolidated a capitalist economic base, with workers being dependent upon employers for their living. Throughout history the class structure has been maintained, and capitalism, under which a worker's labour was expropriated for less than its true value (the value being reflected in the end price of the product), reinforced that class system. A person's social class is determined by his or her position within the relations of production. Those who own the natural resources, or the industrial technology with which to extract natural resources, or own and control industrial output have the power to control all other – lower – classes who are dependent upon the ruling elite. Only the eventual overthrow of capitalism would free society from the shackles of class and lead first to a socialist State and then ultimately to a Communist State in which each person would be truly equal under a system of common ownership of the infrastructure.

Laws, which are superstructural, reflect the economic base in society. There are two principal interpretations of Marx's views on law. First, that law

---

[50] For reasons of space, it is impossible to offer more than the briefest introduction to the central themes in Marxist theory which is both vast and complex and comprises many differing interpretations.

[51] *Op cit*, Collins, fn 47, Chapter 1. (See *Sourcebook*, pp 329–31.)

[52] See Marx, K, 'Preface: a contribution to the critique of political economy', in Colletti, L (ed), *Early Writings*, 1975, London: Penguin.

[53] Tenures (Abolition) Act 1660.

operates as a means of class oppression by supporting the capitalist system. Secondly, that law – whilst not being directly and overtly an instrument of class oppression – maintains and sustains the capitalist system which is itself an instrument of class oppression. Law is, under both interpretations, coercive and supportive of the capitalist status quo. With the overthrow of capitalism, law will 'wither away'.

From a feminist perspective, it is the writing of Friedrich Engels which provides the focus for most analysis. In *The Origins of the Family, Private Property and the State*,[54] Engels argues that the position of women in society has been determined by the changing structure of marriage which itself is determined by economic forces. While group marriage was prevalent in 'savage society', with the introduction of private property and the need for its legitimate succession, paring marriage became the norm. It is Engels' thesis that, in early society, women determined the line of succession. This 'mother right' needed to be destroyed if male supremacy was to be secured. With the successful destruction of mother right, women's subordinate status in society was ensured. The introduction of machinery which facilitated more efficient agriculture enabled man to enslave other men and to exclude women from their traditional economic role. Thus women were confined to the 'domestic sphere' – to the hearth, home and children. The introduction of private property and the destruction of mother right represented 'the greatest historical defeat of the feminine sex'.

Only with the destruction of capitalism would women be able to emerge as the equal partners of men, able to compete on equal terms in the means of production. However, this analysis is both essentialist and exclusionary. Essentialist because of the centrality of economic determinism, exclusionary in its failure to examine the position of women in society. Women are merely *assumed* to be coextensive with men: their subjectivities are subsumed within the male subjectivity, resulting in women's 'disappearance'. Ignoring women's child-bearing and child-rearing roles, Marxist theory *assumes* the lack of differentiation in women's lives. Woman's identity becomes invisible. Woman's labour is multi- rather than uni-dimentional. To locate women's oppression within the class structure, and no more, is to miss the whole dimension of patriarchal society. Woman's economic and social equality will not become reality by 'simply' dismantling the capitalist economic base and enabling women to operate on the basis of equality with men in the public sphere. Women's role within the sexual division of labour is categorised as part of the 'natural relations' in society.[55] As Nancy Hartsock has written:

---

[54] Engels, F, *The Origins of the Family, Private Property and the State* (1884), 1940, London: Lawrence & Wishart.

[55] Marx, K and Engels, F, *The German Ideology*, Arthur, C (ed), 1970, New York: International Publishers.

Marx's procedure was in fact to set out from men's labour and to ignore the specificity of women's labour.[56]

For the most part, women and gender relations were ignored in classical marxist theory. In *The German Ideology*,[57] Marx and Engels offer a seemingly contradictory analysis of production. At one point production is linked to both the production of self within labour, and to the reproduction of the species. Yet, later in the same passage the meaning of production becomes confined to production within 'industry and exchange' – material production within industrial society.[58] Thus economic relations within the economy form the foundation of society – the infrastructure – on which the legal and political superstructure depend. Women within the family thus become invisible in Marx's thought. However, in *The Origins of the Family, Private Property and the State*,[59] Engels states that the first-class oppression 'coincides with the development of the antagonism between man and woman in the monogamous marriage, and the first-class oppression with that of the female sex by the male'.[60] Whereas many societies adopted a matrilineal line of succession (albeit one controlled by men),[61] virtually all transformed into patrilineal systems once wealth started to accrue. With industrial development, women became excluded from the public world of work and confined to work in the home. The reintroduction of women into the marketplace, the key to removing women's oppression, could only come about if 'the quality possessed by the individual family of being the economic unit of society be abolished'.[62] Socialist feminism seeks to put the woman back into socialist theory, to show how the original class oppression was the oppression of women by men.

Socialist feminism criticises alternative feminist analyses for disregarding class as an oppressive concept, and for seeing feminism as essentially a bourgeois movement. However, the insistence that the relations of production and capitalism determine class structure appears to ignore the particular interests of all women, irrespective of class, or State ideology, whether socialist or capitalist. As seen, Marxist-socialism, for the most part (and Engels aside), has little to say of the conditions of most women in society, as if women are simply attachments to, or the property of men. Whereas, from a Marxist-socialist perspective, it is the capitalist system, and the laws which

---

[56] Hartsock, N, *Money, Sex and Power: Toward a Feminist Historical Materialism*, 1983, London: Longman, p 146.
[57] *Op cit*, Marx and Engels, fn 55.
[58] *Op cit*, Marx and Engels, fn 55, p 41.
[59] 1848. See *op cit*, Engels, fn 54.
[60] *Op cit*, Engels, fn 54, p 225.
[61] See, eg, Malinowski, B, *Sex and Repression in Savage Society* (1927), 1960, London: Routledge & Kegan Paul.
[62] *Ibid*, Malinowski, p 233.

support that system, which oppresses the 'working class', from a feminist perspective, it is patriarchy which oppresses all women irrespective of their class. Eradicating the class structure and replacing capitalism with socialism – without more – would leave the first and original form of oppression – patriarchy – unaffected.

What Engels also failed to address in a satisfactory manner is the precise relationship between the introduction of private property and women's oppression. Why should the original division of labour – attendant upon the development of tools – have been one of oppression and not co-operation?[63] Equating women's inequality with class inequality exacerbated by capitalism does little to clarify and much to obfuscate the reality of women's condition. The suggestion that women's condition is the result of economic forces which follow some predetermined self-driving evolutionary process, masks the fact (and does little to explain the causes) of women's traditional oppression irrespective of their class.

The problem is not satisfactorily avoided either by Engel's view that once women enter into the marketplace of work their oppression will end, for the experience of most women is that not only are they in the marketplace, but they also labour in the home. Why this should be the case, other than as a remnant of a male-perceived 'natural division of labour' between men and women, is unclear. Despite both Marx's and Engel's assumptions about the natural role of women, there is nothing 'natural' about women being particularly fitted to dust, clean and to undertake all the other domestic chores which they traditionally undertake not only (or not even primarily) for themselves, but for their male partners and children, unless one accepts Marx's view that the division of labour within the family 'springs up naturally ... caused by differences of sex and age, a division that is consequently based on a purely physical foundation'.[64] Where the origins of the division of labour between men and women does carry explanatory power is in the combined fact of woman's biological reproductive capacity allied to the historical reality of the separation of family economics from the home. However, to characterise woman's position in the home as a 'natural condition', is at one and the same time to distinguish between the home (the private) and the outside world (the public, the social), and to place men firmly in the latter sphere and to relegate women to the private domain, excluded by implication and fact from the world of social relations.

One further problem with Marx's writing is the ambivalence in the meaning of 'production' which lies at the heart of Marxist theory. In the analysis of the emergence of capitalism, the production of goods became

---

[63] On this, see, further, de Beauvoir, S, *The Second Sex* (1949), Parshley, H (ed and trans), 1989, London: Picador.
[64] Marx, K, *Capital*, Vol I, 1967, New York: International Publishers, Vol I, p 351.

separated from the home – thus creating the conceptual divide between the private sphere – the home – and the public sphere of economic relations. By focusing on the economic sphere, now equated with the public sphere, the role of women within the family and their productive and reproductive role becomes separated from Marxist analysis. Far from the family being identified as central to the 'relations of production', the family, and woman's role within the family, is marginalised, as is the significance of gender to the issue of class. By focusing on production of material goods, Marx ignores women's reproductive and nurturing role.

Some socialist feminists have attempted to find a solution for this dilemma by focusing on the role of women, both inside and outside of the family, and in demonstrating the economic value of child-rearing and domestic work, and also demanding recognition by the State of this economic resource.[65] Free labour is antithetical to equality between individuals and to respect for women's domestic work, and thus recognising not just the social value of such work, but also its economic value, is perceived as an appropriate solution. One perceived solution is payment for housework. However, whilst recognising the value of domestic labour and thus bringing 'women's work' conceptually into the economy, this solution also has an effect which results in the woman becoming an employee of her husband which is not consistent with the idea of liberation of women as free independent economic beings and would further enslave women and keep them confined to the home.[66]

Socialist feminists have also focused on the analysis of women's oppression within the family (in addition to women's domestic labour within the home). The ordering of reproduction and childcare is a public, political issue, and not one which should be viewed as situated within the private sphere of the individual family. Only by analysing the conditions within which women's labour is sited, can the political dimension of women's inequality by understood. A Marxist theory which focuses almost exclusively on production within capitalism, and class, is both uni-dimensional and blind to the concerns of women. When the family and women's role is viewed, not as irrelevant to the market economy, but as central in creating the conditions of that economy, then issues such as contraception, abortion, childbirth conditions, responsibility for child-rearing and domestic labour can be viewed as political activities which must be encompassed in any analysis of economic relations.

Alienation is also a concept central to Marxist analysis of economic relations, and one theorised by socialist feminists. Marx focuses on the alienation of the labourer from the product of his own labour, and alienation within the conditions of his labour over which the worker has no control.

---

[65] See Malos, E (ed), *The Politics of Housework*, 1980, London: Alison and Busby.
[66] See, further, Pateman, C, *The Sexual Contract*, 1988, London: Polity. (See *Sourcebook*, pp 339–41.)

Applying the concept of alienation to women's condition within the domestic economy, socialist feminism endeavours to give voice to the isolation of women within the social structure which determines the conditions of many women's lives – domestic responsibilities. While it may be argued that nowadays many women are in full time employment and thus women's alienation caused by domesticity is a feature of past society, the statistics reveal that domestic responsibilities remain – irrespective of women's involvement in the 'public' economy – women's responsibilities. In the United Kingdom, more than 75 per cent of women between the ages of 35 and 45 are economically active. Nevertheless a high proportion, nearly 50 per cent, continue to work only part time on low wages, compared with one in 15 men.[67]

Socialist feminists analyse also – as do other feminists – the mechanisms of control which perpetuate women's alienation, isolation and inequality in the public sphere. Social control is identified with the imagery of women as sexual objects. The construction of woman, by men, as desirable, (hetero)sexually feminine – in the capitalist media and advertising industry – reinforces women's inequality, on this view, by objectifying her and making less visible her equal personhood, and reinforcing her traditional role as (no more than) 'wife and mother'. Many women also continue to identify with such constructions, thus rendering themselves open to the charge of complicity in their own male-constructed inferiority.[68]

The socialist feminist agenda includes the struggle for women's reproductive freedom, the 'right to choose' motherhood or not; the right also for publicly funded childcare in order to release women for employment in the public sphere; the recognition of the economic value of now unpaid domestic labour; equality for women within the workforce, and its organisation on gender-neutral grounds. Thus, while women have conventionally been viewed as most suited to positions of 'support' – the clerk, the nurse, the primary school teacher – equality can only be realised by reconceptualising employment on terms which render gender irrelevant to economic activity. However, as will be seen in the next chapter, cultural feminism, which has exerted much influence on feminist social and political theory and legal analysis, insists on the significance of gender difference, an insistence which leads to fundamentally different conclusions.

---

[67] See (1994) 24 Social Trends 24, charts 4.7 and 4.12 and pp 59–60. See, also, Witherspoon, S, 'Interim report: a woman's work', in Jowell, R, Witherspoon, S and Brook, L (eds), *British Social Attitudes, the Fifth Report,* 1988, Aldershot: Gower; Gershuny, J, Godwin, M and Jones, S, 'The domestic labour revolution: a process of lagged adaptation?', in Anderson, M *et al* (eds), *The Social and Political Economy of the Household,* 1994, New York: OUP.

[68] See, eg, Bartky, S, 'On psychological oppression', in Bishop, S and Weinzweig, M (eds), *Philosophy and Women,* 1979, Belmont, California: Wadsworth, p 33. See also Rich, A, *Of Woman Born: Motherhood as Experience and Institution,* 1976, New York: WW Norton; Firestone, S, *The Dialectic of Sex: The Case for a Feminist Revolution,* 1974, New York: Bantam.

CHAPTER 7

SCHOOLS OF FEMINIST JURISPRUDENTIAL THOUGHT: II

DIFFERENCE FEMINISM/CULTURAL FEMINISM

An alternative approach to women's equality is that which espouses the recognition of women's difference from men – physical and psychological and social – and demands that law adapt to include women on the basis of their differing characteristics and also their innate right to equality with men. Cultural feminism inquires into the perceived differences between women and men and emphasises, and celebrates, women's psychological and physical differences from men, whilst analysing the consequences of women's difference in socio-political terms.

The work of very differing cultural feminists such as Nancy Chodorow, Luce Irigaray and educational psychologist Carol Gilligan[1] have done much to advance an understanding of the differing forces which contribute to the 'making of a woman' and how woman's experience is different from that of man's. In the complex and diverse multidisciplinary writings of philosopher and psychoanalyst Luce Irigaray, the analysis of woman's difference; women's exclusion from society and language and the search for woman's subjectivity represents a profound challenge to both liberal and radical feminism. In Gilligan's work, research into the moral reasoning of girls and boys reveals that girls and boys in facing moral dilemmas did respond with *different* reasoning methods. That this should only have been made clear by research published in 1982 raises serious questions about the previous adequacy of psychological knowledge about women and psychoanalytic practice, deficiencies highlighted, in differing ways, in the work of both Irigaray[2] and Gilligan. Gilligan herself has written that at the time of writing *In a Different Voice*, 'women's voices were inconspicuously missing' and that a 'societal and cultural disconnection was being maintained by a psychological dissociation'.[3]

Feminist developmental theories

Writing in 1978, Nancy Chodorow traces the development of children through to adulthood, drawing on sociological and psychoanalytical theory to explain

---

[1] Professor of Education, Harvard University.
[2] See, in particular, Irigaray, L, 'The poverty of psychoanalysis', in Whitford, M (ed), *The Irigaray Reader*, 1991, Oxford: Basil Blackwell, Chapter 5.
[3] Gilligan, C, 'Getting civilized' (1992) LXIII Fordham L Rev 17.

the phenomenon of mothering.[4, 5] Mothering is what women traditionally do. There is a 'natural assumption' that because of childbirth and lactation, women *should* mother. Mothering thus has a central significance to the relationships within the family, to the division of labour in society, and to the opportunities and difficulties which women face as individuals who strive to be more than 'just a mother'.

Chodorow argues that mothering is not merely a 'product of physiology', but is rather perpetuated 'through social-structurally induced psychological mechanisms'.[6] This, at root, is an instance of the movement from nature to culture, and one which has the capacity to stultify women's capacities as rational, free and equal individuals. Chodorow, through using psychoanalytical data, establishes that by the age of five, children are conditioned into their lifelong gender identities. For girls, the implication of this is that they are conditioned to become mothers, not just in the biological sense, but also with all the now induced psychological implications which create and maintain barriers to full emancipation. Chodorow argues that women, through mothering, 'overinvest' in their children. From sons, strength and support is demanded; from girls, the emotional investment leads to a perpetuation of the mother's need for her own mother. Where, Chodorow argues, women have satisfactory adult relationships, this 'overinvestment' may be limited but, she argues, the capitalist system has established precisely the conditions under which women are less likely to have such relationships. Where mothers enter the workforce, the traditional stereotyping of women in the mothering role imposes additional strains. Men also are harmed by this social construction of the mothering role by which they are isolated from their children, expected to be the economic 'hunters and gatherers' of old, to be 'masculine', 'virile', 'competitive', 'detached' from the emotional world of the family. The system thus feeds on itself, perpetuating women's confinement to the home; perpetuating the barriers to their full entry into employment on equal terms with men.

In Chodorow's analysis the exclusive mother/child relationship damages all parties, and she argues that what is needed is a recognition that children should have equal parenting from both mothers and fathers in order to inculcate an individuated sense of self in relation to both parents. The cycle in which children regard their mother (to the exclusion of their father) as the primary nurturer, carer and provider of emotional support, emphasises the mother's role in the private world of the family as an unequal and dependent partner within the family. Chodorow demands social change in order to facilitate greater gender equality, for the benefit of all society. In the author's

---

[4] Chodorow, N, *The Reproduction of Mothering: Psychoanalysis and the Sociology of Gender*, 1978, Berkeley, California: California UP.
[5] See, also, Dinnerstein, D, *Rocking the Cradle*, 1978, London: Souvenir.
[6] *Ibid*, Chodorow, fn 4, p 211.

analysis, motherhood, as socially constructed, lies at the heart of the problem of social change. The socialisation of children within the family with the mother as the primary care-giver, results in the socialisation of girl children in preparation for motherhood, and the socialisation of boys in preparation for life in the public sphere. Only by breaking the cycle of the primacy of maternal care, will the socialisation of children lead to a society in which women and men play substantively equal roles in both the public and the private spheres of life.

However, there are difficulties with the realisation of the goal of equal parenting, and thus equal relations for the child with each parent which would break the cycle of the girls' overly relational identification with the mother, while simultaneously situating the father in a more relational role. Where lies the catalyst for change? If boys are socialised to 'be men', and that socialisation requires, as Luce Irigaray argues from a psychoanalytic perspective, the separation from – and rejection of – the mother in order to 'become a man', how then can the boy both retain his 'manhood' and also retain the capacity for mothering/parenting?[7]

From a postmodern perspective, there is also the theoretical argument that Chodorow is postulating a universalising 'meta-narrative'. There is the assumption that women and men are – irrespective of culture, race and class – 'mother' and 'father', and that the socialisation of children, under the primary care of the mother, will – also irrespective of culture, race and class – become socialised in the respective role models provided by their parents. From a postmodern perspective, this reduction of the causes of continued gender stereotypes is too grand a theory, too monocausal, too essentialising.

Carol Gilligan's psychological/developmental research

One of the most influential contributions to feminist theory located within cultural feminism/difference feminism, comes from psychologist Carol Gilligan, whose research published under the title *In a Different Voice:*

---

[7] Nancy Chodorow takes psychoanalysis specifically to task in *Femininities, Masculinities, Sexualities: Freud and Beyond*, 1994, London: Free Association Books. Chodorow identifies two principal difficulties in Freud's theories. First, in common with Luce Irigaray, discussed below, is the absence of the maternal in psychoanalytic theory, and secondly, that Freud's portrayal of adult female desire and heterosexuality is, 'at worst, female desire and sexuality ... seen through male eyes'. Psychoanalytic theory also, Chodorow demonstrates, focuses on heterosexuality and the heterosexual underpinning of gender difference as the norm and thus fails to develop theoretical analyses of homosexuality. Chodorow criticises the overgeneralisations and universalising nature of psychoanalytic theory, which tends to ignore the multiplicities of ways in which men and women love, thus ignoring both important cultural forces and the individuality and differences of and between men and women. While generalisations have their uses, if they lead to a failure to recognise other forces at work in gender and its analysis, then stereotypical categorisations will continue at the expense of understanding each individual's gender.

Psychological Theory and Women's Development,[8] has had a profound impact on feminist theory. Gilligan sought, through studying the reactions of children to differing situations, to explicate the manner in which boys and girls reason. Two of these children, Amy and Jake, who were of comparable intellect, age (11 years) and social background, were faced with moral dilemmas, one of which concerned Heinz who needed drugs for his sick wife, but who could not afford the price of the drugs. Should Heinz steal the drugs? Gilligan established that Jake and Amy adopted very different modes of reasoning in tackling this problem. Jake's reasoning follows a detached, logical pattern. Jake argues that life is of a higher value than property, and therefore Heinz should steal the drug, regardless of the fact that this would be a criminal offence. Jake argues that if caught, the judge should be lenient, and also that, in any event, the law which convicted Heinz under these circumstances would be a bad law. Amy's reasoning followed a different line, which Gilligan initially describes as 'an image of development stunted by a failure of logic, an inability to think for herself'. Amy is at first vague in her response and considers whether there are any viable alternatives to stealing the drug ('a loan or something'). Amy then considers the impact of the situation on the relationship between Heinz and his wife. On the one hand, if Heinz does not get the drug, his wife might get worse and die; on the other hand if he stole the drug and went to prison, his wife might also get 'more sick'. Amy, unlike Jake, views the problem as one primarily involving relationships, not logic: her responses revolve around this concern for relationships and a reliance on the connectedness of people. In Amy's view, it is the druggist who is in the wrong in this situation for failing to respond to Heinz's dilemma.

Gilligan concludes that Amy's judgments contain the 'insights central to an ethic of care, just as Jake's judgments reflect the logic of the justice approach'. Each child has argued in sophisticated fashion, but each adopts a very different approach to reasoning through this moral dilemma. Gilligan's research proved a catalyst for feminists and further fuelled the gender debate which ensued.[9]

French feminism

Feminism in France may be traced to the French Revolution of 1789, with women, excluded from male organisations, forming their own campaigns for economic and political life.[10] Throughout the nineteenth century the struggle

---

[8] Gilligan, C, *In a Different Voice: Psychological Theory and Women's Development*, 1982, Cambridge, Mass: Harvard UP. (See *Sourcebook*, Chapter 6.)

[9] On the application of Gilligan's research to legal practice, see Chapter 1 and references therein.

[10] Olympe de Gouges, eg, in 1791, rewrote the *Declaration of the Rights of Man*, substituting the word 'man' for 'woman'.

for equal rights continued, with women's newspapers and campaign groups fighting for equality across all aspects of life, including education and politics. The right to vote, however, was only achieved in 1944. Feminism was revived in France with Simone de Beauvoir's *The Second Sex*, published in 1949, the influence of which on feminist analysis and thought continues.

It was to be the political unrest and violence of the late 1960s, however, which revitalised French feminism. Political protests, originating in the universities and focusing on the perceived deficiencies of the education and social system, evolved as the left wing May Movement, a loose, unco-ordinated alliance of Marxists, Maoists, Trotskyists and socialists. Out of the political protest emerged the MLF, the *Mouvement de Liberation des Femmes*.[11] The movement was neither unified nor harmonious. By 1973, the influential group *Psychoanalyse et Politique* – '*psych et po*' (Psychoanalysis and Politics) – was formed with the explicit focus on women's difference, a focus which proved contentious among other feminists who regarded the concentration of women's difference as the equivalent to maintaining women's traditional inferiority, and yet others who opposed the assumed heterosexuality of women and thereby, as lesbians, felt excluded. The focus of *psych et po* was psychoanalytic rather than purely political. The task was, primarily, to unravel the socially and linguistically constructed 'Other'. It is with this latter group that the 'Holy Trinity' of French feminism, Luce Irigaray, Helene Cixous and Julia Kristeva, is most closely associated.[12]

The influence of both psychoanalytic and philosophical thought in French feminism cannot be underestimated. Not only does it produce analyses which are founded in particular theoretical disciplines, but it also results in feminist theory which is – for Anglophone jurists – particularly abstract, difficult, and abstruse. Whereas much feminist theorising in the common law world has a direct legal and political focus, French feminist thought is most appropriately situated within the distinctive continental philosophical, psychoanalytic and linguistic tradition, in a manner and style which makes it less accessible to feminist legal scholars than is overtly legal and political analysis. Moreover, as JG Merquior has pointed out in another context, whereas English philosophy is characterised by academic style and 'tightly analytic', French philosophy's leanings are more towards interdisciplinarity – the application of philosophy to diverse areas of knowledge such as linguistics, psychology, structural

---

[11] On which see Duchen, C, *Feminism in France: From May '68 to Mitterand*, 1986, London: Routledge and Kegan Paul, Chapter 1.

[12] Discussion is confined to introducing the thought of Luce Irigaray. This should not be taken to suggest that the work of Julia Kristeva and Hélène Cixous is not important to an understanding of difference feminism. For students wishing to explore Kristeva's and Cixous's thought, see, initially, Grosz, E, *Sexual Subversions: Three French Feminists*, 1989, London: Allen & Unwin.

anthropology, the arts and literature – and adopts a looser, more literary style than that of English philosophy.[13]

There is a further distinguishing feature between French feminist thought and feminisms in common law jurisdictions which must be borne in mind, and that is the political backcloth or landscape within which post-War French feminist thought resides. While – in the broadest possible terms – liberalism, within the confines of capitalism, has provided the organising focus of much feminist work in English speaking common law jurisdictions, French feminist thought has been far more influenced by the Marxist-socialist tradition which has a more natural accommodation in French political thought than elsewhere. Thus, the analysis of women in relation to social class and to capitalism has had deeper resonances than is apparent elsewhere. This is not to imply that French feminism, such as that exemplified by Luce Irigaray, is directly informed by or concerned with the relationship between feminism and socialism, but rather to give a flavour of the differing political influences as between French feminist thought and that of English speaking feminist analyses.

Luce Irigaray

Luce Irigaray, French feminist philosopher and psychoanalyst, stands in a complex relationship with psychoanalysis, as identified with Sigmund Freud and Jacques Lacan, and her contemporary, the deconstructionist philosopher Jacques Derrida. The prolific writings of Irigaray in psycholinguistics, psychoanalysis and philosophy and science represents a powerful and challenging body of feminist thought which has both provoked intense controversy and been much misunderstood. Indeed, as differing interpretations of Irigaray's work demonstrate, Irigaray is more easily misunderstood than understood. Without a sound grounding of linguistics, psychoanalysis and philosophy, Irigaray's work remains vulnerable to misdirected interpretations and evaluations.[14] As Margaret Whitford,[15] who has both written widely on Irigaray and made Irigaray's writings more accessible to English speaking audiences,[16] herself admits: '[S]he is more than a little inaccessible; she is associative rather than systematic in her reasoning.'[17] Similarly, Irigarayan scholar Elizabeth Grosz has commented that 'Irigaray's writings are extremely difficult to write about. They are

---

[13] Merquior, J, *Foucault*, 1985, London: Fontana, pp 12–13.
[14] See, in particular, *op cit*, Whitford, fn 2, Chapter 1.
[15] Professor of French, Queen Mary and Westfield College, University of London.
[16] See *op cit*, Whitford, fn 2.
[17] Whitford, M, 'Introductory remarks', in *Luce Irigaray: Philosophy in the Feminine*, 1991, London: Routledge, p 4.

exceptionally elusive, fluid and ambiguous ...'.[18] Because of the breadth and complexity of Irigaray's work, it is not possible within an introductory work to do justice to the author: that would require a/several separate volume(s).[19] However, notwithstanding the complexities and the dangers of reductionism and simplistic interpretation and presentation in *any* introduction, her insights into the philosophical and psychoanalytical positioning of women as Other, of women as 'excluded', have an importance to feminist jurisprudence which cannot be ignored. Irigaray's work has had a marked influence on feminist thought and analysis both within and outside France, and while there has been a time lag between publication in French and translation of her work, her work has been the focus for much argument, particularly in relation to her insistence on women's difference from men, and the apparent grounding of her theory in woman's body, which has tempted some critics to accuse her of essentialism,[20] and others of, in some sense, propping up the patriarchal ordering of society by not seeking to overcome the problem of difference but rather to promote the reality of women's difference.[21]

As noted above, consistent with the continental approach, Irigaray's primary focus is philosophical, psychoanalytic and linguistic, rather than legal or political. Irigaray's rich and diverse work, situated within the civil law tradition, provides a controversial theory of gender difference within the feminist debate. It is, however, essential to note that Irigaray herself has remarked that she cannot be reduced to 'commentaries'. Furthermore, not only is her work prolific, and her approach multidisciplinary, but also Irigaray's interests and intellectual foci have changed over time – a feature which compounds complexity upon complexity.

The publication of *Speculum of the Other Woman*, in 1974, led to Irigaray's dismissal from her post in the École Freudienne, the Department of Psychoanalysis at the University of Paris at Vincennes. The work represents a powerful feminist critique against the orthodoxies of established psychoanalytic theory as developed by Freud and later Jacques Lacan. Psychoanalysis, in Irigaray's analysis was, as Margaret Whitford explains, 'unaware' of the 'philosophical and historical determinants of its own discourse'; has been unable to explain the 'unconscious fantasies' which govern psychoanalysis, and is patriarchal, in so far as the role of the mother in the social order – which psychoanalysis reflects – is not acknowledged.[22] The

---

[18] *Op cit*, Grosz, fn 12, p 101.
[19] See *op cit*, *The Irigaray Reader*, fn 2, and *Luce Irigaray: Philosophy in the Feminine*, fn 17.
[20] See, eg, Segal, L, *Is the Future Female: Troubled Thoughts on Contemporary Feminism*, 1987, London: Virago.
[21] See Plaza, M, '"Phallomorphic power and the psychology of "woman": a patriarchal vicious circle' (1980) 1 Feminist Issues 73.
[22] *Op cit*, Whitford, fn 2, p 6.

forgotten mother in psychoanalysis is a focus for Irigaray's difference theory, as is the female body.

As a 'natural successor' to Simone de Beauvoir, Irigaray develops the concept of woman as Other.[23] There are, however, seminal differences between the two writers' work. Whereas for de Beauvoir, women needed to achieve equality with men in all fields of public life, for Irigaray such a demand is the equivalent to demanding that women become as men; that the differences between women and men remain masked. This women cannot do, it is argued, for their identity would then be subsumed within the patriarchal order. Rather, women must seek an identity *of their own*, and not just 'disappear' into the mirror-image of men. Equality for the sake of equality within the established patriarchal order is not Irigaray's agenda. Irigaray states 'Demanding to be equal presupposes a term of comparison', and asks 'Equal to what? What do women want to be equal to? Men? A Wage? A public position? Equal to what? Why not to themselves?'.[24] Thus, while Simone de Beauvoir argued that woman was a culturally determined – as opposed to biologically determined – construct, and that woman must be recognised as a subject in equal relation to man: 'mutually recognising each other as subject, each will yet remain for the other an *other*',[25] Irigaray seeks to construct woman's specific, unique, subjectivity and not to merely allow woman to enter the dominant patriarchal world on terms under which woman's subjectivity would remain hidden.

Thus women cannot simply be assimilated into a patriarchal world. To demand egalitarianism, without more, is too short sighted. What is required is an analysis of woman, a defining of the 'rights and duties of each sex, insofar as they are *different*'.[26] For feminism to have a future, it must 'go beyond' the stage of demanding equality *per se*. Irigaray's stated task is to 'challenge *the foundation of our social and cultural order*.[27] The achievement of equal political, social and economic rights with men cannot represent the end-point of women's achievement for Irigaray: woman would become 'a potential man'.[28] Rejecting the 'egalitarian dreams about sexual difference'[29] is Irigaray's objective. That equality is not enough is revealed through women's role in the social order. Women reproduce. Woman is a 'product', a 'commodity' to be exchanged in the marketplace by men. Women's role in the marketplace is as

---

[23] Irigaray expressed regret that de Beauvoir never responded to her request for commentary on her early work *Speculum of the Other Woman*, Gill, G, (trans), 1985, New York: Cornell UP; Irigaray, L, 'Equal or different?', in Whitford, *op cit*, fn 17, p 31.

[24] *Ibid*, 'Equal or different?', p 32.

[25] de Beauvoir, S, *The Second Sex* (1949), Parshley, H (ed and trans), 1989, London: Picador, p 740.

[26] *Ibid*, de Beauvoir, p 33.

[27] *Ibid*, 'Equal or different?', fn 23, p 165.

[28] See Irigaray, L, 'The power of discourse', in Whitford, *op cit*, fn 2, p 131.

[29] Irigaray, L, *Sexes et Parentés*, Macey, D (trans), 1993, New York: Columbia UP, back cover.

an object, never a subject – for the marketplace has been constructed by men, as has women's identity. Women do not have a voice in the marketplace in which to speak as subjects.[30] It should be understood, however, that Irigaray is not concerned – as some commentators have taken her to be[31] – with constructing a 'theory of women'. Rather Irigaray's emphasis is on constructing an understanding of woman's psychoanalytic and sexual self which challenges the patriarchal dominance of psychoanalytic, philosophical and linguistic – and hence social and political – analysis.[32] As Irigaray has stated:

> ... the issue is not one of elaborating a new theory of which woman would be the subject or the object, but to jam the theoretical machinery itself, of suspending its pretension to the production of a truth and a meaning that are excessively univocal.[33]

In *Sexual Differences*,[34] Irigaray states that 'sexual difference is one of the important issues of our age, if not in fact the burning issue' and argues that in philosophy, science and religion the issue remains 'silenced'. What is needed is nothing less than 'a revolution in thought and politics':[35] 'What is at stake is the ethical, ontological, and social status of women.'[36]

It is in Irigaray's analysis of the forming of and substance of subjectivity that Irigaray takes male psychoanalysis to task. Indebted to Freud and to his disciple Jacques Lacan, Irigaray the psychoanalyst challenges their philosophy of the subject. The dominant philosophy centres on the phallus, the discourse is 'phallogocentric'. The identity and role of the maternal is suppressed. Women thus cannot be heard as women, they are heard only as 'different from men': in Irigaray's terms, 'the Other as the same'. Irigaray's challenge to conventional philosophy and psychoanalysis cannot be reduced to the criticism that Irigaray is championing or establishing some form of theory which is best characterised by 'biological determinism', the consequence of which is the over-identification of women and women's role in society with the maternal function. Rather, Irigaray is seeking the means by which to identify the specifically female 'voice' – in psychoanalytical terms – in order

---

[30] Irigaray's theories may be contrasted with those of her contemporary philosopher and psychoanalyst Julia Kristeva, who, while working within the confines of Lacanian and Derridean frameworks and seeking to deconstruct sexuality, aims to deconstruct the 'repressed masculinity' of women and the 'repressed femininity' of men. Thus, far from seeking 'women's distinctive voice', Kristeva collapses the concepts of masculinity and femininity, and gendered subjectivity. See *op cit*, Grosz, fn 12, Chapters 2 and 3.

[31] See, eg, Moi, T (ed), *French Feminist Thought: A Reader*, 1987, Oxford: Blackwells.

[32] On this, see *op cit*, Grosz, fn 12, Chapter 4.

[33] *Op cit, Speculum of the Other Woman*, fn 23, pp 77–78.

[34] Irigaray, L, *Sexual Differences*, Hand, S (trans), in Moi, *ibid*, Chapter 10.

[35] *Ibid*, Moi, p 166.

[36] *Op cit*, fn 17, Whitford, p 22.

that women, as well as men, become the subjects of philosophy, psychoanalysis and society.[37]

Freud's theory of the Oedipal complex, adopted and developed by Jacques Lacan, which Irigaray deconstructs, requires that, in order to enter the symbolic world of language, and hence society, – the phallocentric, or phallogocentric, world – boys must reject their mothers. Mothers and girls cannot enter the symbolic order – they are left outside.[38] Because language is knowledge, language constructs the subject. Language, as Claude Levi-Strauss and Lacan argue, is a system of signs – signifiers and signified – a Symbolic Order. The Symbolic Order is already in existence and must be entered into by the child. The dominant male language is not a language into which women can enter: the Symbolic Order is patriarchal – hence Lacan insists that 'women do not exist'. Women, being unable to enter into the Symbolic Order remain outside phallic discourse and thus cannot be heard within it. It is in order to counteract this exclusion of women that Irigaray seeks for a 'voice for women' – one not yet heard, for it exists within the unconscious.

Irigaray aims to deconstruct the Freudian concept of motherhood, and the mother-daughter relationship, not in order to reduce women to mothers, but to reveal the complex psychological relationship between a child and its parents, and to demonstrate the phallocentric nature of traditional, and Freudian, psychoanalytic theory which theorises women 'out' of theory. Freudian and Lacanian psychoanalysis, according to Irigaray, has obliterated the maternal. Freud's thesis of the Oedipal child entails the girl child's letting go of its attachment to its mother, in order to 'attach' herself to the father. She must 'relinquish her primary libidinal attachment to the mother in order eventually to take her father as love object'.[39] However, the child must also remain attached to her mother in order to assimilate the feminine attributes. In Elizabeth Grosz's analysis the effect of this is that the girl child 'must abandon not the woman-in-the-mother but a *phallic mother*. And later, she must identify with the *castrated mother*, the powerless mother who has submitted to and acts as a representative of the symbolic father'. Neither of these symbols – the phallic mother nor the castrated, powerless mother, can provide 'an adequate basis for autonomous identity'.[40]

The relationship between mother and daughter is thus central to Irigaray's analysis of the patriarchal order. In rejecting the mother, the seeds for subordination are planted. Psychoanalysis, history and language denies female genealogies which Irigaray argues must be reinstated. Irigaray develops her theory of women's genealogies, in part, through her

---

[37] On Irigaray and psychoanalysis, see *op cit*, Whitford, fn 2, Part I; on philosophy, see Part II.
[38] See, further, the discussion of Irigaray's analysis of Plato's myth of the Cave in Chapter 4.
[39] *Op cit*, Grosz, fn 12, p 119.
[40] *Op cit*, Grosz, fn 12, p 119.

deconstruction of myths. Myths, for Irigaray, express history 'in narratives which illustrate the major lines of development of a given period'.[41] In Aeschylus's *Oresteia*, King Agamemnon is murdered by Clytemnestra, his wife. Orestes, their son, together with his sister Electra, murders their mother to avenge their father. Orestes, pursued by the Furies, escapes to Delphi, where he recovers from madness, whereas Electra, also driven to madness, is to remain consigned to that madness. In Irigaray's analysis, the murder of the mother represents the founding moment of patriarchy. In order to reinstate the mother-daughter relationship, and thereby facilitate a woman-to-woman relationship, psychoanalytic theory must be reconfigured to deal with the matricide entailed in the separation of both the father and son from the mother in the Oedipal stage. Women's genealogies – the relationship between mother and daughter and woman-to-woman – must be reinstated. Such reinstatement would create a space in which women can relate initially between themselves, and ultimately to an ethical society in which both men and women may peacefully co-exist.

For Irigaray, the maternal function is separate from womanhood: Irigaray neither identifies woman-as-mother, nor demands that women must free themselves, as Shulamith Firestone argued,[42] of motherhood. Rather, motherhood must be seen as a political issue and must, in psychoanalytic theory, be reconceptualised so as to replace the maternal into an understanding of psychological development. Where the child has no concept of the mother as woman, but only of woman as mother, the child can develop no sense or understanding of sexual difference, but enters into the patriarchal order – the boy rejecting the mother to identify with the father, the girl rejecting the mother to relate as woman to her father. The resistance of male psychoanalytic theory to such reconceptualisation of motherhood is explained by Irigaray as lying in the fear of disrupting accepted 'truths' about the maternal role. Woman must be accorded full subjectivity, not denied identity which causes woman to be reduced to motherhood, to be invisible in the social order, to be subordinated beneath the father in the patriarchal world, to be the Other.

Before women can move beyond being the Other, women must find a voice: 'speaking (as) woman', *parler femme*, rather than 'speaking of woman', is Irigaray's elusive formulation of women's need. The dominant discourse is male. Women cannot enter into that discourse because the terms of the discourse, the language of the discourse, is male. Irigaray, however, does not portray for us what 'speaking (as) woman' entails.[43] It is not 'speaking of

---

[41] Irigaray, L, *Le Temps de la Différence*, 1989, p 112, published in English as *Thinking the Difference: For a Peaceful Revolution*, Montin, K (trans), 1994, London: Athlone.
[42] Firestone, S, *The Dialectic of Sex*, 1970, New York: Bantam.
[43] See Irigaray, L, *This Sex Which Is Not One*, Porter, C and Burke, C (trans), 1985, New York: Cornell UP.

woman', for that is to enter the dominant patriarchal linguistic paradigm. Culture and language, cast in its Oedipal structure, 'distributes different roles to men and women'.[44] What is required is not so much a different language, but an understanding and counterpoise to the socially-determined (male) linguistic practices which deny women a voice, and to develop women's distinctive voice alongside that of man's.[45]

'Speaking (as) woman' is thus both undefined and undefinable. How, then, may it be understood? Irigaray, the psychoanalyst, argues that under psychoanalytic conditions, woman's different voice is the expression of her unconscious. Margaret Whitford was to write in 1986, that:

> ... if we keep in mind the model of the psychoanalytic session, we might understand the idea of a woman's language as the articulation of the unconscious which cannot speak *about* itself, but which can nonetheless make itself heard if the listener is attentive enough.[46]

The theory that women have a 'different voice' from the paradigmatic male meta-language is one which has met with opposition and misinterpretation from some quarters. Irigaray has been variously accused of being anti-feminist in the sense that her work represents a 'celebration of femininity' which is capable of reinforcing male stereotypes about women. By denying that women can enter the meta-language of men, and seeking an alternative voice for women within the *polis*, Irigaray has also been criticised as perpetuating the patriarchal order. Gender difference theories, for some critics, undermine the feminist attempt to eliminate patriarchy: 'gender differentiation is in and of itself an evil, because it circumscribes difference and denies access to the "other" in each one of us.'[47] Irigaray's close linkage of biological and sexual identity also leads to the charge of 'biological essentialism' – that women's destiny is determined by biology. The charge of essentialism is also made by those who object to the unitary concept of 'woman', on the basis that 'woman' as a class does not exist: there are only differing women whose lives are affected not just by gender but by age, class, colour and race. This, however, is not ignored by Irigaray. In *This Sex Which Is Not One*,[48] Irigaray directly addresses women's multiplicity of experience, but seeks to 'expose the exploitation common to all women' and also to discover the 'struggles that are appropriate for each women, right where she is, depending upon her

---

[44] *Op cit*, Whitford, fn 2, p 4. Margaret Whitford states that in her later work, Irigaray recognises that there will need to be 'big shifts' in society and culture 'if transformations in language are to come about'.

[45] *Ibid*, p 5.

[46] Whitford, M, 'Speaking as a woman: Luce Irigaray and the female imaginary' (1986) 43 Radical Philosophy 3.

[47] Cornell, D and Thruschwell, A, 'Feminism, negativity and intersubjectivity', in Benhabib, S and Cornell, D (eds), *Feminism as Critique: Essays on the Politics of Gender in Late-Capitalist Societies*, 1987, London: Polity.

[48] *Op cit*, Irigaray, fn 43.

nationality, her job, her social class, her sexual experience ...'.[49] Irigaray's emphasis on identifying women's different voice, finding women's subjectivities through language, has also been criticised as ignoring the need for the identification of and elimination of inequalities suffered by women on the basis of their difference from men. But, as Margaret Whitford demonstrates in her scholarly explanation(s) of Irigaray's work, each of these charges reveal a misunderstanding of Irigaray's position – which is both difficult to 'pin down', and to understand, in light of Irigaray's classical, multidisciplinary scholarship.

Perhaps the most controversial aspect of Irigaray's work lies in her theorising on women's bodies and the symbolic, which some critics have interpreted to mean that 'women's language' is closer to the body, to nature, than is man's, and that, accordingly, there is a direct relationship between the body and language.[50] This Irigaray herself has specifically denied. The basis for much misunderstanding of Irigaray lies in her explication of woman's sexuality. Lacan argues that the Symbolic Order creates the Subject and Object – the 'I' and the 'Other'. Since men and women are defined by their 'natural' characteristics – that is, their bodies and sexuality – it is man's sexuality which is present within the Symbolic Order. Women – as excluded – and women's sexuality cannot exist, or be articulated, within the Symbolic Order as philosophically determined. For Lacan this exclusion is inevitable. For Irigaray it is not. Irigaray seeks to give women an existence, and in the process to disrupt the Symbolic Order. Thus Irigaray's task is more than 'just' a feminism of difference, a feminism which condemns women to remain outside the Symbolic; Irigaray seeks women's identity, women's language, as a means by which to secure political and social equality for women. Women would no longer be the 'Other of the same', but would be truly the 'other' of the 'other', as would men to women: equal in their difference, with neither excluded.[51]

In *This Sex Which is Not One*,[52] Irigaray argues that psychoanalysis is a discourse on sexuality, but one which, in relation to feminine sexuality, ignores the patriarchal order. Irigaray states that '[A]cknowledgment of a "specific" feminine sexuality disturbs the monopoly over values that the masculine sex has ...'.[53] Irigaray's affirmation of the feminine is thus more than an explanation of what women *are*, and represents rather a demand for entry into the social and political order – not in a position of inferiority – as

---

[49] *Op cit*, Irigaray, fn 43, pp 166–67.
[50] See *op cit*, Whitford, fn 2, Chapter 2.
[51] Compare Julia Kristeva on this point. Kristeva, a fellow psychoanalyst, follows Lacan (and Derrida), and argues that women exist outside the Symbolic Order as a challenge to that order: women cannot be brought into that order without undermining feminism's challenging nature: see *op cit*, Duchen, fn 11, pp 85–87.
[52] *Op cit*, Irigaray, fn 43.
[53] *Op cit*, Irigaray, fn 43, pp 62–63.

Object – but as an equal Other – as Subject. In Drucilla Cornell's sympathetic analysis, '[W]riting from the position of the feminine involves an explicit, ethical affirmation which in itself is a performative challenge to the devaluation of the feminine'.[54]

The exclusion of feminine sexuality from the patriarchal order thus demands the search for feminine identity. Irigaray argues that whereas man has a unified sexuality, identified and identifiable with the phallus, women's sexuality is 'plural', it has multiplicity. It is at the level of anatomy, and women's sexuality, that women's different characteristic is found. Male sexuality is unified, female sexuality is represented by its pluralism – the concept of 'two lips', and its fluidity.[55] Sexual difference is found in women's sexuality, in feminine *jouissance*, but extends beyond sexuality to the social and political world. Feminine sexuality, which is denied in the Oedipal, patriarchal, Symbolic Order, requires identity and analysis, and is central to giving women a voice, and thus enabling women to enter the Symbolic Order, the social contract, not as subordinate, 'shadow Other men', but as full Subject in equal relation with men. Thus, Irigaray is not theorising the sexual and women's sexuality, at the level of nature, of anatomy, but rather using women's difference in order to challenge the patriarchal Symbolic Order, and to carve a place for women in society – within, rather than with-out, the social contract.

Irigaray's insistence on the centrality of woman's sexuality to her subjectivity, and the need for a woman-to-woman discourse in a system of social relations devoid of phallocentrism has been more welcomed by lesbian feminists than by heterosexual feminists. However, positioning Irigaray within either homosexuality or heterosexuality is complex and not free from ambiguity. Elizabeth Grosz has written that Irigaray's position could be described 'as a theory of the *hetero-sexual* rather than the homo-sexual',[56] and warns against identifying Irigaray as promoting lesbian sexuality, in that Irigaray views all cultural sexual practices as being 'the effects of an underlying phallocentrism that renders women socially and representationally subordinate'.[57] In 'The bodily encounter with the mother',[58] Irigaray writes that the love for 'women-sisters' must be

---

[54] Cornell, D, *Beyond Accommodation: Ethical Feminism, Deconstruction and the Law*, 1991, London: Routledge, p 150.

[55] Margaret Whitford states that the concept of 'two lips' can be 'read as representation of whatever interpretation of Irigaray the interpreter wishes to highlight': see *op cit*, fn 2, p 171 *et seq*.

[56] Grosz, E, 'The hetero and the homo: the sexual ethics of Luce Irigaray', in Burke, C, Schor, N and Whitford, M (eds), *Engaging with Irigaray: Feminist Philosophy and Modern European Thought*, 1994, New York: Columbia UP, p 335.

[57] *Ibid*, Grosz.

[58] Reproduced in Whitford, *op cit*, fn 2, Chapter 2.

distinguished from the love between a mother and daughter, and that the former 'is necessary if we are not to remain the servants of the phallic cult, objects to be used by and exchanged between men ...'.[59] However, in Elizabeth Grosz's analysis, Irigaray is not advocating homosexuality as a substitute for heterosexuality, nor attempting to undermine heterosexual relations. Rather, the withdrawal from 'heterosexual commerce' is a 'provisional manoeuvre' and 'tactical and temporary' – it is a 'political strategy in achieving women's autonomy'. And the autonomy which women seek entails the autonomy to make a free choice as to woman's relation with either men or women.

Whereas much of Luce Irigaray's earlier work was firmly rooted in psychoanalysis and psycho-linguistics, her later work has become more related to changes in the legal order which will facilitate the inclusion of women.[60] It is with Irigaray's *Sexes et Parentés*[61] that women's different civic rights become articulated.[62] Irigaray argues that laws and the legal profession are male constructs which exclude women's difference. Questing for equality on the same terms as men in terms of equality in the workforce, without recognising women's difference, will be accomplished at women's expense. The workplace is organised along male lines: to succeed in the male world, women must conceal their differences; must adapt to male criteria. For law masks difference by its purportedly neutral language and forms. Thus, those struggling to achieve equality should, according to Irigaray, do so in order to 'bring out differences' – not to disguise them.

Women's 'sexuate rights' should be defined and protected in law. Among these, Irigaray calls for an end to the commercial use of women's bodies and women's images; a right to respect for a woman's bodily integrity and for a girl's virginity not to be 'exchanged among men in our cultures', or 'traded for money'; a right to human dignity, in which the right to motherhood is recognised as a specific sexuate right, and the mutual duties between mother and child are defined; a right to financial parity, including equal taxation and the equal representation of women in the media, and the right of equal representation in arenas in which civil or religious decision are taken.[63]

---

[59] *Op cit*, Whitford, fn 2, p 43.

[60] But see, also, *op cit*, Irigaray, 1985, fn 23, pp 119–23 and 214–26. On political and social rights see, also, *op cit*, Irigaray, fn 43.

[61] Macey, D (trans), 1993, New York: Columbia UP, repr in Whitford, *op cit*, fn 2, Chapters 13 and 14.

[62] Formulated within the context of the French civil law.

[63] *Op cit*, Irigaray, 1994, fn 41, Chapter 3, and Irigaray, L, 'How to define sexuate rights', in Whitford, *op cit*, fn 56, Chapter 14.

Luce Irigaray and the charge of 'essentialism'

Irigaray's insistence upon women's need to achieve subjectivity, without 'disappearing' into the phallogocentric world, through women's language – speaking as woman – together with her imagery of woman as identified through her sexuality and her body, has led to the charge that Irigaray is positing an essentialist theory – that she is universalising the concept of 'woman'.[64] Essentialism, it will be recalled, denotes that 'woman' has a particular essence which defines woman as woman. There are a number of possible responses to this difficulty.

As Naomi Schor has demonstrated in her excellent analysis 'This essentialism which is not one: getting to grips with Luce Irigaray',[65] essentialism itself does not have a single property. A deconstruction of essentialism leads the author to conclude that essentialism may be critiqued from a 'liberationist' stance, a 'linguistic' stance or a 'philosophical' stance, or a 'feminist' stance. The liberationist critique is that which analyses the cultural forces which 'produce' women – as epitomised in Simone de Beauvoir's classic pronouncement that '[O]ne is not born, but rather becomes a woman'. Thus, from this perspective, the social construction of woman must be deconstructed in order to reveal the forces which operate in the formulation of woman. The linguistic critique of essentialism focuses on the role of language in the construction of woman. As Irigaray has so vividly argued, women cannot enter into the world dominated by the phallic discourse of man – rather woman must 'speak as woman', rather than *speak of woman*, the latter of which is to adopt the phallogocentric male language. The philosophical critique of essentialism, according to Naomi Schor, is that which deconstructs the meanings and identities of 'woman' as she is placed in the inferior half of the binary opposition man/woman. Finally, the feminist critique of essentialism, which for Schor is the 'most compelling', rejects the notion that there is an identity of 'woman', or a single female subjectivity, and insists that what must be deconstructed is the concept of woman which precludes, excludes, ignores, the differences between women. Essentialism, as deconstructed by Schor, becomes a rather more complicated concept than at first sight it appears.

In Margaret Whitford's analysis of the trenchant criticisms which were launched against Irigaray's early work, the essentialism which is detected in Irigaray's work is a necessary tactic employed to reach the goal of social and

---

[64] See Moi, T, *Sexual/Textual Politics*, 1985, London: Methuen; Plaza, M, '"Phallomorphic power" and the psychology of "woman": a patriarchal vicious circle' (1980) 1 Feminist Issues 73; see, also, Judith Butler's criticism that Irigaray's analysis 'is undercut precisely by its globalising reach': Butler, J, *Gender Trouble: Feminism and the Subversion of Identity*, 1990, New York: Routledge.

[65] Reproduced in Burke, Schor and Whitford, *op cit*, fn 56, Chapter 4.

political transformation which Irigaray seeks: '[I]f this is interpreted as essentialism or phallogocentrism, it is because what has been lost sight of is the horizon. It is to fix a moment of becoming as if it were the goal.'[66] Elizabeth Grosz also directly confronts the criticisms of Irigaray from the perspective of strategy:

> Contrary to Moi's assertion that she [Irigaray] aims to develop a 'theory of "woman"', Irigaray's main concerns up to 1979 are largely negative: to place phallocentrism 'on trial', not to oppose it or reject it once and for all (which is in any case both phallocentric and utopian), but to devise a series of tactics which *continually* question phallocentrism, destroying its apparently naturalistic self-evidence and demonstrating the possibility of alternatives. Instead of devising a 'theory' of women's oppression, Irigaray's aim is largely methodological and tactical. Indeed she refuses either to define woman or to present a theory about women (which she sees as politically problematic insofar as one voice then represents all others in an insidious representationalist politics).[67]

Perhaps the key to understanding the criticisms of essentialism levelled at Irigaray's theories lies in a deconstruction of essentialism, as propounded by Naomi Schor, which reveals that 'essentialism' itself is an 'essentialist concept' until deconstructed. Throughout Irigaray's work, the centrality of woman, and woman's body, must be read as a deconstructive challenge to male-linguistic and psychoanalytic formulations of woman. Irigaray seeks social and political change, not by defining the 'essence' of woman, but by identifying and theorising the patriarchal exclusions which have confined women to inferiority, and through recovering women's voice, through speaking as woman, enabling women to move out from and beyond the dark confines of patriarchy and into the light of equal citizenship. An essentialist account of women would centre on theorising women's essence *without more*. Of this Irigaray cannot justly be accused.

Drucilla Cornell

The work of both Carol Gilligan and Luce Irigaray receives partial endorsement from Drucilla Cornell.[68] Utilising her interpretation of Lacanian psychoanalysis and Derridean deconstruction, and sympathetic to French feminism's approach, Drucilla Cornell develops her own distinctive feminist jurisprudence. Whilst Cornell is sympathetic to Catharine MacKinnon's identification of the causes of female inequality with male dominance, and female subordination, Cornell is deeply critical of the implications of

---

[66] *Op cit*, Whitford, fn 17, p 143.
[67] *Op cit*, Grosz, fn 12, p 113.
[68] Professor of Law, Cardozo School of Law, New York.

MacKinnon's work.[69] In Cornell's analysis, MacKinnon's theory reduces women to their sexuality – in her blunt terms, to 'fuckees' – and offers no hope for women to alter their subordinate position. MacKinnon, in this analysis, identifies women's subordination but leaves them within that subordination. Not only is this pessimistic for female equality, but it also, in Cornell's view, represents Grand Theory which adopts an essentialist and universalising theory of women. Cornell, on the other hand, offers a more optimistic, if yet unrealised, vision of equality for women focused on women's difference.[70] As Cornell writes:

> My position is that without the affirmation of feminine sexual difference, we will unconsciously perpetuate the gender hierarchy under which the feminine is *necessarily* devalued.[71]

Drucilla Cornell seeks to develop an ethical feminism which is 'an alternative to both liberal and radical feminism',[72] a feminism which emphasises not description of the way women are, but rather what 'should be'. On Carol Gilligan's work, Cornell writes that it represents 'at least a moderate, ethical affirmation of female experience as valuable',[73] unlike MacKinnon, who, in Cornell's analysis, identifies the reality of women's oppression but fails to offer any real 'way out' of that oppression. Both theorists, however, are critiqued for representing the current position of women, the way women are, rather than a world which could be. Cornell does not accept that women are to remain within the identity constructed for women by men and male language. There needs to be a deconstruction of the language which creates women, and a way developed in which women can both affirm their difference, and the value of that difference, in order to realign gender relations in an equal and constructive manner, without replicating either essentialism or universalism. Jacques Derrida denies that there can be any 'unshakeable biological entities, through his concept of *différence* which is not to be understood as the same as sexual difference as understood in Anglo-American terms). For Cornell:

> ... it is politically, and even legally, important to affirm the 'other' dream of a new choreography of sexual difference, a dream which I have suggested involves the writing of sexual difference as the feminine, and not simply the

---

[69] See, further, Chapter 9, in which Cornell's crique of radical feminism is more fully discussed.

[70] Drucilla Cornell's work is prolific. For her critique of Catharine MacKinnon's theory, see 'Sexual difference, the feminine, and equivalency: a critique of MacKinnon's *Toward a Feminist Theory of the State*' (1990) 100 Yale LJ 2247. See, also, *Beyond Accommodation: Ethical Feminism, Deconstruction, and the Law*, 1991, London: Routledge; *The Philosophy of the Limit*, 1992, London: Routledge; *Transformations: Recollective Imagination and Sexual Difference*, 1993, London: Routledge; *The Imaginary Domain*, 1995, London: Routledge.

[71] Ibid, Cornell, *Transformations*, p 5.

[72] Ibid, Cornell, *Transformations*, p 59.

[73] Ibid, Cornell, *Beyond Accommodation*, p 137.

postulation of a neutral person, no longer defined by the bipolarity of our current representations of gender identity.[74]

Current representations of gender identity must be undermined, deconstructed, in order to affirm the feminine, otherwise any legal changes achieved within the legal system to eliminate female inequality will be 'undermined by the law of gender in which the feminine is only our difference from them, as is devalued as inferior'.[75] What is required is a reconfiguration of gender relations, the 'imaginary domain' in which women may affirm their equal but different subjectivities. By thinking that which cannot yet be, 'the doubly prized world' which is 'stranger than the facts' feminism can challenge the gender hierarchy in 'which the masculine is privileged'.

What Cornell seeks is 'a new choreography of sexual difference, in which love and intimacy are other than the lacklustre lassitude of tired and cynical collusion in women's oppression'.[76] Translated into law, Cornell calls for a programme of 'equivalent rights'. Rights such as restrictions on pornography which, through 'reinforcing women's sexual shame' and in denying women the 'equivalent protection of inviolability', damages women's equality, and rights also to abortion[77] to ensure women's control over their reproductivity. Cornell's work, together with Chodorow's, Gilligan's and Irigaray's theses stands in direct opposition to the tenets of radical feminism, which is considered in Chapter 8.

---

[74] *Op cit*, Cornell, *Beyond Accommodation*, fn 73, p 151.
[75] *Op cit*, Cornell, *Beyond Accommodation*, fn 73, p 152.
[76] *Op cit*, Cornell, *Beyond Accommodation*, fn 73, p 101.
[77] On which see, further, Chapter 10.

CHAPTER 8

SCHOOLS OF FEMINIST JURISPRUDENTIAL THOUGHT: III

RADICAL FEMINISM

In one sense, all feminism is by definition 'radical', challenging the central tenets of legal and political thought and demanding full citizenship for women in society. The emergent woman's movement of the late 1960s and the political activity of women in confronting the prevailing mores in Western society, represented a radical departure from women's conventional roles and stereotypes. Radical feminism has, however, developed its own distinctive critique of society which separates it from – although intersections remain – liberal feminism, cultural/difference feminism and Marxist-socialist feminism. Where liberal feminists accept the meritorious tenets of liberalism and work within the dominant political ideology to achieve reforms of the law, radical feminists demand a root and branch reform of society. As with alternative feminist theory, radical feminism has many exponents and takes diverse forms, and this introduction attempts merely to synthesise some of the central tenets of radical feminism, rather than to explicate all aspects of it.

Liberal ideology, as has been seen in Chapter 6, insists on formal equality between men and women, whilst either failing to recognise women's continuing inequality, or rationalising it as 'natural'. As women have been subordinated in all aspects of life from time immemorial, and men accordingly hold power, the standard by which equality is judged is that of the male. With the male as referent, women are forced into two possible modes of argument. First, women may argue that while biological differences between the sexes exists, women nevertheless have the same capacities (intellectual and otherwise) to participate fully in society. This, in part, was Plato's argument back in the third century BC.[1] Secondly, women may argue that indeed they are different from men (biologically, psychologically and intellectually), but worthy of equal respect and, accordingly, claim the right to equality on this basis.

Radical feminism, by contrast, adopts as its organising focus the problem of the universal dominance of men over women, and women's correlative subordination to men. Women's sexuality lies at the heart of the radical feminist debate. Thus, radical feminists analyse the means by which men's sexuality is expressed in forms which result in women's inequality. Radical feminism, therefore, unlike liberal feminism, does not accept that equality will

---

[1] See, further, Chapter 4.

be achieved for women provided the legal inequalities and disabilities are removed from law. Rather than concentrating on specific legal inequalities, radical feminism challenges the core structure of society and law by focusing on its patriarchal ordering and its representation of patriarchal culture and mores. Radical feminism is thus deeply critical at the level of society's structure.

From its broadly left wing political origins in the 1960s, and characterised principally by white, middle-class, heterosexual, academic women, radical feminism has evolved as a key challenger to the societal status quo. In the 1970s, radical feminists subjected patriarchal legal and social attitudes and concepts to analysis. Inquiries into rape, for example, led to a feminist analysis of the *meaning* of rape, with its inherent representation of male sexual power and domination, and the obliterating consequences for women victims, as a political act of dominance and aggression, accompanied by fear.[2] The legal system, with its emphasis in rape trials on the question of the woman's consent to sexual intercourse, rather than the fact of male aggression, reinforces the patriarchal view that somehow 'rape is all right'.[3] The feminist analysis of prostitution and pornography also focuses on the extent to which society and law 'legitimates' the subordination of women, through labelling them as sexual objects. Shulamith Firestone's analysis of the oppressive force of child-bearing, and her call for technology to free women from its force, also falls within the radical 1970s analysis of woman's condition.[4]

It should not be assumed that radical feminism represents a 'single school of thought': radical feminism is diverse. However, in radical feminism's insistence on the universality of patriarchy and women's oppression, on the basis of woman's sexuality, and on consciousness raising as a technique for the expression of women's oppression, radical feminism occupies a distinctive vantage point. Radical feminism has also proved to be challenging, not only to men, but to women of colour and lesbian women. The universalising nature of radical feminism, and its close alignment with sexuality, to the exclusion of women with differing sexual orientation and to women of colour who view black women's oppression as more complex than the radical feminism of the 1970s and 1980s acknowledged, has led to friction within feminism. Nevertheless, radical feminism provides deep insights into the social structures within which women operate, and calls for nothing less than a reconceptualisation of women and their equality.

---

[2] See Griffin, S, *Rape: The Power of Consciousness*, 1979, New York: Harper & Row; Brownmiller, S, *Against Our Will: Men, Women and Rape*, 1976, New York: Simon & Schuster (see *Sourcebook*, pp 398–404); Morgan, R, 'Theory and practice: pornography and rape', in Lederer, L (ed), *Take Back the Night: Women and Pornography*, 1980, New York: William Morrow. See, also, Millett, K, *Sexual Politics*, 1972, London: Virago.

[3] See, further, Chapter 11.

[4] Firestone, S, *The Dialectic of Sex: The Case for Feminist Revolution*, 1971, New York: Bantam.

Catharine MacKinnon's dominance theory

Since the 1980s, radical feminism has been epitomised by the writings of Professor Catharine MacKinnon.[5] It is to MacKinnon's theory that attention is now turned.[6]

Difference is the velvet glove on the iron fist of domination.[7]

In *Feminism Unmodified: Discourses on Life and Law*,[8] Catharine MacKinnon addresses the gender question.[9] Considering gender within the context of sex discrimination law, MacKinnon identifies a central dilemma, namely that the law relating to sex discrimination is based on the sameness of the sexes – in the sense that no discrimination is justified on the basis of sex alone – whereas gender is socially constructed on the basis of the differences between men and women. MacKinnon rejects the emphasis on either sameness or difference in relation to the achievement of sexual equality. Her objection to the sameness/difference approach lies in her perception of its futility. As she argues, theorists who emphasise 'sameness' (we're the same, we're the same, we're the same), are opposed by those who seek to highlight gender differences (we're different, we're different, we're different). The futility lies in large measure in the fact that both of these approaches are, unwittingly or unreflectively, using the male standard by which to assess whether women are the same or different *from men*. As MacKinnon states, 'man has become the measure of all things'.[10]

Catharine MacKinnon argues that the equality question must be conceptualised in another manner. Principally it must be recognised that the central issue is neither the extent to which women are the same as or different from men. The real issue, for MacKinnon, is that of male power and dominance. Citing material poverty through lack of opportunity or discrimination, violence against women, prostitution and pornography, MacKinnon argues that these phenomena are unique in that they only happen to women. These are uniquely female experiences and they represent the subjugation of women to the power of men. Women do not become prostitutes for enjoyment; women do not participate in hard-core, sadistic

---

[5] Professor of Law, University of Michigan.
[6] The central tenets of Catharine MacKinnon's work are considered in this chapter. MacKinnon's and Andrea Dworkin's analysis of pornography will be discussed in Chapter 12, while the postmodern critiques of essentialism in MacKinnon's work will be considered in Chapter 9.
[7] MacKinnon, C, *Toward a Feminist Theory of the State*, 1989, Cambridge, Mass: Harvard UP, p 8.
[8] MacKinnon, C, *Feminism Unmodified: Discourses on Life and Law*, 1987, Cambridge, Mass: Harvard UP.
[9] See 'Difference and dominance: on sex discrimination' in MacKinnon, *ibid*, fn 8. (See *Sourcebook*, pp 211–221.)
[10] *Ibid*.

pornography for enjoyment. Women do not enjoy sexual and other physical violence at the hands of strangers and their partners. These are conditions largely forced on women because of their economic vulnerability, and vulnerability encouraged and supported by male control of the economy, and of political power. As MacKinnon states gender is 'constructed as a socially relevant differentiation in order to keep [that] inequality in place'. Thus the issue of sexual inequality raises questions of systematic male dominance and supremacy which is not at all 'abstract and is anything but a mistake'.[11]

The question of power distribution, of inclusion and exclusion in civic life, of equality, is a political question: it concerns male power, male dominance, male control. That this is patently the case may be demonstrated by a brief glance back into ancient history. In Ancient Greece, the philosophers Plato and his successor Aristotle discussed the role of women in society. The questions posed were both timeless and enduring: to what extent and in what manner should women participate in society? Should women participate in the defence of the realm and train alongside men for that purpose? Should women have equal authority in the family? In what sense are there *relevant* differences between men and women which indicate the allocation of rights and responsibilities?[12] Even at that time man was the measure against which woman was measured: woman was 'Other', the 'object' and not the subject. Men controlled the public world, the *polis*. Men, holding political power, determined what women could and could not, should and should not do in that world; whether women were equal or different from men. For centuries this position has endured, with women being the recipients of male largesse, at the discretion of men. Only when women struggled to attain, and attained, equality as full citizens would the power disparity be removed.

For MacKinnon, feminist theorising which emphasises women's difference, cultural feminism, is fundamentally flawed and leads to the subliminal endorsement of women's inequality by adopting the male standard against which to measure women's equality. On the other hand, the dominance approach, in MacKinnon's view, is truly feminist in that it looks at the world through the eyes of subordinated women. MacKinnon draws an analogy between women's demands for true equality and that of the emancipation of African-Americans in America. In that movement, there came a point of time when no matter what the differences between blacks and whites, no further discrimination could be tolerated. The 'differences' simply became irrelevant: overborne by the overarching need for equal treatment as human beings.

In Catharine MacKinnon's view, liberalism – with its insistence of equality regardless of an individual's attributes – represents a false ideology.

---

[11] *Op cit*, MacKinnon, fn 9.
[12] See, further, Chapter 4.

Liberalism is false because it ignores the realities of *power*, and hierarchies of power which are determined on the basis of gender. Catharine MacKinnon sees the gender issue as not one centrally concerned with analysing physiological or psychological differences between men and women, but rather the question of the distribution of *power* between men and women. As Professor Robin West[13] expresses the matter (whilst putting forward an alternative thesis), '[R]adical feminists appear to be more attuned to power disparities between men and women than are cultural feminists'.[14] Men have power, women do not. Men dominate, women are subordinate and subordinated *because* they are women. MacKinnon's view is encapsulated in the demand that gender hierarchy be eradicated. The 'difference strategy' reinforces economic, political and social subordination. Feminism must 'empower women on our own terms'.[15]

Here MacKinnon is demanding power for women – not on the basis of some false equation with men as the referent standard – but in women's own right. In order to achieve this equality, the key to power in society must be understood. That power, according to radical feminism, lies in the constant and consistent oppression of women on the basis of their sex. Male dominance and women's subordination reveals itself in many ways. The setting of cultural mores[16] which require young girls to be circumcised, or their feet bound, or women's bodies burned on the funeral pyre of their husband, are all designed to ensure the continuation of male supremacy. In the West, laws (which were slow to be reformed) which limited women's right to own and manage property, freedom to divorce, limited their rights over their children, denied women the right to abortion, all evidence the hierarchical male-dominated societal structure. Dominance nowadays is revealed in the statistics on rape, violence, child abuse and sexual harassment of women. From a radical feminist perspective, male dominance is revealed in the prostitution and pornography industries. It is revealed in less obvious, but nonetheless crucial, ways in employment, where despite the many victories achieved in the quest for equality, women remain as the lowest paid sector of the workforce; women are still faced with a 'glass ceiling' in promotion terms in the professions. Through all of these, and other means, men have secured and maintained power over women.

Andrea Dworkin, whose writing on pornography will be considered in detail in Chapter 13, analyses men's power over women and identifies several aspects of power. First, men have assumed a 'metaphysical assertion of self', supported by customs and laws, which women are denied. This is the 'first

---

[13] Professor of Law, University of Maryland.
[14] West, R, 'Jurisprudence and gender' (1988) 55 Chicago UL Rev 1. (See *Sourcebook*, pp 227–44.)
[15] *Op cit*, MacKinnon, fn 8, p 22.
[16] See, further, Chapter 2.

Introduction to Feminist Jurisprudence

tenet of male-supremacist ideology'. This sense of self which men assume, needs no justification or apology – as Dworkin puts it 'it just is'. This natural assertion of selfhood which is denied to women, manifests itself in man's natural superiority. From childhood man is nurtured first by his mother and later in life by other females to whom he has a 'parasitic' attachment and who continue to feed and support his supremacy through their inferiority. Secondly, man has physical strength and strength equals power over others. As Dworkin expresses it '[T]he power of physical strength combines with the power of self so that he not only is, he is stronger; he not only takes, he takes by force'.[17] Thirdly, the power accrued through the innate sense of self and physical strength enables man to dominate others, to suppress those who lack his attributes through sheer force. The symbols of this force, for Dworkin, are the 'gun, the knife, the bomb, the fist' but above all there exists a 'hidden symbol of terror, the penis'. Fourthly, men have the 'power of naming'. This is a complex and subtle power – essentially meaning the power to 'define experience, to articulate boundaries and values, to designate to each thing its realm and qualities, to determine what can and cannot be expressed, to control perception itself'.[18] Through this power, men define (or name) women as sexual objects to be used, brutalised, raped, demeaned through pornography. Through this power also, men define women as most appropriately confined to the home – to bear and raise children, to nurture and care for the male and the children, to be denied full participation in civic life. Woman, in short, is what man defines her to be: what he wants her to be.

The fifth aspect of the power assumed by man is the power of owning. This power can clearly be seen in the laws relating to the family cited above, among others the historical power of ownership and management of a woman's property upon marriage; the right to sexual access to a wife, irrespective of the woman's willingness, through the fictitious doctrine of 'one flesh' imposed upon consent to marriage; the right to damages at law from another man if a woman has been adulterous; the absolute control over the children of the marriage; the ostracisation of a woman bearing a child outside a marriage whereupon she became a burden on the State and the child was regarded as *fillius nullius,* no-one's child. And whilst laws have been reformed to remove the ostensibly most discriminatory disabilities heaped upon women, men still largely control the economic purse, men still assume ownership rights in relation to sex with victims of rape and harassment. Sixth, and allied to the above, men have economic power. Money in the hands of man buys women; confirms power. This economic power is not confined to a man's personal life but extends also to the marketplace: men still largely

---

[17] Dworkin, A, *Power in Pornography: Men Possessing Women*, 1981, London: The Women's Press, p 15.
[18] *Ibid*, p 17.

control employment, control entry to professions, control promotion, control the Boards of companies. Finally, the final tenet of male supremacy is the power of sex. The power of sex defines woman and her role – that of sexual object to be owned and used by man. As Dworkin graphically expresses this power, '[T]he woman is acted on; the man acts and through action expresses sexual power, the power of masculinity'.[19] This power is manifested everywhere – in literature, music and art man's virility is celebrated.

For Catharine MacKinnon, the task of feminist analysis is to unmask, unravel, women's subordination and lack of power. In this task MacKinnon draws the analogy with Marxist reasoning within the context of gender: as labour is to Marxism so gender is to feminism. Female gender, the male and socially constructed sexuality of women, reduces women to their sexuality, and keeps them there. Women's 'reality' is that she is objectivised by male constructs as a sexual object for men's use. 'Man fucks woman; subject verb object.'[20] The world is divided on gendered lines which ensure that women are positioned in the subordinate. Thus, the task of feminism is not to 'see' women as 'different', or the 'same' because so to do is to identify women's position in relation to man. As MacKinnon expresses it, '[W]e are not allowed to be women on our own terms'.[21] Accordingly, in relation to sex discrimination, the sameness approach demands that women 'measure our similarity with men to see if we are or can be men's equals',[22] where as the difference approach 'views women as men view women: in need of special protection, help, or indulgence'.[23] By reconceptualising the debate as an issue not of difference or sameness, but as a matter of legal, political and social power, feminism can break free from the sterility of the sameness/difference debate.

By understanding the power relationship, and power inequality, and the manner in which this is translated into laws and legal practices, women can use the law to struggle against the female-specific harms of sexual discrimination, sexual harassment, denial of reproductive rights, sexual and other physical violence, inequalities in pay and employment opportunities, etc, which have proven so resistant to change. The language of sameness and difference merely provides legitimating norms for continued unequal treatment. Seeing the power relationships maintained by law, enables women to understand and resist the reality of the maleness of the State and law, and to understand the social reality that women's gender has been constructed by men: 'Gender is what gender means. It has no basis in anything other than the

---

[19] *Op cit*, Dworkin, fn 17, p 23.
[20] *Op cit*, MacKinnon, fn 8, p 124.
[21] *Op cit*, MacKinnon, fn 8, p 71.
[22] *Op cit*, MacKinnon, fn 8, p 71.
[23] *Op cit*, MacKinnon, fn 8, p 71.

social reality its hegemony constructs. The process that gives sexuality its male supremacist meaning is therefore the process through which gender inequality becomes socially real.'[24]

To adopt either the sameness or difference approach, for MacKinnon, is to remain trapped within the system of the male, dominant, referent; to accept the construction of woman as defined by men and male language. For this reason, to theorise woman's distinctive mode of moral reasoning as does Carol Gilligan, or to develop the concept of woman's distinctive voice as in Irigaray's 'speaking as woman',[25] inevitably reaffirms the supremacy of maleness against which woman is defined and judged. There is no 'beyond' of the reality of unequal power relationships: the power relationships themselves must be deconstructed and restructured in a manner which makes gender difference irrelevant to law. From MacKinnon's perspective, alternative feminist theories, by refusing to recognise the real power relationships which determine women's inequality, not only fail to explain the reality of women's condition, but also continue to affirm the status quo.

The liberal State 'coercively and authoritatively constitutes the social order in the interest of men as a gender – through its legitimating norms, forms, relation to society, and substantive policies'.[26] Thus, the liberal concept of equality of all persons in life and before law, disguises the reality of power relationships which are inherently gendered. Woman's reality can only be understood, and her position improved under the law, if the ideology of the liberal State is challenged and decoded to reveal its gendered reality.

In MacKinnon's analysis relations within society, otherwise constrained in liberal sameness/difference theory with its acceptance of the public/private divide, can be better understood when reconceptualised on the basis of those with power – men, and those without power – women. Dominance theory, in rejecting the public/private split, enables issues such as marital rape and other domestic violence to be identified as political issues: the personal is the political. Moreover, MacKinnon's dominance theory has explanatory power which sameness/difference theories cannot provide. In relation, for example, to rape, sameness/difference theories cannot provide satisfactory explanations. Women, predominantly, are raped, and raped by men. Stating that women are raped because they are different from men, seems to be saying not very much, and does not facilitate placing rape as an issue on the political agenda for women. Reconceptualised by dominance theory, however, the issue of rape can be clearly seen and explained as a disparate power relationship between the powerful man and the powerless woman: it is thus both a public and political issue. Sexual harassment is also more clearly

---

[24] *Op cit*, MacKinnon, fn 8, p 149.
[25] On which see Chapter 8.
[26] *Op cit*, MacKinnon, fn 8, p 162.

explained by dominance theory. Sexual harassment in the workplace cannot be explained only by women's difference from men. A particular woman's sexuality may result in her harassment by a particular man: thus conceptualised, the issue remains at the level of whether or not sexual harassment is a 'natural' feature of gender difference. Reconstituted as an issue of dominance versus subordination, and raising the experience of the individual woman to the level of understanding that sexual harassment is consistently and pervasively experienced by all women, and perpetrated by men, redefines sexual harassment as an issue of sexual discrimination which is actionable in law, and also renders sexual harassment a political issue. The success of this approach was evident in the case of *Meritor Savings Bank, FSB v Vinson*, decided by the United States' Supreme Court.[27] In that case, the issue of sexual harassment was understood to involve more than the single issue 'did this woman consent to the sexual advances of this man?' and a recognition that the particular victim was a victim because she belonged to a class of persons to which sexual harassment occurred. The sameness/difference approach does not lead to an analysis of sexual harassment as a political issue concerning sexual discrimination. Sameness theory is inapplicable to sexual harassment; difference theory fails to have political explanatory power: dominance theory has that power, a power which can translate into legal recognition of the harm of sexual harassment to all women.

The sexual abuse of children, pre-eminently conducted in the 'private' sphere of the home and family, is most clearly explained by Catharine MacKinnon's dominance theory. Sameness and/or difference theory simply cannot tackle child sexual abuse at a level at which it can be understood as an urgent, public, political issue concerning power and powerlessness, dominance and subordination. Dominance theory enables a reconceptualisation of child sexual abuse as a matter of public concern and a political issue in which the subordination of women is carried over to the most vulnerable and powerless members of society, and represents an issue of sexual discrimination.

Sameness/difference theory also fails to explain sexually-specific issues such as prostitution and pornography, the latter of which has been the focus of much of MacKinnon's analysis. Prostitution, into which women are coerced on economic grounds, and often remain coerced by their male pimps, is, however, understandable once the dominance approach is adopted. Prostitution is the expression of power of (privileged) men – economic, physical, sexual – over (underprivileged) subordinated women. Prostitution is thus not 'just' a matter of individual choice of a free and equal female agent – it represents MacKinnon's argument that women are objects, and objectified, in prostitution, for the use of men. Pornography[28] carries with it the same

---

[27] 477 US 57 (1986).
[28] Discussed further in Chapter 12.

messages: women are sexual objects – and no more than that. Entitled to no respect, enjoying no autonomy, women are portrayed as violated, degraded, mutilated, for the sexual arousal of male consumers. Difference theory cannot explain pornography in a political manner: difference theory would leave pornography at the level of a recognition of women's difference as a causal explanation for a phenomenon which is predominantly an expression of power relationships.

Notwithstanding MacKinnon's aversion to difference feminism, there are nonetheless, features about both difference and radical approaches which reflect common aspirations which are too easily missed in a compartmentalised reading of either approach. Difference feminism – especially as characterised by French philosopher Luce Irigaray – and radical feminism – characterised by Catharine MacKinnon's work – are both concerned with the construction of woman. While Irigaray focuses on woman's potential different-but-equal voice as the medium through which women may find full subjectivity, MacKinnon also demands a recognition of woman's contemporary lack of identity. In *Feminism Unmodified: Discourses on Life and Law*,[29] MacKinnon writes:

> I'm evoking for women a role that we have yet to make, in the name of a voice that, unsilenced, might say something that has never been heard.[30]

The 'personhood' that women lack, for both Irigaray and MacKinnon, lies in women's inability to speak. Pornography, in MacKinnon's analysis is representative of the silencing of women, but by no means exclusively so, for all law is constructed on male lines and reflects male conceptions of self and 'otherness' (women) against which otherness must be judged. But to remain with pornography as representative of the problem of women's silencing under law, pornography's representation of women as sexually available objects for (male) use and abuse, silences women in rendering women's voices unequal and not worthy of respect. In MacKinnon's vision, the silence must be removed, to enable women to achieve a voice. What MacKinnon does not do, which Irigaray explicitly does, is to argue that that voice, when heard, will be a distinctively 'feminine voice'. However, the value of 'woman's voice' – whether pursued through women's political consciousness raising and campaign for the removal of legal inequalities or linguistic and philosophical analysis – lies, albeit in very differing ways, at the heart of both theorists' conception of the equality of women and social transformation. It is in the *consequences* of social and legal change that the point of departure is represented for Irigaray and MacKinnon. Irigaray seeks to explicate women's differences, and to prophesy women's distinctive voice which will be both equal to and different from men's voice. MacKinnon, on the other hand, seeks

---

[29] *Op cit*, MacKinnon, fn 8.
[30] *Op cit*, MacKinnon, fn 8, p 77.

to dismantle the dominance/subordinate dichotomy through empowering women's voice – killing the silence – in order that legal, political and social equality may be achieved: an equal society in which gender will have no relevance.

Catharine MacKinnon's challenging, erudite and visionary jurisprudence has been subjected to numerous analyses and criticisms, which have been pursued with a vigour reminiscent of engagement in a blood sport in permanent open season. It is to some of these critiques that attention is now turned.

Radical feminism and the critiques of 'essentialism'

Two major alleged difficulties in radical feminism, and indeed any form of modernist theory, involve forms of *essentialism*. Essentialism has been defined as:

> [in philosophy] One of a number of related doctrines which hold that there are necessary properties of things, that these are logically prior to the existence of the individuals which instantiate them, and that their classification depends upon their satisfaction of sets of necessary conditions.[31]

The first criticism which has been voiced relates to the apparent reduction of women, in Catharine MacKinnon's work, to being little else other than sexual objects: her theory is accordingly critiqued as being essentialist and universalist. The second objection lies in feminist theoretical assumptions about the inherent characteristics of all women, as if any one woman stands as representative of all women, irrespective of age, race, nationality or social class.

In relation to the first critique, Professor Drucilla Cornell[32] takes MacKinnon to task for what she perceives to be MacKinnon's overemphasis of women's sexuality. Drucilla Cornell argues that MacKinnon is unable to develop her theory of feminism fully because she is 'unable to affirm feminine sexual difference as other than victimisation'.[33] Cornell does not deny that gender lies at the heart of the social construction of femininity nor that patriarchy lies at the heart of this construction. Nor does Cornell disagree with MacKinnon's insistence that woman's condition is intimately connected with male domination. What Cornell advocates is a theory which encompasses both a recognition of the causes and forms of subordination which are imposed upon women and a positive construction of women's femininity.

---

[31] *Collins English Dictionary*, 3rd edn, 1991, London: HarperCollins, p 531.
[32] Professor of Law, Benjamin Cardozo School of Law, Yeshiva University.
[33] Cornell, D, 'Sexual difference, the feminine and equivalency: a critique of MacKinnon's *Toward a Feminist Theory of the State*' (1990) 100 Yale LJ 2247. (See *Sourcebook*, pp 227–44.)

Cornell insists that 'women's sexuality cannot be reduced to women's sex'. What MacKinnon does, according to Cornell, is to reduce women to 'fuckees' which has the effect of supporting and endorsing men's fantasies about women and their role, which is both demeaning and damaging to women and women's image of women. Thus, a more positive programme is called for in which women – far from accepting men's view of women as mere objects of, and for, sex – work towards a more equal society through the recognition of women's unique capabilities. Sexual difference should not be denied, decried or viewed as a matter of shame, but rather celebrated and brought centre stage in the quest for a feminist jurisprudence and the realisation of full equality.

In 'Feminism always modified: the affirmation of feminine difference rethought',[34] Drucilla Cornell returns to MacKinnon's work, in both constructive and critical style. Cornell's critique is undertaken from the standpoint of a sympathetic analysis of French feminists', and particularly Luce Irigaray's, analyses of women's difference, and its potentiality for the achievement of women's equal-but-different subjectivity in society and law. MacKinnon's jurisprudence, in Cornell's critique, is one in which women 'are fated to remain victims within patriarchal reality',[35] obliged to limit women's reformist role to that of the litigant who, operating within the patriarchal reality, seeks to remove the specific discriminations enforced through law. By contrast, Cornell argues, Luce Irigaray's analysis enables women to avoid the trap of entering into the dominant male discourse by empowering women through women's distinctive voice: 'speaking as woman'. Irigaray's work, as has been discussed in Chapter 7, is challenging the very basis of social and political life as it is expressed in male discourse, and advocating social and legal change through the recognition and articulation of women's different sexuality – woman's *jouissance* – thus conferring on women full subjectivity in equal relationship to men: no longer 'mirrored' as the 'other of the other', but realising the status in equality of 'other to the other'. MacKinnon, in rejecting women's difference (and women's 'sameness'), is forced into an account of women's victimisation in society and law, without being able to transcend that victimisation other than through the more limited appeal to law and litigation in order to remove specific inequalities. Thus, from this perspective, MacKinnon is driven to analysing *what women are,* without being able to move forward into a vision, albeit idealistic and utopian and as yet unrealised, which offers women full and equal status as citizens, but imbued with women's own distinctive feminine voice. By 'seeing' woman's identity as sexuality defined on male supremacist terms, MacKinnon has limited the potential of her analysis by remaining within the confines of the masculine

---

[34] See Cornell, D, *Beyond Accommodation: Ethical Feminism Deconstruction, and the Law,* 1991, London: Routledge, Chapter 3.
[35] *Ibid,* p 151.

perspective. In order, therefore, to break out of the 'old dream of symmetry' in which women are identified and judged according to male norms, Cornell supports Irigaray's quest for the identity of the 'feminine' not in male constructions, but in women's own terms, expressed through the voice of the feminine, in order precisely to escape from the 'old dream of symmetry' which MacKinnon is both forced to deny and yet cannot move beyond.

Drucilla Cornell also questions what she perceives to be MacKinnon's insistence that the foundation of women's inequality lies in women's bodies and hence the identification with women as those 'who are fucked' (by men). Cornell's questions concern the need to define women's sexuality in these terms – terms which position women as the victims of heterosexual sex. Cornell's argument with MacKinnon becomes clearer if Cornell's alternative interpretation of the female body is considered. Instead of 'figuring' the body as a site of imposition of sexual dominance by way of penetration, if sexual penetration is reconceptualised as 'receptivity', it becomes possible to recognise not women's victimisation, but rather women's participation in a reciprocal act which represents an expression of women's sexuality – her *jouissance*, not her defensiveness in the light of sexual threat.

Cornell's analysis of Irigaray and MacKinnon is both insightful and interesting. There are, however, difficulties entailed in the comparative analysis. First, despite the apparent difference in their work, there is also much common ground. Both accept that societal ordering is patriarchal; both accept that women have been relegated to the position of the inferior of the binary coupling: man/woman; dominant/subordinate and so on. Both theorists are radical and utopian and seek a way forward; a means by which to permanently transform society and to gain women's equality within that society. However, the work of Irigaray and MacKinnon – unsurprisingly given their respective intellectual backgrounds – French philosophy, psychoanalysis and linguistics for the former, political science and law for the latter, is informed by very differing discourses. Placing Irigaray and MacKinnon within the context of a comparative analysis, in which Irigaray is favoured and privileged and MacKinnon is not, inevitably results in an apparently damaging critique of the latter. Irigaray undoubtedly has a utopian vision of woman's equality, one which through the evolution of woman's voice – woman-speaking-as-woman – offers the potential for woman's subjectivity and the destruction of woman's position as Object, the inferior partner to the Subject. MacKinnon's work, however, has more direct and immediate legal, social and political, transformative potential. This potential has been realised in relation to the acceptance in law that sexual harassment is within the domain of sexual discrimination. The reconceptualisation of pornography, whilst not succeeding in overcoming the American preoccupation with the First Amendment guarantee of free speech, has, as discussed in Chapter 13, reformulated the issue as one related directly to the political position of women. MacKinnon has reconceptualised the gender debate, through analysing the male/female power relationship, rather than resting within an exploration of the sameness/difference debate. Accordingly, notwithstanding the strength of Cornell's comparative analysis, it is important not to lose sight of the transformative power of MacKinnon's analysis.

The second anti-essentialist critique relates to the assumption that all women are in fact represented in feminist jurisprudence. This critique is not confined to radical feminism alone, but extends to all feminist theories which seek to universalise women's oppression. The anti-essentialist critique is both a general theoretical critique and a critique advanced by minority groups who have felt marginalised by feminist modernist theory. Because this critique is most appropriately situated within the postmodern climate of intellectual thought, it is necessary to consider the central tenets of postmodernism which represents the focus of the next chapter.

CHAPTER 9

POSTMODERNISM AND CRITICAL LEGAL STUDIES

All that is solid melts into the air, all that is holy is profaned.[1]

INTRODUCTION

The age of modernity

The pre-modern age is that age in which there exists cultural homogeneity within (a) society – shared identities and beliefs.[2] The origins of the age of modernity lie in the eighteenth century and the Enlightenment.[3] While France and the United States were to be racked by revolution in the eighteenth century,[4] by the mid nineteenth century economic, political and social upheavals were experienced throughout continental Europe, culminating in the revolutions of 1848. Throughout Europe urbanisation and industrialisation also changed the social and political map. The former certainties of the Age of Enlightenment were unsettled and the age of modernism ushered in. In place of orthodoxy and coherence came fragmentation, experimentation, contingency, diversity and transitoriness. In art, architecture, literature and language the 'creative destructiveness' of the modern age made its mark. Picasso's *Guernica* represents clear testimony to that concept. But while the age of modernism, in its heyday between 1848 and the onset of the First World War, is characterised by a reaction against newly perceived false certainties of the Age of Enlightenment, modernism is also characterised by a desire for certainty and coherence. There is thus a schizophrenic quality to the age of modernism, summed up by Baudelaire: '[M]odernity is the transient, the fleeting, the contingent; it is the one half of art, the other being the eternal and the immutable.'[5] This conflict between the 'chaos' of modernism and its questing for certainty amongst the chaos, characterises the age of modernism.[6]

---

[1] Marx, K, *The Communist Manifesto* (1848), Wayne, J (ed), 1987, Toronto: Canadian Scholars.
[2] On the influence of René Descartes, see Chapter 5.
[3] See, further, Chapter 5. See also Nesbit, R, *History of the Idea of Progress*, 1980, New York: Basic Books.
[4] 1789 and 1775–88 respectively.
[5] Baudelaire, CP, *The Painter of Modern Life* (1863), Mayne, J (trans), 1964: London: Phaidon.
[6] Saussure's linguistic structuralism, epitomising the search for coherence, emerged in 1911, and provides the intellectual backcloth to poststructuralism, discussed below.

The First World War represented a catalyst against which the quest for certainty became more urgent. As Taylor has written, 'modernist subjectivity ... was simply unable to cope with the crisis into which Europe in 1914 was plunged'.[7]

If the First World War represented a threat to modernity, it is with the Holocaust and Nazi Germany that modernity faced its most critical challenge. The Holocaust, Hitler's final solution to the 'problem' of Jews and other non-Aryan peoples, eliminated an estimated one-third of the world's Jewish population. Sociologist Max Weber had warned that the pursuit of rationality would lead to an 'iron cage of domination'.[8] *Par excellence,* Nazism represented that iron cage. The elimination of the Jews was pursued with a cold rationality: racial purity, Aryan racial purity, underpinned the drive for the elimination of those who did not fit the mould of Hitler's mad, cold logic.[9]

The aspect of modernism which reflected the search for rationality within the reality of the chaos of society, seeks to look behind that which is apparently self-evident, to seek meanings in the arts and social sciences which are both coherent and reveal the structures of thought which underlie 'reality'. Modernism is the era in which society, the arts, economics, politics, law and psychology are theorised around central organising concepts. In relation to law, the attempt to provide an all-embracing theory of the origins and structure of law, is a project of modernism. Thus, utilitarianism, positivism, Marxism and theories of justice are part of the project of modernity, positing universalist, monocausal explanations of law and justice.

The age of postmodernism

At some undefinable point in time in the late 1960s the postmodern age was born. As with its predecessors, its origins are neither fully documented nor understood, but rest in a major shift in society, rather than a clear break with the past. It remains unclear whether postmodernism represents the latest stage of modernity or marks a clear change in perspective. The post-War demise of colonialism and the rise of independent nation States, heightened perceptions about national and cultural self-determination and racial and sexual equality; economic globalisation and the technological revolution, all impacted on former cultural, economic, social and political certainties. The Civil Rights Movement in the United States of America of the 1950s and 1960s,

---

[7] Taylor, B, *Modernism, Post-modernism, Realism: a Critical Perspective for Art,* 1987, Winchester, p 127.

[8] For discussion, see Cotterrell, RBM, *The Sociology of Law: An Introduction,* 1985, London: Butterworths.

[9] On the Holocaust, see Morrison, W, *Jurisprudence: From the Greeks to Post-modernism,* 1997, London: Cavendish Publishing, Chapter 11.

the Vietnam War and the violent opposition to the United States' involvement therein, characterised disunity and dissent. Throughout Europe in 1968 student unrest disrupted the calm of academic life. The cultural change again reflected itself within culture and intellectual thought. Art, architecture, literature, linguistic analysis, law and legal theory have all been affected by the cultural and intellectual sea-change.

Postmodernism, by contrast to that aspect of modernism which sought certainty, seeks to dismantle the 'meta-narratives' of modernity, to disrupt the foundations of now conventional, comforting certainties and to expose the lack of rationality and coherence in grand theory.

Traditional theories of history, architecture, anthropology, the arts and literature, philosophy, psychology, language, politics, law and science are all subjected to the postmodern reaction against the certainties which they suggest. In place of certainty, there is uncertainty, contingency, fragmentation, diversity. In place of the 'big story', there are only 'little stories'. Not only is the meta-narrative denied, but the uncertainty produced is one which is accepted: there is *no meaning, no truth,* beyond the fragmented, the incoherent.

Theories based on sweeping generalisations about law, and centred on single, fundamental concepts of modernist thought are challenged. Postmodernism then is both a reaction against the theorising of the past and a critique of former modes of thought. To understand the world from the postmodern perspective is to be deeply critical and questioning of the theories produced by modernism – to replace 'grand theory' with disparate, specific, competing discourses. That this is unsettling is undeniable – the world seems to dissolve into a myriad of intersecting, conflicting, yet-to-be-analysed or unanalysable categories and concepts. What was once 'known' becomes unknown and unknowable. Fragmentation replaces totality. The individual – the Subject of law – as constructed in modernism, in postmodern thought is scrutinised and deconstructed. The 'death of the Subject' is announced.[10] Social identity becomes fractured and indeterminate. Psychoanalytic theory becomes a primary site for deconstructing the 'myth' of the formerly identifiable Subject. The meta-narrative of Freudian psychoanalytic theory has provided a natural focus for postmodern and poststructuralist psychoanalytic thought. Thus, formerly accepted central organising concepts around which theory developed are deconstructed to reveal the fragmented nature of the Subject. Patriarchy, woman, gender, sexuality: under the deconstructive technique become fragile concepts. Subjectivity is understood as socially constructed rather than confined within predetermined closed categories of thought. Deconstructing the Subject entails recognising the multiplicity of subjectivities, identities, which inhere in the individual and recognising that each individual is comprised of multiple subjectivities. The postmodern

---

10 Foucault, M, *Power/Knowledge,* 1972, New York: Pantheon, p 117.

Subject has multiple identities as he or she moves in and out of differing milieux. This critique and deconstruction of the modern Subject lies at the heart of postmodern thought. The deconstruction of the Subject of life, of law, poses particularly difficult challenges to feminist thought, but also opens up new avenues of inquiry.

Postmodernism represents reactions against past orthodoxies concerning the individual and society, and provides the intellectual backcloth against which the Critical Legal Studies (CLS) movement, discussed below, came into being. Postmodern thought has permeated every aspect of culture and intellectual life.

Since the late 1960s, postmodern thought has emerged as a challenge to the 'grand theories' of modernism which present themselves as coherent, all-embracing 'meta-narratives' of culture and language. While not directly 'jurisprudential', in the sense that the focus of many engaged with postmodernism is not 'law', the influence on legal theorists, including feminist theorists, has been marked. To introduce the important insights into knowledge and language which postmodernism and poststructuralism and critical legal scholars provide as separate, distinctive approaches is not possible, for there exist intersecting, overlapping sites of scholarship. Postmodernism employs the deconstructive techniques of postsructuralism; Critical Legal Studies is itself a postmodern, poststructuralist enterprise. The interrelatedness must be borne in mind when reflecting on each sphere of analysis.

From a legal-theoretical perspective, the postmodernist rejects the 'grand' concepts of traditional theory: rights, equality, rationality must be rethought and reunderstood from a critical standpoint which dismantles the perceived false certainties and reveals the realities of life. As noted above, fragmentation, contingency and diversity must replace coherence, uncertainty displace certainty. The implications of the postmodern critique for feminist jurisprudence are profound. If 'grand theory' is no longer sufficient to explain women's condition, concepts such as patriarchy and gender, the public and the private, lose their explanatory force, and throw doubt on the potential for a convincing coherent theoretical understanding of women's lives and conditions. In place of grand theory, there must be developed critiques which concentrate on the reality of the diversity of individual women's lives and conditions, critiques which reject the universalist, foundationalist philosophical and political understandings offered by modernism. With the 'age of innocence' lost, in its place there exists diversity, plurality, competing rationalities, competing perspectives and uncertainty as to the potentiality of theory.

Structuralism and poststructuralism, modes of thought and understanding sited respectively within the modern and postmodern, are most readily located within the linguistic philosophical tradition, but extend also to anthropology, architecture and the arts. Structuralism may be defined as an analysis which uncovers patterns and structures within a given discipline. Structuralism suggests a coherence, a continuity in form which is revealed by analysis. By way of illustration, in the field of anthropology, Claude Levi-Strauss analysed the structural norms and patterns within the family: the taboos on incest, for example, which appear universal and historical.[11] Structuralists are therefore concerned to reveal the patterns which are replicated within different structures. Rather than relying on some form of modernist historical theory, such as Marx's theory with its emphasis of historical determinism, structuralists analyse the perceived reality of structures at a given point in time. It is with the analysis of the human subject that structuralism has most relevance to feminist jurisprudence, and poses the greatest challenge to any coherence in theory.

Poststructuralism challenges the orthodoxies of structuralism. In essence, the task of poststructuralists is to imbue doubt in the former certainties of the structures designated to anthropology, architecture, language, philosophy, psychoanalysis and society. Poststructuralists focus on the ambivalences and discontinuities in structures, and on the relationship between the signifier and the signified: the Subject and the Object. In structuralist linguistics, two concepts which make up language pertain: the signifier and the signified. The signifier is the word, the signified that which is indicated by the signifier. In structuralism, the signifier and the signified are but two sides of the same coin. Poststructuralists reveal the underlying deficiencies in such formulations.

Four postmodern/poststructuralist theorists have provided a particular focus for feminist thought:[12] Michel Foucault,[13] poststructuralist historian; Jean-Francois Lyotard, postmodernist philosopher; postmodernist psychoanalyst, Jacques Lacan, and professor of the history of philosophy at the École Normale Supérieure in Paris and architect of the deconstructive school of literary criticism, Jacques Derrida.[14]

---

[11] See Levi-Strauss, C, 'Patterns of kinship', in *The Savage Mind*, 1966, London: Weidenfeld and Nicolson.

[12] The list of those who have *influenced* feminist theorising encompasses all theorists from Ancient Greece through to postmodernism.

[13] 1926–84. Author of *Madness and Civilization: A History of Insanity in the Age of Reason*, 1971, London: Routledge; *Discipline and Punish: The Birth of the Prison*, Sheridan Smith, A (trans), 1998, Harmondsworth: Penguin; *History of Sexuality*, 1990, London: Penguin; *The Archaeology of Knowledge and the Discourse on Language*, Sheridan Smith, A (trans), 1972, London: Tavistock; *Power/Knowledge: Selected Interviews and other Writings, 1972–77*, 1980, Brighton: Harvester.

[14] Rorty has been labelled a postmodernist, although this label he has himself questioned while recognising the similarities between his work and that of postmodernists: see Rorty, R, 'Feminism and pragmatism', in Peterrson, G (ed), *The Tanner Lectures on Human Values*, 1990, Salt Lake City: Utah UP, p 1, repr in Patterson, D (ed), *Postmodernism and Law*, 1994, Aldershot: Dartmouth, Chapter 2.

Michel Foucault

French postmodernist and poststructuralist, Michel Foucault, focuses on the concept of power and the relationship between power and knowledge. Foucault himself refused to be categorised, denying that he had been a Freudian, a Marxist or structuralist. In Foucault's analysis of power, power does not mysteriously reside within the State, power exists within the multiple and multifarious sites of relationships within society – power from this perspective cannot accurately or adequately be theorised, in the legal positivist sense, as some 'sovereign body'. Rather, an analysis of power must be located within the local, the specific, in order to understand power relations. Thus, the family, the psychoanalytic session, the prison, the asylum, must all be examined. The power relationships within each cannot simply be explained by some meta-narrative of State power. Indebted to Nietzsche and his historical analysis of genealogy,[15] Foucault rejects the Hegelian notion of an inevitable unfolding of history in favour of difference theory – the practice of digging beneath the surface explanations of history and unearthing the irrational, the local, the forgotten incidents. Thus totalising historical theorising is rejected: '... the traditional devices for constructing a comprehensive view of history and for retracing the past as a patient and continuous development must be systematically dismantled.'[16]

Foucault thus attacks all totalising theory, including 'all forms of general discourse'.[17] The deconstructive endeavour is to remove the false certainties about knowledge entailed in totalising theory, and to reveal the multiplicity of the sites of power in society – without constructing yet another totalising theory. A significant theme in Foucault's work is that of the Subject. Whereas traditional historians posit the individual Subject at the heart of history, Foucault argues that the construction of the Subject is the effect of power relations, and that the 'constitution of the subjectivity of the individual is simultaneously the constitution of his or her subjection'.[18] Thus, a focus on the Subject and subjectivity is, for Foucault, false, for the Subject is nothing but the product of power relationships which must be resisted.

While Foucault systematically deconstructs universalising theories of history and State, he simultaneously refuses to envisage an alternative theory: any theory being totalising and thus dangerous. Foucault's commitment is thus not to imagine a different world, for that is identified with Utopianism

---

[15] See Foucault, M, 'Nietzsche, genealogy, history', in Bouchard, D (ed), *Language, Counter-Memory, Practice: Selected Essays and Interviews*, 1977, Oxford: Basil Blackwell.

[16] Foucault, M, *Language, Counter-Memory, Practice: Selected Essays and Interviews*, 1977, New York: Cornell UP, p 153.

[17] Ibid, Foucault, p 231.

[18] Balbus, I, 'Disciplining women: Michel Foucault and the power of feminist discourse', in Benhabib, S and Cornell, D (eds), *Feminism as Critique: Essays on the Politics of Gender in Late Capitalist Societies*, 1987, London: Polity, Chapter 6.

and the substitution of one form of universal theory for another, but to analyse the power relationships within society which constitute knowledge, and to resist the disciplinary effects of power.

Foucault developed the concept of *discourse* which has become central to postmodern thought. Discourse, of which language is a facet, is distinguishable from language and is the term which focuses on the indeterminacy of meaning, and incorporates an awareness of the importance of the context in which words are spoken (or written).[19] Foucault does not offer a single definition of discourse, but states that:

> In the most general, and vaguest way, it denoted a group of verbal performances; and by discourse, then, I mean that which was produced (perhaps all that was produced) by the groups of signs. But I also meant a group of acts of formulation, a series of sentences or propositions.

Further:

> [Discourses] are practices that systematically form the objects of which they speak ...

and

> Of course, discourses are composed of signs; but what they do is more than use these signs to designate things. It is this *more* that renders them irreducible to the language *(langue)* and to speech. It is this 'more' that we must reveal and describe.[20]

Discourse is central to an understanding of power and power relationships. Through discourse, which assumes a particular way of thinking, and shared conceptions of subject matter, the indeterminacy of language, its 'gaps, its discontinuities, its entanglement, its incompatibilities, its replacement, and its substitutions'[21] are revealed, and the dependence of language on context for meaning, becomes clearer.

Jean-Francois Lyotard

Postmodernist Jean-Francois Lyotard[22] also argues against the meta-narratives such as those of Hegel and Marx, and theories of justice, which offer universalising explanations of history and society: theories which provide monocausal explanations: 'I will use the term modern to designate any science that legitimates itself with reference to a meta-discourse of this kind making an explicit appeal to some grand narrative.'[23] Such modernist

---

[19] See Foucault, M, *The Archaeology of Knowledge and the Discourse on Language*, Sheridan Smith, A (trans), 1972, London: Tavistock.
[20] *Ibid*, Foucault, pp 108–49.
[21] *Ibid*, Foucault, p 72.
[22] Professor of Philosophy at the University of Paris at Vincennes.
[23] Lyotard, J-F, *The Postmodern Condition: A Report on Knowledge*, Bennington, G and Massumi, B (trans), 1984, Manchester: Manchester UP, p xxiii.

theories claim a privileged position – legitimating or delegitimating particular facets or practices of society. Lyotard defines the postmodern 'as incredulity towards meta-narratives'.[24] The 'postmodern condition'[25] is rooted in diversity rather than coherence, the local rather than the global, the specific rather than the general. Lyotard focuses on language and the subject. The 'social bond is linguistic' but it 'is not woven with a single thread' but by an 'indeterminate number' of 'language games'.

Lyotards's *The Postmodern Condition: A Report on Knowledge*[26] was commissioned by the president of the Conseil des Universities of the Government of Quebec. Lyotard worked from the hypothesis that 'the status of knowledge is altered as societies enter what is known as the postindustrial age and cultures enter what is known as the postmodern age'.[27] The technological revolution, 'the computerisation of society', evolution and growth in multinational corporations, and globalisation all have impacts on 'knowledge'. Language transmits knowledge. Utilising the categorisation of JL Austin, discussed in Chapter 13, of locutionary, illocutionary and perlocutionary speech, Lyotard examines language games – Wittgenstein's term for the categories of speech which are defined in terms of rules which specify 'their properties and the uses to which they can be put'.[28] Speech falls 'within the domain of a general agonistics' (competition, eagerness to win in discussion/argument).

The narrative form of speech plays a dominant, or pre-eminent, role in the formation of customary, traditional, knowledge (as opposed to scientific knowledge). In the narrative form there is the sender (of knowledge), the addressee and the subject. The sender or narrator has knowledge because he or she was once the addressee. The term knowledge is not confined to sets of (denotative) statements, but requires also ideas of 'know how', 'knowing how to live', and 'knowing how to listen'.[29] In the narrative form, the rules of the society are set out, and the social bond is created through the rules of the game. With scientific knowledge matters differ. The researcher develops knowledge and transmits that knowledge to the addressee who does not have the knowledge. Only the competence of the sender is at issue: not the competence of the addressee. With scientific knowledge, the central issue is the legitimation of knowledge, a feature absent from the narrative form. For the scientist 'Narratives are fables, myths, legends, fit only for women and children'.[30]

---

[24] *Op cit*, Lyotard, fn 23, p xxiv.
[25] *Op cit*, Lyotard, fn 23, p xxiv.
[26] *Op cit*, Lyotard, fn 23, p xxiv.
[27] *Op cit*, Lyotard, fn 23, p 3.
[28] *Op cit*, Lyotard, fn 23, p 10.
[29] *Op cit*, Lyotard, fn 23, p 18.
[30] *Op cit*, Lyotard, fn 23, p 27.

Jacques Derrida

Jacques Derrida is the founder of poststructuralism.[31] Language is a complex web of signs and, for Derrida, is metaphorical. Metaphor is 'a figure of speech in which a word or phrase is applied to an object or action that it does not literally denote in order to imply a resemblance, as in *he is a lion in battle*. Language can never mean literally what it says – language is made up of metaphors and symbolisms. Thus language is not a reflection of reality, but rather plays a role in constituting reality. Derrida,[32] whose work extends that of Nietzsche, Freud and Heidegger, argues that the sign (the word, the signifier) is not co-extensive with that which is signified. Rather than leading to a direct correlation with the signified, the signifier leads only to other signs and signifiers. The signified is never identical to the signifier: there is fluidity, adaptability and uncertainty as to the meaning of that which is signified. Thus language is indeterminate. The signified cannot be identified, it is absent, has no identity in reality. The signified can only be understood, on this analysis, in relation to the signifier, the sign, and yet what is indicated by the signifier has no presence. Derived from Martin Heidegger,[33] Derrida adopts the technique of *sous rature* (under erasure). Thus, the signified (for example, the word n~~atur~~e) – crossed out but left legible – alerts the reader that the word 'nature' is uncertain – an inadequate word to capture the essence of 'nature', yet essential to convey the idea of 'nature'. The word 'woman' therefore, cannot itself define woman – it merely conveys an idea about 'woman', the interpretation of which is dependent upon the reader's construction of woman. The word, the signifier, woman indicates the *idea of woman*, the reality of woman is missing – absent. Words are thus indeterminate – the signifier has no meaning independent of the signified – the signifier signifies something else; all that remains is a chain of signifiers.

Central to the project of deconstruction is the study of binary opposites. It is this feature of Derrida's work which has become so crucial for feminist scholars, and most particularly the French feminist school. According to Jacques Derrida, '[W]estern thought ... has always been structured in terms of dichotomies or polarities'. Thus, 'good vs evil, being vs nothingness, presence vs absence, truth vs error, identity vs difference, mind vs matter, man vs woman, soul vs body, life vs death, nature vs culture, speech vs writing', these 'polar opposites' do not stand in equal relationship. 'The second term in each pair is considered in the negative, corrupt, undesirable version of the first ... [T]he two terms are not simply opposed in their meanings, but are arranged in

---

31 See Derrida, J, *Of Grammatology*, 1976, Baltimore: Johns Hopkins UP; *Speech and Phenomena, and Other Essays on Husserl's Theory of Signs*, 1973, Chicago, Illinois: Northwestern UP; *Writing and Difference*, 1978, London: Routledge and Kegan Paul.
32 Professor of Philosophy at the École Normale Supérieure in Paris.
33 1889–1946.

a hierarchical order which gives the first term priority ...'[34] The signifier is in the dominant position; the signified subordinate. By insisting that the signified cannot be adequately represented by the signifier, and calling for the deconstruction of the signified – which is 'under erasure', thereby reversing the balance of superiority and inferiority as between the signifier and signified, Derrida provides a linguistic technique which has been adopted by feminists in the quest to understand language, society and law. The significance of this technique in feminist theory will be discussed below.

Jacques Derrida's focus lies in a rejection of modernist linguistic structures and a reformulation of the relationship between the 'producer', the artist or author, the painting or text, and the 'consumer' of that work. Aesthetic deconstruction is a technique for 'reading' texts. The writing or the reading of a text, and what is understood by the writer and reader, is not explained by the text itself, but rather by the influences and situation of the writer and the use made of the text – the interpretation of the text – by the reader who constructs her own 'text'. The critic of the text will produce yet another interrelated text. Cultural life, then, is represented not by a series of disconnected, isolated, 'texts', but rather by intersecting, interrelated texts. This is the problem of language: language cannot be isolated from the words expressed, or the reading of the words. The authority of the author of the text is diminished. The continuity of the discourse is broken, 'and leads necessarily to a double reading: that of the fragment perceived in relation to its text of origin; that of the fragment as incorporated into a new whole, a different totality'.[35] Thus linguistic and other representations have shifting meanings – there can be no unified monolithic representation of the world. The individual Subject moves through differing relations, and as the text, the 'reading' of the Subject may differ from the Subject's self-image, just as that self-image is localised, determined by time and place. Subjectivity therefore cannot be fixed any more than can the meaning of an author's words. It follows that unifying classifications – woman, white women, women of colour – are too simplistic formulations on which to fix identity. The question 'what is woman' thus presents a problem. Derrida states that '[I]t is impossible to dissociate the questions of art, style and truth from the question of the woman'. Further, '[O]ne can no longer seek her, no more than one could search for women's femininity or female sexuality and she is certainly not to be found in any of the familiar modes of concept or knowledge. Yet ... it is impossible to resist looking for her'.[36]

---

[34] Derrida, J, *Dissemination*, 1972, Paris: Éditions du Seuil.
[35] Derrida, J, cited in Foster, H (ed), *The Anti-Aesthetic: Essays on Postmodern Culture*, 1983, Washington: Port Townsend, p 142.
[36] *Ibid*, Derrida, 1983, p 71.

Postmodernism and Critical Legal Studies

Postmodern and poststructuralist thought and analysis contains its own contradictions. The master narrative must give way to the inclusion of and predominance of the individual, the subjective, the atomised, the contemporary (non-historical), the local. As Wayne Morrison writes:

> ... postmodernity is characterised by a feeling of extreme ambivalence to the hopes and social structures of the last 200 years; a mood of nostalgia; cultural relativism; moral conventionalism; scepticism and pragmatism; a dialectic of localism amidst globalism; ambivalence towards organised, principled political activity; and a distrust of all strong forms of ethical or anthropological foundations.[37]

Past modernist theory 'stands in the dock', under prosecution, found guilty and awaiting sentence, rejected and useful only for its role in rejection. However, it must be noted that to speak of postmodernism, with the implication that postmodernism is a coherent school of thought, is to mislead. Postmodernism comes in many forms – there exist postmodernisms rather than postmodernism. In Pauline Marie Rosenau's analysis, the two principal forms of postmodernism are sceptical postmodernism and affirmative postmodernism. Sceptical postmodernists, epitomised by Heidegger and Nietzsche, focus on the negative: the uncertainties and ambiguities of existence, the 'impossibilities of truth', 'characterised by all that is grim, cruel, alienating, hopeless, tired and ambiguous'.[38] Affirmative postmodernists, on the other hand, according to Rosenau, while agreeing with the critique of modernity, adopt less dogmatic, negative, ideological attitudes to the present and future. Not all socio-political action is decried, not all values are rejected. Neither sceptical nor affirmative postmodernist approaches are mutually exclusive – there are overlaps, intersections. In each there exists both the extreme and the moderate. While sceptical postmodernism offers little constructive potential for feminist (or indeed any) theorising, affirmative postmodernism offers avenues for development.

Sceptical postmodernism, in its denial of theory, paradoxically itself presents its own formulated theory: that of the impossibility of theory. Thus, in seeking to distance itself from all grand theory, postmodernism postulates a grand theory of non-theory: the postmodern conundrum.[39]

---

[37] *Op cit*, Morrison, fn 9, p 513.
[38] Rosenau, P, 'Affirmatives and skeptics', in Anderson, W (ed), *The Fontana Postmodernism Reader*, 1996, London: Fontana, p 103.
[39] On the potentialities and problems posed by postmodernism for jurisprudence in general, see *op cit*, Morrison, fn 9, Chapter 16.

CRITICAL LEGAL STUDIES

Critical Legal Studies (CLS) is the term applied to those legal scholars who, from the late 1970s, reacted against the 'grand theorising' of 'traditional' jurisprudence. Critical Legal Studies began life with a conference in 1977, the agenda of which was undefined beyond an invitation to discuss critical approaches to law and society:[40] intellectual punk thus entered the legal academy with all the irreverence and innovative vitality of its artistic counterparts.

Consistent with poststructuralism and postmodernism, CLS abjures theory which is abstracted from society, which posits 'grand truths' about society and law. Scepticism and self-doubt about law and legal theory are the hallmarks of CLS:

> Traditional legal scholarship implicitly tells us that everything is as it should be and that our role as lawyers, or thinkers about law, is assured. The law is the tool of modernity and modernity is sane, rational, functional, efficient – CLS writings points out the underbelly of modernity's claims to universality, reason and coherence.[41]

The distrust of 'meta-narratives' about law has not escaped feminist jurisprudential attention. The assumption that law is centrestage in the recognition of the rectification of women's disabilities has been criticised, for example, by Carol Smart,[42] who argues that law, far from being rational, objective and coherent, often exhibits irrationality, subjectivity and incoherence.[43] Also characterising much CLS writing is the distrust on the traditional insistence on the value of legal rights. Debunking, or 'trashing' the myths of law comes to the fore. In place of law's centrality and certainty, so prevalent in positivist theory and the liberal rule of law, is exhibited distrust for law and a yearning for a society characterised not by atomised individuals each relying on legal rights, but based on co-operation and sharing within a spirit of community. Moreover, the 'science of law', characterised by positivism and its attempted rationality, so evident in the centrality of fixed rules and principles, masks the law's interaction with and dependence upon other disciplines, such as anthropology, politics, psychology and sociology. CLS thus seeks to open up the legal mind to fresh interpretations of law and the legal enterprise and to see law as a political enterprise within its social setting. This demands that law be looked at through fresh eyes: get away from the concentration on formality and rationality, understand the causes and

---

[40] *Op cit*, Morrison, fn 9, p 454.
[41] *Op cit*, Morrison, fn 9, p 458.
[42] See Smart, C, *Feminism and the Power of Law*, 1989, London: Routledge and Kegan Paul.
[43] See, also, Olsen, F, 'Feminism and critical legal theory: an American perspective' (1990) 18 Int J Soc L 199.

effects of legal change. Legal education came under early attack, especially from CLS scholars Robert Gordon[44] and Duncan Kennedy,[45] as artificial, sterile and not fitting law students for the 'real world' of legal practice. 'Grand theory', whether liberalist or Marxist also falls under attack. Wayne Morrison identifies four 'assumptions' of liberalism which attract CLS critique:

(a) the assumption of law's neutrality ...;
(b) the assumption that legal reasoning is somehow an unproblematic matter ...;
(c) the assumption that laws are positive data of social life, ie, that they have fixed objective meanings which cannot really be challenged; that their validity and significance are settled by objective unchallengeable methods ...;
(d) the radical contingency and openness of modernity and hence the meaning of social progress ...;[46]

Sweeping away the assumptions of modernity's grand theories; postulating the radical view of law's inherent indeterminacy, law's lack of formal rationality, CLS, typifying postmodernism's doubt and uncertainty about knowledge and reality, demands that law be seen as a 'cluster of beliefs'[47] held about law which mask the fact that law is a representation of power, and a mechanism for maintaining power in society. Law thus has an ideological function, which becomes hidden under liberalism.

The uncertainties and fragmentation which characterises postmodernism and CLS has both positive and negative implications for feminist jurisprudence. First, freeing the mind from the certainties about law and legal theory, has led to considerable feminist scholarship on law and women's subjectivities. Secondly, and related, 'grand theory', such as liberalism and also feminist 'grand theory', for example, that of legal scholar Catharine MacKinnon, has come under closer scrutiny. Thirdly, the CLS distrust of legal rights has come under criticism from feminist scholars for whom the concept of rights, and the struggle for the achievement of equal legal rights for women in society, has played a central role in the quest for gender equality.

FEMINISM, POSTMODERNISM AND CRITICAL LEGAL STUDIES

It is with the critique of essentialism, and the appeal for an all-embracing feminist jurisprudence, that the demands for diversity and inclusion arise.

---

[44] Gordon, R, 'New developments in legal theory', in Kairys, D (ed), *The Politics of Law: A Progressive Critique,* 1982, New York: Pantheon.
[45] Kennedy, D, 'Legal education as training for hierarchy', in Kairys, *ibid*, .
[46] *Op cit*, Morrison, fn 9, p 460.
[47] *Ibid*, Gordon.

Thus, any theory – whether it be liberal, cultural, Marxist-socialist or radical – which fails to attend to the diversity of women's reality falls under attack.

The history of jurisprudence as a mainstream discipline within the academy has advanced through the certainties of positivism which unsettled natural law thought and asserted rationality, objectivity and order into legal theory. In its turn, positivism was to be unsettled in the 1920s and 1930s, particularly in the United States of America, by the school of legal realism. Legal realists assert, in essence, that a closed system of legal theory, one which excludes the practice of law, the *reality* of law, cannot be sustained. Instead the focus of inquiry must shift to encompass the work of the courts; an analysis of legal judgments; the problems in the evaluation of both facts and the legal reasoning employed to reach decisions. Early perceptions concerning the cultural origins of law, and law's dependency on culture, expanded further the boundaries of understanding about the complex relationship between society and law.[48] The developing sociology of law and sociological jurisprudence, evolving out of this realist movement, further challenged positivist assumptions about law as a discrete, autonomous discipline. However, conventional legal theory has maintained a tenacious hold on presenting law as a discrete autonomous theoretical domain. Hart's *The Concept of Law*,[49] Rawls's *A Theory of Justice*,[50] and Ronald Dworkin's *Law's Empire*[51] reside firmly within modernist thought, as does liberal feminism, difference feminism, Marxist-socialist feminism and radical feminism.

The charge put forward by critics is that the predominant modernist feminist legal thought, particularly of the 1980s, and in the United States of America, was propounded by white, educated and privileged, academics whose backgrounds and experience were ethnically and culturally limited. This is the accusation of feminist 'essentialism' or 'reductionism'.

In *Inessential Woman: Problems of Exclusion in Feminist Thought*,[52] Elizabeth Spelman[53] subjects feminist writing to critical analysis, arguing that from the time of Plato and Aristotle through to contemporary feminist writers, too many assumptions have been made about the nature of women which have resulted in the virtual exclusion of women oppressed by other forces such as class and race. Spelman's thesis centres on women's diversity and the difficulties in extrapolating from one woman to all women in the creation of a

---

[48] See, eg, Ehrlich, E, *The Fundamental Principles of the Sociology of Law* (1936), 1975: New York: Arno Press; Sumner, W, *Folkways* (1906), 1940, Boston, Mass: Ginn.
[49] Hart, HLA, *The Concept of Law*, 1961, Oxford: OUP.
[50] Rawls, J, *A Theory of Justice*, 1972, Oxford: OUP.
[51] Dworkin, R, *Law's Empire*, 1986, London: Fontana.
[52] Spelman, E, *Inessential Woman: Problems of Exclusion in Feminist Thought*, 1990, London: The Women's Press.
[53] At the time of writing, Associate Professor of Philosophy, Smith College, Massachusetts.

satisfactorily coherent feminist theory. In an insightful, pithy passage, Spelman observes that:

> ... essentialism invites me to take what I understand to be true of me 'as a woman' for some golden nugget of womanness all women have as women; and it makes the participation of other women inessential to the production of the story. How lovely: the many turn out to be one, and the one that they are is me.[54]

The question which arises from this perspective, is whether there can be developed a feminist jurisprudence which is all-inclusive of all women, or whether – if gender is not the sole force of oppression in society, but rather one of many – gender can legitimately continue to be used as a foundation for feminist theory. Elizabeth Spelman, among others, argues not. For her, gender is but one basis for the oppression of women in society. For privileged, white, middle-class women, gender may be the only basis for oppression. For other women, however, the issue is less clear-cut. Can a white, middle-class professional woman, share the same concerns about her position in society, about the forces which dictate that position, as a middle-class woman of colour, or a poor, white or black woman, or a Muslim woman living in traditional society? For any woman to assume that merely because 'I am a woman I am entitled to speak for all women' suggests both arrogance and naiveté about the forces which determine most other women's lives. For a particular individual may not be oppressed by one particular factor such as gender, race, or by class, or by religion, or by male constructions of cultural norms which have a particular bearing on particular women. An individual may alternatively be oppressed by a combination of one or more factors.

Accordingly, from this perspective it is not possible for any individual to 'know', trapped in his or her own particular characteristics/psyche/consciousness, the discrimination or oppression from which another woman with differing characteristics suffers. However much this discrimination may be understood intellectually, however much reading and research is undertaken, a person cannot '*know*' precisely what another, different, woman experiences. Part of the postmodern agenda is to deconstruct the concept of 'woman' and 'gender' and to provide a theoretical perspective, reconstructed with a critical awareness of the danger of conceptual generalisation.

In Spelman's view, what is needed is not so much an abandonment of theorising about the position of women, all woman, vis à vis men, but rather an opening up of the debate in order that the many and different voices of women are all heard. From this perspective there is an overwhelming need to recognise the differences between women, and when theorising to make it clear from which standpoint the author is speaking, in order to avoid the problem of appearing to assume that 'I am all women'. Only by opening up

---

[54] *Op cit*, Spelman, fn 52, p 159.

the debate further, and making feminist jurisprudence truly inclusive of all women's concerns, will the feminist endeavour develop in a manner which avoids Spelman's charge of 'feminist ethnocentrism'.

Angela Harris[55] shares the concerns about feminist jurisprudence being the preserve of the white, privileged woman, and excluding too many other women's concerns. In 'Race and essentialism in feminist legal theory',[56] Angela Harris argues that radical feminist scholars adopt a gender essentialism which not only excludes the voices of women of colour but also in so doing, privileges those women who fall within the characterisation of the 'essential woman'. Harris criticises Catharine MacKinnon's dominance theory for its claim to be a total theory capable of representing all women, irrespective of race, ethnicity, class or sexual orientation. Despite MacKinnon's frequent reference to the needs and interests of woman of colour, Harris accuses MacKinnon of justifying essentialism on the basis that irrespective of particular women's particular situation and characteristics, all women are dominated and subordinated by men, and this is the central organising fact for a total feminist theory. By way of example, Angela Harris cites the differing experiences of white and black women in relation to rape. MacKinnon defines the rape experience as being 'a strange man knowing a woman does not want sex and going ahead anyway'. For Harris, this is a white woman's account of rape which ignores the complexities of rape for women of colour. The historical experience of women of colour was rape by a white employer; during slavery, the rape of a black woman was not even considered a crime, and after the Civil War the law was rarely used to protect women of colour. Furthermore, the charge of rape against a black man was often used by whites as an excuse for a lynching.[57] Thus, rape for women of colour represents more than forced sex by a stranger; to understand rape from the perspective of women of colour is to understand also the oppression through colour expressed in slavery and the master/slave relationship. Angela Harris calls for a movement beyond essentialism, for the abandonment of 'grand theorising' about women's oppression as women, and women 'as victim', and argues for positive action to understand the differences between women, to root out and overcome discriminations and to build a confident future for all women.

Professor Patricia Williams[58] has also written of the need to recognise and accommodate the experiences of women of colour within feminist theory. In

---

[55] Professor of Law, University of California at Berkeley.

[56] Harris, A, 'Race and essentialism in feminist legal theory' (1990) 42 Stanford L Rev 581 (see *Sourcebook*, p 249).

[57] See, also, Smith, V, 'Split affinities: the case of interracial rape', in Hirsch, M and Fox Keller, E (eds), *Conflicts in Feminism*, 1990, London: Routledge.

[58] At the time of writing, Associate Professor of Law, University of Wisconsin.

'The pain of word bondage',[59] Williams describes the difficulties faced by black women in their relationships with white people, and writes of the stereotypical construction of black women as 'unreliable, untrustworthy, hostile, angry, powerless, irrational and probably destitute'.[60] Because of this perceived reaction, Patricia Williams argues against both essentialism and against critical legal theorists, that legal rights are of particular significance to people of colour. Whereas for her white, male colleague renting an apartment, informality and trust regulated the transaction, for her there was a real need for a binding legal contract. For her white male colleague, any insistence of formality would damage the relationship between himself and the lessor by introducing distrust, but for Williams, lacking the commonality of a shared background with the lessor, formality represented the protection of legal rights without which she would have experienced insecurity. These two very differing examples – the black experience of rape and the entering into of contractual relations – show the extent to which white, middle-class essentialism inevitably fails to recognise the very differing histories, experiences and perceptions of women of colour.

In 'Race, reform and retrenchment: transformation and legitimation in anti-discrimination law',[61] Kimberlé Crenshaw identifies the binary opposites of language which have typically been employed to define black identity. First, white is privileged over black: black is the negative and subordinate image of white. Secondly, racist ideology employs traditional stereotypical images of people of colour. Accordingly, Crenshaw argues, white images are those of industriousness, intelligence, moral, knowledgeable, responsible, etc, whereas the opposite, negative and subordinate black images are lazy, unintelligent, immoral, ignorant, shiftless etc. Historically, American society regarded people of colour as 'the other', the 'subordinate' and reinforced this otherness – this exclusion – through both what Crenshaw labels 'symbolic' and 'material' forms. Symbolic subordination was effected through 'the formal denial of social and political equality to all people of colour, regardless of their accomplishments', while material subordination was reinforced by segregation and 'other forms of social exclusion'. American history is thus characterised as privileging white identity at the expense of people of colour. Formal equality for Afro-Americans was secured through the rhetoric of rights – rights consciousness and the language of rights was crucial in the struggles for formal equality. However, Crenshaw argues, formal equality is not enough, and itself masks the continuing subordination of people of colour. Where law can present itself as a rational and equal ordering of society, the real remaining inequalities are hidden. Legal reforms have provided 'an ideological framework that makes the present conditions facing underclass

---

[59] From *The Alchemy of Race and Rights*, 1991, Cambridge, Mass: Harvard UP, p 146.
[60] *Ibid*, Williams, p 147.
[61] Crenshaw, K, 'Race, reform and retrenchment: transformation and legitimation in anti-discrimination law' (1988) 101 Harv L Rev 1331.

blacks appear fair and reasonable'. Paradoxically, the achievement of rights which has enabled some people of colour to secure real equality has also, Crenshaw writes, fragmented the solidarity among black people. What is called for is the development of an understanding of the oppositional black 'subordinate Other', and the struggle to defeat 'Otherness' in the quest for meaningful equality.

Both similar and different objections to modernist feminist theory come from lesbian scholars. Two charges are pertinent here. The first is essentialism as discussed above. The second charge is that radical dominance theory, fails to accommodate lesbian women who, whatever oppression they may experience, are not oppressed by men. Patricia Cain[62] has taken heterosexual feminism to task. In 'Feminist jurisprudence: grounding the theories',[63] Cain argues that a feminist theory cannot successfully be built unless and until feminism becomes inclusive of all women's voices. Cain argues that radical feminist theory, while insisting on the importance of feminist method (listening to the voices of real women) and whilst making passing reference to the differences among women, is a theory of heterosexual relations which relegates lesbian women to the margins by treating them as either irrelevant to the core of dominance theory, or alternatively suggesting that even though lesbian women do not directly experience male dominance in their relationships, they nevertheless remain in a world constructed on the basis of male dominance. This represents, according to Cain, a failure to listen to the voices of lesbian women, in the same way that radical (and other) feminism has allegedly failed to listen to the voices of those oppressed by race and class.

Given these debates within feminist theory, centred on sameness/difference or dominance, there remains the central question of the way forward for feminist jurisprudence. On the one hand, 'sameness' feminists would seek the assimilation of women within the male world: remove the remaining obstacles to full equality; allow women their rightful place alongside men. On the other hand, difference feminists seek women's distinctive 'voice'. Conversely, if social relations are – as MacKinnon argues – constructed on the basis of dominance (by men) and submission (of women), then the liberal assimilationist ideal is no more than an ideal: an unrealisable goal – only apparently realisable whilst in reality unattainable without a fundamental reordering of gender relations. Further, the charges of essentialism – quite aside from the debate about 'sameness' and 'difference' – appear to undermine the feminist quest. There is thus an apparently unfathomable conundrum which offers no clear future direction for a coherent feminist jurisprudence. This uncomfortable suspicion, however, is one entirely consistent with the postmodern condition.

---

[62] Professor of Law, University of Texas.
[63] Cain, P, 'Feminist jurisprudence: grounding the theories' (1989) Women's LJ 191. (See *Sourcebook*, pp 256–67.)

POSTMODERN FEMINIST JURISPRUDENCE

Postmodern legal thought emphasises critique and seeks to unravel the uncertainties, irrationalities and diversities of law. The values of the Enlightenment which inform modern(ist) thought – liberalism, rationality, equality and freedom – fall under scrutiny. Thus the very foundations of traditional, modern(ist) legal thought are challenged. Theories about law, whether they be conventional, male, jurisprudential theories, or more recent feminist theorising about law, are critiqued for portraying legal theory as 'closure'.[64] Postmodernist theorists seek to explode the previously foreclosed boundaries of law.

The feminist reaction to postmodernism and poststructuralism is both positive and negative, alternatively viewed as offering new techniques for analysis of concepts, law and legal systems or viewed as a danger to the potentiality of feminist theory as coherence. The concept of essentialism, discussed above, is a manifestation of postmodern feminist thought. Deconstruction, moreover, located originally primarily in the postmodern field of linguistics, becomes an accessible tool for the analysis of law and legal theory.

The construction of gender

As understood in modern(ist) thought, gender is a socially constructed identity. This identity fixes the subject of law. Gender constructs reside within the linguistic system of binary opposites: man/woman; Subject/Other. As Luce Irigaray's analysis has shown, psychoanalytic theory is premised on gender, and in its modernist theorising about the origins of gender, the focus is male. Using Lacanian theory, but moving beyond it, Irigaray argues that this traditional male psychoanalytical theorising, in privileging the male, constructs woman as Other. The boy's identity with his mother, his dependency on the mother, must be rejected if he is to assume his gender-assigned role as a male. This Irigaray terms 'matricide': the mother is destroyed in order to free the boy-child to develop 'as a man'. In order for the woman to become a Subject (as opposed to the Other, or object), to have a voice, she must learn to speak (as) woman; develop her own language which can then be admitted to, accommodated within, the male-dominant language. Only when women's different voices are heard, will women be recognised as having subjectivity, and thus become, as Irigaray puts it, 'the other of the other', rather than the 'Other of the same'.

---

[64] See Norrie, A (ed), *Closure or Critique: New Directions in Legal Theory,* 1993, Edinburgh: Edinburgh UP.

As has been seen, postmodernism constitutes an unsettling of fixities, and a denial of the determinacy of concepts. Postmodernism challenges the traditional modes of thought which form the foundation of theory, whether philosophical, linguistic or legal. Postmodernism seeks explanation and critiques which are not dependent upon former theoretical foundations. Neither philosophy nor linguistics – as understood in modern(ist) terms – nor even theory itself, can avoid the postmodern deconstructive process. Thus, the very terms gender and woman come under scrutiny, as does theorising which focuses on any particular concept. The very existence of, or possibility of, a feminist jurisprudence appears threatened. The postmodern analysis seeks to collapse the meaning attributed to 'gender', 'woman', 'man' – to render gender a non-viable linguistic construct on which to found theories about society and law. For modernist feminism, gender has proved an invaluable construct in unravelling law's maleness and exclusion. In modernist thought, gender has been formulated as a culturally and socially induced construct into which to situate women and men. There is a coherence in the term 'woman', which is readily comprehensible, and which forms an organising focus for theorising about women and as a political tool with which to press for legal and social equality. If that coherence is lost – if 'woman', along with gender, is deconstructed – it becomes possible to argue, as does French psychoanalyst and poststructuralist theorist Julia Kristeva,[65] that woman cannot be said 'to exist'.[66]

The feminist reaction to postmodern thought has accordingly been ambivalent. Feminism, as a political enterprise, requires organising concepts. Woman and gender provided that focus which facilitates the campaign for equality, non-discrimination and a non-patriarchal society. Postmodernism in challenging the use of any meta-narrative organised around a single, unifying concept, and thus feminist modernist theory, unsettles former certainties. As women have started to find a voice, to analyse their subjectivities and demand equal incorporation into life, politics and law, postmodernism steps in the undermine the feminist quest. In Susan Bordo's view, postmodernism not only distracts feminists from pursuing 'crucial feminist concerns' but also denies the legitimacy of feminist theorising.[67]

While postmodernism and poststructuralism unsettle the certainties of modernity, and criticise theory based on essential organising foci, such as

---

[65] Kristeva, a contemporary of Luce Irigaray, also analyses the subject from a psychoanalytic and linguistic standpoint. Her deconstruction of language, however, leads to a very different conclusion from that of Irigaray. Rather than women needing a distinctive voice and subjectivity, Kristeva argues that there is no specifically feminine voice. See Moi, T (ed), *French Feminist Thought: A Reader*, 1987, Oxford: Blackwells, Chapter 5.

[66] Kristeva, J, 'Woman can never be defined', in Marks, E and de Courtivron, I (eds), *New French Feminism*, 1984, New York: Schocken.

[67] See Bordo, S, 'Feminism postmodernism and gender-scepticism', in Nicholson, L (ed), *Feminism/Postmodernism*, 1990, London: Routledge, p 136.

woman, or gender, or even feminism itself, the postmodern approach also offers new insights and suggests new directions for feminist jurisprudence. The challenge to some forms of modernist feminism, based on its essentialism – its assumptions about the nature of women – discussed above, compels feminist theorising to recognise its own self-imposed boundaries: its closure. 'Women' are not necessarily white, heterosexual, middle-class. While the essentialist 'woman' facilitates discourses about women's (inferior) status in relation to men's (superior) status, it also masks characteristics of disparate women's characteristics and lives. Women, vis à vis men, have traditionally been constructed as the inferior half of the binary opposition. Nevertheless, this perception, whilst credible at one level, ignores the impact of culture, race, class, age and sexual orientation. Status is culturally dependent: women's status cannot be universalised but must be set within its cultural and historical context – both time and place are essential features in the analysis of women's condition. Feminist theory which fails to identify the differences between women, and the impact which those differences have on women's lives, fails to be inclusive. Thus scepticism with gender may be helpful in so far as it obliges feminist scholarship to 'demote' gender as an organising concept, in so far as it has been the *dominant* concept in feminist modernist theory, and to set gender alongside crucial other factors such as race, class, age, sexual orientation, the local and specific (as opposed to universalising and general), and so forth.[68] Thus a postmodern feminism must focus on the specificities of women's lives, rather than assuming the commonality of all women's lives. Feminist pluralism must replace feminist modernism.

Nonetheless, such challenges entail their own difficulties. Whereas gender as a central, unifying construct, may fail to encompass alternative realities of women's lives, gender also remains the basis on which women can challenge the dominant male discourse. As has been said before, gender represents a simple (too simple?) categorisation for the political pursuit of women's equality. Some political issues *are* specifically issues of gender – abortion, childbirth for example – and whilst, as will be discussed in Chapter 10, issues of race and class do affect the manner in which abortion and childbirth are handled by law and medical practice, these issues are most appropriately dealt with as gender-issues; with gender as the principal organising construct, and race and class as subordinate organising constructs. Alternatively expressed, abortion rights and childbirth management are issues which potentially affect *all* women; additionally *some* women will be affected in particular ways because of their race or class. Thus there is a necessity to identify, and recognise, that there are two, probably more, levels at which women's issues may be conceptualised and organised.

---

[68] See, in particular, Fraser, N and Nicholson, L, 'Social criticism without philosophy', in Nicholson, *op cit*, fn 67, Chapter 1.

Postmodernism is troubling to a feminist perspective in a different regard. Postmodernism smacks of intellectual and theoretical elitism. To those who struggle to achieve equality in the harsh reality of life and law, and those who seek to theorise the causes of the inequality handed down by male-constructed and male-dominated history, the intellectual postmodern theorising of white, privileged men in industrial societies which denies the disadvantaged a theoretical legitimacy – on theoretical grounds – is problematic. Feminist goals are both practical and political. To deny legitimacy to theoretical concerns located in gender on the basis that the theoretical premises are inadequate is to deny or delegitimate – in the interests of those who have – the aspirations of those who traditionally have not, and must fight to have. While society and law remain gendered, while women are classified as women with all the attendant inequalities, whatever merits the tools of analysis offered by postmodernism are for feminist analysis, feminists should resist the overarching prescription of postmodernism in so far as it proscribes the centrality of organising concepts. Sceptical postmodernism invites a loss of direction, of identity, with the potential for undermining feminist goals. Relativism and nihilism loom on the horizon.

On the other hand, feminist jurisprudence can develop in a more radically and constructively self-conscious manner by utilising the tools of postmodernism/poststructuralism. While postmodern scholarship invites/demands the collapsing of organising concepts, the rigorous logic of postmodern deconstruction must be utilised in a constructive manner by feminist scholars in the task of unearthing the wiring of patriarchy. At the same time, the merits of the postmodernist deconstructive exercise must be weighed in the balance against the social and political, legal, *practical,* goals of feminist jurisprudence. The scepticism of black feminist author and scholar bell hooks, which echoes that of Jane Flax[69, 70] must be borne in mind. As bell hooks asks:

> Should we not be suspicious of postmodern critiques of the 'subject' when they surface at a historical moment when many subjugated people feel themselves coming to voice for the first time?[71]

Bordo echoes this perception when she asks: 'Do we want to delegitimate *a priori* the exploration of experiential continuity and structural common ground among women?'[72]

---

[69] See Flax, J, 'Postmodernism and gender relations in feminist theory', in Nicholson, *op cit*, fn 67, p 39.

[70] See, also, Hartsock, N, 'Rethinking modernism: minority vs majority theories' (1987) 7 Cultural Critique 187.

[71] hooks, b, 'Postmodern blackness', in *Yearning: Race, Gender, and Cultural Politics*, 1991, Boston: South End, repr in Anderson, *op cit*, fn 38, p 117.

[72] *Op cit*, Anderson, fn 38, p 142.

Postmodernism and Critical Legal Studies

It has been seen that from a postmodernist/poststructuralist perspective, all forms of theorising which focus on a unifying, totalising concept, are anathema. Thus, as a project, feminist jurisprudence, focusing on women and women's inferiority under and before the law, as theory – on this logic – is problematic.[73] However, such a conclusion need not follow. Feminist jurisprudence over the past decade at least has absorbed some of the strictures of postmodernism and used them to its advantage. Recognising the limitations of 'grand theory' which makes essentialist assumptions about women without recognising the diversity among and between women, has given way to more specific analyses of women's conditions and situations. Generality has given way to specificity, the universal has given way to locality and individuality.

However, there are limits to the postmodern method which feminist jurisprudence should recognise if it is to retain its power to critique social and legal structures which inhibit the potential for women's real equality in society. While postmodernism may decry universalising theory which is monocausal, which demands that theory centred on single concepts should be abandoned, feminists should be wary of the siren call to abandon gender as an organising concept, a *foundational concept* upon which to theorise. Whatever the deconstructionist and philosophical logic of collapsing concepts into themselves, thereby revealing their meaninglessness in theory, gender is too important a conceptual tool for feminists to abandon. Abandoning gender as an organising concept, would lead to the nihilism implicit in much postmodern and Critical Legal Studies thought. Throwing the baby – woman – out with the bathwater – postmodernism and CLS – may be a strategy which would be welcome to anti-feminists, of whom there remain many, but not to the cause of women's equality: that is a political and legal objective, not a 'mere' matter of philosophical speculation on the limits of meta-narratives, and their destruction, from a postmodern/poststructuralist/deconstructive/CLS perspective. As Mary Joe Frug has written:

> Despite the healthy, self-serving respect I have for the influence of legal scholarship and for the role of law as a significant cultural factor (among many) that contributes to the production of femininity, I think 'women' cannot be eliminated from our lexicon very quickly.[74]

Thus, feminist jurisprudence must continue to use postmodernism's deconstructive techniques, while avoiding postmodernism's elitist,

---

[73] See Harding, S, *The Science Question in Feminism*, 1986, New York: Cornell UP; see, also, hooks, b, *Feminist Theory: From Margin to Center*, 1984, Boston: South End.

[74] Frug, M, *Postmodern Legal Feminism*, 1992, London: Routledge, Chapman and Hall, p 131. Mary Joe Frug, formerly Professor of Law at the New England School of Law, was murdered in April 1991. *Postmodern Legal Feminism* was published posthumously.

exclusionary, male and obscurantist language,[75] to analyse and theorise inequalities based on gender, and the complexities within gender analysis. But arguments over *method* must not be destructive of arguments over *substance*. To remain overly concerned with essentialism is to court the danger of losing sight of the feminist quest for woman's equality. As Susan Bordo has written:

> The programmatic appropriation of poststructuralist insight ... in shifting the focus of crucial feminist concerns about the representation of cultural diversity from practical contexts to questions of adequate theory, is highly problematic for feminism.[76]

Postmodernism/poststructuralism and Critical Legal Studies: unravelling law's claim to rationality and objectivity

Consistent with the demands of postmodernism and CLS, feminist scholars have been focusing on the claims made by traditional legal theory to the supposed rationality, logic, objectivity and coherence of law and legal systems.[77] As seen above, positivism perpetuates the mystification of law and the idea that legal rules and principles can satisfactorily be explained in a structural/scientific manner. As emphasised by sociological jurisprudence and CLS, however, there is much evidence which suggests that law is not, either in terms of judicial decisions or in legislation, imbued with these characteristics.

To illustrate by way of concrete example, under the English Children Act 1989, in relation to the private law, section 1 provides that the welfare of the child shall be paramount in any consideration relating to the education and upbringing of the child. Section 1 also provides that where conflict exists between adults with parental responsibility for the child, or an adult with a substantial interest in any particular decision sufficient to entitle that person to *locus standi*, the court shall not make any order unless making an order is better than making no order at all. Thus, within one section of the Act, we find two potentially competing principles at work: the 'welfare of the child', and the 'no order' principle, thus allowing elements of flexibility and discretion into the decision making process.

---

[75] As Walter Truett Anderson has remarked, 'The postmodern era has given the world some really good ideas and some really bad writing'. See the entertaining and irreverent essay by Katz, S, 'How to speak and write postmodern', in Anderson, *op cit*, fn 38.
[76] *Op cit*, Bordo, fn 67, Chapter 6, p 136.
[77] See, eg, *op cit*, Smart, fn 42; *op cit*, Olsen, fn 43. (See *Sourcebook*, p 342.)

In Frances Olsen's analysis,[78] there exist three potential challenges which may be launched against law's rationality. The dualistic structure of thought, which identifies a linguistic system of binary opposites (male/female, culture/nature, rational/irrational, active/passive, power/sensitivity, objective/subjective, etc), identifies the hierarchically superior former half of the dualisms with maleness, the latter with femininity and women. Thus men are rational, active, powerful, objective, rational and so on. As is law, or so is law said to be. Women, on the other hand, are imbued, under this dualistic system, which is a sexualised system, with all the characteristics which fall on the hierarchically inferior side of the dualism: women are irrational, passive, emotional, sensitive, subjective. One approach is to argue that contrary to male ascriptions as to the characteristics of women, women have been wrongly labelled: women can be rational, objective, active, unemotional and so forth. An alternative strategy is to reject the hierarchical nature of the dualisms, and to assert equality for women. From this perspective, it can be argued that even if women are correctly identified with differing characteristics from men, women nevertheless are equal with men: there is no hierarchical ordering of the dualisms, they co-exist. Far from women being viewed as subordinate to men, on the basis of the dualisms, women's unique characteristics entitle them to equality with men. The third strategy involves a rejection of the 'sexualisation and hierarchisation of the dualisms'.[79]

Olsen argues that the sexualisation of law which results in women's categorisation, and relative inferiority, needs to be dismantled. So too must the ascription of particular kinds of law – such as *par excellence*, family law – as 'feminine', and hence irrational etc, whereas commercial law, is traditionally conceived as rational, 'male'. Such classification of legal subjects results in what Olsen terms 'law's irrational, subjective ghettos'. Law is not, Olsen argues, capable of being so rigidly classified: in every aspect of legal regulation, there exist examples of rationality and irrationality. One of the tasks of feminist critical theorists is to break down the traditional classifications which work against women's interests. To see law as inherently rational etc, and hence male, is an historical error. Law is neither male nor female, but since it has traditionally and almost exclusively been practised by men, the identification of law with male qualities is an understandable, but false and damaging, feature of legal analysis which must be eradicated.

As has been discussed, where feminism differs from other critical legal theorists is in the centrality of gender as an organising concept. Only through incorporating women's voices, and women's experience into legal theory and critical theorising about law will gender-based inequality and discrimination

---

[78] See *op cit*, Olsen, fn 43.
[79] *Op cit*, Olsen, fn 43.

be eradicated. This takes us back to the importance of feminist legal method.[80] Feminist legal methods, it will be recalled, include consciousness raising: the retelling of women's experience, a restatement of women's point of view, a demand that women's voices and experience be heard in and by the law.

Feminism differs also from other critical theory in its origins. While CLS, as a derivative of postmodern thought, grew out of a dissatisfaction with legal theory and legal education, critical feminist theory grew out of women's experience of inequality and lack of representation, and women's exclusion from the law. Feminism is thus a political enterprise, grounded in women's experience of gender inequality. With gender as a central organising focus comes the problem caused by the diversity of women, and charges of essentialism levelled at feminist theory. Without reworking the concept of essentialism, it is necessary at least to recall that feminist theory has been criticised on the basis that the concept of 'woman' suggests a homogeneity, a sameness, of all women which excludes women's diversity. Age, class, culture and race all contribute to *differing forms* and experience of discrimination and inequality. Only when these factors are also brought adequately into focus will feminism be able to claim to be representative of women and women's interests. However, while there is much merit in the demand that feminist scholarship be truly inclusive of all women's experience and interests, it should be remembered that the ascription 'woman' is a powerful organising concept: arguing that different women experience discrimination and inequality differently does not mean that all women, irrespective of their similarities or differences, do not suffer inequality and discrimination on the basis of gender alone.

FEMINISM AND THE CLS DISTRUST OF RIGHTS

For many CLS scholars, legal rights build defensive barriers around individuals which inhibit the building of a society constructed on co-operative communitarian foundations. Rights, from this perspective, emphasise individuality, defensiveness and lack of trust. From a feminist perspective, however, the gaining of legal rights has played a central role in the quest for the elimination of discrimination on the basis of gender. The struggle for the franchise, the struggle for equal rights between mothers and fathers over children, the struggle for the right to equal and further education, the struggle for entry on equal terms into the professions, the right to equal pay and equal conditions of work, the campaign for legal recognition and regulation of domestic violence, the removal of a husband's immunity from the law of rape,

---

[80] Discussed in Chapter 1.

the establishment of the offence of sexual harassment, of stalking, all testify to the centrality of rights in the demand for equality for women.

Legal scholars who argue against rights, albeit on the altruistic and idealistic basis that rights undermine community, argue from a privileged male perspective. While it may be acknowledged that law alone cannot produce social change, and that the impact of law as a force for social change is difficult, if not impossible, to measure, rights have played and continue to play an essential role for women in the movement for equality. It may also be argued that the existence of *formal rights* alone does not guarantee that the *substantive equality* provided for will in practice be brought about. To provide legal guarantees against sexual discrimination in recruitment laws, does not secure a guarantee that in practice a prospective employer may reject a female applicant on other grounds: qualifications, unsuitability, etc. To prove in a court of law that a rejection was in fact based on grounds of gender would, for most, be both prohibitively expensive and uncertain in outcome. Moreover, legal systems characterised by white, middle-class, privileged judges does little to convince applicants from alternative backgrounds that their claim would be met with an impartial and fair interpretation, let alone a successful outcome.

Notwithstanding the indeterminacy of rights, legal rights provide an authoritative platform from which to press for greater equality and control. In the United States of America, rights discourse takes on a particular resonance. The written Constitution guaranteeing fundamental rights and freedoms, provides a sound foundation for the securing of equal rights. Thus, for example, the right to privacy has been employed to promote the right of women to control their reproductive lives.[81] The right to equality under the law provides a platform for the campaign against the sexual harassment of women.[82] The right to the equal protection of the law was also instrumental in removing the discriminatory barriers of racial segregation and discrimination.[83] Conversely, however, where rights claimed by women conflict with other rights secured under the Constitution, little progress may be made. An example of this alternative outcome lies in the campaign spearheaded by Catharine MacKinnon and Andrea Dworkin to provide civil remedies for the harm caused by pornographic representations of women. As will be seen in Chapter 12, while the Dworkin/MacKinnon Ordinances were adopted in Minneapolis and Indianapolis, they were ultimately to be struck down as infringing the constitutional guarantee of 'freedom of speech'. One set-back for constitutionally guaranteed rights, however, does not diminish the force of rights rhetoric, or the importance of the existence of a constitution

---

[81] On which see Chapter 10.
[82] On which see Chapter 11.
[83] See *Brown v Education Board of Topeka* 349 US 294 (1954).

which provides a frame of reference against which claims of rights may be adjudicated.[84]

Critical legal scholars overemphasise the 'downside' of rights. Not only is the overemphasis wrong from a feminist perspective, but it is also misleading. Legal rights are not just individualistic: legal rights for women have been secured for all women – not just individual plaintiffs. Rights as class rights, as collective rights for subordinate groups in society, are more important even than individual rights. As Kimberlé Crenshaw has written, '[T]he Critics' product is of limited utility to blacks in its present form. The implications for blacks of trashing liberal legal ideology are troubling, even though it may be proper to assail belief structures that obscure liberating possibilities'.[85]

DECONSTRUCTING THE SUBJECT OF LAW[86]

> The question of 'the subject' is crucial for politics, and for feminist politics in particular, because juridical subjects are invariably produced through certain exclusionary practices that do not 'show' once the juridical structure of politics has been established.[87]

> The problem of the subject is that it has never been part of the story. Until now.[88]

The application of postmodern deconstructive techniques to the identity of law's subject has become a fruitful and vibrant site of feminist analysis. The formerly accepted constructions of sex and gender as the appropriate binary pairing in which the biological attributes of women have been downgraded in favour of the social construction of the human subject of law as the principal focus for analysis. This process has been prompted by several perceptions. First, while prioritising gender over sex avoided the tendency to perpetuate women's inequality through forms of biological essentialism, gender itself has been critiqued for its essentialist portrayal of women in legal theory as uniformly heterosexual, white and middle-class. Second, feminist theory which is cast in the mould of 'grand theory', whether it be labelled dominance theory or cultural feminism, when subjected to critique from alternative

---

[84] The position under an unwritten constitution, such as that of the United Kingdom, deprives citizens of this point of reference. The constitutional differences between the USA and the United Kingdom, above all, explain the relatively muted feminist campaigns in the latter country.

[85] *Op cit*, Crenshaw, fn 61.

[86] For in-depth analyses, see Naffine, N and Owens, R (eds), *Sexing the Subject of Law*, 1997, London: LBS Information Services/Sweet & Maxwell.

[87] Butler, J, *Gender Trouble: Feminism and the Subversion of Identity*, 1990, New York: Routledge, p 2.

[88] Schlag, P, 'The problem of the subject' (1991) 69 Texas L Rev 1627.

perspectives, revealed its inherent weaknesses. Either grand theory 'said too much' about women's inequality by positing single causal explanations, or it 'said too little' by ignoring or denying alternative perspectives. The postmodern challenge to the meta-narrative has forced postmodern feminism to re-evaluate its methods and objectives in order to avoid the alleged implicit dangers of universalising theory. Furthermore, the conceptualisation of biological sex – male and female – and culturally-constructed gender – men and women – fails to mirror the diversity of human experience, and privileges the conventionally accepted pairings. Thus 'men' are heterosexual, 'masculine', 'virile', rational and objective; 'women' are heterosexual, feminine, frail, emotional and subjective. Law, based on this conventional stereotype, reflects all that is 'male', and little that is 'female', other than calculating, when relevant, the extent to which women do not reach the 'male' standards of law. Not only is this discrimination in law, but it also represents a false conceptualisation of both men and women. The conceptualisation of the subject of law in binary manner fails to recognise the diversity of the subject – irrespective of maleness or femaleness. Men are not all rational, unemotional, objective. Women are not all emotional, irrational and frail. By characterising law's subject as if it were an autonomous, disembodied individual – the conventional privileging of mind over body – law fails also to recognise the interconnectedness of human beings, their relatedness and the manner in which their embodiment interacts with the manner in which the subject is socially constructed. From a postmodern feminist perspective, law is thus premised on overly narrow perceptions of sex and gender which, through deconstruction, can – without positing a new essentialism in place of the old – reveal the multiplicity and diversity of the subject of law, and thus debunk law's claims to objectivity and rationality, and the notion of the universalised, masculine, subject of law.

The analysis of the legal subject has thus become a central focus of attention. From the time of Descartes, through to contemporary liberal theory, the subject of law is portrayed as the autonomous, rational, gender-neutral individual. In conventional (masculine) jurisprudence, law is theorised consistently as a rational gender-neutral ordering of human conduct. Accordingly, law and the subject of law, are presented in terms which mask the gendered reality of law and individual subjects. When the focus shifts from the analysis of law to the analysis of the subject and the concept of subjectivity, it becomes possible to broaden theory to expose the reality of individual lives, without forcing the subjects of law into the conceptual straightjacket represented by concepts of sex and gender. As many feminists have long argued neither sex nor gender are adequate constructions for reflecting the multiplicity of human realities. The concept of sex not only implies biological determinism, but also fails, in its compartmentalisation of man/woman, adequately to reflect the diversity of human sexual life. Gender fails also in this regard by implying universal heterosexuality, and in reifying the conventional social attributes of maleness and femaleness. Highlighting subjectivity through deconstructing sex and gender, leads not to nihilism and emptiness, but to a rigorous analysis which opens up spaces in which all subjects of law can find accommodation – irrespective of their individual sex or gender orientation.

The ongoing analysis of the legal subject also entails the recognition and analysis of the manner in which the law fixes legal subjects with identities which are universalising and false. The 'reasonable man' of the common law is perhaps the most obvious of law's falsehoods. The reasonable man of law is characterised as being rational and objective, thus privileging the mind over emotion, and suggesting that reasonableness is a male, and not female, trait. With the masculine identified with the rational, the feminine is cast in the mould of rationality's subordinate, inferior binary opposite – irrationality and emotionality. For feminist analysis, both the law of provocation and rape, discussed in Chapter 11, have provided fertile areas for research in exposing law's gendered nature. As has been well documented, the law of provocation when applied to women who kill their violent partners, reveals itself to be steeped in masculinity: the law is premised on two individuals of roughly equivalent physical strength, one of whom provokes an immediate and sudden loss of control in the other, who responds instantly with a degree of force which is deemed reasonable to the provocation which prompted the reaction. Women, particularly women who have been victims of violence in domestic relationships, do not, as research into the psychological effects of domestic violence which leads to battered woman syndrome, testifies, respond in this fashion: rather they bide their time until it is safe to react. The law of provocation, constructed in its male-gendered fashion, thus cannot accommodate women's subjectivity. The English law of rape is equally problematic in its gendering. As will be seen, the law of rape centres not on the fact of unlawful, non-consensual sexual intercourse suffered by the victim, nor on the reasonableness of the man's belief as to whether or not the woman consented to sexual intercourse, but on whether the man – reasonably or not – actually believed that the woman was consenting. Thus, in both instances – provocation and rape – the law genders, or 'sexes', the subject of law as male to the exclusion of other identities and subjectivities. The 'abstract' subject of law is masculine, and masculine in the conventional sense: the 'reasonable man' of law is characterised as white, heterosexual and middle-class. Thus viewed, the law is gendered to construct the subject of law in a manner which is exclusionary not only of women but of men who do not share the paradigmatic characteristics of law's preferred subject. The potential for the deconstructive project is well summarised by Margaret Davies:

> When it is widely recognised that the law sexes its subjects, it will no longer be possible to present any subject as an abstract person before the law, meaning that if it is to retain its ideal of equality, the law will have to begin to deal with

its inbuilt prejudices in some way, or at least invent new ways of masking them.[89]

---

[89] Davies, M, 'Taking the inside out', in Naffine and Owens, *op cit*, fn 86, pp 25–27.

PART IV

KEY ISSUES IN FEMINIST JURISPRUDENCE

CHAPTER 10

WOMEN AND MEDICINE

INTRODUCTION

In this chapter, feminist concerns over law, medicine and medical practice are considered. The hallmark of autonomy and integrity of the self is the right to make decisions concerning one's own body, including the right, among others, to regulate one's own fertility. A woman's right to autonomy over decisions relating to her body is circumscribed by culture, law and medical practice. The traditional role of women, defined and reinforced by traditional patriarchal society, lies at the heart of the debate concerning a woman's right to autonomy. As Frances Olsen has written:

> By refusing to grant women autonomy and by protecting them in ways that men are not protected, the State treats women's bodies – and therefore women themselves – as objects. Men are treated differently. Their bodies are regarded as part of them, subject to their free control.[1]

Women's traditional role in child-bearing and nurturing, her *private* role within the *private sphere* of life, continues to exert its historical influence over contemporary matters of medicine and medical practice. Furthermore, women's rights to control over their bodies, especially in relation to issues of fertility, are traditionally viewed as rights which are placed in competition with, if not opposition to, the claims of others: of husbands, partners, children and the yet unborn. The conventional family exerts its control – directly or obliquely – over a woman's right to determine her own destiny. Thus, operating within the context of medical decisions, there exists an interacting web of controls and influences: the family, the State and law; the medical profession; and the traditional conceptualisation of woman as mother and the primary carer in society.

Within this context, the principal issue for consideration is the extent to which law and medical practice respects, or does not respect, women's autonomy. Subsumed beneath this far-ranging enquiry lie a number of further and specific issues for consideration. The availability and safety of means of contraception, the availability of abortion, the management of pregnancy and childbirth, reproductive technology and surrogacy, sterilisation – voluntary and involuntary – and the use of mental health legislation in relation to this

---

[1] Olsen, F, 'Statutory rape: a feminist critique of rights analysis', in Bartlett, KT and Kennedy, R (eds), *Feminist Legal Theory: Readings in Law and Gender*, 1991, Boulder: Westview, pp 306–08.

and other medical treatment, and the forcible treatment of victims of anorexia nervosa are discussed below.

In addition to issues relating to individual autonomy in medical matters, consideration needs to be given to State policies such as population control programmes. The means adopted in the pursuit of population control goals, which undermine the individual's claim to autonomy and respect, are several, although a common element – that of focusing on controlling women's rather than men's reproductive capacity – may be discerned.

Each of the issues considered involves questions of a woman's autonomy, competing individual interests, the interests of the State, the status and role of the medical profession, and most particularly in relation to abortion, a clash of ideologies concerning individual women's rights and the claimed 'rights' of the unborn. What also becomes apparent from a study of the differing aspects of 'women and medicine' is the extent to which different cultural, institutional, legal, political, religious and social factors coalesce to produce a position of inferiority for women as compared with men. This web of interacting factors represents subtle control by the State, judiciary and the medical profession, a further manifestation of the patriarchal ordering of, and hierarchical male power in society. A person's body and his or her sexuality is *par excellence* a site of autonomy and privacy. When autonomy and privacy are taken away or delimited, individuality itself is harmed. For women, sexuality, conception and contraception, pregnancy and childbirth are all central to female identity. As will be seen below, the rise in medical professionalism in the nineteenth century was accompanied by the increasing medicalisation of reproductive issues: that which was once natural and unregulated – reproductive capacity – became increasingly the subject of regulation by predominantly male doctors and surgeons, to the exclusion of women medical practitioners. Pathology entered the natural.[2] Devoid of experience of womanness, male theories about women and their 'conditions' – be it premenstrual tension, pregnancy or the demand for abortion – informed medical practice and law.

The traditional linguistic analysis of binary opposites hold clues to this phenomenon and has great explanatory power in relation to the construction of women by men, and, conversely, of men by men. Male/female; objective/subjective; rational/emotional; responsible/irresponsible; strong/weak: all these binary oppositions come into play in the construction of women. Thus, woman is emotional, irrational, irresponsible, subjective and weak (physically and psychologically). Conversely man, and in this instance the male-dominated medical profession, is rational, responsible, objective and authoritative.

---

[2] Pathology: the branch of medicine dealing with the origins, cause and nature of disease.

Woman's unique reproductive capacity has accorded her 'special status' historically and universally. Woman is ostensibly cherished for her capacity to reproduce. On this male rationale, woman must be protected from the reality and ravages of the public sphere for which she – by virtue of her talent for nurturing and caring – is deemed to be unsuited. Woman must be confined, for her own good, and the good of future generations, in the private sphere, under the care, power and tutelage of, firstly her father, and then her husband. The idealisation of motherhood, the capacity (apparently unique to women) to nurture and care, represents a mask for male power and control; a justification for women's exclusion from the public sphere of government, the professions and other paid employment.

Without reworking the discussion on cultural feminism, the celebration of woman's uniqueness in terms of reproduction and nurture, or of her differing faculties of moral reasoning, tend to reinforce the constructions of women by the medical profession, to the detriment of women. This difficulty is exacerbated by the fact, dictated by the originally male exclusivity of the medical profession, that the profession itself is organised on the lines of differences between men and women and a hierarchical professional ordering which has evolved in a manner which reflects male dominance and female subordination; male rationality and authority with the correlative of women's 'capacity for caring' (nursing rather than doctoring; obstetrics and gynaecology and physiotherapy rather than orthopaedic surgery) resulting in inferior career status for women while upholding the traditional authority and power of men.

THE MEDICAL PROFESSION IN WESTERN SOCIETY

Whereas early medical and legal developments in Australia and the United States of America largely followed those of the United Kingdom, and continue to employ similar concepts in relation to fertility management, differing constitutional arrangements between the three countries have resulted in very differing juridical bases for the resolution of disputes over various issues. The medical profession has traditionally, as with every other profession, been dominated by men. The struggle for entry into the profession was considered in Chapter 2. Nowadays, while women enjoy equal rights of entry,[3] the profession is characterised by unequal sexual distribution and unequal rates of career advancement. General surgery remains a male province.[4] Women consultants are mainly located in field of gynaecology, obstetrics, paediatrics

---

[3] In the 1950s, the University of Cambridge restricted entry of women to read medicine to 10% of students: see Savage, W, *A Savage Enquiry: Who Controls Childbirth?*, 1986, London: Virago. In 1997, the proportion of female medical students in the United Kingdom has risen to 51%, 48% of whom graduate.

[4] Bock, G and James, S, *Beyond Equality and Difference*, 1992, London: Routledge.

and psychiatry. In general practice, which is less lucrative than surgery, whereas men used to outnumber women, fewer men than women now enter into general practice. In 1980, in England, there were 19,500 men and 4,000 women in general practice. By 1991, there had been an increase of 3,500 female GPs, but only 800 more male GPs.[5] It is no coincidence that in that decade general practice became less lucrative and attractive, compared with consultancy work. Within the National Health Service, in 1991, 15.5 per cent of consultants were women, and only 18 per cent of National Health Service General Managers were female.[6] At the other end of the spectrum, in nursing, women predominate. A third of all nurses work part time.[7] 'Bank' nurses, temporary staff employed to deal with shortages of full time staff, are increasingly employed by the United Kingdom's National Health Service. Ninety eight per cent of all bank nurses work part time; receive no sick or maternity pay, nor pension or annual leave.

The male control of the upper echelons of the medical profession provides a 'natural' site for the imposition of male perceptions of health and norms of practice which both reflect male perceptions about women's health and which simultaneously exclude women and their perceptions. The doctor/patient relationship is inherently a power relationship: with the power invested in the male profession, and exercised according to male constructions of women and women's health, reinforced by legal norms, women's role as object rather than equal subject is reinforced. The imbalance in power is supported and extended by the symbiotic relationship between the medical profession and the medico-scientific technology industry and pharmaceutical industry. Fuelled by medical and scientific advancement and the profit motive, the pharmaceutical and medico-scientific industries have posed a number of significant threats to women's health. In the 1960s, for example, the prescription of the drug Thalidomide, designed to suppress morning sickness in pregnancy, resulted in the birth of deformed children. In the 1960s and 1970s, the development of the contraceptive pill provided women with sexual liberation, with also with the threat of yet undiagnosed side-effects.[8] In the 1980s, the introduction of contraceptives by injection or implants, Depo Provera and Norplant, provided 'long term' protection from conception to women, but again at the cost of severe side-effects, including prolonged bleeding, weight gain or weight loss.[9] In 1979, 30.7 million benzodiazepine

---

[5] See *Health and Personnel Social Services Statistics for England*, 1992, London: HMSO.
[6] Department of Health, *Departmental Report*, 1994, London: HMSO.
[7] See Seccombe, I and Ball, J, *Motivation, Morale and Mobility: A Profile of Qualified Nurses in the 1990s*, 1992, London: Institute of Manpower Studies, No 233, October.
[8] See Mosse, J and Heaton, J, *The Fertility and Contraception Book*, 1990, London: Faber & Faber.
[9] Bunkle, P, 'Calling the shots: the international politics of Depo-Provera', in Arditti, R, Klein, R and Minden, S (eds), *Test-tube Women*, 1984, London: Pandora.

prescriptions for Librium, Valium, Mogadon and Mandrax, were dispensed, decreasing by 1991, following increased concerns over their over use, to 19 million. In the late 1980s, 'there were over one million long-term users, two-thirds of whom were women'.[10] The use of the anti-depressant 'miracle' drug Prozac, prescribed predominantly to women, who, according to medically defined criteria, are most susceptible to depression, has created a climate in which the individual is able to cope with daily routine, but prevented from addressing the underlying socially induced circumstances of her depression.

Obstetrics[11] and gynaecology[12]

Gynaecology and obstetrics, as a male medical discipline dealing with women's bodies, developed in the nineteenth century. Matters relating to abortion, pregnancy and childbirth had, in pre-industrial society, been regarded as private matters dealt with by non-medically-trained female midwives, with knowledge being handed down from generation to generation.[13] Pregnancy and its management at that time was mainly an all-woman affair:[14] a service by women for women, unregulated by the State and not a concern of either surgeons or physicians.[15] Female midwives provided an abortion service as well as natal care. As English society became industrialised, much of the specialist female knowledge of midwifery skills was lost. At the same time, there was a rise in the availability of chemical substances to terminate pregnancies which could be purchased from apothecaries and self-administered. Significant also in this period was the invention of mechanical aids to childbirth: the introduction of extracting foetal slings and forceps. Designed by men, and used by men, the process of childbirth became associated with technology, a development which was to have profound and lasting effects on the question of the medicalisation of pregnancy and childbirth.[16]

---

[10] Foster, P, *Women and the Health Care Industry: An Unhealthy Relationship?*, 1995, Buckingham: Open University, p 90, citing research findings: Gabe, J (ed), *Understanding Tranquiliser Use*, 1991, London: Routledge; *Mental Illness: The Fundamental Facts*, 1993, London: Mental Health Foundation.

[11] The branch of the medical profession specialising in childbirth and related matters.

[12] The branch of medical profession specialising in women's diseases, especially those of the genitourinary tract.

[13] See, *inter alia*, Castiglioni, A, *A History of Medicine* (1941), 2nd edn, 1958, Alfred A Knopf; Oakley, A, 'Wisewoman and medicine man: changes in the management of childbirth', in Oakley, A and Mitchell, J (eds), *The Rights and Wrongs of Woman*, 1976, London: Penguin.

[14] There were some male abortionists, but they were at that time in the minority: see *ibid*, Oakley, p 33.

[15] The two principal divisions within the emergent medical profession.

[16] See Martin, E, *The Woman in the Body: A Cultural Analysis of Reproduction*, 1987, Buckingham: Open University, Chapter 4.

THE MEDICALISATION OF REPRODUCTION

As seen above, in pre-industrial Western society, and still nowadays in existing small-scale societies, the management of conception control, abortion, pregnancy and childbirth was regarded as a non-medical matter within the informal jurisdiction of women themselves. Paralleling the developments noted above which resulted in women no longer controlling pregnancy and birth, was a relatively far more significant factor: the rise of the medical profession and usurping of traditional 'non-medical' skills relating to reproduction matters through a reconceptualisation of such issues as medical issues within the province, alone, of the medical profession. Ann Oakley writes that:

> The main change in the social and medical management of childbirth and reproductive care in industrialised cultures over the last century has been the transition from a structure of control located in a community of untrained women, to one based on a profession of formally trained men. Thus, a process of professionalisation has been accompanied by a transfer of control from women to men.[17]

Feminist theologian Mary Daly writes that the medical profession in the United States of America in the nineteenth century was regarded as: 'flamboyant, drastic, risky, and [with the] instant use of the knife.'[18]

However, even before the medicalisation of pregnancy and childbirth, female midwives had not been unchallenged in society. There was an early associative relationship between witches, midwives, and female healers. In Marianne Hester's analysis the persecution of female witches could be explained largely as an attempt by men to control women who were unmarried and therefore outside of normal patriarchal controls.[19] Further, as Ann Oakley documents, society was regulated by the Church, which in the sixteenth century had assumed control over midwives through the introduction of a licensing system designed in large measure to prevent witches becoming midwives.[20]

With women excluded from university education, and the right to practice medicine being confined to those with a university education and training, it was inevitable that the medical profession would become dominated by men. The Royal College of Physicians was founded in 1518 by Royal Charter.

---

[17] *Op cit*, Oakley, fn 13, p 18.

[18] Barker-Benfield, GJ, *Horrors of the Half-Known Life: Male Attitudes Toward Women and Sexuality in Nineteenth Century America*, 1976, New York: Harper and Row, p 81, cited in Daly, M, *Gyn/Ecology: the Metaethics of Radical Feminism*, 1979, London: The Women's Press, p 226.

[19] See Hester, M, *Lewd Women and Wicked Witches: A Study of the Dynamics of Male Domination*, 1992, London: Routledge and Kegan Paul. (See *Sourcebook*, p 35.)

[20] See *op cit*, Oakley, fn 13, p 26.

Physicians were not permitted to perform surgery. That right was confined to surgeons, who had a lesser status than physicians, and were trained via apprenticeship rather than at university. The Royal College of Surgeons was established in 1745. Male midwives started to practice in the seventeenth century, and the invention of forceps in 1647, initially undisclosed, and when publicised, accompanied with a prohibition against their use by women, contributed to the rise in male control over obstetrics and the exclusion of women. The power and control of the medical profession, especially in industrialised Western society, manifests itself in numerous ways, most particularly in relation to that most intimate and private issue of reproductive rights, including the right not to reproduce, and reproductive technologies.

In relation to abortion, for example, under English and Australian law, it is one or two doctors who must certify that a woman meets the legal criterion for an abortion – not the woman who may seek an abortion as of right. In relation to the English Abortion Act 1967,[21] two doctors must certify that a woman seeking an abortion within 24 weeks of her pregnancy would be at risk of injury to her physical or mental health, a risk which must be deemed to be greater than if the pregnancy were terminated, or, alternatively, that the termination of the pregnancy is necessary 'to prevent grave permanent injury to the physical or mental health of the pregnant woman'; or that continuance of the pregnancy would involve risk to the life of the pregnant woman, greater than if the pregnancy were terminated; or that if the child were born it would suffer serious physical or mental abnormalities. The criteria are thus framed on medical grounds, with those medical grounds being determined by doctors. In no sense does the Act convey the concept of a 'right' to terminate the pregnancy – even within the first trimester – which may be exercised autonomously by the woman. That this is so should cause little surprise when the composition of the Parliament which introduced the Abortion Act 1967 is considered. Simply stated, Parliament being traditionally a male domain, the law was framed by men, and as has been well documented by research, the debates in Parliament portray women seeking abortions as variously, irresponsible, feckless, weak and irrational. Set in opposition is the medical profession categorised as authoritative, responsible and rational.[22]

Further, as the case law of the Supreme Court of the United States of America reveals, even though the Court continues to uphold the rhetoric of a 'woman's right to choose' in the first trimester,[23] the Court has subsequently so whittled away a woman's autonomy, by upholding restrictive procedural requirements of State law, that the woman's 'right' has become virtually

---

[21] As amended by the Human Fertilisation and Embryology Act 1990, s 37.
[22] See Sheldon, S, 'Who is the mother to make the judgment? Construction of woman in English abortion law' [1993] 1 Feminist Legal Studies 3. (See *Sourcebook*, pp 507–18.) See, also, Sheldon, S, *Beyond Control*, 1997, London: Pluto.
[23] See *Roe v Wade* (1973) and subsequent interpretations of the law discussed below.

devoid of substance and conditional upon meeting the procedural and other requirements deemed constitutional by the Court.

Similar considerations apply to the contemporary medical control of pregnancy and childbirth throughout the West. The insistence on childbirth in hospital as opposed to birthing at home – on the basis of maternal and foetal welfare – is opposed to the long tradition of midwifery in the community. Before 1914, less than one per cent of births took place in hospital: in 1990, 99 per cent of births in England and Wales took place in hospital. The manifest readiness of doctors to insist on delivering babies by forceps delivery or Caesarean section is also testament to the medicalisation of childbirth. As Emily Martin has shown in her detailed research in the United States, a woman's desire to give birth at home is too often frustrated by doctors insistence on hospitalisation for the event, an insistence avoided only by the most obdurate women.[24] To quote Emily Martin, '[O]ne has to ask: whose baby, whose life, whose birth, whose timing, and who has the power to decide?'.[25]

Emily Martin's research also covers the question of race and class in the United States of America, with some disturbing findings. It is apparent from the research findings cited that a woman's social class background, and her colour, adversely affect both her health and medical treatment, and that of her baby. A study in New York City, in the early 1960s, for example, revealed that not only was there a '50 per cent difference in neonatal mortality between children of professional and managerial fathers at the top and service workers and labourers at the bottom, but also that the 'neonatal mortality rate among blacks in the highest socio-economic class is close to the rate in the labourer and service worker category among the whites'.[26] In terms of medical treatment, Martin finds that whereas – given the relative high cost of Caesarean section – it would be expected that these would be primarily made available to those in the highest socio-economic group, in fact, and notwithstanding the complexity of interpreting such data, in some areas the use of Caesarean sections on non-white women of low socio-economic class is disproportionately higher than those available to white, higher class women.[27]

---

[24] See *op cit*, Martin, fn 16, especially Chapter 6.
[25] *Op cit*, Martin, fn 16, p 148.
[26] Shapiro, S, Schlesinger, E and Nesbitt, R, *Infant, Perinatal, Maternal and Childhood Mortality in the United States*, 1968, Cambridge, Mass: Harvard UP, pp 66–67, cited in Martin, *op cit*, fn 16, p 148.
[27] See *op cit*, Martin, fn 16, pp 149–55.

STERILISATION

Sterilisation also raises questions concerning the appropriate balance to be struck between a woman's autonomous decision making, her health, and the interests of the State. In many parts of the world, the State interest is that of population control, where sterilisation programmes – usually focused on women – represent a form of contraception. The data on the use of forced or coerced sterilisation around the world reveals the extent to which law and medical practice combines to restrict women's reproductive autonomy. Even in industrialised societies there exists evidence of sterilisations being performed on minority groups and on mentally incompetent adults who are incapable of giving full and informed consent.[28] The whole issue of sterilisation and its uses becomes confused with a number of competing claims which need to be unravelled before any sound judgment may be reached as to the justification for its imposition on women without consent.

On the positive side, it is undeniable that for some women, who have either achieved the family size that they desire, or who have made the firm decision not to bear children, sterilisation, as the most permanent form of contraception, frees them from the need for constant vigilance over contraceptive devices or methods, and from concerns over the side-effects which such methods or devices may produce. However, data suggests that such women – exercising their free choice – are in a minority of those women who undergo sterilisation. A further preliminary point may be made: namely that the focus on female – as opposed to male – sterilisation, which is a statistical feature in most countries, places the full responsibility for the control of fertility and pregnancy on the shoulders of the woman, to the exclusion of men, thus reinforcing already unequal power relationships.

Sterilisation, whether by division of the fallopian tubes[29] or by hysterectomy is a generally non-reversible termination of a woman's right to reproduce, recognised in life and law as a fundamental human right. Where a woman voluntarily chooses sterilisation as a means of achieving freedom from reproductive risks, there is little controversy – other than in the eyes of the Roman Catholic Church or Islam – both of which oppose sterilisation, on the basis that it is contrary to God's will. However, in other situations, sterilisation is one of the most controversial issues in reproductive ethics.

Historically, there is much evidence that sterilisation was performed on men and women for eugenic reasons. Earlier in this century, in the United States, a number of States had legislative provisions for the sterilisation on

---

[28] See, eg, the recent admission of the Japanese Department of Social Justice and Welfare that mentally incompetent women had been routinely sterilised until the programme ceased in 1995.

[29] Laparotomy, laparoscopy and colpotomy.

mentally incompetent persons, those suffering from genetically transmissible diseases and criminal recidivists.[30] Nowadays, several States retain legislation permitting compulsory sterilisation, while under the common law the courts have the power to authorise the sterilisation of legally incompetent minors and adults.[31] It is from the dismal eugenic legacy that the law inherits its powers in relation to the authorisation of involuntary sterilisation.

Sterilisation may be sought for either therapeutic or non-therapeutic reasons, and this distinction has raised a number of basic issues which have been treated differently in different common law jurisdictions. Sterilisation as a form of therapeutic medical treatment is one accepted use. Sterilisation as a means of ending menstruation, or for contraceptive purposes,[32] or sterilisation of mentally incompetent minors and adults is more controversial.

The case law

In 1976, the case of *Re D*[33] was decided by the English Court of Appeal. An 11 year old girl, D, suffered from Sotos' syndrome, and had an IQ of approximately 80. On an application by a mother, supported by her doctor, to the courts to authorise the sterilisation of D, the judge, Heilbron J, ruled that given the girl's IQ and that her condition was improving rather than deteriorating, her 'basic human right to reproduce' should not be removed from her. While the girl was not capable of giving her own informed consent at this young age, she should not be forced to undergo an operation the consequences of which were so final and which she might, at a later age, come to understand and regret.[34]

A decade later the Supreme Court of Canada was to hand down a seminal and controversial judgment. In *Re Eve*,[35] while citing *Re D* with approval, the Court ruled that the determining issue was the best interests of the woman, a 24 year old suffering from 'extreme expressive aphasia'. Relying on the 'best interests' test, the Court ruled that a distinction should be drawn between therapeutic sterilisation and non-therapeutic sterilisation, and that the former was permissible, the latter unlawful. In La Forest J's opinion:

---

[30] See Reilly, P, 'Eugenic sterilization in the United States', in Milunsky, A and Annas, G (eds), *Genetics and the Law – III*, 1985, Aldershot: Dartmouth, Chapter 17; Norrie, S, *Family Planning Practice and the Law*, 1991, Aldershot: Dartmouth.

[31] See *Re Grady* 405 A 2d 851 (Md, 1979).

[32] In Canada, sterilisation for contraceptive purposes is regarded as a major form of contraceptive: see *Sterilization Decisions: Minors and Mentally Incompetent Adults*, 1988, Institute of Law Research and Reform: Edmonton, Alberta.

[33] *Re D (A Minor) (Wardship: Sterilisation)* [1976] Fam 185; [1976] 1 All ER 326.

[34] See Bainham, A, 'Handicapped girls and judicial parents' (1987) 103 LQR 334.

[35] (1986) 31 DLR (4th) 1.

The grave intrusion on a person's rights and the certain physical damage that ensues from non-therapeutic sterilisation without consent, when compared to the highly questionable advantages that can result from it, have persuaded me that it can never safely be determined that such a procedure is for the benefit of that person. Accordingly, the procedure should never be authorised for non-therapeutic purposes under the *parens patriae* jurisdiction.[36]

From the perspective of a woman's right to autonomy over her reproductive decisions, the Canadian Supreme Court's decision had the most far-reaching implications. To restrict authorisation for sterilisation only to cases where the operation is used for therapeutic reasons denies to mentally incompetent women access to sterilisation as the safest permanent form of contraception for other social, non-therapeutic, reasons and limits the right of all women to choose a permanent form of contraception in order to lead a secure child-free life.

Sterilisation was to return to the English courts in 1987 with the case of *Re B (A Minor) (Wardship: Sterilisation)*.[37] The first case of its kind to reach the House of Lords, the court in *Re B* gave careful consideration to the judgment of the Canadian Supreme Court in *Re Eve*. The English decision has been much criticised – not least on the basis that the House of Lords felt compelled to reach a speedy decision[38] because the girl in question was aged 17 and about to pass out of the English wardship jurisdiction.[39] B, then aged 17, had a mental age of about five years and, unless institutionalised, was in danger of becoming pregnant. There was general consensus that any ensuing pregnancy would have to be terminated. Thus, what was being sought was authorisation for a sterilisation based not on therapeutic grounds, but rather on non-therapeutic, social, grounds. The House of Lords ruled that the welfare of the girl required that the sterilisation be authorised. Her welfare, and her welfare alone, dictated the result.[40] Lord Hailsham LC made particular reference to *Re Eve*, and declared that the Canadian court's decision that sterilisation should never be considered for non-therapeutic purposes was 'totally unconvincing' and 'in startling contradiction to the welfare principle'.[41] The House of Lords, and Lord Hailsham LC in particular, considered the nature of a woman's 'right to reproduce', which he linked clearly to a woman's capacity to reach an informed decision on whether or not to reproduce:

---

[36] (1986) 31 DLR (4th) 1, p 32.
[37] [1988] AC 199; [1987] 2 All ER 206, HL.
[38] See Kennedy, I and Lee, S, 'This rush to judgment' (1987) *The Times*, 1 April, p 12.
[39] The position in Canada differs, with the wardship jurisdiction being retained by the courts in relation to such issues after the age of majority.
[40] For a critical analysis, see Kennedy, I, *Treat Me Right: Essays in Medical Law and Ethics*, 1994, Oxford: OUP, Chapter 20.
[41] [1988] AC 199, p 203; [1987] 2 All ER 206, p 213. In the Australian High Court case *of Re Jane* [1989] FLC 92, the court followed similar reasoning to that of the House of Lords in *Re B*. See Boldhar, J, 'The right to reproduce' (1989) 63 Law Inst J 708.

To talk of the 'basic right' to reproduce of an individual who is not capable of knowing the causal connection between intercourse and childbirth ... [or who] is unable to form any maternal instincts or to care for a child, appears to me wholly to part company with reality.[42]

Re B was followed by *Re F (Mental Patient: Sterilisation).*[43] The patient, a 36 year old woman, was mentally handicapped,[44] having a mental age of about four or five years. The House of Lords accepted that it had no jurisdiction, either by statute or derived from the *parens patriae* jurisdiction, to either give or withhold consent to the medical treatment of an adult. In order to avoid the logical trap of being unable to reach a decision, the House of Lords held that a decision could be reached either on the basis of necessity,[45] or as being in the public interest,[46] and that these criteria necessitated a decision when that decision would be in the patient's best interests. In the instant case, the House of Lords granted a declaration that the treatment – sterilisation without consent – would not be unlawful.

In F's case, she had apparently formed a relationship with a male patient, and was thought to be engaging in sexual intercourse about twice a month. Concern arose over her ability to manage pregnancy and childbirth.[47] Griffiths LJ reviewed the position in Australia, Canada and the United States of America.[48] In his judgment, there was a need for a common law rule which required that before a sterilisation operation was performed on a mentally incompetent minor or adult, those proposing the operation must come to the High Court for a judicial inquiry and sanction.[49] That position was strongly supported by Lord Goff of Chieveley, who rejected the suggestion put to the court by counsel for the Mental Health Act Commission, that a court should never depart from the expert medical evidence put before it, and ruled that an independent judicial determination of the issue in each case must be made. On the basis that F had a 'right' to relationships, including sexual relations, it

---

[42] [1988] AC 199 p 205; [1987] 2 All ER 206, p 213. See, also, *Re P (A Minor) (Wardship: Sterilisation)* [1989] 1 FLR 182; [1989] Fam Law 102.

[43] [1989] 2 All ER 193.

[44] But did not fall within the Mental Health Act 1983 criteria, on which see below.

[45] See the judgments of Lords Brandon and Goff.

[46] *Per* Lord Griffiths.

[47] The Official Solicitor had argued before the House of Lords that sterilisation of an adult of unsound mind could never be authorised. His submission turned on a woman's right of reproductive autonomy and on the fact that sterilisation represents irreversible interference with the 'patient's most important organs' and that sterilisation is an issue over which there exist divided medical opinions.

[48] In the United States, no sterilisation operation may be performed on an incompetent minor or adult without the consent of the court.

[49] The *parens patriae* jurisdiction over minors was less appropriate in his Lordship's judgment, depending as it does on an interested party making an application to the court, and thus not guaranteeing that every such decision would be authorised by the High Court.

was in F's best interests for her to be forcibly sterilised. As Ian Kennedy pithily remarks:

> F is entitled to enjoy her rights to society including sexual intercourse (and, as a consequence, should be sterilised), but she is incapable of understanding sexual relationships and their consequences (hence she should be sterilised).[50]

The question which needs asking[51] is why it is that F, rather than her sexual partner, who was allegedly also having sexual relations with other patients, should be sterilised? The answer to that, presumably, is that sterilising her current partner did not guarantee that she would not form future relationships with other men, and that the risk of pregnancy would remain. That, however, remained a speculative judgment, for which no evidence could exist.

Circumstances do exist in the United Kingdom, however, in which sterilisation may be undertaken without the authorisation of the court, where sterilisation is the only available alternative and is being performed for therapeutic purposes.[52]

The Australian courts departed from both the English and Canadian approaches as expressed in *Re D* and *Re Eve*, in *Department of Health v JWB and SWB*.[53] In reaching its decision to authorise the sterilisation of a mentally incompetent 14 year old, the court ruled that there was a distinction between therapeutic and non-therapeutic sterilisation, but that non-therapeutic sterilisation could be authorised judicially on the basis of the best interests of the patient.

COURT ORDERED CAESAREAN SECTIONS

Between 1992 and May 1997, there were eight cases of legally enforced Caesareans in the United Kingdom.[54] In seven of these cases, the women concerned were not legally represented in court. Concern has been expressed at the use of mental health legislation in order to raise the jurisdiction of the courts for the issue to be decided.[55] It is accepted that the courts have no

---

50 *Op cit*, Kennedy, fn 40.
51 As Ian Kennedy asked.
52 See *Re E (A Minor) (Medical Treatment)* [1991] 2 FLR 585; *Re GF* [1992] 1 FLR 293; [1993] 4 Med LR 77.
53 (1992) 66 ALJR 300. See Cica, N, 'Sterilising the intellectually disabled' (1993) 1 Med L Rev 186.
54 An American survey in 1987 revealed that court orders had been obtained in 11 different States. A disproportionate number of forced Caesareans were authorised in relation to non-English speaking women and women from ethnic minorities. In 88% of cases, the orders were obtained within six hours. See Kolder, V, Gallagher, J and Parsons, M, 'Court-ordered obstetrical interventions' (1987) 316 New England Journal of Medicine 1192.
55 In particular by the Royal College of Midwives: see (1997) *The Times*, 16 May.

parens patriae jurisdiction over mentally incompetent adults which would confer power to give or withhold consent to medical treatment. Nevertheless, the courts have held that the court does have jurisdiction to grant a declaration that a given procedure is lawful and in the patient's best interests.[56] A mentally competent adult, on the other hand, has the absolute right to consent to or to refuse medical or surgical treatment:

> An adult patient who suffers from no mental incapacity has an absolute right to choose whether to consent to medical treatment, to refuse it or to choose one rather than another of the treatments being offered.[57]

Furthermore, the decision to refuse treatment by a mentally competent adult does not 'have to be sensible, rational or well considered'.[58] The fact that a woman is pregnant has no effect on her capacity to give or withhold informed consent.[59] However, when the court seizes jurisdiction over a situation in which a pregnant woman refuses consent to treatment, it is possible that the court, invoking the doctrine of the patient's best interests, may deem the patient's capacity to consent to be impaired and thus undermine the 'absolute right' of the otherwise mentally competent patient to decide.

This situation arose in *Re T (Refusal of Treatment).*[60] The woman, a 20 year old who was 34 weeks pregnant, was involved in a motor accident. Following her admission to hospital her condition deteriorated and she gave birth to a stillborn child. A blood transfusion was necessary, but this she refused on the basis that she was a Jehovah's Witness. When her condition became critical, her father and boyfriend applied to the courts for a declaration that a blood transfusion would not be unlawful. The Court of Appeal, having reiterated the doctrine of a patient's right to refuse treatment, granted the declaration on the basis that the effect of her condition, together with misinformation, rendered her refusal of consent ineffective. Lord Donaldson noted a possible exception to the absolute right to refuse treatment in the case of a pregnant woman: namely that the court might intervene in a competent patient's refusal to consent to treatment where that refusal 'may lead to the death of a viable foetus'. That situation did not pertain in *Re T*.

Possibly the most bizarre case relating to forced Caesarean sections, and the capacity to consent, to reach the English courts is that of *Re MB*.[61] MB, an

---

[56] See *Re F (Mental Patient: Sterilisation)* [1990] 2 AC 1; *Airdale NHS Trust v Bland* [1994] 1 FCR 485; *Re T (Adult: Refusal of Treatment)* [1992] 2 FCR 861; *Re C (Adult: Refusal of Treatment)* [1994] 2 FCR 151; *Thameside and Glossop Acute Services Trust v CH* [1996] 1 FCR 753.

[57] *Re T (Refusal of Treatment)* [1992] 3 WLR 783.

[58] Per Butler Sloss LJ, *Re T (Refusal of Treatment)* [1992] 2 FCR 861.

[59] On informed consent under English Law, see *Sidaway v Governors of the Bethlem Royal Hospital* [1985] AC 871; [1985] 2 WLR 480; [1985] 1 All ER 643; *Bolam v Friern Hospital Management Committee* [1957] 1 WLR 582. See also the Law Commission's proposals on mental incapacity: Law Commission, *Mental Incapacity*, Law Com No 231, 1995, London: HMSO.

[60] [1992] 3 WLR 783.

[61] [1997] 2 FCR 541.

adult woman, suffered from a phobia to injections. Whilst in hospital and in labour, doctors considered that a Caesarean section was required. MB refused to consent, on the basis of her fear of the anaesthetic injection. A declaration that the administration of the requisite treatment was not unlawful was sought from the court. The Court of Appeal, whilst affirming the right of a mentally competent adult to consent to, or refuse to consent to treatment, and specifically stating that women in labour have that same right, overrode MB's refusal. That right to refuse was accepted to exist even though 'the consequences may be the death or serious handicap of the child she bears, or her own death'. However, in MB's case, her needle phobia rendered her less than mentally competent to make the correct decision.[62]

However, the Court of Appeal ruled, in 1998, that a woman whose mental faculties were not impaired, was entitled to refuse medical treatment even where that refusal would result in the death of her unborn child.[63] Ms S, when in her thirty sixth week of pregnancy, was advised that she needed urgent hospital treatment for pre-enclampsia. She refused. Two doctors signed the necessary forms for her compulsory admission to hospital under the Mental Health Act 1983. Doctors then sought the consent of a court to administer treatment and the court dispensed with Ms S's consent. While confined no treatment for any mental disorder was prescribed. Ms S gave birth to a daughter delivered by Caesarian section. The Court of Appeal ruled that Ms S had been unlawfully detained. The fact of pregnancy *per se* did not diminish her capacity to refuse treatment. Moreover, there was no conflict between her autonomy and her foetus, and her autonomy could not be lawfully overridden even though her thinking process was 'unusual, even apparently bizarre and irrational'.

Treatment under the Mental Health Act 1983

Under the Mental Health Act 1983, provision is made for the treatment of a medically incompetent person. That treatment is defined as being treatment which is given for the mental condition itself, subject to restrictions imposed against the use of certain irreversible procedures and hazardous procedures or treatment:[64] Section 63 provides:

---

[62] The Court of Appeal laid down guidelines of the procedure to be followed when clinicians seek declarations from the courts. *Inter alia*, applications will only be entertained by the courts when the issue of mental competence is in doubt; rulings should be sought from the High Court; the mother should be legally represented and the hearing *inter partes*. The Official Solicitor should act as *amicus curiae*, in order to develop a body of expertise; there should be some evidence – preferably that of a psychiatrist – as to the competence of the patient. Decisions will be made by the court on the basis of the patient's best interests.

[63] *St George's Healthcare National Health Service Trust v S; Regina v Collins and Others ex p S* (1998) *The Times*, 8 May.

[64] Mental Health Act 1983, ss 57 and 58.

The consent of a patient shall not be required for any medical treatment given to him for the mental disorder from which he is suffering, not being treatment falling within section 57 or 58 above, if the treatment is given by or under the direction of the responsible medical officer.

The question which inevitably arises is the basis on which the court can authorise a forced Caesarean on a mentally incompetent adult. It was this question which was directly addressed in *Tameside and Glossop Acute Services Trust v CH*. The patient, a diagnosed schizophrenic aged 41, was admitted to hospital under section 3 of the Mental Health Act in 1995 and was subsequently found to be pregnant. When problems arose over the pregnancy in the thirty eighth week, doctors were concerned that, whilst the patient had indicated her consent to induction, and, if necessary, a Caesarean, she might change her mind. It was accepted by the doctors that if the patient were of sound mind, she would have the absolute right to refuse any particular course of treatment.[65] However, the medical opinion was that for the patient to give birth to a live child would maximise her chances of recovery from her mental condition, and that accordingly there was a direct link between the treatment for her mental condition and the treatment necessary to ensure a healthy live child.[66] The hospital trust applied to the court for a declaration that a Caesarean section, and any necessary restraint, would be lawful. The court granted the declaration as to the lawfulness of the Caesarean section, accepting that treatment not directly related to the mental disorder in question, but ancillary to it, was authorised under the Act.[67] In relation to the issue of the possible need for restraint to be applied, the court ruled that such restraint which was reasonably necessary as an incident of treatment was lawful, and did not require a declaration to that effect.[68]

---

[65] [1996] 1 FCR 753. Per the Guidelines laid down by the Royal College of Obstetricians and Gynaecologists following *Re S (An Adult: Medical Treatment)* [1992] 2 FCR 893.

[66] Compare the case of *Re C (An Adult: Refusal of Treatment)* [1994] 2 FCR 151, in which a male paranoid schizophrenic patient refused medical treatment (amputation of a gangrenous leg) which would have saved his life, and the court granted the patient's application for an injunction preventing amputation without his consent.

[67] This reasoning has been judicially accepted in relation to the treatment of anorexic patients by forcible feeding: see further below.

[68] See, also, *Norfolk and Norwich Healthcare (NHS) Trust v W* [1997] 1 FCR 269, in which the High Court granted a declaration authorising medical treatment to bring to an end a patient's labour, whether by forceps delivery or if necessary a Caesarean. The court ruled that, notwithstanding that the patient was not suffering from a mental disorder, she lacked the necessary competence to make a decision, and that terminating the pregnancy would be both in the interests of her health and that of the foetus.

INFERTILITY TREATMENT

Infertility treatment[69] raises several difficult issues from a feminist perspective. Whilst the relief of infertility, for those whose lives are blighted by infertility, is an unquestioned good, the conceptualisation of infertility as a disease for which treatment is increasingly available is more questionable. The issue also involves unstated assumptions about the appropriate role of women: that of child-bearing and nurturing and of being 'incomplete' unless able to bear children, which has not been welcomed by many feminist critics. The emphasis on woman's 'natural maternal' role aside, Renate Duelli Klein, for example, has argued that techniques designed to relieve female infertility 'deconstruct' women. Rather than the woman being seen as a whole, a unique identity, women are now fragmented – reduced to their bodily parts – to ovaries and uteruses.[70] Michelle Stanworth also argues that the new techniques mean that women are reduced to their parts – and fragmented in such a way that the idea of the 'mother' can no longer be conceived in the natural way, but must be seen as 'ovarian mothers', 'uterine mothers', and, in the case of surrogacy, 'social mothers'.[71]

Furthermore, in the United Kingdom, whilst the techniques continue to be developed, and the demand for the relief of infertility continues to grow, the potential success rate of treatment, which involves extensive, invasive and often painful techniques, is poor. Citing research, Peggy Foster states that, in the 1980s, the overall success rate in the United Kingdom was only 9.7 per cent of couples treated and that by the early 1990s, the success rate of 'larger, more established British clinics in a population of "carefully selected" couples were only approaching 50 per cent after three cycles of treatment'.[72]

The phenomenon of professional medical control, allied to male constructions of women, is also evident in the criteria to be established before a woman may qualify for treatment for infertility. No infertile woman has an entitlement to infertility treatment, and in the United Kingdom State funding is limited and strictly controlled.[73] In 1984, the influential Warnock Report

---

[69] Artificial insemination by donor (AID); *in vitro* fertilisation (IVF); gamete intra fallopian tube transfer (GIFT).

[70] Klein, R, 'What's new about the "new" reproductive technologies', in Corea, G *et al* (eds), *Man-made Women: How New Reproductive Technologies Affect Women*, 1985, London: Hutchinson, p 64.

[71] Stanworth, M, 'The deconstruction of motherhood', in Stanworth, M (ed), *Reproductive Technologies: Gender, Motherhood and Medicine*, 1987, Cambridge: Polity, p 16.

[72] *Op cit*, Foster, fn 10, p 51.

[73] See Harman, H, *Trying for a Baby: A Report on the Inadequacy of NHS Infertility Services*, 1990, London: HMSO.

was published.[74] The report, which reviewed the ethical and legal implications of techniques to relieve infertility in the United Kingdom, formed the basis for the current statutory regime for regulating infertility techniques, and for research into causes of and treatment for infertility, now contained in the Human Fertilisation and Embryology Act 1990. The moral and ethical dilemmas which such techniques entail – especially the issue of experimentation on embryos – were given detailed analysis, although it may be argued that a consistent moral stance was not evident in the final report.[75] Certain preconceptions about the role of women, and the centrality of the conventional family, however, are clear from the Report.

The Committee expressed its preference for treatment to be given to women who were either married, or could demonstrate that they were in a stable, heterosexual two-parent family, thus placing the interests of the potential unborn child above that of the potential mother:

> To judge from the evidence, many believe that the interests of the child dictate that it should be born into a home where there is a loving, stable, heterosexual relationship and that, therefore, the deliberate creation of a child for a woman who is not a partner in such a relationship is morally wrong ... we believe that as a general rule it is better for children to be born into a two-parent family, with both father and mother, although we recognise that it is impossible to predict with any certainty how lasting such a relationship will be.[76]

This preference for a two-parent, heterosexual family has not only led to the exclusion of those women who cannot satisfy the immediate criteria, but to those who, having been an infertile partner in a marriage, find that posthumous use of a deceased husband's frozen sperm, taken without his consent at the time, but consistent with his desire for his wife to have his child/children, is prohibited. This precise issue came before the English courts in the case of Diane Blood,[77] whose husband contracted bacterial meningitis which led to his coma and death, and had been unable to sign the required consent form which would have enabled his wife to use his sperm for posthumous fertility treatment. Following a two year campaign against the ruling of the Human Fertilisation and Embryology Authority which led to the Court of Appeal, Diane Blood finally won the right to seek the necessary treatment in Belgium.[78]

---

[74] The Warnock Committee, *Report of the Committee of Inquiry into Fertilisation and Embryology*, Cmnd 9314, 1984, London: HMSO; and see Warnock, M, *A Question of Life*, 1985, Oxford: Basil Blackwell.

[75] The issue of abortion was considered by the Committee to be outside its terms of reference.

[76] *Ibid*, Warnock Report, para 2.11. See, also, paras 4.16 and 5.10.

[77] *R v Human Fertilisation and Embryology Authority ex p Blood* (1997) *The Times*, 7 February, CA.

[78] The Court of Appeal laid much emphasis on a citizen's right to receive medical treatment in another Member State of the EC, under the EC Treaty, Arts 59 and 60.

Issues of class also enter the picture. Given that the National Health Service allocation of funds for such infertility treatment is finite, an evaluation of the potential of the applicant woman/couple inevitably involves an evaluation of their social capacity to provide for the child. Further, the scarcity of resources also inevitably leads to the greater capacity of the relatively affluent and confidently articulate to seek treatment for infertility, even at the cost of mortgaging their home and future.

ABORTION RIGHTS

One's philosophy, one's experiences, one's exposure to the raw edges of human existence, one's religious training, one's attitude toward life and family and their values, and the moral standards one establishes and seeks to observe, are all likely to influence and to colour one's thinking and conclusions about abortion.

In addition, population growth, pollution, poverty, and racial overtones tend to complicate and not simplify the problem.[79]

State parties should ensure that measures are taken to prevent coercion in regard to fertility and reproduction, and to ensure that women are not forced to seek unsafe medical procedures such as illegal abortion because of lack of appropriate services in regard to fertility control.[80]

Introduction

The World Health Organisation estimates that 'globally 20 million unsafe abortions are performed each year, resulting in the death of 70,000 women'.[81] The incidence of unsafe abortions is highest in South America, but also very high in parts of Africa. In Asia, the rate of unsafe abortions is relatively low among developing regions, although in southern Asia the total number of deaths from abortion is high. Female infertility is also associated with unhygenic abortions and obstetric practices. The United Nations Report records that 'more than half a million women are estimated to die each year for want of adequate reproductive health care'. In Latin America, abortion is prohibited in most countries due to the pervading influence of the Roman Catholic Church, and it is estimated that between one-fifth and one-half of maternal deaths are due to illegal abortions. In Bolivia, some 60 per cent of

---

[79] Blackmun J, *Roe v Wade* 410 US 113 (1973).
[80] United Nations Convention on the Elimination of All Forms of Discrimination Against Women (CEDAW), GA Res 34/180, UN GAOR, 34th Sess Supp No 46 at 193, UN Doc A/34/46 (1979).
[81] United Nations Report, *The World's Women 1995: Trends and Statistics*, 1995, London: HMSO, p 79.

Introduction to Feminist Jurisprudence

funds spent on obstetrical and gynaecological care are committed to treating complications from illegal abortions.[82] In Africa, the risk of a woman dying from pregnancy related causes is one in 12, whereas in North America the figure is one in 4,000.[83]

A woman's right to autonomy entails the right to control her fertility. The availability of contraception and abortion is thus critical for women who do not wish to spend their lives as reproductive instruments confined within the private world of the home and family. As Luce Irigaray has pointed out, contraception and abortion enable women to be conceptualised as *women* and not merely as *mothers*: 'contraception and abortion ... imply the possibility of *modifying women's social status,* and thus of modifying the modes of social relations between men and women.'[84]

The struggle for the right to abortion across the Western world has represented one of the sites of intractable difficulties and conflict. While in the West the battle for abortion rights has largely been won, the debate continues to arouse passionate debate, particularly in the United States of America, where it remains a live and contentious issue.

Blackmun J, in the extract from his judgment cited above, explains many of the influences and issues which confront the question of abortion law reform and practice. What is left out of his opinion above, is the question of a woman's right to choose, a right to control her own reproductive life.[85] Conflicting interests, personal and political, intrude on the abortion debate: the rights of natural fathers, the 'rights' of the unborn child oppose the woman's right to choose. The traditional Western liberal separation of the private and public spheres of life, and perceptions about woman's role within the family, the power and control of the (predominantly male) medical profession and the (predominantly male) legislature and judiciary also compound the issue. Abortion thus represents an amalgam of issues, of philosophies, of politics and morality.

The evolution of abortion law in England[86]

The debate about abortion law is of relatively recent origins. Under the common law of the United States of America and the United Kingdom,

---

[82] Newland, K, *The Sisterhood of Man*, p 612, cited in Hartmann, B, *Reproductive Rights and Wrongs: The Global Politics of Population Control*, 1995, Boston, Mass: South End.
[83] *Op cit*, United Nations Report, fn 81, p 77.
[84] Irigaray, L, 'The power of discourse', in Whitford, M (ed), *The Irigaray Reader*, 1991, Oxford: Basil Blackwell, p 130.
[85] *Roe v Wade* was decided on the basis of a woman's right to privacy as guaranteed by the Fourteenth Amendment to the United States' Constitution.
[86] In 1996, 177,225 abortions were performed in England and Wales.

abortion was permissible before the 'quickening'[87] of the foetus, occurring at around the fifth month of pregnancy. In the nineteenth century, with the confinement of middle and upper class women to 'the home' and the production and care of children, and the development of the medical profession as a male-dominated domain, abortion became criminalised.[88]

The English Offences Against the Persons Act 1861 made abortion illegal. Notwithstanding that Act, abortions continued to be performed in England and Wales where a woman's life would otherwise be in danger. The legal position in Scotland was more relaxed: a doctor could lawfully perform an abortion provided that it was, in his clinical judgment, necessary. In England, the Abortion Law Reform Association was founded in 1936. The volume of illegal abortions performed in England and Wales was estimated, in 1939, to be in the order of 50,000 a year.[89] By 1949, the estimate rose to 250,000. In 1938, a doctor was prosecuted for performing an abortion on an 14 year old rape victim.[90] The doctor, Mr Bourne, performed the abortion and reported his 'offence' to the police whereupon he was duly prosecuted. The prosecution failed, the judge concluding that an abortion was lawful where the woman's physical or mental health was at risk through the continuation of the pregnancy. This seminal case expanded the law to include the effects on a woman's mental health, a ground which has since remained in the law.

It was to be 1967 before the English Parliament acted to regulate abortion. A Private Members' Bill introduced by David Steel MP,[91] opposed by both the Conservative right and Roman Catholic MPs, amidst much controversy, reached the statute book. The Act confirmed the legality of abortion under the conditions specified in *R v Bourne*. Abortion was also to be permitted where the mother risked giving birth to a seriously handicapped child. In addition to the health of the mother, the Act included a clause which would require doctors to consider whether an abortion should be performed where the pregnancy would seriously affect the existing children of the family, and where the woman's social environment dictated the need for abortion. Abortion was permissible up to the twenty seventh week of pregnancy. After sustained pressure for a tightening of the law, and especially the problem of terminations in late pregnancy, the time limit was reduced to 24 weeks, with exceptions being permitted on the basis of serious handicap of the foetus.

---

[87] The time at which movement of the foetus is experienced by the carrying mother.

[88] See Kaulfmann, K, 'Abortion, a woman's matter: an explanation of who controls abortion and how and why they do it', in Arditti, Klein and Minden, *op cit*, fn 9.

[89] See Birkett Committee, *Report of the Committee of Inquiry into Abortion*, 1939, London: HMSO.

[90] See *R v Bourne* [1939] 1 KB 687; [1938] 3 All ER 615. See, also, Bourne, A, 'Abortion and the Law' (1938) 2 BMJ 254.

[91] As he then was.

Opposition to the Act came from the Society for the Protection of the Unborn Child (SPUC) and *Life*. Each received support from the Roman Catholic Church. The principal objection came in the form of the claim to legal protection for the foetus, more emotively labelled the 'unborn child'.

'Foetal rights'? and the law

Under English law, the foetus enjoys no legal protection until it is developed to the stage where it is 'capable of being born alive'.[92] However, an action in negligence may lie if damage is done to the foetus through carelessness.[93] Equally under United States' law, '[T]he unborn have never been recognised in the law as persons in the whole sense'.[94] Whilst this position ostensibly protects women's autonomy from being restricted by the foetus, at least in the early months of pregnancy, it is clear that in both the United Kingdom and the United States of America, the status of the foetus is by no means clear-cut, and that as a pregnancy progresses, the *prima facie* right of the foetus to the protection of its mother from harm, increases to the point of denying the carrying mother autonomy over her body.

Given that under English law the foetus has no rights to protection from its mother, other than the right conferred on the child born alive to sue, through its 'next friend', for compensation to injury suffered whilst in the womb, it is unsurprising that the issue of foetal welfare has not given way to judicial and medical perceptions about the 'best interest of the mother', rather than the foetus. Such perceptions have, however, been repeatedly enunciated by courts in the United States of America. By way of illustration, rather than full analysis, the courts have, in relation to the issue of forced Caesarean sections, as with the judicial control of the woman's 'right to choose' abortion, repeatedly placed in the balance the right of the mother to autonomy over her body, and the State's interest in the near viable or viable foetus. For example, in 1981, in *Jefferson v Giffin Spalding County Hospital*,[95] the Supreme Court of Georgia placed an unborn foetus in the custody of the Department of Family and Children Services, and conferred power on the Department to make all medical decisions in relation to the birth of the foetus, including that relating to a Caesarean section, if needed, on the basis that the woman would not consent to such treatment as a result of her religious beliefs. Although the court recognised that in general the powers of the court in respect of mentally competent adults was exceedingly limited, on the facts of the case, power would be exercised in order to protect the child's right to live. Such an

---

[92] Infant Life Preservation Act 1929.
[93] Congenital Disabilities (Civil Liability) Act 1976, s 1.
[94] Blackmun J, *Roe v Wade* 410 US 113 (1973).
[95] 247 Ga 86, 274 SE 2d 457. Discussed in Kennedy, *op cit*, fn 40, Chapter 19.

approach reinforces the view that in relation to pregnancy, American courts will weigh in the balance the woman's rights over her body and the incipient rights of the unborn, despite ostensibly adhering to the view that the unborn foetus has no rights which can be protected by law.

The Warnock Committee Report

It was the question of the point at which an embryo should be accorded legal protection which dominated the Committee on Human Fertilisation and Embryology's (the Warnock Committee) considerations on the regulation of *in vitro* fertilisation and other techniques for the relief of infertility.[96] Whilst the Committee regarded the law relating to abortion as being outside its terms of reference, the Committee's Report represents a comprehensive review of the complex moral, legal, political and social issues relating to the foetus. The Committee, while endorsing the production of, and experimentation on, foetuses surplus to the requirements of the infertile woman receiving fertility treatment, nevertheless did not recommend that medical scientists should be granted a *carte blanche* in relation to medical experimentation. In a compromise decision, the Committee, whilst recognising the legal position concerning the absence of foetal rights up until the time at which the foetus could be born alive, refused to countenance experimentation on embryos beyond a period of 14 days from conception: thus implicitly recognising the uniqueness of human life whilst also recognising and respecting the value of medical experimentation in the search for solutions to infertility.

The legal position of the father of the child

Under English law, the natural father possesses no right to control his wife or partner in relation to the question of abortion. The issue has been raised in three cases. In *Re Paton v British Pregnancy Advisory Service Trustees*,[97] the husband sought an injunction restraining his wife from undergoing an abortion. The application was refused. This decision was followed in *C v S*,[98] in which a student father tried to seek legal support to stop the termination of his girlfriend's pregnancy. In *Re F (in utero)*,[99] the Court of Appeal ruled unequivocally that a foetus could not be subject to the wardship jurisdiction – the protective jurisdiction of the High Court – thus implicitly respecting a mother's right to choose whether to carry a foetus to term.

---

[96] *Op cit*, Warnock Report, fn 74.
[97] [1979] QB 276; [1978] 2 All ER 987. See Kennedy, I, 'Husband denied a say in abortion decision' (1979) 42 MLR 324; Lowe, N, 'Wardship and abortion prevention' (1996) 96 LQR 29.
[98] [1988] QB 135; [1987] 1 All ER 1230.
[99] [1988] Fam 122; [1988] 2 All ER 193. See Fortin, J, 'Can you ward a foetus?' (1988) 51 MLR 768.

The interaction between abortion, contraception and sterilisation

Increasingly, with legal abortion becoming more widely available, the availability of abortion is linked to medical practices and procedures designed to control future fertility. The most extreme practice is that of sterilisation of the woman during the course of, and as a precondition to, abortion, although evidence suggests that sterilisation is often undertaken without the full informed consent of the woman. Less drastically, but with serious medical and psychological implications, in some Third World countries, Inter-Uterine Devices (IUDs) may be inserted into women who have undergone an illegal abortion and present themselves for treatment at a hospital. Alternatively, in India, for example, where abortion is lawful, sterilisation or the insertion of an IUD to prevent subsequent pregnancies, may be a precondition for the abortion.[100] In Indonesia, the woman must either agree to the insertion of a contraceptive implant (Norplant), or their husbands agree to undergo a vasectomy where there are already two or more children in the family. In attempts to regulate population control, women in the Third World are actively encouraged in the use of Depo-Prevura – a contraceptive injection which provides between three and six months protection from pregnancy. Depo-Prevura has had a controversial history in the West, carrying with it the risk of many short term, and some suspected long term, side-effects. Despite the risks, both the World Health Organisation and the Office of Planned Parenthood allegedly promotes its use as a means of population control, without adequate information being provided as to its risks, or safeguards undertaken to limit those risks.[101]

Abortion rights in the United States of America

With the medical profession seizing jurisdiction over pregnancy and childbirth from women who in previous centuries provided a self-regulating, self-administering, informal system of services, pregnancy – its continuation or discontinuance – became a public, rather than a private, matter. As the law intervened to provide a formal system of regulation, the termination of pregnancy became an overtly political issue. Nowhere is this more clearly seen than in the United States of America, with its high proportion of Roman Catholics and a written Constitution, interpreted and enforced by the Supreme Court. Whereas under the unwritten Constitution of the United Kingdom, abortion regulation falls under statutory provisions which may be

---

[100] See Ravindran, 'Women and the politics of population', and Karkal, M, 'Abortion laws and the abortion situation in India' [1991] 4 Reproductive and Genetic Engineering 3.

[101] On population planning programmes see, further, below.

amended by Parliament with the minimum of procedural technicality, in the United States the issue is regulated by State law, subject only to the constitutionality of that law under the Constitution. The highwatermark in terms of judicial decision making lies in *Roe v Wade*.[102] The case was a class action suit, representing the interests of many women, not just the parties to the litigation. In *Roe v Wade*,[103] three different issues were involved: a pregnant woman wanting an abortion; a couple trying to avoid pregnancy but wanting abortion available as a 'last resort', and a doctor being sued for performing abortions.[104] The decision of the Supreme Court was reached by a majority of seven to two. The law under challenge was a statute of the State of Texas, passed in 1857, which made procuring an abortion, other than to save the life of the mother, a criminal offence. Jane Roe challenged the law, seeking a declaration that it was unconstitutional in so far as it denied her access to a lawful and safe abortion conducted by a competent physician. While the Supreme Court ruled in Jane Doe's favour, and granted the declaration, its judgment was not a licence for the absolute availability of abortion at any stage of a pregnancy. The Court ruled that the concepts of liberty and privacy enshrined in the Constitution entitled a woman, in the first trimester of pregnancy, to choose whether to continue with that pregnancy or not. After the first trimester, however, other competing interests were given recognition which effectively limited a woman's right to abortion. The woman's right diminished as the pregnancy progressed: by the second trimester of pregnancy State law could regulate abortion, and by the onset of the third trimester the State could absolutely prohibit abortion, other than where the abortion was necessary to save the life of the mother. Thus the 'right to choose' was confined to the first three months of pregnancy, after which the competing interests of the foetus, and of the State in relation to its respect for the life of the unborn, assumed greater significance, culminating in the last three months of pregnancy into overriding interests.

While at the time the decision was greeted by feminist groups as a legal triumph, especially in affirming that decision making at least in the first trimester of pregnancy was a matter for the woman alone as an aspect of her constitutional right to privacy, it did not go so far as to require doctors or hospitals to perform abortions, nor did it have any impact on additional funding being given for such services to be set up, nor for the provision of funds under Medicaid[105] to enable women to have financial access to abortions. Such battles lay ahead. For the anti-abortion, 'pro-life', lobby, the

---

[102] 410 US 113 (1973).

[103] See, also, *Doe v Bolton* 410 US 179 (1973).

[104] For a full analysis, see Rubin, E, *Abortion, Politics, and the Courts: Roe v Wade and its Aftermath*, 1987, New York: Greenwood.

[105] State funding for meeting the medical costs of those meeting the need criteria: Title XIX Social Security Act 1965. The fund is administered by States but regulated by the Federal Government.

strong majority of seven to two justices was a disappointment, but given the balance of the judgment, hope still remained that future litigation would turn the tide their way.

Individual States reacted in a variety of ways to the decision of the Supreme Court: and whilst complying with the letter of the law, many imposed more or less stringent conditions and requirements which had to be met before abortion would become available. The issue of informed consent played a central role, as did the requirement for the consent of a minor's parent(s). In some States, a waiting period was imposed. In some States abortion could only be performed within a hospital licensed for that purpose, others required that abortions could only be performed by physicians. Some States prohibited the advertising of the availability of legal abortions. A majority of States introduced 'conscience clauses' permitting physicians to refuse to perform abortions on the basis of moral or religious objections to abortion.

At a national level, the abortion issue became overtly political, and became a central issue in the 1976 presidential election campaign and in subsequent gubernatorial campaigns across the country. The Roman Catholic Church entered into the political battle, and drew in its support the Moral Right: a coalition of conservative 'family-centred', 'pro-life' activists. The rights of women to liberty and privacy were set in political opposition to competing values: a position which remains dominant in the political debate on abortion in the United States.

In 1976, the Supreme Court affirmed its judgment in *Roe v Wade* in *Planned Parenthood v Danforth*,[106] and made it clear that not only was the woman's decision final in the first trimester, but also that no State law could give a right of veto over that decision either to the father of the foetus, or to the parents of an under-age minor. However, set-backs for women's rights were to follow. In *Beal v Doe*[107] and *Maher v Roe*,[108] the Court was to hold that States were not required to provide funds for elective abortions through Medicaid, and that the fact that State funding was available for child-bearing costs did not mean that such funding had to be provided for elective abortions: States could legitimately give preference to child-bearing over abortion. Moreover, even in relation to medically necessary abortions, in *Harris v McRae*,[109] the Court ruled that States had no obligation to provide financial assistance to meet their costs. Worse, the refusal of a State to fund programmes designed to counsel and advise on abortion, was upheld as constitutional in *Rust v Sullivan*,[110]

---

[106] 428 US 52 (1976).
[107] 432 US 438 (1977).
[108] 432 US 464 (1977).
[109] 448 US 297 (1980).
[110] No 89–1391 (1991).

despite the argument that such a decision effectively controlled the doctor/patient relationship and infringed the constitutional guarantee of free speech.

Abortion laws returned to the Supreme Court for adjudication in 1982, and provided the opportunity to test the Court's willingness or otherwise to conform to its decision in *Roe v Wade*. In 1978, the city council of Akron, Ohio, drafted an Ordinance which comprised some 17 provisions which restricted access to abortions. These Ordinances were duly challenged in the courts, and reached the Supreme Court in 1982.[111] In *City of Akron v Akron Center for Reproductive Health, Planned Parenthood, Kansas City; Missouri v Ashcroft and Simpoulos v Virginia,* the Court reaffirmed the central principle decided in the 1973 case: namely that a woman in the first trimester of pregnancy had the right to choose. The Court also ruled that the requirements imposed by the city council of Akron represented excessive restrictions on that right. The Court, however, in this case, was now divided by six to three in its decision.

In 1985, the Supreme Court once again considered the law. In *Thornburgh v American College of Obstetricians*[112] and *Diamond v Charles,*[113] State laws of Pennsylvania and Illinois were under challenge. Both concerned restrictions on access to abortion and/or restrictive abortion procedures. The Supreme Court, by a majority of five to four, ruled six provisions of the Pennsylvania law unconstitutional, on the basis of imposing too restrictive a regime.

In 1989, however, came a landmark case for the anti-abortion lobby. In *William Webster*[114] *v Reproductive Health Services,*[115] the Court was once again asked to review its decision in *Roe v Wade*. Under challenge was the requirement under State law that a woman seeking an abortion, who was thought to be 20 weeks pregnant, should be required to undergo tests for foetal viability. The law also prohibited the performance of abortions in publicly funded institutions. The Supreme Court by that time had a change in its composition, with two new appointees to the Court. Four justices voted to uphold the regulations. Four other judges held that the right to choose abortion as stipulated in *Roe v Wade* should be upheld. The deciding vote was that of Justice O'Connor. Justice O'Connor held that a regulation would be unconstitutional if that regulation had the effect of imposing an 'undue burden' on a woman's decision. In her view, the requirements of the State law of Missouri did not place such an undue burden on the woman, and would therefore be upheld.

---

[111] 462 US 416 (1983).
[112] 106 S Ct 2169 (1986).
[113] 106 S Ct 1697 (1986).
[114] Webster was Missouri's Attorney General.
[115] 109 S Ct 3040 (1989).

The reaction to *Webster* varied. Whilst some claimed that the original decision in *Roe v Wade* remained unaltered,[116] others were more sceptical. The decision left it open for State legislature to test the limits of regulation of abortion availability, whilst ostensibly upholding the constitutional right of women to choose. The tide appeared, for the first time since 1973, to have swung against that proclaimed 'absolute' right. In two subsequent cases that trend appeared to be confirmed. In *Hodgson v Minnesota*,[117] the Court upheld a State requirement that a minor must either obtain parental consent to the operation, or obtain the consent of a court. *Ohio v Akron Center for Reproductive Health*[118] upheld the requirement of State law, that the physician proposing to perform an abortion on a minor should notify her parents in advance.

In 1992, came another seminal Supreme Court case, which threw further doubt on a woman's right to choose. By this time, yet another change had taken place regarding the composition of the Court. While the majority of the bench ruled to uphold the principal thrust of *Roe v Wade*, four justices openly called for that decision to be overruled. In *Planned Parenthood of Southeastern Pennsylvania v Casey*,[119] the issue once again was the right of States to introduce regulatory requirements in relation to abortion. The Pennsylvania Abortion Control Act of 1982, as amended in 1988 and 1989, requires a woman seeking an abortion to give her informed consent, and requires that she be provided with information at least 24 hours before the operation is performed. In addition, in relation to minors, the Act requires the minor to seek either the consent of one or both of her parents, or alternatively, to seek judicial sanction for the operation. Further, in the case of a married woman, when seeking an abortion she must certify that her husband has been notified of her intention. The only exemption granted from these provisions relates to situations of medical emergency.

The Court ruled that the fundamental principle enshrined in *Roe v Wade* should be maintained. Much in evidence in the judgment is the Court's perception of its own authority and standing, and the importance of certainty in the law and compliance with the doctrine of *stare decisis*, at least in the absence of any other compelling force which demanded a departure from that doctrine. The Court reaffirmed the centrality of a woman's individual liberty, under the doctrine of the due process of law enshrined in the Fourteenth Amendment, to choose, within the first trimester of pregnancy, whether to terminate the pregnancy or not. Thereafter, the Court ruled, a woman who had not acted within the first trimester could be deemed to have recognised

---

[116] See, eg, Dworkin, R, 'The future of abortion' (1989) New York Review of Books, 28 September.
[117] 497 US 417 (1990).
[118] 497 US 502 (1990).
[119] 112 S Ct 2791 (1992).

and acquiesced in the State's legitimate interest in the protection of unborn human life, which provided the rationale for a more restrictive approach to abortion.

Where the Court departed from its 1973 decision, however, was in the area of the trimester structure itself, which in *Casey* the Court ruled to be excessively rigid, and unnecessary in securing the objective of the woman's right to choose. The trimester structure, was not part of the 'essential holding of *Roe*' according to the Court. Further, the woman's right to choose a termination within the first trimester was not itself a principle which could preclude States from ensuring that her decision to abort was 'thoughtful and informed'. The State interest in protecting the life of the unborn, an interest which after the first trimester increases, legitimated State laws which were framed with the purpose of ensuring thoughtful and informed decision making. Moreover, such regulations did not, the Court ruled, offend against the central principle of *Roe*. In *Roe*, it had been recognised that there was a balance to be struck between the woman's right to choose and the State's increasing interest in potential human life. Accordingly, States could legitimately enact rules and regulations which:

> ... serve[s] a valid purpose, one not designed to strike at the right itself, has the incidental effect of making it more difficult or more expensive to procure an abortion cannot be enough to invalidate it. Only where State regulation imposes an undue burden on a woman's ability to make this decision does the power of the State reach into the heart of the liberty protected by the Due Process Clause.[120]

Thus, while in *Roe* the Court's principal concern had been to recognise and enunciate the existence and scope of a woman's right to choose, in 1992 with the decision of *Casey* is found a shift of emphasis towards an enunciation of the power and right of the State to regulate access to abortion even in the first trimester, provided that such regulation does not impose an 'undue burden'. The balance of the scales had now tilted towards the protection of unborn life through the imposition of restrictions designed to ensure full and informed rational decision making on the part of the woman. Where, however, the purpose of a State law is not to facilitate a woman's free choice, but to hinder it, that law would be invalid.

In relation to the Pennsylvania law under consideration, the Court ruled that a 24 hour waiting period, while it may be for some women (for example, those who had to travel long distances and for whom the explanation of a 24 hour absence could be difficult) 'particularly burdensome' as the court below held, that did not of itself establish that it placed an 'undue burden' on a particular woman within that group. Accordingly, the Court was not 'convinced that the 24 hour waiting period constitutes an undue burden ...'.

---

[120] *Planned Parenthood of Southeastern Pennsylvania v Casey* 112 S Ct 2791 (1992).

As to the requirement that a married woman, save in a medical emergency, should provide a signed statement that she has notified her spouse that she intends to undergo an abortion, or alternatively certifying that it was not her husband who impregnated her, or that her husband could not be located, or that she had been the victim of spousal sexual assault which had been notified to the State, or that the woman believes that notifying her husband will lead to violent repercussions, the Court ruled that these provisions were inconsistent with the woman's right to choose, in imposing an undue burden on her, and were thus invalid.

In relation to the State law's requirement that minors under the age of 18 required the consent of one of her parents or the approval of the courts before undergoing an abortion, the Court held that the parental consent requirement was valid, provided that a 'judicial bypass' procedure was also in place.

Finally, with respect to the record keeping and reporting requirements of Pennsylvania, the Court ruled that all the provisions, save the requirement of spousal notice, were valid. Accordingly, State law is entitled to claim, in the interests of 'maternal health', that a report be filed identifying the physicians involved, the institution, the woman's age, any previous pregnancies or abortions, any pre-existing medical conditions which might affect pregnancy, any medical complications with the abortion, and the weight of the aborted foetus. Further, all institutions must file a quarterly report detailing the number of abortions performed, and details as to the trimester breakdowns. In all cases, the identity of the woman concerned remains confidential, although the records in relation to publicly funded institutions is a matter of public record.[121]

WOMEN'S REPRODUCTIVE RIGHTS IN INTERNATIONAL DIMENSION

The Report of the International Conference on Population and Development, 1994, states that:

... reproductive rights rest on 'the basic right of all couples and individuals to decide freely and responsibly the number, spacing and timing of their children and to have the information and means to do so, and the right to attain the highest standard of sexual and reproductive health.

... the right to make decisions concerning reproduction free of discrimination, coercion and violence, as expressed in human right documents.[122]

---

[121] See, also, *NOW v Scheidler* 24 January 1994 (Supreme Court); *Madsen v Women's Health Centre* 30 June 1994 (Supreme Court); *Elizabeth Blackwell Health Center for Women v Knoll* 25 July 1995 (US Court of Appeals 3rd circuit).

[122] Cairo, September 1994 (A/CONF 171/13), Chapter 1, Resolution 1, Annex, para 7.3.

The religious and cultural inheritance and influence

Historically, in many societies, abortion was viewed for centuries as a means of fertility control. Sex selection of children also plays a role in the availability of abortion in both China and India. While the birth of a son is desirable, the birth of a daughter may present serious financial and social problems for a family. The cost of a daughter's marriage, especially in light of the requirements of dowry, dominates the issue of a girl child's desirability. Boys, by contrast, are prized for their capacity to increase the family wealth through marriage. In India, in particular, given the practice of marrying young girls to older men and the unsurprising fact of early widowhood, widows represent a burden on the family and society, and are generally discriminated against and unwanted. The choice between *suttee*[123] and widowhood is a choice between relative fates.[124] The rise in consumerism and the State directed policy of smaller family units also contributes to the explanation of the undesirability of girl babies. Girl babies are, relative to boy babies, socially unwanted babies. Infanticide has long been a means of population control,[125] and represents an alternative to failed contraception or sex selection procedures.

Population control programmes[126]

Population law and policy raises a number of difficult issues. Until the Second World War, there was little concern with population control: a healthy birthrate was considered as right and natural. In the succeeding years, however, with improvements in health and increasing longevity and decreased infant mortality, population growth in many parts of the world came under scrutiny, both within individual States and by the increasingly influential international agencies of the United Nations. With awareness of the economic and social consequences of population growth and control, came increasing awareness of, and standard setting for, the realisation of individual human rights. While the structure and personnel of the United Nations and its agencies has been criticised as being traditionally male-dominated and male-orientated by feminist legal scholars,[127] there has been increasing awareness of those aspects of human rights which are unique to women. As stated in the

---

[123] See, further, Chapter 2.
[124] See, eg, the account of the fate of Indian widows, *The Sunday Times*, 21 June 1997.
[125] For an account of the contemporary position in India, see Venkatachalam, R and Viji, S, *Female Infanticide*, 1993, New Delhi: Har-Anand.
[126] See, for further details, *op cit*, Hartmann, fn 82.
[127] See, eg, Charlesworth, H, Chinkin, C and Wright, S, 'Feminist approaches to international law' (1991) 85 AJIL 613.

Introduction to Feminist Jurisprudence

United Nations Reports documents,[128] internationally, women suffer particular inequalities in the economic and social sphere; particularly high levels of domestic and other violence and health problems connected with fertility and childbirth. Thus, while much of the data in this chapter concerning, for example, the law relating to abortion and sterilisation, is drawn from Western jurisprudence, the broader picture of the particular difficulties facing women worldwide must also be considered.

The most notorious campaign of population control occurred during Indira Ghandi's Prime Ministership of India. In 1976, the Government introduced new laws and regulations requiring individual States to meet sterilisation quotas. If a couple refused sterilisation after the birth of three children, fines and imprisonment could follow. Government aid was also withheld from those who refused to comply with the sterilisation programme. Between July and December 1976, 6.5 million people were sterilised in India. Men were not exempt from the purge: it is recorded that in one village, all men of eligible age were rounded up and forcibly sterilised.[129] Nevertheless, the primary targets were, and remain, women. The conditions under which such operations were performed were often insanitary: increasing the dangers of operative and post-operative infections. Following the fall of the Ghandi Government in 1977, the number of sterilisations fell rapidly. Nevertheless, the programme continues, with the principal emphasis being on pressure and inducements. Women are reportedly paid $22 for submitting to sterilisation: men only $15. External pressure from international funding agencies places further pressure on the Government to control its population, with the United National Fund for Population Activities and the United States Agency for International Development increasing its contributions to the programme.

From a feminist perspective, the issue is not whether or not population control programmes are 'right' or 'wrong', moral or immoral, but rather the means by which such programmes are achieved. First, the principal targets for such programmes are for the most part women, rather than men. This despite the fact that vasectomies are surgically far more simple to perform than are sterilisations and/or hysterectomies. They are also far less costly to perform. Secondly, the side- and after-effects of vasectomies are also far less serious, actually and potentially, on the physical and psychological health of the patient. Thirdly, while sterilisation may be a welcome option for those women who have achieved their desired size of family, sterilisation – that most permanent form of contraception – which is performed by way of force, pressure or inducement, removes a woman's right to choose the future of her fertility and is thus indefensible, notwithstanding the desirability of population control. Fourthly, it is well documented that such programmes,

---

[128] See United Nations Report, *The World's Women 1970–90*, 1991, London: HMSO; United Nations Report, *The World's Women 1985: Trends and Statistics*, 1995, London: HMSO. (See *Sourcebook*, pp 3–19.)

[129] See 'Entire village sterilised' (1978) India Now, August.

whether the method employed is the encouragement of long-term contraception through the use of implants (Norplant) or injections (Depo-Prevura) or by means of abortifacients (RU486), or by sterilisation or hysterectomy, focus on the poorest women in the community who have the worst nutrition and are therefore more likely than women in better health to succumb to side- and after-effects. Fifthly, such programmes are regarded by governments and those international agencies which sponsor and encourage them, as the principal agent to achieve limits to population growth. This preference for the lasting efficacy of the means employed often precludes the alternative of education concerning fertility control, and the promotion of alternative means of contraception – barrier methods, withdrawal practices, 'safe' sexual intercourse only in non-fertile periods ('natural' contraception favoured by the Roman Catholic Church) – which carry none of the adverse medical or health risks.

Sterilisation as a means of voluntary infertility should be regarded – other than from a strict religious perspective – an incontrovertible right. It was so recognised in 1974 by the Symposium on Law and Population which recommended that:

(1) with due regard to the legal and cultural traditions and mores, and the economic needs, of the respective countries, governments adopt such legislation as may be required to make voluntary sterilisation available for contraceptive purposes;

(2) in adopting such legislation governments ensure freedom of choice based upon legally competent and fully informed consent, and subject to proper medical procedures and requirements ...[130]

It is not only in Africa, Asia and South America that non-voluntary sterilisations are performed in the name of population control. In Canada, the United States of America and the United Kingdom, there is evidence of sterilisations being performed in circumstances which do not amount to the free choice of the woman concerned. Again, several issues are involved. On the one hand, there is the question of the availability of sterilisation for those women who choose sterilisation as a permanent means of contraception. This in turn entails the right to sterilisation for social purposes, otherwise labelled non-therapeutic sterilisations, rather than for therapeutic reasons. It is this issue which caused particular judicial disquiet in Canada. On the other hand, there is the question of the use of sterilisation as a means of permanently preventing conception by mentally incompetent women and minors and furthermore, the use of sterilisation as a means of controlling the fertility of women from minority groups and impoverished families. This use of sterilisation is most closely associated with a sterilisation requirement being

---

[130] The Symposium on Law and Population, June 1974 (Tunis). See Lee, L, 'Legal implications of the world population plan of action' (1974) 9 Journal of International Law and Economics 375.

attached to the availability of abortion. Within each of these scenarios lies the question of the right of a woman to choose and to control her own fertility, as opposed to the right of others to decide on her future fertility.

A note of caution should perhaps be entered here, namely that legal rights do not inevitably and invariably ensure real equality of power. As Hilary Charlesworth, Christine Chinkin and Shelley Wright have written:

> The formal acquisition of a right, such as the right to equal treatment, is often assumed to have solved an imbalance of power. In practice, however, the promise of rights is thwarted by the inequalities of power: the economic and social dependence of women on men may discourage the invocation of legal rights that are premised on an adversarial relationship between the rights holder and the infringer. More complex still are rights designed to apply to women only such as the right to reproductive freedom and to choose abortion.[131]

Balanced against a 'woman's right to choose', or a 'woman's right to refuse' must be posited the realities of economic and social power disparities between women and men; the role of the medical profession and the power of the courts to determine issues related to a woman's fertility. Nowhere is this dilemma more apparent than in the United States of America, with its constitutional 'guarantee' of a woman's right to choose, at least in the first trimester of pregnancy, which is then hedged in and severely restricted by other regulations and requirements which *de facto* deny women access to abortion advice, impose time restrictions in the form of waiting periods, the denial of State funding for abortion, whether elective or medically necessary, and restrictions imposed via the doctrine of informed consent.

NON-CONSENSUAL TREATMENT OF PATIENTS SUFFERING FROM ANOREXIA NERVOSA[132]

Each year, an estimated 6,000 new cases of anorexia nervosa are diagnosed in the United Kingdom, swelling the total of sufferers to 3.5 million.[133] The

---

[131] *Op cit*, Charlesworth, Chinkin and Wright, fn 127. In this regard, the scepticism in relation to rights which forms the heart of the Critical Legal Studies school of thought discussed in Chapter 6, and opposed by many feminist scholars, especially those who have been traditionally denied rights, must be recalled. (See *Sourcebook*, pp 537–54.)

[132] On anorexia nervosa see Palmer, R, *Anorexia Nervosa*, 2nd edn, 1988, London: Penguin; Wolf, N, *The Beauty Myth*, 1991, London: Vintage; Bordo, S, *Unbearable Weight: Feminism, Western Culture and the Body*, 1993 Berkeley, California: California UP; Orbach, S, *Fat is a Feminist Issue*, 1993, Harmondsworth: Penguin, and *Hunger Strike: The Anorexic's Struggle as a Metaphor for Our Age*, 1993, Harmondsworth: Penguin.

[133] *Ibid*, Wolf, p 183.

increasing incidence of eating disorders, primarily among women and young girls,[134] has caused the issue of the appropriate treatment for the conditions to come before the courts. What is of interest about this matter, from a feminist perspective, is the manner in which the eating disorders of women have been conceptualised as not only medical matters, but matters in which the patient is classified as being psychologically disturbed, and thus brought within the mental health arena. Starting from the proposition that a medically competent adult is entitled to accept or refuse medical treatment, even where acceptance or refusal would cause harm to the patient, it is only by extending the concept of mental incompetence to cover those whose decisions do not agree with medical or judicial opinion about their welfare, that individuals can find their autonomy over such decisions restricted, if not eliminated.

That minors should not be accorded full autonomy over medical matters, especially where they lack the necessary intelligence and understanding, is relatively uncontroversial, although it becomes contentious where it is perceived that a mature minor has the necessary intelligence and understanding but her decision is overridden by the courts on the basis that the court's perception of her welfare is superior to her own.[135]

However, in relation to adult women, case law reveals the same sleight of hand in relation to the mental health legislation, as is evident in relation to court sanctioned Caesarean sections, of women whose competence to consent to treatment is overridden by interpreting permissible treatment without patient consent as encompassing treatment for disorders not directly related to the mental disorder for which the patient is hospitalised. An illustrative and seminal case is that of *B v Croydon Health Authority*.[136] B, a woman, was admitted to hospital under section 3 of the Mental Health Act 1983 for 'psychopathic disorder'.[137] The treatment prescribed was 'psychotherapeutic psychoanalysis'. B stopped eating. By the time the case came to court, B had started eating, but she and the Health Authority wanted the judgment of the court as to whether forcible feeding by nasogastric tube would have been lawful. Hoffmann LJ ruled that it would. Against the submission that the proposed treatment must be related to the mental disorder itself, Hoffmann LJ stated that medical treatment in the Act[138] was broadly defined to include 'nursing ... care, habilitation and rehabilitation under medical supervision'.

---

[134] On the increasing incidence of anorexia in young men, see Dresser, R, 'Feeding the hungry artist: legal issues in treating anorexia' (1984) 2 Wisconsin L Rev 297; Frost, N, 'Food for thought: Dresser on anorexia' (1984) 2 Wisconsin L Rev 375.

[135] For the English case law, see, in particular, *Gillick v West Norfolk and Wisbech Area Health Authority* [1986] AC 112; [1984] QB 581; *Re R* [1992] Fam 11; *Re W* [1993] Fam 64. See, also, Williams, G, 'The *Gillick* saga' (1985) 135 NLJ 1156 and 1179; Cretney, S, 'Gillick and the concept of legal capacity' (1989) 105 LQR 356.

[136] [1995] 1 All ER 683.

[137] Defined as borderline personality disorder coupled with post-traumatic stress disorder.

[138] Mental Health Act 1983, s 145(1).

Accordingly, a range of ancillary acts to the principal treatment fell within the definition. Given that B was lawfully detained by virtue of a mental disorder, treatment which alleviated 'the consequences of the [mental] disorder' were capable of being ancillary 'to a treatment calculated to alleviate or prevent a deterioration of the psychopathic disorder'. The court endorsed the dicta of Ewbank J in *Re KB (Adult) (Mental Patient: Medical Treatment)*,[139] in which he declared that the test-tube feeding of an anorexic patient 'relieving symptoms is just as much a part of treatment as relieving the underlying cause'.[140]

Where mental health legislation is not, or cannot be, invoked to legitimise medical treatment, the courts lack jurisdiction to override an adult patient's refusal of consent to treatment. In *Secretary of State for Home Department v Robb*,[141] a 27 year old male prison inmate went on hunger strike. The Home Secretary sought a declaration from the court that it was lawful to abide by the prisoner's refusal to receive nutrition. Thorpe J ruled that the right of an adult of sound mind to self-determination prevailed over the interests of the State, and that there was no duty to prolong life. What distinguishes this case from cases concerning anorexic patients, and cases concerning Caesarean sections, is the court's acceptance of the mental competence of the adult male prisoner to decide to end his own life. With anorexia patients, the courts have accepted that the condition itself, which centres on the patients need to control the situation, impairs the patient's mental capacity to make decisions in her own best interests. As Lord Donaldson of Lymington MR stated in *Re W (A Minor) (Medical Treatment: Court's Jurisdiction)*,[142] 'one of the symptoms of anorexia nervosa is a desire by the sufferer to "be in control" and such a refusal [of medical treatment] would be an obvious way of demonstrating this'.[143]

Competence and the 'mature minor'

Section 8 of the The English Family Law Act 1969[144] provides that:
(1) The consent of a minor who has attained the age of 16 years to any surgical, medical or dental treatment which, in the absence of consent, would constitute a trespass to his person, shall be as effective as it would be if he were of full age; and where a minor has by virtue of this section given an effective consent to any treatment it shall not be necessary to obtain any consent for it from his parent or guardian.

---

[139] (1994) 19 BMLR 144, p 146.

[140] See, also, *Riverside Health Trust v Fox* [1994] 1 FLR 614, in which the Court of Appeal set aside a declaration authorising the forcible feeding of a 37 year old anorexic patient, which was granted without the patient being heard.

[141] [1995] 22 British Medical L Rev 43 (Family Division).

[142] [1992] 3 WLR 758.

[143] [1992] 3 WLR 762.

[144] See *The Report of the Committee on the Age of Majority* (the Latey Report), Cmnd 3342, 1967, London: HMSO.

(2) In this section, 'surgical, medical or dental treatment' includes any procedure undertaken for the purposes of diagnosis, and this section applies to any procedure (including, in particular, the administration of an anaesthetic) which is ancillary to any treatment as it applies to that treatment.

(3) Nothing in this section shall be construed as making ineffective any consent which would have been effective if this section had not been enacted.

The position under common law was authoritatively reformulated in *Gillick v West Norfolk and Wisbech Area Health Authority*.[145] In *Gillick*, the issue for decision was whether a 'mature minor' had the right, under statute or common law, to seek and be given contraceptive and abortion advice and treatment, without the consent of her parent(s). The House of Lords ruled that she could. Notwithstanding Lord Brandon's reservations concerning the apparent 'encouragement' that this decision gave to under-age, and hence unlawful, sexual intercourse, the House of Lords ruled that where a girl, under the age of 16, showed sufficient maturity and understanding in relation to the particular matter in question – and that competence would vary according to the difficulty of the subject matter – the girl had the capacity to consent under common law, as preserved by section 8(3) of the Family Law Act 1969.[146] Further, where a mature minor has the competence to consent, that consent is determinative: she cannot be opposed by her parents. As Lord Scarman stated:

> The underlying principle of the law ... is that parental right yields to the child's right to make his own decisions when he reaches a sufficient understanding and intelligence to be capable of making up his own mind on the matter requiring decisions.

A number of issues were left open by the decision. It remained unclear, for example, whether the right to consent to treatment included the right to refuse treatment, and the position of parents and the courts in relation to consent and withholding of consent. Moreover, although *Gillick* was heralded as a 'landmark' decision for children's rights, it soon became apparent that the decision was not to have the widespread application of which it was capable. In no area is this clearer than in relation to a teenage girl's capacity to consent to, or refuse, medical treatment.

---

[145] [1986] AC 112; [1985] 2 WLR 413; [1985] 1 All ER 533, CA; [1985] 3 All ER 402, HL.
[146] On *Gillick*, see Bainham, A, 'The balance of power in family decisions' [1986] CLJ 262; Eekelaar, J, 'The emergence of children's rights' [1986] 6 OJLS 161.

In *Re R (A Minor) (Wardship: Medical Treatment)*,[147] Lord Donaldson MR was to rule that whereas a competent minor could consent to treatment, the minor could not determine whether or not she should receive treatment. Where the girl refused treatment – as opposed to consenting to it – both her parents, who retain power, and the court, could override that refusal. In *Re R* the issue was treatment for anorexia nervosa of a 15 year old girl. She was mentally competent for periods of time, but that competence wavered. The court held that such fluctuating competence did not suffice to fulfil the *Gillick* criteria. Furthermore, Lord Donaldson stated clearly that whereas a *Gillick* competent minor could consent to treatment, she could not refuse consent to treatment, and that her parents and the court retained the power to consent on her behalf. Lord Donaldson referred to the 'keyholders' to the issue of consent: the competent minor, her parents and the courts. Each had the power to unlock the door to consent.

The right to consent, and right to refuse to consent, returned to the courts in 1992 in *Re W (A Minor) (Medical Treatment: Court's Jurisdiction)*.[148] W, a 16 year old girl suffering from anorexia, was in the care of the local authority, having had an unsettled and unhappy childhood. She was being treated in an adolescent residential unit, but refused to eat solids and her weight had dropped to 5 stone 7 lb. Medical evidence suggested that 'within a week' her capacity to bear children later in life would be at risk, and that sooner rather than later her life would be at risk. W was not refusing all treatment, but doctors were uncertain whether she would continue to consent to treatment in the future. It was also considered desirable for her to be transferred to a specialist clinic in London: this W refused to consent to, wishing to stay in a known and supportive environment in her home area. On an application to the court to invoke its inherent jurisdiction and authorise W's transfer, the Court of First Instance held that W had sufficient understanding to make the decision, but notwithstanding that the court had jurisdiction to make the order sought. W appealed. The Court of Appeal dismissed her appeal. While the Family Law Act conferred a right to consent to treatment, it did not confer an absolute right, and in particular the decision of a 16 year old minor, or of a *Gillick* competent minor, could be overridden by the court where her best interests dictated it. Lord Donaldson MR ruled that one of the clinical manifestations of anorexia was 'a firm wish not to be cured, or at least not to be cured unless and until the sufferer wishes to cure herself. In this sense it is

---

[147] [1992] Fam 11; [1991] 4 All ER 177. See Douglas, G, 'The retreat from Gillick' (1992) 55 MLR 569. For critique, see Bainham, A, 'The judge and the competent minor' (1992) 108 LQR 194; Thornton, R, 'Multiple keyholders – wardship and consent to medical treatment' [1992] CLJ 34; Brazier, M, *Medicine, Patients and the Law*, 2nd edn, 1992, Harmondsworth: Penguin, p 345.

[148] [1992] 3 WLR 758.

an addictive illness ...'.[149] Accordingly, 'it is a feature of anorexia nervosa that it is capable of destroying the ability to make an informed choice. It creates a compulsion to refuse treatment or only to accept treatment which is likely to be ineffective'.[150] While the wishes of the anorexic minor were to be respected, they had a 'much reduced significance' as a result of the illness, and could not override a decision which was taken in her best interests. Lord Donaldson regretted his 'keyholder' analogy. Keys can lock as well as unlock, he recognised. What remains startling about his change in terminology, and of view, is that he moved directly from the issue of consent to the issue of the protection of the medical profession. What replaced the 'keyholder' was the 'flak jacket' – the device which protects the doctors from legal liability. As Lord Donaldson expressed it, '[A]nyone who gives him [the doctor] a flak jacket (that is, consent) may take it back, but the doctor only needs one and so long as he continues to have one he has the legal right to proceed.'[151] Once again the law reveals its alliance with and support for its fraternal profession, under which the interests, rights and freedoms on the individual are subsumed.

---

[149] [1992] 3 WLR 758, p 761.
[150] *Ibid*, p 769.
[151] *Ibid*, p 767.

CHAPTER 11

WOMEN, VIOLENCE AND THE LEGAL SYSTEM

INTRODUCTION

In this chapter the physical (sexual or otherwise) and psychological violence against women and the reaction of the legal system to that violence, both in terms of the treatment of women victims of violence and that of women who react against violence with violence, is considered. As the data will reveal, violence against women is a universal, ahistorical, phenomenon. Gender-based violence – in all its many manifestations – occurs throughout the world, irrespective of culture or economic development. The universality of gender-based violence – violence which is predominantly violence inflicted by familial male members against women partners and female children – raises a number of questions.

The first issue to address is the definition of gender-based violence. The second question relates to the causes of such violence. Is domestic violence related to socio-economic deprivation? Is domestic violence explained through an analysis of gender power relationships? Is violence against women explained as a socially learned phenomenon, which gets 'handed down' from generation to generation? Why do some women continue to tolerate economic, physical, psychological and sexual violence? To what extent can the law provide appropriate remedies for victims of violence, either in the form of deterrence or punishment, or through civil law remedies which protect the victim? Given the universalism and a historical nature of gender-based violence, the role of law in this regard is both culturally and historically dependent, but also – given the culturally embedded nature of gender-based violence – destined to play a limited role in the eradication of such violence. Gender-based violence represents one of the greatest challenges to law, and reveals law's limitations in dealing with the extremes of human conduct.

Defining gender-based violence

The United Nations Declaration on the Elimination of Violence Against Women[1]

Article 2

Violence against women shall be understood to encompass, but not be limited to, the following:

---

1 Adopted by the General Assembly on 20 December 1993, GA Res 48/104.

(a) physical, sexual and psychological violence occurring in the family, including battering, sexual abuse of female children in the household, dowry-related violence, marital rape, female genital mutilation and other traditional practices harmful to women, non-spousal violence and violence related to exploitation;

(b) physical, sexual and psychological violence occurring within the general community, including rape, sexual abuse, sexual harassment and intimidation at work, in educational institutions and elsewhere, trafficking in women and forced prostitution;

(c) physical, sexual and psychological violence perpetrated or condoned by the State, wherever it occurs.

Measuring gender-based violence

Any precise measurement of the incidence of violence in society is problematic. Under-reporting of violent crime – especially that committed within the family – has long been recognised. In addition, the failure to prosecute the offender distorts the criminal statistics. What is evident, however, is that violence against women is endemic in all societies, whether that violence be in the form of sexual harassment,[2] assault, sexual violence including rape, or murder. Further, as will be seen from the discussion which follows, not only are women subjected to violence by men, but they also suffer a form of subtle violence inflicted by the legal system itself, especially in prosecutions for a rape of which they were a victim, and for murder or manslaughter when, no longer able to cope with repeated assaults, women are provoked into killing their violent partners.

International data

On a global scale, the United Nations receives reports of violence against women from its Member States, but itself admits that the accuracy of the data is dubious. As the United Nations Report, 1990,[3] records, '... [s]ecrecy, insufficient evidence and social and legal barriers continue to make it difficult to acquire accurate data on domestic violence against women, which many criminologists believe to be the most underreported crime'.[4] Nevertheless, significant data is provided by the report. In developed regions, a majority of reporting States record domestic violence, sexual assault, rape and sexual harassment. In less industrial societies, for example Kuwait, a third of all

---

2   Which may be conceptualised as a form of psychological violence and sexual discrimination.
3   United Nations Report, *The World's Women 1970–90*, 1991, London: HMSO.
4   *Ibid*, p 19. (See *Sourcebook*, pp 554–58.)

women participating in a survey reported assaults. In India, in 1985, there were 999 recorded cases of dowry deaths, in 1986, 1,319 and in 1987, 1,786. In the United Nations Report, 1995,[5] the United Nations records that gender-based violence against women 'crosses all cultural, religious and regional boundaries and is a major problem in every country in which it has been studied'.[6]

Globally, the most prevalent form of gender-based abuse is committed by a husband or other male partner. The United Nations reports that 'studies in 10 countries estimate that between 17 and 38 per cent of women have been physically assaulted by an intimate partner'.[7] Moreover, studies in Africa, Latin America and Asia report 'even higher rates of abuse', in some cases up to 60 per cent of the population studied.

Sexual abuse data reveals that in up to 60 per cent of all sexual cases, the victim is known to the perpetrator. Statistics on rape collated from surveys conducted among college aged women reveal that between eight per cent and 15 per cent of them have been raped, and that, if attempted rape is included, the figure rises to between 20 per cent and 27 per cent. Irrespective of region or culture, the United Nations reports that from 40 per cent to 60 per cent of known sexual assaults are committed against girls aged 15 or younger. In relation to child abuse, in the United States 78 per cent of substantiated child sexual abuse cases involved girls.[8] A South African study recorded that 92 per cent of child victims were girls, and all but one of the perpetrators were male, two-thirds of them being family members.

In addition, the United Nations records that the trafficking of women for prostitution continues despite international legislation. The report reveals that an estimated two million women, of whom roughly 400,000 are under 18 years of age, are engaged in prostitution in India.[9] In Nepal, some 5,000 to 7,000 young girls from Nepal are sold into brothels each year, and an estimated 20,000 Burmese women and girls work in brothels in Thailand.[10]

Trafficking in women is by no means confined to the Far East. The United Nations records that a 1992 report of the Netherlands Advisory Committee on Human Rights and Foreign Policy 'suggests traffic in thousands of women in the Netherlands alone for the purposes of prostitution'.[11] Moreover, an

---

[5] United Nations Report, *The World's Women 1995: Trends and Statistics*, 1995, London: HMSO.
[6] *Ibid*, p 158.
[7] *Ibid*, p 158.
[8] *Ibid*, p 181.
[9] The Commission on Human Rights Working Group on Contemporary Forms of Slavery; see *ibid*, United Nations Report, 1995, p 162.
[10] Asia Watch and the Women's Rights Group; see *ibid*, United Nations Report, 1995, p 162.
[11] *Ibid*, p 162.

increase in trafficking has been recorded in Eastern European countries, and from Eastern Europe to Western Europe.[12]

In Australia, Canada, England, New Zealand and the United States, rape is regarded as one of the most (if not the most) underreported crime. In the United States, research in 1986 found that only 50 per cent of all rapes are reported to the police.[13]

In England, 5,039 rapes were reported to the police in 1994;[14] in the London Metropolitan Police Area, 1,199 rapes were reported in 1992–93.[15] The number of rapes which went to trial in 1994 was 936, or 18.6 per cent of all notifiable offences.[16] In 1996, however, whereas just under 6,000 rapes were reported to the police in England and Wales, the number of prosecutions and convictions had fallen sharply. Only 19 per cent of complaints led to a court case, and half of the defendants acquitted.[17]

Rape in wartime – with women being regarded as part of the 'spoils of war' – continues to be reported. Whilst acknowledging the difficulties in collecting accurate data in this particularly sensitive area, the United Nations nevertheless records estimates of 20,000 rapes in the war in former Yugoslavia. Physicians – using calculations based on pregnancies occurring after a single act of intercourse – estimated that 11,900 rapes had occurred during that conflict.

As the United Nation's evidence reveals, the problem of domestic violence, conceived as gender-based violence, is universal. As the United Nations Report, *Violence Against Women in the Family*,[18] reveals, 'women irrespective of nationality, colour, class, religion or culture are at significant risk of physical psychological and sexual violence in the home from male relatives, most frequently their husbands or partners'.[19] Irrespective of economic conditions, religious and cultural differences between societies, or questions of class, violence against women is a persisting universal phenomenon. In the United Nation's *Declaration on the Elimination of Violence Against Women*,[20] replicated above, gender-based violence is conceived as a general human rights issue and also as an issue of sexual discrimination.

---

[12] Papers presented at the 1994 Utrecht Conference on Traffic in Persons; see *op cit*, United Nations Report, fn 5, 1995, p 162.

[13] US Department of Justice, *Sourcebook of Criminal Justice Statistics*, 1988.

[14] *Criminal Statistics 1994*, Cm 3020, London, HMSO, Table 2.16.

[15] *Report of the Commissioner of Police of the Metropolis*, London: HMSO.

[16] *Criminal Statistics England and Wales 1983–94, Criminal Statistics Supplementary Tables*, Vol 2, 1983–94, London: HMSO.

[17] (1997) *The Times*, 18 September.

[18] UN Centre for Social Development and Humanitarian Affairs, United Nations Report, *Violence Against Women in the Family*, 1989 (United Nations Sales No E.89.IV.5).

[19] Connors, J, 'Violence against women' (see *Sourcebook* p 558). This paper was prepared for presentation at the 1995 United Nations Fourth World Conference on Women.

[20] General Assembly Resolution 48/104, adopted in December 1993.

Violence against women in the United Kingdom

Given the difficulties in assessing statistical data on violence against women, and recalling that domestic violence remains the most highly underreported offence against women, recourse to the Judicial Statistics and Home Office data is helpful but by no means conclusive. Whether the law invoked is the criminal or civil law, recourse to law is often the last resort of many women. For a number of reasons – acceptance, condonation, fear, ignorance, shame, to name a few – women are remarkably reluctant to invoke the law in their own defence against violence. In 1994, 24,034 applications were made under the Domestic Violence and Matrimonial Proceedings Act 1976,[21] of which 3,946 sought exclusion orders, 24,566 non-molestation orders and 9,793 orders had a power of arrest attached.[22] Under the Domestic Proceedings and Magistrates' Courts Act 1978,[23] in 1984, 8,480 orders were granted. By 1988, the rate of applications had fallen to 5,510, and to 3,450 in 1991. In 1993, 1,642 orders were granted.[24, 25]

The criminal statistics for the year 1995 in England and Wales recorded a total of 30,274 sexual offences, of which 16,876 were indecent assaults of a female (compared to 3,150 on males); 4,986 rapes of women (compared with 150 rapes of men).[26] Sexual offences taken as a whole amounted to just under 10 per cent of the total recorded violent crimes in 1995. In terms of convictions, in 1995, 587 offenders were either found guilty or cautioned for rape of a woman; 3,321 offenders were found guilty or cautioned for indecent assault on women.[27]

In terms of the most extreme form of violence – 'spousal' murder – in 1990, of 43 per cent of female murders in the United Kingdom, the principal suspect was the women's partner, whereas the figures for 1983 reveal that in only five per cent of male murders the female partner was the principal suspect. In 1990 there were 226 female murder victims. Of these, 43 per cent were killed by

---

[21] The statute which provided for non-molestation and exclusion orders to be granted by the county court and High Court for married spouses and cohabitees 'living together as husband and wife'. See now the Family Law 1996, Part IV.

[22] Judicial Statistics 1981–94.

[23] The statute conferring jurisdiction on the lower courts to provide injunctive relief for married persons. The jurisdiction is more limited than that under the 1976 Act. Whereas under the latter Act, 'molestation' and psychological violence is covered, the 1978 Act requires actual physical violence or threats of violence.

[24] *Domestic Proceedings: England and Wales, 1983–92*, Home Office Statistical Bulletin, London: HMSO.

[25] The decrease in numbers is attributable in part to the complexity of the grounds to be established for an order, and in part for the increased preference of proceedings in the county court under the 1976 Act (the law is now reformed, see Part IV of the Family Law Act 1996).

[26] Male rape, or forced buggery, was introduced as a specific offence in the Criminal Justice and Public Order Act 1994, s 142.

[27] Source: *Criminal Statistics: England and Wales, 1995*, Cm 3421, 1996, London: The Stationery Office.

their partners and 19 per cent by other members of the family. Of 381 male murder victims, nine per cent were killed by their partners and 17 per cent by another member of the family.[28] 'Wife beating' is regarded as the most under-reported crime.

Explaining gender-based violence

Gender-based violence concerns traditional patriarchal attitudes – the notion of male ownership, control and dominance. Cultural and religious practices have a unique authority within society. 'Cultural violence' such as Hindu suttee, female circumcision, Chinese footbinding, and witchmurders, considered in Chapter 2, whilst very different phenomena, share common explanatory causal characteristics to those of sexual harassment, rape and domestic violence: namely traditional male authority and control. Such an explanation may be met with the charge of 'essentialism' and 'universalisation' of complex phenomena: however, as noted above, the international data reveals that gender-based violence is universal, ahistorical and crosses all cultural boundaries. It is thus a global problem.[29] Gender-based violence, whether it be physical, sexual, psychological or economic represents a form of control:

> Domestic violence is the systematic, ahistorical, acultural manifestation of male power. It is as immutable and enduring as patriarchy which supports and sustains it.[30]

A range of differing explanations is offered in relation to gender-based violence. Writing in the 1970s, English campaigner Erin Pizzey argued that the violent male is psychotic: mentally deranged and in need of incarceration to keep his victims safe.[31] Socio-economic conditions have also been blamed: unemployment, loss of self-esteem and poverty, all undoubtedly play a role in explaining violence. And yet, this explanation is unconvincing: if it is accepted that domestic and (other) sexual violence is primarily and predominantly a male crime, the question must be asked why is it that women in similarly poor socio-economic conditions (and women's economic situation has traditionally been worse than the male's) do not turn to gender-based violence. For others,[32] violent behaviour is learned early in life: violent children will become violent adults; children who have experienced violence in the home –

---

[28] See Home Office, *Gender and the Criminal Justice System*, 1992, London: HMSO.
[29] See Charlesworth, H and Chinkin, C, 'Violence against women: a global issue', in Stubbs, J (ed), *Women, Male Violence and the Law*, 1994, Sydney: Institute of Criminology, Monograph Series No 6, p 1.
[30] Edwards, S, *Sex and Gender in the Legal Process*, 1996, London: Blackstone, p 180.
[31] See Pizzey, E, *Scream Quietly or the Neighbours Will Hear*, 1974, London: Penguin.
[32] Eg, Dobash, R and Dobash, R, below.

whether directly against them or against their mother – are most likely to grow into violent adults. In Dobash and Dobash's study of battered women,[33] women's responses revealed that in 45 per cent of cases, the violence was prompted by possessiveness or sexual jealousy; a further 16 per cent that the aggressor was seeking a confrontation revolving around the domestic sphere; in 15 per cent of cases, the last act of violence occurred in the woman's attempt to escape, of which seven per cent reported that this last violence was also the most violent. It is possessiveness – that concept which has dogged English family law in so many ways – which some psychiatrists point to in explaining male violence: and sexual possessiveness is the most fundamental aspect of this. For a woman to be unfaithful means that she is expressing independence; sexual relations are a source of possession and being possessed.[34]

From a radical feminist perspective, sexual and other domestic violence against women is symptomatic of unequal power relations within society, inherited from the past and upheld by those with power. For Catharine MacKinnon[35] sexual harassment and violence against women are explained best by recognising that the principal factor in gender-based abuse and violence is the traditional role of women as subordinates, men as dominators. Marxist theory tells us that inequality is the result of the relations of production and economic determinism which has resulted in capitalism which denies the worker the true value of his labour and subordinates him to the capitalist elite. For MacKinnon, by contrast, the fundamental and first source of inequality lies in sexuality and the oppression of women: what work is to Marxism, sexuality is to feminism.[36]

Historically, traditionally and conventionally women have been treated as second-class citizens and as sexual objects. Law and legal rules do not exist in a vacuum. They arise, as sociological explanations of the relationship between law and society tell us, out of the 'mores' of society.[37] The mores of society have traditionally placed women in an inferior, or subordinate, position to men, confined to the private sphere, under the dominion of men, to child-bearing and child-nurturing. Traditionally, the male is provider; the dominant figure in the family. The patriarch. The father figure; the husband with full powers of management over the family finances; the husband with full parental rights over any children of the marriage. The husband, as Aristotle

---

[33] Dobash, R and Dobash, R, 'The nature and antecedents of violent events' (1984) 24 Br J Crim 269; see, also, Dobash, R and Dobash, R, *Violence Against Wives: A Case Against the Patriarchy*, 1979, New York: Free Press; *Women, Violence and Social Change*, 1992, New York: Routledge.

[34] Tov-Ruach, L, 'Jealousy, attention and loss', in Rorty, A (ed), *Explaining Emotions*, 1980, Berkeley, California: California UP.

[35] Professor of Law, University of Michigan.

[36] See MacKinnon, C, *Toward a Feminist Theory of the State*, 1989, Cambridge, Mass: Harvard UP.

[37] See, further, Chapter 2.

argued, is the master of the household: or as Sir William Blackstone tells us, the husband has power over the wife, under whose 'couveture' and 'protection' she exists. This conventional political, economic and physical power of men over women results in violence by the powerful against the powerless.

The problem of the liberal analysis of the 'public' and 'private' spheres of life

Liberalism, with its insistence on a private sphere of life, which is immune from legal control, contributes to the idea that somehow violence within the family is a domestic, private, family matter, which 'is not the law's business'. As Katherine O'Donovan has stated, '[H]ome is thought to be a private place, a refuge from society, where relationships can flourish untrammelled by public interference'.[38] The historical legacy which entailed a husband's absolute right to sexual access – irrespective of consent – to his wife's body; and his right to administer discipline (provided that the stick was 'no broader than his thumb') and constructed gender relations within the family as power relations – a feature which in domestic violence is represented in its most extreme form. The reluctance of the police to intervene in domestic disputes;[39] the reluctance of women victims to institute proceedings or to give evidence against their partners; and of the Crown Prosecution Service to prosecute[40] violent partners, the tendency of the courts to avoid custodial sentences, or to confer short custodial sentences, all lend weight to the notion that domestic violence is 'acceptable', 'inevitable' and as a result domestic violence appears trivialised by both the participants and the State. Conduct which the State would not tolerate between strangers in the public sphere, becomes conduct which is largely uncontrollable within the family context. The State, in failing adequately to protect victims of violence, privileges both the private sphere and male power, over protection for the victim, and thus perpetuates patriarchy within the family.

Thus, liberalism, the dominant political theory of the nineteenth and twentieth century, contributes to the problem which women face. By distinguishing between the public sphere of life which is legally regulated, and the private sphere of life which is largely legally unregulated, liberalism carves out a haven for domestic violence. The treatment of women – sexual

---

[38] O'Donovan, K, *Sexual Divisions in Law*, 1985, London: Weidenfeld and Nicolson, p 107.

[39] A Home Office Circular of 1990 emphasised that apprehension of the offender and the protection of the victim was the principal concern in the investigation of domestic violence cases. Domestic Violence Units have also been established in a number of police areas, which has resulted in increased numbers of cases reported, and increases in arrest rates: see *op cit*, Edwards, fn 30, pp 194–95.

[40] On which, see *op cit*, Edwards, fn 30, pp 198–213.

harassment, sexual assaults and rapes – which takes place in the public sphere (outside the home) is a further manifestation of traditional patriarchal views about the role and status of women in society.[41] However, where gender-based violence occurs in the public sphere, and between strangers, the State response is more robust than that which occurs in relation to 'domestic' violence. Nevertheless, as will be seen below, even where the State reacts and brings the offender before the courts, there remain many problems for the victim when she enters the legal arena.

A woman's traditional 'place': the home

Marital rape

In the nineteenth century John Stuart Mill was to write that the sole remaining state of slavery existed within marriage.[42] Women had become confined to the home, denied the right to vote, denied the right to enter into universities and the professions and remaindered to the 'private sphere' of life, so beloved by liberalism, to be the chattel of her husband. The concept of woman as possessed and man as the possessor has a long history. In Sir William Blackstone's *Commentaries on the Laws of England 1765–69*,[43] Blackstone wrote of a husband's right to chastise his wife in the same manner as he could chastise his children.

The English criminal law's traditional attitude to women is also revealed in relation to marital rape. Until 1991, the eighteenth century *dictum* of Sir Matthew Hale held good, namely that:

> But ... the husband cannot be guilty of rape committed by himself upon his lawful wife, for by their matrimonial consent and contract the wife hath given up herself in this kind unto her husband, which she cannot retract.[44]

The law left married men immune from prosecution for rape of their wives, and wives without a remedy for rape by their husbands.[45] The doctrine, which survived for 250 years, was based on the doctrine of 'one flesh' in marriage. Under this doctrine, propounded by Sir William Blackstone in his *Commentaries on the Laws of England 1765–69*, upon marriage a woman was placed under the protection and authority of her husband: they were, in law,

---

[41] From this perspective, prostitution and pornography are but two further illustrations of women's subordinate status in society and the violence which this attracts.

[42] See Mill, JS, *The Subjection of Women* (1869), 1989, Cambridge: CUP.

[43] Blackstone, W, *Commentaries on the Laws of England 1765–69*, 1978, New York: Garland.

[44] Hale, Sir M, *History of the Pleas of the Crown* (1736), 1971, London: London Professional Books; cited as the correct statement of the law in Archbold, JF, *Criminal Law Practice and Proceedings*, Richardson, PJ (ed), 1997, London: Sweet & Maxwell.

[45] See, for the pre-1991 position, Atkins, A and Hoggett, B, *Women and the Law*, 1984, Oxford: Basil Blackwell. (See *Sourcebook*, pp 379–85.)

one flesh, and that flesh was male. Accordingly, a woman's consent to intercourse was implied. As Hawkins J expressed the matter in 1888:

> The intercourse which takes place between husband and wife after marriage is not by virtue of any special consent on her part, but is mere submission to an obligation imposed on her by law.[46]

The United Kingdom Parliament had been exceedingly slow in tackling the issue of marital rape.[47] In 1976, the matter was debated within the context of the Sexual Offences (Amendment) Bill.[48] However, a husband's immunity from the law relating to 'unlawful sexual intercourse' was reserved for the Criminal Law Revision Committee to examine. In 1984, the English Criminal Law Revision Committee's Policy Advisory Committee affirmed the right of husband to have intercourse with his wife, irrespective of consent, adopting the view that in the absence of 'overt injury', non-consensual intercourse was evidence of the 'failure of the marital relationship', not of rape.[49] It was to be 1990 before the Law Commission tackled the issue and recommended provisionally that the immunity be abolished,[50] a view subsequently endorsed by the Law Commission's *Final Report* published in 1992.[51]

It was the English courts rather than Parliament which ultimately resolved the issue. The fiction was finally laid to rest in 1991 in the case of *R v R*,[52] in which the Court of Appeal ruled, and the House of Lords affirmed, that such a fiction had 'become anachronistic and offensive and we consider that it is our duty having reached that conclusion to act upon it'.[53] On an application under the European Convention of Human Rights and Fundamental Freedoms alleging that English law had infringed Article 7 of the Convention which prohibits retrospectivity, the European Court of Human Rights endorsed the decision of the English courts, ruling that such a decision was foreseeable and in line with the principles of gender-equality protected by the Convention.[54, 55] Parliament finally endorsed the decisions of the Law

---

[46] *R v Clarence* (1888), para 4.3. See also *R v Clarke* [1949] 2 All ER 448; *R v Miller* [1954] 2 All ER 529; *R v Reid* [1972] 2 All ER 1350; *R v O'Brien* [1974] 3 All ER 663; *R v Steele* [1976] 65 Cr App Rep 22; *R v Roberts* [1986] Crim LR 188.

[47] The immunity from rape had long been abolished in other common law jurisdictions, eg, Canada, New Zealand, Victoria, New South Wales, Western Australia, Queensland, Tasmania, the Republic of Ireland, Israel and some jurisdictions in the United States of America.

[48] Enacted as the Sexual Offences (Amendment) Act 1976.

[49] *Sexual Offences,* Cmnd 9213, 1984, London: HMSO.

[50] Law Commission Working Paper, No 116, 1990.

[51] *Criminal Law: Rape Within Marriage,* Law Com No 205, 1992, London: HMSO.

[52] [1991] 2 WLR 1065; [1991] 2 All ER 257, CA; [1991] 3 WLR 767, HL.

[53] Lord Lane CJ, *R v R* [1991] 2 WLR 1065, p 1074, CA (Criminal Division). The Australian High Court followed this landmark decision in *R v L* (1991) 103 ALR 577.

[54] *CR v United Kingdom* (48/1994/495/577), judgment 22 November 1995.

[55] See *R v R* [1991] 3 WLR 767. See Laird, V, 'Reflections on *R v R*' (1991) 55 MLR 386; Naffine, N, 'Possession: erotic love in the law of rape' (1994) 57 MLR 10.

Commission and the House of Lords in the Criminal Justice and Public Order Act 1994.[56]

Evolution of the English law relating to domestic violence[57]

> ... all studies that exist indicate that wife abuse is a common and pervasive problem and that men from practically all countries, cultures, classes and income groups indulge in their behaviour. The issue has serious implications from both a short-term and long-term perspective and from an individual and societal perspective. Many victims suffer serious physical and psychological injury, sometimes even death, while the economic and social costs to the community are enormous and the implications for future generations impossible to estimate.[58]

Domestic violence, and also child abuse, was to remain 'undiscovered' by the law until the 1970s. Writer and former activist Erin Pizzey did much to raise the profile of battered women. In *Scream Quietly or the Neighbours Will Hear*,[59] Erin Pizzey detailed the violent physical and sexual abuse suffered by women and the inadequacy of legal remedies to deal with the matter.

The criminal law

The criminal law which applies equally to violence within the home and violence outside of it, has proven inadequate in its application. While the law relating to assault through to murder would be vigorously applied in relation to strangers, the same did not apply to family members. Police traditionally, in the United Kingdom and elsewhere, have shown a marked reluctance to intervene in 'domestic' matters. Moreover, even where a victim of domestic violence is prepared to take action and co-operate in a prosecution, too often the woman later refuses to give evidence against her violent partner. To pursue criminal proceedings is also ineffective in so far as the majority of defendants in domestic violence cases are given non-custodial sentences only to return to their partners and inflict more violence in revenge for being taken to court. Where custodial sentences are passed, these are often of short

---

[56] Section 142 provides a substitute s 1 of the Sexual Offences Act 1956, and provides, in part, that it is an offence for a man to rape a woman or another man, and that rape is committed if a man has sexual intercourse with a person (whether vaginal or anal) who at the time of the intercourse does not consent to it.

[57] On the prevalence of domestic violence and the attitude of the police, see Morley, R and Mullender, A (1992) 6 International Journal of Law and the Family 265; Stanki, B 'Book review: *Women, Violence and Social Change*' (1993) Br J Crim 449.

[58] *Op cit*, United Nations Report, fn 18, p 7.

[59] *Op cit*, Pizzey, fn 31.

duration and have the consequence of further damaging the economic base of the family.

The civil law has also proved inadequate. As Erin Pizzey stated, a pot of black pepper in the pocket is of more use than an injunction when faced with a violent partner.[60] Pizzey was responsible for opening the first women's refuge, in Chiswick. As the refuge filled up, the local authority took her to court for overcrowding. Nor were women safe there: for partners would locate the refuge and attempt to attack their partners: but at least there was some safety in numbers, however overcrowded the accommodation. Pizzey's campaign led to the House of Commons Select Committee Inquiry into domestic violence.[61] The legislative consequence was the passage of the 1976 Domestic Violence and Matrimonial Proceedings Act, and, in 1978, to enable magistrates' courts to grant relief in cases of physical abuse, the Domestic Proceedings and Magistrates' Courts Act. The differing jurisdictional bases and differing remedies provided by differing courts led to substantial complexities in the law. Following detailed Law Commission scrutiny, and its recommendations for reform of the law, the Family Homes and Domestic Violence Bill was introduced into Parliament in 1994. That Bill was lost in 1995, following acrimonious parliamentary debates. The current law is now found in Part IV of the Family Law Act 1996.[62]

The Family Law Act 1996 now provides a unified jurisdiction and unified remedies of the High, county and magistrates' courts. However, while the threshold criteria for a non-molestation order is relatively low, that order may be insufficient to secure the safety of victims of violence. The English Law Commission, in illustrating the English threshold criteria for legal intervention in domestic violence – molestation – defines molestation as encompassing a range of relatively minor incidents which, when their effect on the victim is considered, justify legal action:

> ... [conduct which] extends to abuse beyond the more typical instances of physical assault to include any form of physical, sexual or psychological molestation or harassments which has a serious detrimental effect upon the health and well-being of the victim ... Examples of such 'non-violent' harassment or molestation cover a wide range of behaviour. Common instances include persistent pestering and intimidation through shouting, denigration, threats or argument, nuisance telephone calls, damaging property, following the applicant about and repeatedly calling at her home or place of work. Installing a mistress into the matrimonial home with a wife and

---

[60] *Op cit*, Pizzey, fn 31.
[61] See HC 553 (1974–75).
[62] For analysis of the former law, see Cretney, S and Masson, J, *Principles of Family Law*, 5th edn, 1990, London: Sweet & Maxwell; for analysis of the current English law, see Cretney, S and Masson, J, *Principles of Family Law*, 6th edn, 1997, London: Sweet & Maxwell, Chapter 10.

three children, filling car locks with superglue, writing anonymous letters and pressing one's face against a window whilst brandishing papers ...[63]

Where an order requires one partner to vacate the family home, in order to provide a safe environment for victims of violence and their children, the threshold criteria is more stringent, and reveals a tension in the law between protecting the physical integrity of victims of violence, and the property rights of the abuser. This tension is more marked when considering the differing manner in which the law applies to married spouses and unmarried cohabitants, privileging the former over the latter. Also privileged by law are those spouses or cohabitants who have either 'matrimonial home rights' and/or a legal or equitable interest in the property in question. The tension between personal protection and property rights is one which has long been evident in English law, and which emphasises the priority which property rights are accorded. Under the reformed law, exclusion orders against married partners may be 'for a specified period, until the occurrence of a specified event or until further order',[64] where the married applicant or cohabitee has a legal entitlement to occupy. However, in the case of cohabitees or former cohabitees, applicants who have no occupation entitlement in law, may be granted an order which – irrespective of the nature or duration of the relationship – may last no longer than 12 months. The emphasis on the protection of property rights is perhaps unsurprising, given the historical antecedents of a married woman's incapacity to own and manage property,[65] and more generally, the various legal discriminations against women which survived until the latter half of this century.[66] However, given the 'discovery' of the extensive and pervasive fact of domestic violence, in which women and children are most commonly the victims, the enduring privileging of property rights by law, over personal protection of victims of violence, is one factor which suggests that legislators do not regard domestic violence with the seriousness that the phenomenon demands.

Reconceptualising 'domestic' violence

The term 'domestic violence' undermines the significance of the suffering inflicted on the victim. The word domestic implies privacy – that it is a personal matter for the individuals concerned – and non-State responsibility for the actions within the private sphere. Yet domestic violence which ensures the continued dominance of men – physically, economically and

---

[63] *Report on Domestic Violence and Occupation of the Family Home*, Law Com No 107, 1992, para 2.3.
[64] Family Law Act 1996, s 33(10).
[65] Corrected in 1882 by the Married Woman's Property Act.
[66] See, further, Chapter 2.

psychologically – over women, denies women the right to equality and equal respect as human being. Domestic violence reconceptualised as a violation of human rights, *women's rights*, resonates with more force than does domestic violence. Nor is this reconceptualisation a matter of regrettable essentialism which has so bedevilled recent feminist theory. Gender-based violence is specifically and predominantly violence against women. That this violence takes many forms, and may be culturally specific, does not reduce the force of the argument, supported by much international data, that gender-based violence is violence against women by men.

It is in the international arena that feminist international lawyers have made and continue to make progress in reconceptualising violence against women as a violation of human rights and sexual discrimination.[67] In addition, feminist international law scholars are advancing the case for the imposition of State responsibility for violence against women. Under international law, States have responsibility for both unlawful actions and for failure to provide remedies for unlawful actions. By failing to provide adequate protection of women's human rights, the State, it is argued, assumes responsibility for the violations of human rights experienced by women in the home.[68]

Female victims and the legal system

The legal system has much to answer for in regard to the treatment of female victims of violence and in relation to women who kill their partners. Whether the inquiry is into the personnel of the legal profession, or attitudes towards female victims of crime or defendants in the criminal process, the legal system reveals itself as steeped in tradition.

As seen in Chapter 2, the broad picture of the legal professions in (for example) Australia, Canada and the United Kingdom is one of a primarily male, white, middle-class institution. In England, constructive – if belated – attempts are being made to redress the imbalance between gender and race. The Policy Studies Institute undertook research in 1995 on behalf of the Law Society's research and policy planning unit. The latest research confirms that sexual and racial discrimination remains rife. In 1995, of 63,628 practising solicitors in England and Wales, a mere 18,417 were women, and only 70

---

[67] See, generally, Cook, R (ed), *Human Rights of Women: National and International Perspectives*, 1994, Pennsylvania: Pennsylvania UP.

[68] See, in particular, Charlesworth, H, 'What are "women's international rights"?'; Romany, C, 'State responsibility goes private: a feminist critique of the public/private distinction in international human rights law'; Copelon, R, 'Intimate terror: understanding domestic violence as torture'; Cook, R, 'State accountability under the Convention on the Elimination of All Forms of Discrimination Against Women'; Roth, K, 'Domestic violence as an international human rights issue', in Cook, *ibid*.

practising solicitors were from ethnic minorities. When figures for partnerships are examined, the Young Women Lawyers group have found that only 25 per cent of new partners in 1995 were women; a drop from 1985 when 44 per cent of new partnerships were granted to women. At the Bar, the Bar Council has endorsed a new 'equality code' which is aimed at tackling discrimination within the profession.[69]

The absence of a profession which is balanced on gender and racial lines has inevitable consequences for women who find themselves dealing with law. The continued dominance of the profession by middle-class, middle-aged, white males – the majority of whom it may reasonably be assumed are conservative in outlook (if not political party) ensures a continuance of the traditional stereotypical attitudes to women. With this background in mind, attention can now be turned to the manner in which the legal system is imbued with patriarchal attitudes.

Consistent with the treatment of women as the 'other', as 'different', 'unequal' and subordinated in patriarchal society, the legal process itself reveals evidence of biases being reflected in legal judgments; in defences which the law permits to be advanced for certain crimes, and in the sentencing of women.

The failure of traditional defences to a charge of murder for women victims of violence

Lack of guilt, the failure to prove either the *actus reus* or *mens rea* for murder; provocation and self-defence represent the traditionally accepted defences to a charge of murder which will result in an acquittal. Self-defence, however, is rarely, if ever, successful in relation to women who kill their violent partners. Under English law, self-defence can succeed only if, in response to an imminent danger, the attacker responds with force of a degree which has 'reasonable proportionality' to the perceived danger. Thus, women victims of prolonged violence who wait until there is a 'safe' moment in which to attack – often when the partner is asleep or in a drunken stupor – cannot fit the test of imminent danger. In addition, the partial defences of provocation or diminished responsibility are available to reduce the charge from murder to manslaughter and thus relieve, under English law, the automatic life sentence. The failure of self-defence as a defence to murder for battered women goes some way to explain the significance of provocation or diminished responsibility.[70]

---

[69] (1995) *The Times*, 14 November.
[70] Self-defence succeeded in the Canadian case of *R v Lavallee* [1990] 1 SCR 852, discussed further below.

However, from a feminist perspective, these defences have also proved inadequate, and have resulted in women being found guilty of the crime of murder in circumstances where, were the criminal justice system inclusive of and sensitive to women's particular situations, especially in relation to circumstances of domestic violence, a different result would have been achieved.

Provocation

A plea of provocation or diminished responsibility, where successful, reduces the charge against the defendant from one of murder, which carries an automatic life sentence under English law,[71] to one of manslaughter, for which the sentence lies in the judge's discretion.[72] In order successfully to plead provocation[73] as a defence, the defendant must prove that she or he suffered a 'temporary and sudden loss of self-control so that he or she was no longer "master of her or his own mind"'. In *R v Duffy*,[74] however, a woman killed her husband, whilst he was asleep, having previously had a violent quarrel and endured years of violence from him. Devlin J, having defined provocation, went on to rule that where a woman waited until the opportunity arose, rather than reacting immediately, this amounted to a killing for revenge – not provocation. Where provocation pertains, the defendant has the right to have the issue put to the jury.[75] However, whether that matter is put to the jury in turn depends on whether the trial judge accepts that there is evidence of provocation in the facts before the courts.

A build-up of tension resulting in a delayed reaction to the violence suffered (cumulative provocation) is not considered a defence under English law. However, in Jeremy Hordern's analysis, the law as expressed in *R v Duffy* represented a restriction of the law of provocation, which previously could have accommodated 'slow-burn' cases. Hordern writes:

---

[71] A House of Lords Select Committee on Murder and Life Imprisonment in 1989 recommended that the mandatory life sentence for murder be abolished. That recommendation has been supported by two Lord Chief Justices, Lord Lane and Lord Taylor.

[72] Subject to the requirements of s 1 of the Murder (Abolition of Death Penalty) Act 1965.

[73] Homicide Act 1957, s 3, provides that: 'Where on a charge of murder there is evidence on which the jury can find that the person charged was provoked (whether by things done or by things said or by both together) to lose his self-control, the question whether the provocation was enough to make a reasonable man do as he did shall be left to be determined by the jury; and in determining that question the jury shall take into account everything both done and said according to the effect which, in their opinion, it would have on a reasonable man.' The burden of proof is on the prosecution to prove beyond all reasonable doubt that the case is not one of provocation.

[74] [1949] 1 All ER 932.

[75] *R v Ballard* [1957] AC 635.

The root of the trouble and misunderstanding has been the recent failure to recognise that the law's conception of anger has never always been loss of self-control alone, but has historically included outrage.[76]

Accordingly, the 'person who boils up when her long-term violent abuser is asleep in his chair may well be acting out of provoked outrage, despite the absence of any immediate provocation. Such a person's anger would always historically have fallen within the scope of the defence'. Thus, what is needed, Hordern argues, is a reinstatement of the former legal pre-*Duffy* position, with the substitution 'of references to provoked angry retaliation in place of references to provoked loss of self-control in the Homicide Act 1957, section 3'.[77]

Cumulative provocation – or slow-burn, or provoked angry retaliation – has been defined by Martin Wasik as involving:

> ... a course of cruel or violent conduct by the deceased, often in a violent setting, lasting over a substantial period of time, which culminates in the victim of that conduct ... intentionally killing the tormentor.[78]

Accordingly, when women victims wait until the moment is safe before reacting to their ordeals, the provocation they have suffered – over months or years – cannot be deemed to be within the English legal definition of provocation.[79] In *Ibrams and Gregory*,[80] for example, a time lapse of seven days between the act of provocation and the woman's attack, resulted in the judge withdrawing the issue of provocation from the jury.[81] What is revealed in an analysis of the law of provocation is that the law is constructed according to male criteria – the law excludes the particular circumstances in which women victims may kill, namely an accumulation of fear and hatred which is reacted to, not 'in the heat of the moment' following a particular violent incident, but when the woman victim feels it is safe to react to her treatment. This the law does not recognise – for the law is gendered, and accordingly defines provocation in relation to male standards of equal physical strength and fails to recognise that domestic violence – sexual or otherwise – consistently perpetrated, can result in a 'slow-burn' reaction which will only be given

---

[76] Hordern, J, *Provocation and Responsibility*, 1992, Oxford: Clarendon, p 190.
[77] *Ibid*.
[78] Wasik, M, 'Cumulative provocation and domestic killing' [1982] Crim LR 29.
[79] The position in Australia differs in the significant respect that 'cumulative provocation' may be considered as sufficient provocation to murder. See, generally, Kennedy, H, *Eve Was Framed*, 1992, London: Vintage.
[80] (1982) 74 Cr App R 154.
[81] A fresh approach was evident in *R v Ahluwalia* [1992] 4 All ER 889, discussed further below.

physical expression when the victim of that violence is confident of her own physical safety.[82] The criminal law has been fashioned, in relation to self-defence to murder, on the paradigm which relies on violent confrontation, generally spontaneous, between two equally physically strong males. It does not, conventionally, encompass situations in which a woman – after the sustained physical and psychological pressure of violence within the home – finally snaps and, from a position of relative safety (typically when he is asleep), kills her violent partner.[83]

In Jeremy Hordern's analysis, the law of provocation should be abolished. From a feminist perspective, he argues that the mitigating effect of a successful plea of provocation, reinforces in the law 'that which public institutions ought in fact to be seeking to eradicate, namely, the acceptance that there is something natural, inevitable, and hence in some (legal) sense-to-be-recognised forgivable about men's violence against women ...'.[84] The role which provocation should play in law lies, for Hordern, not in its role as a defence, but as a mitigating factor to be considered in sentencing, provided only that English law would finally be reformed to abolish the automatic life sentence for murder.

Diminished responsibility

A person shall not be found guilty of murder where a plea of diminished responsibility is successful.[85] Whereas a defence of provocation requires that the defendant justify her action and meet the masculine standard of 'reasonableness', and 'immediacy', a defence of diminished responsibility

---

[82] A relatively early reform of the law relating to provocation occurred in New South Wales, Australia. Fuelled by feminist activism following the prosecution of women for the murder of their violent husbands, the Crimes Act 1900 (NSW) was amended, in 1982, to provide that:
For the purpose of determining whether an act or omission causing death was an act done or omitted under provocation ... there is no rule of law that provocation is negatived if:
  (a) there was not a reasonable proportion between the act or omission causing death and the conduct of the deceased that induced the act or omission;
  (b) the act of omission causing death was not an act done or omitted suddenly; or
  (c) the act or omission causing death was an act done or omitted with any intent to take life or inflict grievous bodily harm.

[83] For analysis of the case law, see Hordern, J, 'Sex violence and sentencing in provocation cases' [1989] Crim LR 546; op cit, Hordern, fn 76, Chapter 9; Edwards, S, 'Battered women who kill' (1990) 5 NLJ 1380; op cit, Edwards, fn 30, Chapters 6, 8, 9.

[84] Op cit, Hordern, fn 76, p 194.

[85] Homicide Act 1957, s 2(1), provides that: 'Where a person kills or is party to the killing of another, he shall not be convicted of murder if he was suffering from such an abnormality of mind (whether arising from a condition of arrested or retarded development of mind or any inherent causes or induced by disease or injury) as substantially impaired his mental responsibility for his acts and omissions in doing or being a party to the killing.' The burden of proof lies with the defence, and the standard of proof is the balance of probability.

involves the court accepting that the defendant's mental state was such that she was not responsible for her actions, and hence there is no issue of justification before the court.[86] The issue before the court becomes whether, at the time of the 'crime', the defendant's mental state was impaired. In determining this, the court considers not just mental illness or insanity, but the whole personality of the defendant, including her 'perception, understanding, judgment and will'.[87] Accordingly, expert psychiatric evidence will be adduced in order to determine the defendant's mental state, and this evidence may include the defendant's depression induced by domestic violence.[88] Susan Edwards, citing research findings,[89] states that 'pleas of diminished responsibility are accepted by the prosecution in about 80 per cent of cases'.[90] Where the prosecution and defence differ over the plea, the matter must be established by the court. Where this occurs, according to research, the jury rejected the defence evidence and convicted on a charge of murder in 64 per cent of cases.[91]

Whether women should be encouraged to have recourse to diminished responsibility is a difficult question. On the one hand, pleading diminished responsibility has led to a number of successful defences, resulting in acquittal or lesser sentencing, and it is thus understandable that legal advisers should encourage women to plead diminished responsibility, especially given the relative lack of success in relation to self-defence or provocation. On the other hand, pleading diminished responsibility – in cases in which the woman's mental state has been induced by the violence of her partner – places the emphasis not on the wrongdoing of the violent partner, but on the woman's weakness and fragility. Diminished responsibility represents an *excuse* for a killing, but not exoneration for that killing as in the case of self-defence or provocation. Diminished responsibility also, at a conceptual level, reinforces the construction of woman as irrational, as the 'Other'.

---

[86] Battered woman syndrome, on which see below, is now recognised as being within the British classification of mental diseases which enable the defendant to claim diminished responsibility: see *R v Hobson* (1997) *The Times*, 25 June, in which a murder conviction was quashed and a retrial ordered in light of fresh psychiatric evidence which suggested that the defendant was suffering from battered woman syndrome at the time of the murder, which occurred before the recognition of battered woman syndrome.

[87] *Op cit*, Edwards, fn 30, p 386.

[88] See *R v Irons* (1995) 16 Cr App R (S) 46, cited in Edwards, *op cit*, fn 30.

[89] Conducted by S Dell: see Dell, S, *Murder Into Manslaughter*, 1984, Institute of Psychiatry, Maudsley Monographs, Oxford: OUP.

[90] *Op cit*, Edwards, fn 30, p 387.

[91] According to Susan Edwards, where the jury rejects unanimous medical evidence, the Court of Appeal may substitute a verdict of diminished responsibility: see *op cit*, Edwards, fn 30, p 389.

Recognising the impact of domestic violence

Law's failure in relation to women who kill their violent abusing partners, is a failure to give adequate weight to the social and political background to domestic violence, and to continue to develop the law in a gendered fashion, determined by male experience.[92] By ignoring the context in which the violence took place, and the disparity in the power relations between the partners, judges can continue to rely on gendered reasoning. Thus, questions which arise, and which are used against women defendants, are typified by questions such as 'why didn't she leave?', 'Why did she not seek a non-molestation or exclusion order?', 'Why did she not involve the police and invoke the criminal law to have her partner prosecuted?'. In other words, the questions raised all presuppose that women in constantly violent situations, at constant risk of violent sexual or other physical and psychological violence, retain the same capacity for autonomy as do men, and the same rationality and power which would enable them to escape from the situation. What has not been adequately understood and accommodated by the law, is the reality of the woman victim's circumstances. The victim may not have the means to leave. Alternative accommodation may not be available. In any event, it has been well documented for many years that women who leave are often pursued and subjected to further recriminatory violence, as are women who seek to escape by invoking the criminal justice system against their violent spouses.[93] Furthermore, the reasonableness of expecting a woman to escape from a violent relationship is negatived by evidence which supports the view that women who have sustained persistent violent abuse becomes passive, the victim has 'learned helplessness' and exists in a state of persistent chronic fear. Thus, notwithstanding the physical possibility of her escape, psychologically the victim of spousal abuse is frequently unable to act to protect herself by removing herself from her physical proximity to the abuser: she is suffering from 'battered woman syndrome'. Battered woman syndrome has been developed not as a discrete defence to a charge of murder, but in support for the traditional defences of self-defence, provocation and diminished responsibility.

Battered woman syndrome

Battered woman syndrome, a concept developed by American clinical psychologist Lenore Walker, explains the psychological effects of persistent long-term violence on women. The syndrome characteristically has three

---

[92] It is instructive to note that the judgment in the landmark Canadian case of *R v Lavallee*, below, was drafted by a female judge.
[93] See Wilson, M and Daly, M, 'Spousal homicide' (1994) 148 Juristat Service Bulletin, Canadian Centre for Justice Statistics.

phases: '(1) tension building, (2) the acute battering incident, and (3) loving contrition'.[94] Being forgiven, the violence recommences. By now, the woman's loss of self-esteem, depression and sense of helplessness have trapped her into a situation from which she is psychologically and hence physically unable to escape. As Lenore Walker records, over time 'the first phase of tension building becomes more common, and loving contrition, or the third phase, declines'.[95]

In Lenore Walker's study of 435 battered women, half of the women reported having been punched, two-thirds had suffered pushing, slapping, hitting and arm twisting, and a third of these reported having been choked or strangled. Others had been burned or attacked with knives or guns. Fifty-nine per cent had been forced into 'unusual sexual acts', and 75 per cent had been raped. A high proportion of the victims were also controlled through having no access to cash or bank accounts. Each of the victims had suffered what Amnesty International has labelled 'psychological torture': social isolation; exhaustion from deprivation of food and sleep; obsessive or possessive behaviour; threats; humiliation; administration of drugs and alcohol; induction of altered states of consciousness and 'indulgences' which 'maintained the woman's hope that the abuse would cease'.[96] The psychological consequence of the treatment received results in the victim's 'learned helplessness' – feelings of despair – and an inability to leave their abusing partners or seek other redress. Women who kill are women who finally react against the violence, not in the heat of the moment as a response to a triggering specific event, but in a violent action caused by the long term suffering of abuse and a final attempt to escape from their abuser. In Walker's research study, more than one-third of the victims had attempted to commit suicide, and a proportion of these had suddenly killed their abusing partners while in the very process of attempting suicide.

Learned helplessness, according to its author Martin Seligman, involves:

[O]rganisms, when exposed to uncontrollable events, learn that responding is futile. Such learning undermines the incentive to respond, and so it produces a profound interference with the motivation of instrumental behaviour. It also proactively interferes with learning that responding works when events become controllable, and so produces cognitive distortions.[97]

In Charles P Ewing's analysis, battered women who kill, do so in 'psychological self-defence'. Ewing notes that:

---

[94] Walker, L, *The Battered Woman Syndrome*, 1984, New York: Springer, p 95.
[95] *Ibid*, p 101.
[96] Ewing, C, *Battered Women Who Kill: Psychological Self-defence as Legal Justification*, 1987, Lexington Books, DC Heath, pp 8–9.
[97] Seligman, M, *Helplessness: On Depression, Development and Death*, 1975, cited in Ewing, *ibid*, p 20.

... almost all battered women who kill claim to have done so to protect themselves from imminent death or serious bodily injury at the hand of their batterers.[98]

Thus, from a battered woman's perspective, the issue of killing her partner is not so much an issue of provocation, or diminished responsibility, but pure self-defence. It was this explanation on which Kuranjit Ahluwalia relied – she had not intended to kill her husband, or even inflict really serious harm on him – she wanted to stop him 'running after her'.

R v Ahluwalia, R v Thornton[99]

In England, two, now seminal, cases provided the catalyst for feminist demands for reform of the law of homicide. Those cases reveal the difficulties under which female defendants labour in establishing a defence to murder of their male partners under English law. In the case of *R v Ahluwalia*,[100] the defendant had suffered years of violent abuse at the hands of her husband, and under threat of a further attack, set fire to his bedding and killed him. Ahluwalia was convicted of murder in 1989. The defence of provocation failed. The court, however, having admitted psychiatric evidence[101] relating to battered woman syndrome, ordered a retrial. When the matter went on appeal to the Court of Appeal, on the basis that the trial judge had ignored the effect of battered woman syndrome, the Court of Appeal quashed the conviction for murder and substituted one of manslaughter. Evidence of battered woman syndrome was adduced, not under a plea of provocation, but under the plea of diminished responsibility.[102]

In the later case of *R v Thornton*,[103] a similar factual situation existed. Sara Thornton had also endured years of violence at the hands of her husband. When her partner threatened to kill her when she was asleep, Thornton went to the kitchen, selected and sharpened a knife, and attacked him. She was convicted of murder and sentenced to life imprisonment, the court ruling that the defence of provocation was unavailable by virtue of the fact that Sara Thornton had not reacted instantly to the provocation by her husband.

---

[98] *Op cit*, Ewing, fn 96, p 61.
[99] [1992] 4 All ER 889; [1992] 1 All ER 306 and *(No 2)* (1995) NLJ 1888; (1995) *The Times*, 14 December; see, also, *R v Humphries* (1995) NLJ 1032.
[100] [1992] 4 All ER 889.
[101] For a feminist critique of expert evidence, see O'Donovan, K, 'Law's knowledge: the judge, the expert, the battered woman, and her syndrome' (1993) 20 JLS 427.
[102] Ahluwalia was released, having served her prison term whilst awaiting appeal.
[103] (1995) *The Times*, 14 December; (1995) 145 NLJ 1888.

On appeal, the Court of Appeal ruled, for the first time, that battered woman syndrome could be a relevant characteristic for the jury's consideration of a plea of provocation.[104]

The deficiency of English criminal law in relation to victims of domestic violence is all too apparent from the cases of Kuranjit Ahluwalia and Sara Thornton. The former refusal of the law to recognise the physical and psychological inability for an immediate provoked response to violence, led, in these and other cases, to the victim being cast into jail for murder. In Sara Thornton's case, the Secretary of State for the Home Department referred the matter back to the Court of Appeal for retrial.

To date, notwithstanding the above cases, the English courts have been more cautious about admitting evidence in relation to battered woman syndrome than their Australian, Canadian or United States counterparts. Space precludes a substantial analysis of the case law in each jurisdiction, nevertheless an outline of the major case law is instructive.

Battered woman syndrome in Australia and Canada

R v Lavallee:[105] *success for self-defence and battered woman syndrome*

Angelique Lavallee killed her partner by shooting him in the back of the head. Having endured persistent violence, her partner had threatened to kill her once guests at a party had left. Rather than wait for the inevitable attack, Lavallee killed him. On the basis of existing precedent, self-defence would not succeed, given that the threatened attack was neither imminent nor in the process of being inflicted. The Supreme Court, having admitted expert psychiatric evidence on Lavallee's state of mind, ruled that the defendant's actual state of mind – and not that of the 'reasonable man' – must be considered and given weight to. By broadening the concept of reasonableness to include the actual psychological state of the victim of violence whose control finally broke, the Court was able to depart from strict precedent and to rule that battered woman syndrome was capable of inducing a mental state in which the action of the woman was reasonable *within the context of the violence suffered by her.*[106] The Supreme Court bench comprised seven judges, including three women, of whom Madam Justice Bertha Wilson gave the leading judgment of the Court. Wilson J made it clear that battered woman syndrome had to be recognised in order to correct the gender bias in the

---

[104] *Op cit, R v Thornton (No 2)*, fn 99.

[105] *Op cit, R v Lavallee*, fn 70.

[106] See Young, A, 'Conjugal homicide and legal violence: a comparative analysis' (1993) 31 Osgoode Hall LJ 761.

criminal law, and that battered woman syndrome enabled the standard of reasonableness required by law to be expanded to include women's experiences. Furthermore Wilson J stated that recognition of battered woman syndrome highlighted the fact of domestic violence, highlighting which was necessary to counteract the impression given by application of the gendered defences to murder that domestic violence was acceptable. In Elizabeth Sheehy's analysis of 10 reported cases between 1991 and 1993, following *R v Lavallee*, in which battered woman syndrome was relied on in defence, in eight cases the evidence was used to support a plea in mitigation of sentence; in one evidence of battered woman syndrome was adduced which negatived the accused's *mens rea*; in the tenth case the plea failed on the basis that the defendant could have called for third party help and did not have to rely on self-help.[107]

Following *Lavallee*, battered woman syndrome has been recognised extensively by the Australian courts.[108] However, as Julie Stubbs and Julia Tolmie demonstrate in their careful analysis of the case law, there have been revealed a number of difficulties with the application of battered woman syndrome to traditional defences to murder.[109] In the authors' analysis, these may be summarised as follows. First, battered woman syndrome overemphasises the psychology of the defendant, and as a result underemphasises the violent context in which the attack took place. Secondly, the syndrome reinforces 'notions of women's irrationality or emotional instability', thereby introducing 'the danger of developing a new stereotype by which the battered woman is to be measured in such cases' and reinforcing 'the notion that battered women as a group share certain psychological characteristics'.[110] The danger of essentialising battered women's psychological states is, in the authors' analysis, particularly dangerous when a battered woman is stereotyped in a manner which ignores racial and cultural factors. In relation to Aboriginal and Torres Straight Island women, for example, Stubbs and Tolmie explain, Aboriginal women – contrary to popular mythology – are frequently the heads of households, and responsible for the economic well being of the family. Accordingly, as the case law demonstrates, Aboriginal women are often assertive, able to seek help and to take positive steps to enlist, albeit often unsuccessfully, the aid of State agencies for their protection. Where the battered woman has taken such positive, protective

---

[107] See Sheehy, E, 'Battered woman syndrome: developments in Canadian law after *R v Lavalee*', in Stubbs, *op cit*, fn 29, p 175.

[108] In South Australia, New South Wales, Tasmania, Queensland, the Australian Capital Territory, Western Australia and the Northern Territory. The first case to admit battered woman syndrome evidence was *Runjanjic and Kontinnen* (1991) 53 A Crim R 362.

[109] Stubbs, J and Tolmie, J, 'Battered woman syndrome in Australia: a challenge to gender bias in the law?', in Stubbs, *op cit*, fn 29, Chapter 9.

[110] *Op cit*, Stubbs, fn 29, p 199.

steps, it is the more difficult for that woman to be characterised as in a psychological state of helplessness. Furthermore, it is demonstrated that Aboriginal women suffer from particular forms of discrimination in society, for example lower educational and employment opportunities. However, as the case of *Hickey*[111] demonstrates, battered woman syndrome was admitted in evidence, with her low educational level and unemployment being cited in support of her 'personal inadequacy', without those factors being placed within the wider context of circumstances shared by a large proportion of Aboriginal women. Moreover, although IQ tests are used in the psychological assessment of the defendant, these tests are themselves culturally specific, and thus not necessarily reliable guides in relation to Aboriginal or Torres Straight Islander women.

Women on trial: rape

As has been well documented by feminist legal scholars, although the victim of the crime of rape is the woman, the victim of the legal system in any prosecution for rape is the victim herself.[112] While rape is clearly an aspect of gender-based violence, rape – representing that most intimate and destructive form of violence – has formed a specific site of inquiry for feminist scholarship. Rape, as with all gender-orientated violence, is a manifestation of power. Rape controls women. The social fact of rape not only subordinates its victims, but also controls all women through the instillation of fear in women, irrespective of age, race or class. As Susan Brownmiller expresses it:

> ... the incidence of actual rape combined with the looming spectre of the rapist in the mind's eye ... must be understood as a control mechanism against the freedom, mobility and aspirations of all women, white and black.[113]

Furthermore:

> That *some* men rape provides a sufficient threat to keep all women in a constant state of intimidation, forever conscious of the knowledge that the biological tool must be held in awe for it may turn to weapon with sudden swiftness born of harmful intent.[114]

In the case of a man on trial for alleged murder or rape of a woman, the conduct, lifestyle and personality of the woman are central to the question of guilt or innocence of the man. If the English legal system has hitherto been

---

[111] Unreported, Supreme Court New South Wales, 14 April 1992, discussed in Stubbs and Tolmie, *op cit*, fn 109.

[112] See, eg, Duncan, S, 'The mirror tells its tale: constructions of gender in criminal law', in Bottomley, A (ed), *Feminist Perspectives on the Foundational Subjects of Law*, 1996, London: Cavendish Publishing.

[113] Brownmiller, S, *Against Our Will: Men, Women and Rape*, 1975, New York: Simon & Schuster, p 255. (See *Sourcebook*, pp 398–404.)

[114] *Ibid*, Brownmiller, p 209.

either blind or unsympathetic to the problems of women trapped into violent and ultimately fatal relationships, the system demonstrates an unremitting harshness when the issue of liability for rape is considered. As with victims of 'ordinary', 'domestic' violence, rape victims are themselves on trial in the courtroom. The issue is not whether intercourse took place against a woman's will, but whether the woman did, or did not, consent to sexual intercourse. Thus, the woman's mental attitude, the issue of consent, not the sexual intercourse forced on her by the defendant, lies at the heart of rape trials. As students of English criminal law will know, in rape prosecutions the crucial, determining factor is the issue of whether or not the victim consented to sexual intercourse. Where consent lies, no conviction may follow. Accordingly, notwithstanding the prosecution's belief that there is a case to answer, it is not so much the mind of the accused which is at issue, but rather the mind of the victim. However, as will become clear, in operation the English criminal justice system, in evaluating the question of the woman's consent, focuses on whether or not the defendant held an 'honest belief' as to the woman's consent or non-consent. This test reduces the centrality of the issue of the victim's true consent, and elevates the issue of the man's belief, thereby underemphasising the experience of the victim. The criminal justice system once again victimises the injured party. This point is reinforced by the occasional (but too frequent) dicta of judges which suggests that in some way the woman victim has acted (or dressed) in a manner which suggests an element of 'contribution' to the offence.[115]

Traditionally under English common law, lack of consent could only be proven where the woman had sustained physical injury, or by evidence of resistance, fraud or fear. In *R v Camplin*,[116] for example, the victim alleged that she had been drugged with alcohol: the court ruled that the relevant legal test for liability was not whether or not the intercourse took place 'against her will', but rather 'without her consent'. The issue of fraud negativing consent was considered in *R v Linekar*,[117] in which it was emphasised that it was the absence of consent, not the issue of the fraudulent acquisition of consent, which prevailed.

Two principal questions fall for answer in rape trials: first, did the woman consent; secondly, did the defendant believe that she was consenting. The current law on consent derives from *R v Morgan*, decided ultimately by the House of Lords.[118] Under English law, the alleged rapist does not have to establish that he *reasonably believed* that the woman was consenting, rather the

---

[115] Consider, eg, Sir Melford Stevenson's comment that the victim, who had been hitch-hiking, had been 'asking for it', and the rapist received a suspended sentence. See *op cit*, Kennedy, fn 79, p 120.
[116] (1845) 1 Den 89; ER 169.
[117] [1995] Crim LR 320.
[118] [1976] AC 182.

legal test is, did the defendant have an *honest belief, irrespective of its reasonableness,* that the woman was consenting. In *Morgan,* the husband had returned home with three other men, with the intention that each would have sexual intercourse with his wife.[119] The other men had been told that his wife would be a 'willing partner', but that they could expect her to resist sexual intercourse. The House of Lords, abandoning law's usually tenacious hold on the concept of reasonableness as the central criterion for liability, ruled that provided the belief in consent was honest, there was no liability in law for rape, *even where* the woman was not consenting.[120]

In Sheila Duncan's analysis, the criminal law of rape denies women subjectivity and privileges the man as the subject of law, to the exclusion of the woman:

> This is the literal and symbolic construction of the female as other and the man as desiring subject. Mrs Morgan was not consenting, the jury and both appeal courts accepted that, but the defendants were allowed to legitimately construct consent on the word of her husband and there was *nothing* she could do to undermine this.[121]

Moreover, as Sheila Duncan discusses, the law relating to consent to rape is very different from that applying to consent to other sexual acts. In *R v Brown,*[122] the House of Lords ruled that consent to participate in sexual activities – in this case sado-masochism – could not be given where such activities cause physical harm. One cannot consent to being assaulted, even where one may wish so to be, unless the harm caused is 'transient or trifling'.[123] In Duncan's analysis:

> In respect of visible violence outside of that very limited space [ie 'manly sports', 'innocent horseplay'] a male subject will not be allowed to consent, just as in the very considerable space for heterosexual male sexual violence, the law does not in its construction of rape allow the female other not to consent.[124]

The 1994 amendment to the Sexual Offences Act 1956[125] defines rape in gender-neutral terms for the first time.[127] Notwithstanding revised definitions, rape remains a gender-dependent offence. First, there is the

---

[119] Morgan was charged with aiding and abetting rape, since before 1991 a husband could not be prosecuted for the rape of his wife.

[120] For a full analysis of *Morgan,* see Duncan, S, 'Law as literature: deconstructing the legal text' (1994) 5.1 Law and Critique; see, also, *op cit,* Duncan, S, fn 112. (See *Sourcebook,* p 186.)

[121] *Op cit,* Duncan, fn 112, p 183.

[122] [1994] 1 AC 212.

[123] *R v Donovan* [1934] 2 KB 498.

[124] *Op cit,* Duncan, fn 113, p 187. See, also, Duncan, S, 'Law's sexual discipline: visibility, violence and consent' (1995) 22.3 JLS 326.

[125] Criminal Justice and Public Order Act 1994, s 142.

[126] Canada and some jurisdictions in the United States have also adopted gender-neutral definitions of rape.

concentration on whether or not the woman did, or did not, consent – rather than concentration on the man's *actus reus* and *mens rea*. Secondly, while section 2 of the Sexual Offences (Amendment) Act 1976, as amended, prohibits questions being posed as to the victim's past moral character and sexual behaviour, section 2(2) undermines this prohibition by permitting a judge to waive the rule on an application made, in the absence of the jury, to him by the defence, on the basis that it would be 'unfair to the defendant to refuse to allow the evidence to be adduced or the question to be asked'. It has been established in one study that of 45 rape trials, an application was made in 40 per cent of cases.[127] So relaxed has the judicial attitude been to application under sub-section 2, that Jennifer Temkin has commented that in rape cases it 'appears all too often to have given defence counsel a free rein'.[128] Whereas the issue of a woman's past 'moral character' may have some relevance to the question of the plausibility of the man's assertion that the woman consented and as to whether the woman can plausibly be believed – the 'credit' of her story – it can have no bearing whatsoever on whether or not the woman did in fact consent to the alleged offence. The blurring of the lines between 'credit' and the main issue has, however, been demonstrated time and time again by the English Court of Appeal.[129] It is for reasons such as these that Lisa Longstaff and Anne Neale call for 'a change in priorities at every stage of the criminal justice system', including the removal of the right to raise the victim's past sexual history, in order to emphasise 'that in rape cases, consent is the issue'.[130]

The right of the defendant to cross-examine his accuser has been regarded as an important constitutional right. The exercise of that right, however, entails considerable costs, emotional and psychological costs for the victim of rape, and represents her further humiliation, heaping trauma caused by legal procedure on to the trauma of rape. In one instance in 1996, the alleged rapist cross-examined his victim in court for six days, wearing the same clothes as he had in the attack. In November 1997, another defendant forced the victims of a double rape attack to relive their experience.[131] The 1991 Criminal Justice Act provided for the protection of victims of child abuse by removing the right of suspects to cross-examine their victims: the Home Secretary is now considering how similar protection could be given to victims of rape.

Moreover, judicial reactions to rape victims have included breathtaking illustrations of traditional patriarchal attitudes, which indicate that the male

---

[127] Adler, Z, *Rape on Trial*, 1987, London: Routledge, p 73.
[128] Temkin, J, 'Sexual history evidence – the ravishment of section 2' [1993] Crim LR 3.
[129] See, eg, *R v Redguard* [1991] Crim LR 213; *R v Barnes* [1994] Crim LR 691; *R v SMS* [1992] Crim LR 310; *R v Said* [1992] Crim LR 433.
[130] Longstaff, L and Neale, A, 'The convicted rapist feels unlucky – rarely guilty' (1997) *The Times*, 18 November.
[131] He was sentenced to a total of 21 years' imprisonment.

personnel of the legal system are far from the required rational objectivity required of the judiciary where sexual offences are concerned. Helena Kennedy QC has examined such attitudes.[132] She cites Sir Melford Stevenson being lenient in sentencing a rapist on the basis that the victim, a 16 year old, had been hitch-hiking; Mr Justice Jupp in 1990 passing a suspended sentence on a husband who had twice raped his wife on the basis of some distinction between rape within the home and rape by a stranger; Mr Justice Leonard passing a reduced sentence on the perpetrators of a violent multiple rape on the basis that the victim had made a 'remarkable recovery'.[133, 134] Moreover, judicial ambivalence towards the issue of consent was apparent in the direction to the jury by Judge Wild in 1982:

> Women who say no do not always mean no. It is not just a question of how she says it, how she shows and makes it clear. If she doesn't want it she only has to keep her legs shut and she would not get it without force and then there would be the marks of force being used.[135]

What is revealed by such judicial comments is the extent of prejudice against women on the part of the judiciary – as if sex, consensual or not – is, in their minds, 'what women are for'. Such remarks evidence the fact that women are not regarded as equal citizens with equal rights and entitlements to privacy, security and respect under the law. This point is also borne out when considering the position of married women in relation to rape by their husbands.[136]

In the next chapter, feminist analyses of pornography and prostitution are considered. While pornography has been the major focus for feminist debate, prostitution also raises a number of difficult issues. Both pornography and prostitution raise their own particular problems for feminist analysis. Both, however, share a common identity – involving potentially or actually physical and sexual violence against women, and conceptualising women as products for male consumption.

---

[132] See *op cit*, Kennedy, fn 79.

[133] See *op cit*, Kennedy, fn 79, pp 120–21.

[134] More recently, a judge apologised for a remark made 'bad taste', when he likened a victim's ordeal of forced oral sex to being in the dentist's chair. Another judge rebuked a 14 year old victim of rape for 'sulking' when she had difficulty in giving evidence. However, Lord Justice Henry, who heads the training of the judiciary, has defended the work of judges in handling rape cases, pointing out that judges receive considerable training in dealing with such sensitive cases: (1997) *The Times*, 9 December 1997.

[135] *Op cit*, Kennedy, fn 79, p 111.

[136] However, the case for allowing cross-examination by the accused is supported by civil liberties lawyers: John Wadham, Director of Liberty, the civil rights group, has stated that '... there is a fundamental right of trial in the open where the defendant can confront his or her accuser. That should not be given away lightly' (1997) *The Times*, 18 September 1997.

CHAPTER 12

PORNOGRAPHY AND PROSTITUTION

INTRODUCTION

Pornography and prostitution raise a number of similar issues for feminist jurisprudence. In this chapter, the differing interpretations of pornography and prostitution are considered. While the major focus of the discussion is pornography, the arguments concerning prostitution are also introduced.

PORNOGRAPHY

Few issues have engaged such a wide range of feminist scholars in debate as pornography, which has proven a difficult and contentious issue on which little consensus has been reached. For radical anti-pornography feminists, pornography is the graphic representation of woman's inferior status, and thus needs to be exposed for what it is: not sexual imagery for pleasure, but a political statement on woman's equality. For others, pornography – with its difficulties of definition, its different interpretations, the problems of evaluating its impact, and the dangers of feminist theorising against pornography, make pornography an inappropriate and damaging site of inquiry in the pursuit of a society free from sexual discrimination. The complexity inherent in the pornography debate reflects differing political persuasions and philosophies, some of which intersect and interact with (differing) feminist approaches, others which stand opposed to the feminist quest for freedom from the adverse effects of pornography. Conservatism, liberalism and feminism are uneasy protagonists in the debate. In the discussion which follows, the differing approaches are examined.

The evolution of the pornography industry

Explicit depictions of sexuality – pornographic or not – have existed for as long as the human race has had the ability to create lasting images, whether in stone carvings or artefacts. Research demonstrates that, from as early as the sixth to the fourth centuries BC, sexually explicit materials were being produced in Athens and Attica.[1] In the sixteenth century, Italian artist Pietro

---

1 See Richlin, A (ed), *Pornography and Representation in Ancient Rome*, 1992, New York: OUP.

Aretino produced sexually explicit sonnets illustrated with engravings.[2] It was, however, with the development of technologies for the reproduction of the printed word and images in the late eighteenth century that the production of pornographic representations exploded. The Marquis de Sade, 1740–1814, has been attributed with the dishonour of being the 'world's foremost pornographer': 'His life and writing were of a piece, a whole cloth soaked in the blood of women imagined and real.'[3] The development of photographic techniques in the nineteenth century, the evolution of videos in the 1970s and, in the 1990s, CD-Rom and the Internet, are all media through which pornography circulates.

In 1979, the United Kingdom's *Report of the Committee on Obscenity and Film Censorship*[4] recorded that the circulation figures in the United Kingdom and Eire[5] (defined as retail sales) for five monthly magazines surveyed[6] amounted to 913,848 copies.[7] The readership was deemed to be some five per cent of the adult population, with men from all social classes accounting for 80 to 90 per cent of the 'readership'.[8] In the United States of America in 1981, an estimated $7 billion profit – or three per cent of all corporate profits – were attributable to sales of pornographic 'literature'.[9] In 1990, estimates for sales of monthly pornography magazines (and excluding the video market) were 2.25 million copies, although since some publishers do not release figures this figure may well be an underrepresentation.[10]

Defining pornography

Literally defined, pornography has been argued to mean 'writing about whores, prostitutes or female captives'. Derived from Greek, *porno* means whores; *graphos* means writing.[11] Pornography is thus distinguishable from both erotica (deriving from the Greek *eros* meaning passionate love), images

---

[2] See Hunt, L, *The Invention of Pornography*, 1993, New York: Zone.
[3] See Dworkin, A, *Pornography: Men Possessing Women*, 1981, London: The Women's Press, Chapter 3, p 70. (See *Sourcebook*, pp 443–50.)
[4] The Williams Committee, *Report of the Committee on Obscenity and Film Censorship*, Cmnd 7772, 1979, London: HMSO.
[5] Club International, Mayfair, Men Only.
[6] Club International, Mayfair, Men Only, Penthouse, Playboy.
[7] See Appendix 6 of the *Report, ibid*, fn 4.
[8] See the *Report, ibid*, fn 4, Appendix 6, paras 18–52.
[9] See Russo, A, 'Conflicts and contradictions among feminists over issues of pornography and sexual freedom' (1987) 102 Women's Studies International 103.
[10] Cohen, N, 'Reaping rich rewards from the profits of pornography' (1989) *The Independent*, 19 December, cited in Itzin, C (ed), *Pornography: Women, Violence and Civil Liberties: A Radical New View*, 1992, Oxford: OUP, p 39.
[11] See Steinem, G, 'Erotica and pornography: a clear and present difference' (1978) MS Magazine, repr in Dwyer, S, *The Problem of Pornography*, 1995, Belmont, California: Wadsworth; *ibid*, Dworkin, fn 3, pp 199–200.

and materials concerned with ideas of 'positive choice, free will, the yearning for a particular person'[12] and obscenity, the legal umbrella term under which pornography is regulated, which may be far broader in scope than pornography. After all, articles may be 'obscene' without necessarily depicting women as 'whores or female captives'.[13]

Legal definitions

Under English law, as in the United States and Canada, legal regulation is concerned neither with 'erotica', nor with pornography, *per se*, but rather with *obscene* materials. An article[14] is 'obscene' if:

> ... its effect ... is ... such as to tend to deprave and corrupt persons who are likely, having regard to all relevant circumstances, to read, see or hear the matter contained or embodied in it.[15]

As defined by the Williams Committee on Pornography and Obscenity, pornography is a representation which:

> ... combines two features: it has a certain function or intention, to arouse its audience sexually, and also a certain content, explicit representations of sexual material (organs, postures, activity, etc). A work has to have both this function and this content to be a piece of pornography.[16]

Alternatively, as defined by section 163(8) of the Canadian Criminal Code:

> For the purposes of this Act, any publication a dominant characteristic of which is the undue exploitation of sex, or of sex and any one or more of the following subjects, namely, crime, horror, cruelty and violence, shall be deemed to be obscene.[17]

Or, according to the United States' Supreme Court in *Roth v United States*:[18] 'material which deals with sex in a manner appealing to prurient interest', where the prurient interest refers to 'having a tendency to excite lustful thoughts ... [or] as '[a] shameful and morbid interest in sex' which is 'utterly without redeeming social importance'.

A central feature of pornography, as opposed to erotica, is that it exists in the largely hidden, subverted and inaccessible world. Pornography, as traditionally conceived, is the expression of that which should not be

---

[12] *Op cit*, Steinem, fn 11.
[13] As in the case of *Handyside v United Kingdom*, concerning a publication encouraging sexual relations amongst school aged children, *The Little Red Schoolbook*.
[14] Which covers books, pictures, films, records and video cassettes.
[15] Obscene Publications Act 1959, s 1(1).
[16] *Op cit*, *Report*, fn 4, para 8.2.
[17] See 'Legal appendix' in Dwyer, *op cit*, fn 11, p 240.
[18] 354 US 476 (1973).

expressed: the realm of shameful fantasised sexual imaginings. While the erotic may fall within the category of art, pornography does not.

Defining pornography is central to an understanding of the political and legal approaches to pornography. Definition is thus an ideological tool, with definitions framed in such a manner which suggests the appropriate response to pornography. Thus, from the liberal perspective, pornography is a form of representation of sex, which, without proof of substantive harm to an identifiable subject, should remain legally unregulated in the interests of individual liberty to engage with whatever images the individual chooses. From a radical feminist standpoint, however, pornography is defined in terms of the damage it does to the imagery and equality of women. As Catharine MacKinnon argues, the liberal tradition conceptualises pornography '... as not about women as such at all, but about sex, hence about morality, and as not about acts or practices, but about ideas'. Reconceptualised from a radical feminist perspective, however, '[P]ornography contributes causally to attitudes and behaviours of violence and discrimination which define the treatment and status of half the population'. The legal definitions, cast in the language of obscenity, reflect the liberal position of pornography as a moral issue. Radical feminism, on the other hand, views pornography as a political practice 'that is predicated on power and powerlessness'.[19]

Differing constitutional contexts

Before briefly considering the legal regulation of pornography, it is necessary to recall the differing constitutional arrangements between the United Kingdom and, for example, Australia, Canada and the United States of America. In the United Kingdom, having no formally drafted 'written' constitution and lacking a domestic Bill of Rights, legal regulation of obscenity and pornography is by way of Acts of Parliament which are immune from challenge from the domestic courts of law.[20] In Australia, having a written constitution, but no overriding Bill of Rights, the legal regulation of pornography is largely a matter for State regulation.[21] Conversely, in the United States, with a written constitution enshrining an inviolate and overriding Bill of Rights, legislation purporting to regulate such materials may

---

[19] MacKinnon, C, *Toward a Feminist Theory of State*, 1989, Cambridge, Mass: Harvard UP, p 196.

[20] It is to be noted that the Human Rights Act 1998 incorporates the European Convention on Human Rights. Incorporation, however, will not enable judges to question the validity of Acts of Parliament. See Barnett, H, *Constitutional & Administrative Law*, 2nd edn, 1998, London: Cavendish Publishing, Chapter 22.

[21] Federal law regulates customs and excise restrictions on pornographic imports, and in some instances films and computer games.

be challenged against the constitutional guarantees of the right to free speech. The First Amendment to the United States Constitution provides that:

> Congress shall make no law respecting an establishment of religion, or prohibiting the free exercise thereof; or abridging the freedom of speech, or of the press; or the right of the people peaceably to assemble, and to petition the Government for a redress of grievances.

Accordingly, the validity of attempted legal regulation of pornography is a constitutional matter, ultimately for the judges of the Supreme Court to determine. In Canada, whilst freedom of 'thought, belief, opinion and expression, including freedom of the press and other media of communication' is protected under section 2 of the Canadian Charter of Rights and Freedoms, these rights may be restricted under section 1 of the Charter of Rights and Freedoms which provides that:

> The Canadian Charter of Rights and Freedoms guarantees the rights and freedoms set out in it subject to reasonable limits prescribed by law and can be demonstrably justified in a free and democratic society.

As will be seen below, these differing constitutional arrangements have had an important impact on the manner in which courts in the differing jurisdictions have treated the 'pornography problem'.

Under the constitutions of Australia and the United Kingdom, citizens do not have 'rights' – only 'freedoms' to do what the law does not prohibit. Notwithstanding that legal fact, there is the presumption that the individual should have maximum freedom – compatible with the freedom of others – in society. This doctrine holds particularly strongly in areas of personal morality. The legal approach in Canada and the United States may be contrasted with that of Australia and the United Kingdom. As noted above, freedom of speech has an absolutist quality under the United States' Constitution (First Amendment), a position which is not reflected in the Canadian Charter of Fundamental Rights and Freedoms, which while guaranteeing constitutional protection for freedom of speech, provides through section 1 of the Charter for such guaranteed rights to be restricted in order to protect other rights and freedoms, for example the right to equality.

The United States has adopted the same terminology as the United Kingdom in relation to pornography, namely 'obscenity'.[22] In 1842, the first federal statute was enacted to regulate obscenity.[23] In *United States v Bennett* (1879),[24] the federal courts adopted the test previously laid down by the English courts in *R v Hicklin* (1868), namely that:

---

[22] For analysis of the United States case law, see Sunstein, C, 'Pornography, sex discrimination and free speech', in Gostin, L (ed), *Civil Liberties in Conflict*, 1988, London: Routledge, p 152.
[23] Act of 30 August 1842, ch 270, s 28, 5 Stat 548 (1842).
[24] 24 F Cas 1093 (No 14, 571) (CCSDNY 1879).

... the test of obscenity is this, whether the tendency of the matter charged as obscenity is to deprave and corrupt those whose minds are open to such immoral influences, and into whose hands a publication of this sort may fall.[25]

However, in *United States v One Book Called Ulysses*[26] the courts rejected the *Hicklin* test and included in its assessment of the material, the author's intention, the literary merit of the matter and the effect of the material on the average person. An early constitutional challenge to pornographic material arose in *Roth v United States*[27] in 1957, wherein the Supreme Court considered the issue of obscenity law within the context of the First Amendment. For the majority, Justice Brennan argued that obscenity was not protected by the First Amendment on the basis that it is 'utterly without redeeming social importance'.[28] The test to be adopted as to whether or not material was obscene and therefore capable of prohibition is stringent. According to Chief Justice Burger in *Miller v California*,[29] material is obscene, if '(a) the average person, applying contemporary community standards, would find that the work, taken as whole, appeals to the prurient interest; (b) the work depicts or describes, in a patently offensive way, sexual conduct specifically defined by the applicable State law; and (c) the work, taken as a whole, lacks serious literary, artistic, political, or scientific value (the LAPS test)'. The test was modified in *Pope v Illinois*,[30] in which the Court ruled that the test to be applied was not linked to the relevant 'community standards' but rather to the 'reasonable' person.

The Canadian Supreme Court has takes a more robust approach to restricting pornography than has the United States' Supreme Court, and has found legitimate means by which to limit the range and availability of pornography. In *R v Butler*,[31] the Canadian Supreme Court held that whilst restrictions[32] on pornography were *prima facie* a violation of section 2 of the Charter, restrictions could be justified under section 1 as a necessary restraint in the interests of a free and democratic society. In *Butler*, the Court ruled that 'harm' was to be construed in terms of predisposing people to act in an 'anti-social manner', and that it was the 'community standards'[33] test which was to decide what is, and is not, harmful. The forms of pornography which are liable to restriction, according to the Supreme Court, are those which represent either explicit sex with violence, horror, or cruelty, or explicit sex in

---

[25] *R v Hicklin* (1868) LR 3 QB 360, *per* Lord Cockburn, p 371.
[26] 5 F Supp 182 (SDNY, 1933).
[27] 354 US 476 (1957).
[28] 354 US 476 (1957), p 484.
[29] 413 US 15 (1973).
[30] 481 US 497 (1987).
[31] [1992] 1 SCR 452.
[32] In that case, the Criminal Code, s 163(8).
[33] Lord Devlin's 12 jury persons.

which one or more of the participants is degraded or dehumanised. Explicit sex without violence, on the other hand, that is neither degrading nor dehumanising was not vulnerable to restriction.

Empirical evidence concerning pornography[34]

In 1979, the Williams Committee on Obscenity and Pornography reached the pithy conclusion that 'research [into the effects of pornography and violence on human behaviour] tends, over and over again, to be inconclusive'.[35] Not only was the evidence taken as a whole 'inconclusive', but much of the empirical data was contradictory, and in the case of evidence submitted by one witness, criticised for the inaccuracy of its conclusions. Harms which the Committee considered included the alleged increase in rape and other sexual crimes; the exploitation of workers in the pornography industry; general 'cultural pollution'; the effect on human relationships; the effect of engendering hate and aggression; risking 'the normal development of the young'; causing 'desensitisation' and callousness. The issue of the degradation of women through pornography, played a comparatively minor part in the Committee's deliberations, although reference was made to evidence submitted which turned on 'aspects of pornography which degrade women in that much material is not only offensive, but encourages a view of women as subservient and as properly the object of, or even desirous of, sexual subjugation or assault'.[36]

Among the Committee's general proposals – despite the ambivalence in the empirical evidence as to 'harms' – the Committee stated that the law 'should rest partly on the basis of harms caused by or involved in the existence of the materials: these alone can justify prohibitions; and partly on the basis of the public's legitimate interest in not being offended by the display and availability of the material ...'.[37] Further, 'the principal object of the law should be to prevent certain kinds of material causing offence to reasonable people or being made available to young people',[38] and restrictions should apply on the basis that participants appeared to be under the age of 16, or on the basis that 'the materials give reason to believe that

---

[34] See, *inter alia*, Einsiedel, E, 'The experimental research evidence: effect on pornography on the "average individual"'; Russell, D, 'Pornography and rape: a causal model'; Check, J, 'The effects of violent pornography, non-violent dehumanising pornography, and erotica: some legal implications from a Canadian perspective', all repr in Itzin, *op cit*, fn 10.

[35] *Op cit, Report,* fn 4, para 1.10

[36] *Op cit, Report,* fn 4, para 5.29. The Committee's membership was 13, of whom three were women.

[37] *Op cit, Report,* fn 4, para 13.4.3.

[38] *Op cit, Report,* fn 4, para 13.4.4.

actual physical harm was inflicted on the [participant] person'.[39] The status of women in society, their equality and the effects of pornography on women in general did not receive in depth consideration and represents a shortcoming in the whole, otherwise well measured and authoritative, report. This perceived deficiency, may, however, be explained by the sheer complexity of the evidence and the difficulty of conclusively establishing the nature of the harm caused 'beyond all reasonable doubt' which was the Committee's required standard of proof. The Committee was, overall, primarily concerned with freedom from censorship: censorship being harm in itself. Accordingly, without the clearest of proof regarding harm, the Committee was unprepared to depart from the priority of freedom. A 'hands-off' approach towards the regulation of pornography was also adopted by the United States' Attorney General's Commission on Pornography.[40]

The evidence of the harm caused by pornography itself, as the terms of the debate and related research is currently formulated, is equivocal and provides no clear basis on which to draw conclusions.[41] Thus, for example, the United States Commission on Obscenity and Pornography concluded (by a majority), in 1970, that the evidence was insufficient to establish that 'pornography is a central causal factor in acts of sexual violence'.[42] Conversely, the Canadian Attorney General's Commission on Pornography, reporting in 1986, concluded that:

> The available evidence strongly supports the hypothesis that substantial exposure to sexually violent materials as described here bears a causal relationship to anti-social acts of violence and, for some subgroups, possibly to unlawful acts of sexual violence.[43]

To become embroiled in arguments about evidence concerning the cause and effect relationships between pornography and sexual violence, given the ambivalence of that evidence, is an exercise in futility. Moreover, research method strategies have been criticised for manipulation of data, and for the construction of research projects designed to prove the researcher's own beliefs about cause and effect.[44] Cause and effect is also a debate which misses much about the feminist arguments concerning pornography which form the core of the radical feminist approach. A consideration of differing types of harm which may be involved here reveals the complexity of the issue.

---

[39] *Op cit, Report*, fn 4, para 10.6(a) and (b).
[40] The Meese Commission 1986, Washington: US Department of Justice.
[41] See Howitt, D and Cumberbatch, G, *Pornography: Impacts and influences*, 1990, London: Home Office.
[42] See 'Legal appendix' in Dwyer, *op cit*, fn 11, p 241.
[43] *Op cit*, Dwyer, fn 11, p 245.
[44] For a critique of research methods, see King, A, 'Mystery and imagination: the case of pornography effects studies', in Assiter, A and Carol, A (eds), *Bad Girls and Dirty Pictures: The Challenge to Radical Feminism*, 1993, London: Pluto, p 88.

Moreover, as Deborah Cameron and Elizabeth Frazer have argued, even though the causal link between sexual violence and pornography cannot be conclusively established, that does not mean that there *is* no causal link. Neither does it mean that pornography does not play a significant role in forming attitudes and 'certain forms of desire'.[45] Pornography, in Cameron and Frazer's view, is characterised not only by its explicit sexual representations, but also by the attractiveness it generates for certain consumers by virtue of its illicitness; its secretness. This aspect of pornography, the authors state, results in pornography having a 'normative aspect' to it – it tells the viewer 'how to do sex', and 'because it purports to be describing the forbidden, the normative model it presents is much more appealing and powerful than something presented overtly as normative ...'.[46] Pornography thus creates meaning, reinforced by its illicit and transgressive nature, and that meaning – the construction of forms of desire based on violent gratification – in the hands of those predisposed to violence, can have a particularly potent and damaging effect.[47]

From a feminist perspective, however, in addition to understanding pornography's meaning, irrespective of the empirical evidence concerning a causal connection between pornography and physical and sexual violence against women, the appropriate focus of enquiry is the effect of pornography on women's equality and status in society, and pornography's role in reinforcing traditional economic, political and social inequalities.[48]

Reformulating pornography from a feminist perspective

It will be apparent from the above brief overview of contemporary legal approaches to pornography that legal definitions focus on the effect which pornography has on the consumer(s) of the material. Accordingly, in Australia, the United Kingdom and the United States of America – but not in

---

[45] Cameron, D and Frazer, E, 'Moving beyond cause and effect', in Itzin, *op cit*, fn 10, pp 359, 376.

[46] *Ibid*, Cameron and Frazer, p 377.

[47] The most recent British research into the linkage between violent videos and violent behaviour (albeit non-sexual), conducted on behalf of the Home Office, also proved inconclusive. Dr Kevin Browne, of the University of Birmingham, and Amanda Pennell undertook research into the effects of film and video violence on young offenders. The research involved 122 males aged 15–21, 54 violent offenders, 28 non-violent criminals and 40 non-offenders. The research concluded that offenders brought up in a violent family background are most likely to choose to watch violent films, and identify with violent figures, although that did not lead to crime. However, once the taste for violent videos was established, it was more likely that that diet would 'nurture increasingly anti-social behaviour'. The British Board of Film Classification's response was that some 'violent and potentially dangerous young people' could be influenced: *The Effect of Video Violence on Young Offenders*, 1998, London: Home Office.

[48] For a feminist evaluation of the ambivalent evidence on pornography, see *op cit*, Itzin, fn 10.

Introduction to Feminist Jurisprudence

Canada[49] – the impact which pornography has on women, whether individual workers in the pornography industry, or women as a class, is ignored. Thus, from a legal standpoint, women, who are the central focus of most pornographic materials, do not exist in the determination of whether or not the material in question is in fact pornographic as defined by law. Were the legal focus to be altered so that the central question became not whether or not the (principally male) consumer was 'depraved or corrupted', but whether *women* are injured by pornography, then women victims of pornography would be included, rather than excluded, from the law. Legal approaches to pornography, with the notable exception of the Supreme Court of Canada, have hitherto been masculine approaches: does this material 'deprave and corrupt' the male consumer. If the question is reformulated from a feminist, legally inclusive rather than exclusive, perspective, the central question becomes: does this material 'harm' women.[50] Such a reformulation would act as a lodestar for sociological and psychological research with an entirely different focus from that which has been conducted to date. To date, the primary research foci have been the measurable effects of pornography on its male consumers, as if such consumers were themselves the 'victims' of pornography, whereas from a feminist perspective, it is women who are the true victims of pornography – both individually and collectively. Such an approach radically alters perceptions about the value of the empirical research which has been undertaken to date.

Alternative theoretical approaches to pornography

A number of theoretical arguments are advanced in relation to the issue of 'what to do about pornography'? Several approaches may be taken, among which the dominant approaches are:

(a) Pornography represents violence and discrimination against women and accordingly should be actionable under civil law on the basis that it offends against women's right to economic, political and social equality and reinforces male supremacist attitudes (the radical feminist approach advanced by Andrea Dworkin and Catharine MacKinnon).

(b) Pornography is an aspect of free speech. In the absence of clear evidence of 'harm', pornography cannot be restricted (the extreme liberal approach).

(c) Pornography is an aspect of free speech. Access to pornography may be restricted, however, provided that the restrictions are 'reasonable' (the moderated liberal approach).

---

[49] Under the authority of *R v Butler*, discussed above.
[50] Harm here is intended to encompass both women directly and physically harmed by pornography and the imagery, equality and status of women collectively.

(d) Pornography offends society's morality. Accordingly, the law must protect society against pornography (the conservative approach).

(e) Pornography has no single meaning or message, but many. Furthermore, the feminist focus on pornography damages the quest for women's equality, in emphasising woman as 'victim'. Accordingly, there is no justification for regulation other than for laws protecting children and those on whom unlawful violence is afflicted in the making of pornography (the postmodern approach).

FEMINIST APPROACHES TO PORNOGRAPHY

Radical feminism[51]

From a radical feminist perspective, the issue of the harm caused by pornography is less whether, and the extent to which, there can be proven to be a specific cause and effect relationship between pornography and sexual violence against women, but rather that pornography, in its often sadistic depiction of women being generally degraded, hurt and violated, and always submitting to male domination, is itself – without more – the harm caused. The harm from this perspective, as argued by Andrea Dworkin and Catharine MacKinnon, is caused to all women, the *image* of all women, the *equality* of all women and not only those participating in the acts portrayed.

Feminist author Andrea Dworkin in *Pornography: Men Possessing Women*[52] presents a powerful radical feminist critique of the meaning of and evils of pornography.[53] For Dworkin, pornography is the portrayal, in words, on film, of whores. Men retain – as they always have retained – the power[54] of physical possession of women, and this power is most graphically depicted in pornography which reduces all women to the status of a whore: '[I]n the male system, women are sex; sex is the whore.'[55] Male sexual domination over women exhibits itself through the institutions of 'law, marriage, prostitution, pornography, health care, the economy, organised religion, and the systematised physical aggression against women (for instance, in rape and battery)'.[56] All women's lives are defined by male power which finds its most violent and damaging expression in pornography. Pornography is a political issue, and used by both Left and Right to legitimise the subordination of

---

[51] See Chapter 8.
[52] *Op cit*, Dworkin, fn 3.
[53] See now, also, Dworkin, A, *Life and Death: Unapologetic Writings on the Continuing War Against Women*, 1997, London: Virago.
[54] On Andrea Dworkin's analysis of power, see, further, Chapter 2.
[55] *Op cit*, Dworkin, fn 3, p 202.
[56] *Op cit*, Dworkin, fn 3, p 203.

women. The 'men of the Right' regard prostitution – 'real whores' – as a dirty trade to be engaged in secret. The 'men of the Left' regard and use prostitution while proclaiming the equality of women, the joy of sex, the liberality of prostitution and pornography as an industry: '[F]reedom is the mass-marketing of woman as whore.'[57]

Professor Catharine MacKinnon endorses much of Andrea Dworkin's writing on pornography and presents powerful legal arguments against pornography. Like Dworkin, for MacKinnon pornography is a representation of male power and domination and the correlative subordination of women. Pornography is sexual discrimination: maintaining and reinforcing women's inequality in society by representing women as sexual objects, whose primary function in life is portrayed as being sexually available for men's use. MacKinnon's feminism is a theory of 'power and its unequal distribution'.[58] The difference gender makes is a difference in power, and the difference is demonstrated in the statistics on rape, attempted rape, incest, the sexual abuse of women and children and sexual harassment.[59] Male power enables men to define women: women are defined as sexual beings. Rape and sexual violence is an exercise in power. Pornography is an expression of that power:

> [P]ornography not only teaches the reality of male dominance. It is one way its reality is imposed as well as experienced. It is a way of seeing and using women.[60]

Pornography is an institution of the inequality which women suffer as a result of their gender: pornography identifies, defines and constructs women's gender. Women are what pornography portrays.[61] And the law – in the United States, under the First Amendment to the Constitution – protects and endorses pornography as freedom of speech. Freedom of men's free speech: not women's free equal speech, for that is taken away from them by pornographic representations.[62] In 'Francis Biddle's sister: pornography, civil rights, and speech',[63] Catharine MacKinnon draws the analogy between racial discrimination and pornography.[64]

---

[57] *Op cit*, Dworkin, fn 3, p 209.

[58] MacKinnon, C, 'Desire and power', in *Feminism Unmodified: Discourses on Life and Law*, 1987, Cambridge, Mass: Harvard UP, p 49.

[59] MacKinnon presents the following statistics: the rate of rape and attempted rape being 44 per cent of all women; the rate of incest and sexual abuse within the family being 43 per cent of all girls under the age of 18; the rate of sexual harassment at work 'about 85 per cent': see *ibid*, p 49.

[60] 'Linda's life and Andrea's work', in MacKinnon, *ibid*, p 130.

[61] See MacKinnon, C, 'Not a moral issue', in MacKinnon, *ibid*, p 148.

[62] *Ibid*, pp 157–58.

[63] MacKinnon, C, 'Francis Biddle's sister: pornography, civil rights and speech' in MacKinnon, *ibid*, 1987, Chapter 14.

[64] See, also, Catharine MacKinnon's analysis of racial and sexual discrimination law and pornography and the 'collision course' between women's equality and free speech, in MacKinnon, C, *Only Words*, 1994, London: HarperCollins, Part II. (See *Sourcebook*, pp 460–63.)

Racial discrimination and pornography

In both the United States and the United Kingdom, racial and sexual discrimination is prohibited by law.[65] In the United States, the seminal case of *Brown v Board of Education of Topeka*[66] overturned the United States Supreme Court decision in *Plessey v Ferguson*[67] in which 'separate but equal treatment' of black people was held to be constitutional. In the United Kingdom, the Race Relations Act 1976 was enacted to prohibit racial discrimination in employment and the provision of public services and the Public Order Act 1986[68] makes it a criminal offence to publish material 'intended or likely to stir up racial hatred'. Thus, English law goes further than American law in infringing 'free speech' in relation to racial matters. There has been little heartsearching in the United Kingdom over the justification for such a restriction on freedom of expression; no tortured arguments over the need for a 'free market place of ideas' or 'slippery slopes' (what next will be prohibited?). Indeed to voice such views within the context of the need to protect minority groups from racially offensive expression – whether verbal or written – would be considered, in contemporary parlance, 'politically incorrect' and offensive. Neither has there been an exhaustive inquiry into the effects of racial hatred speech: no scientifically proven data on which such speech is prohibited; no analysis of precisely – in Millian terms – the 'harm' caused which justifies the restrictions. The justification for such restrictions in the United Kingdom lies purely in the political perception of the need to protect, on the basis of equality under the law, those who are, or may be, 'harmed' (howsoever analysed) by such expression.

In the United States, however, there has developed substantial case law which demonstrates that the use of graphic sexual depictions and words in the workplace have been construed as racial and/or sexual harassment, thus removing such actions and words from the protection of the First Amendment. In relation to pornography, however, there is no sign of official realisation or recognition of the need to protect women as a whole against the deleterious effect of pornography. So entrenched, it would appear, is the inferiority of women in the minds of men – and hence society – that the issue of the achievement of real equality – the issue of protecting half of the population from both the direct and insidious effects of being constantly violated and demeaned – is simply not considered; not on the formal political agenda. Which brings us back to the power base in society: the governance of man for man, the male controlled pornography and media industry which continues to portray women as inferior sexual objects.

---

[65] But see, further, below for discussion of the limits of this protection.
[66] 347 US 483 (1954).
[67] 163 US 537 (1896).
[68] Section 19. As amended by the Criminal Justice and Public Order Act 1994, s 155.

From a radical feminist perspective, pornography is a form of sexual harassment, a form of sexual discrimination, a means of reinforcing sexual inequality and should be recognised for what it is – a freedom not of expression, but to dominate and subordinate and exploit. Pornography presents images of women which reach far beyond the individual consumer of pornography: the portrayal of women as sexual objects sends a very fundamental message to society: this – sexual violence and abuse – this is what women are, what women are for. From television advertisements which reduce women to domestic workers or sexually desirable adornments for cars, through page three of *The Sun* newspaper to sadistic hard core pornography, the industry shrieks its message, and yet the message is not heard at a political level, although it is absorbed subliminally by those exposed to its pervasive influence. And when the real message is heard and a serious attempt to generate change is made, the messenger is treated with ridicule, derision or contempt as if even to question the existence of pornography, and its effects on women, is a question only a fool (or a killjoy, a bore, a woman) would ask.

In *Only Words*,[69] MacKinnon opens the chapter entitled 'Equality and speech' by stating that '[T]he law of equality and the law of freedom of speech are on a collision course'. So intoxicated are the American courts with the need to protect free speech that the need to protect equality – ostensibly protected under the Fourteenth Amendment to the Constitution – goes unnoticed when in potential or actual conflict with freedom of expression. The First Amendment, originally designed to protect free political argument from governmental suppression, has become the protector of race hate speech and pornographers. So mindful is the law of the dangers of suppressing 'speech' that the protection of freedom of expression has grown to encompass all forms of expression, however abhorrent. As MacKinnon ironically comments: '... [y]ou can tell you are being principled by the degree to which you abhor what you allow. The worse the speech protected, the more principled the result.'[70]

There is, for MacKinnon, a direct link between racial hatred expression and pornography. Both are designed to denigrate their victims; to affirm and maintain the inferiority of a despised group; to instil fear; to enhance the power of the already powerful. From a radical feminist perspective, pornography has all of these effects. Pornography, through its depiction of women as sexual objects for the consumption of man, expresses power over all women. Pornography affirms women's inferiority and inequality. Pornography instils fear in women – all women, for this is what 'a woman is', an object, a thing to be used by the all-powerful, superior male. If equality of women – rather than freedom of expression – were the goal to be achieved by law, then what amounts to legitimate freedom of expression, the exchange of ideas, would require redefinition.

---

[69] *Op cit*, MacKinnon, fn 64, p 51.
[70] *Op cit*, MacKinnon, fn 64, p 54.

As discussed above, the problem, in part, is the law's reliance on the concept of obscenity. Obscenity, by setting tests of material having the effect of depraving and corrupting the average consumer, has nothing to do with the equality of those who are depicted in the materials concerned. Moreover, by introducing the 'contemporary community standards test',[71] the inevitable result ensures that the more pornography there is, and the worse it is, the more desensitised community standards in relation to pornography will be. By focusing on obscenity and the standard of tolerance in the community, the law loses sight totally of the equality issue and fails completely to consider the harm perpetrated on women.[72]

The Dworkin (Andrea) and MacKinnon Indianapolis and Minneapolis Civil Rights Ordinances

In 1983, in an attempt to provide legal remedies for the harm caused by pornography, Catharine MacKinnon and Andrea Dworkin drafted an amendment to the Minneapolis Civil Rights Ordinance.[73] The amendment both defined what is to be regarded as pornography and also defined pornography as 'a form of discrimination on the basis of sex' which would be actionable in law. In 1984, the Indianapolis City and County Council adopted a modified version of the Dworkin-MacKinnon Model Anti-Pornography Ordinance. The Indianapolis Ordinance prohibited any 'production, sale, exhibition, or distribution' of the material defined as pornographic. Pornography is defined in the Minneapolis Civil Rights Ordinance as the portrayal – whether in words or pictures – of the 'explicit subordination of women', where women are, *inter alia*, portrayed as 'dehumanised as sexual objects', as sexual objects who enjoy pain or humiliation, or who experience sexual pleasure from being raped, or as sexual objects tied up or mutilated or physically hurt; in postures of sexual submission, or the portrayal of women's body parts such that women are reduced to those parts; or being penetrated by objects or animals, or presented in scenarios of 'degradation, injury, abasement, torture, shown as filthy or inferior, bleeding, bruised, or hurt in a context that makes those conditions sexual'. The Ordinances did not represent an attempt at censorship – to which both Dworkin and MacKinnon are opposed – but rather made provision for civil actions for damages to be available to individuals or groups harmed by pornographic representations.

---

[71] See *Miller v California* 413 US 15 (1973); *Dominion News and Gifts (1962) Ltd v R* [1964] SCR 251.

[72] The United States' position in relation to child pornography is different: restrictions are based on the assumption of harm to children through participation in pornography. See *New York v Ferber* 458 US 747 (1982); *Osborne v Ohio* 495 US 103 (1990).

[73] On which see, further, below.

The draft Ordinances thus provided for civil, as opposed to criminal, remedies. The 1983 Minneapolis Civil Rights Ordinance was framed in sex discrimination language and made four practices actionable: (a) discrimination by trafficking in pornography; (b) coercion into pornographic performances; (c) forcing pornography on a person; and (d) assault or attack due to pornography. The first head would have made actionable the production, sale, exhibition or distribution of pornography, not on the basis of obscenity, but on the basis of its discriminatory effects on women. 'Coercion into pornography' was designed to provide a remedy for victims of pornography such as Linda Marchiano who, in the course of making the film *Deep Throat*, was imprisoned, beaten, constantly watched, tortured and threatened.[74] 'Forcing pornography on a person' was designed to prevent children and adults from the effects of having pornographic materials thrust upon them, whether at home, in the work place or in public. 'Action for assault or attack due to pornography' would have involved all the problems associated with the cause and effect debate.

Challenges to the Ordinances came rapidly, with challengers basing their claims on the constitutionality of the Ordinances. The result was that the Ordinances were declared unconstitutional on the basis of violating the First Amendment to the United States Constitution: the right to freedom of speech.[75] The Circuit Court for the Seventh Circuit upheld the District Court's ruling and the Supreme Court refused to review that decision. Judge Easterbrook, accepting the premises of the anti-pornography Ordinances, nevertheless in the Circuit Court ruled that nothing must be censored 'because the message it seeks to deliver is a bad one, or because it expresses ideas that should not be heard at all'.[76] The failing of the courts, in relation to the Ordinances, lies in the traditional and intransigent 'liberal' American approach which insists on aligning pornography with 'speech'. Only if pornography were reconceptualised as sexual hatred and/or sexual discrimination, or if pornography were to be reclassified as action against women rather than representation of women, would a way forward be achieved leading out of the constitutional and conceptual clutches of First Amendment protection.

As Catharine MacKinnon documents, the American courts have accepted for some years that racial or sexual harassment in the workplace does not, irrespective of its expression, attract the protection of the First Amendment of the Constitution. Sexual harassment, accordingly, is treated differently from

---

[74] See Lovelace, L and McGrady, M, *Ordeal*, 1980; see Catharine MacKinnon's account in MacKinnon, *op cit*, fn 63, pp 179–83.

[75] *American Booksellers Association Inc v Hudnut* 771 F2d aff'd S Ct 1172 [1986].

[76] Cited in Dworkin, A, 'Liberty and pornography' (1993) *The New York Review of Books*, 21 October, p 117, repr in Dwyer, *op cit*, fn 11.

other forms of expression and is thus legally actionable.[77] The juridical basis for this distinction is the conceptual distinction, accepted by the American courts, between *action* and *words*. Sexual harassment is judicially interpreted and understood to be a form of sexual discrimination. Thus, the legal test of obscenity does not apply to sexually discriminatory acts. However, an issue which has caused fierce debate and much litigation in the United States, and which produces a very different legal result, is that of racially inflammatory or insulting policies, practices and expressions on university and other academic campuses. In this context, the courts have determinedly struck down as unconstitutional any attempted prohibition of free expression on racial grounds, notwithstanding the similar content and effect of both racial and sexual harassment. What is significant here, within the pornography context, is not so much the complex reasoning (right or wrong) involved in this curious distinction, but rather the importance, from the United States constitutional perspective, which lies in what does and does not amount to 'speech' which is constitutionally protected, and 'actions' which may be actionable at law. For as Catharine MacKinnon demonstrates in her analysis of racial and sexual harassment under American law,[78] the two phenomena, which bear more than a superficial resemblance to each other, will be treated differently under law according to whether they are classified as either 'speech' or 'acts'.

Several conceptual issues need to be considered within this context. These may be identified in the form of the following two principal headings:

(a) the meaning of the right to freedom of expression;
(b) whether, and under what conditions, 'speech', or 'expression', may be regarded as conterminous with 'acts' (speech act theory).

Freedom of expression reconsidered

From the time of John Stuart Mill to Ronald Dworkin, liberal philosophers have asserted by primacy of the right to freedom of expression as a core constitutional element of democracy and participation in the democratic process. Under English law, however, this 'right' has no constitutional protection, and is hedged in by limitations deemed to be necessary for the working of a healthy democracy which accords equal respect to citizens irrespective of class or race, and irrespective of sex, other than in the regulation of pornographic materials.[79] In the United States, however, the

---

[77] See *op cit*, MacKinnon, fn 64, Part II.
[78] 'Racial and sexual harassment', in MacKinnon, *op cit*, fn 64, Part II.
[79] European Convention on Human Rights and Individual Freedoms, Art 10, guarantees freedom of expression, subject to such limits as 'are prescribed by law and are necessary in a democratic society'. The Human Rights Act 1998 incorporates the Convention into English law.

First Amendment of the Constitution has produced a situation where under the law, both racial and sexual hatred, other than where sexual hatred is formulated as a form of sexual discrimination in the workplace, is protected. On what justification does this protection lie? From Ronald Dworkin's standpoint, freedom of expression – however vile or morally reprehensible – is justified on the basis that, '... the speech we hate is as much entitled to protection as any other'.[80]

There are, however, other, alternative, arguments which must be considered. The principal argument which will be introduced here is that pursued so effectively by Stanley Fish.[81] In *There's No Such Thing as Free Speech, and It's a Good Thing, Too*,[82] Fish argues that the First Amendment dilemma, namely its use in protecting pornography, sexist language and campus hate speech, lies in a misunderstanding of the meaning of and context within which 'speech' lies. 'Free speech' he tells us, and all the rhetoric which surrounds it in the United States, has no substantive content whatsoever, but is a means of verbal expression which is used to pursue whatever political purpose an individual chooses. Speech is thus contextual: nothing of itself, but a means to an end – an end which for the most part, is political in context. According to the jurisprudence of the Supreme Court, only where 'speech' may be interpreted as 'acts' – as in sexual discrimination law – or where speech is interpreted not purely as speech on the grounds that it acts as incitement to forms of public disorder – can the trap of constitutional protection be avoided. What courts do, when interpreting whether or not 'speech' is 'speech', or 'speech' is 'action', is to classify forms of 'speech' according to their own political agenda: a balancing of what should, or should not, be protected. While courts refuse to articulate the political underpinnings of their judgments and continue to affirm the juristic justifications for the primacy of First Amendment guarantees, those political underpinnings are in fact central to judges' reasoning.

Freedom of speech, being devoid of substantive content and contextually dependent, Fish argues, should not be accorded the blanket primacy which it attracts. Rather, freedom of speech, and its protection, should lie within the context of consideration of the specific forum in which it operates, and be balanced against competing principles – such as equality – in order to determine the appropriate extent and limits of the protection:

> ... the thesis that there is no such thing as free speech, [which] is not, after all, a thesis as startling or corrosive as may first have seemed. It merely says that there is no class of utterances separable from the world of conduct and that therefore the identification of some utterances as members of that non-existent

---

[80] *Op cit*, Dworkin, fn 76, p 12.
[81] Professor of English and Professor of Law, Duke University.
[82] Fish, S, *There's No Such Thing as Free Speech, and It's a Good Thing, Too*, 1993, Oxford: OUP.

class will always be evidence that a political line has been drawn rather than a line that denies politics entry into the forum of public discourse.

'Speech act' theory

Speech act theory derives from linguistic philosophy, and most particularly from the work of JL Austin.[83] The principal thrust of the theory is expressed in Austin's slogan, 'to say something is to *do* something'. Speech act theory is utilised by Catharine MacKinnon when she argues that pornography is an act of subordination, and an act of silencing women's voices. In order to understand the efficacy of speech act theory in advancing the argument against pornography, it is necessary briefly to outline the constituent elements of the theory.

First, the terminology. Speech act theory entails three principal forms of words which effect differing acts: the locutionary, the perlocutionary and the illocutionary. To make a *locutionary* statement is to describe a state of affairs: 'the economy is in recession', for example. Such a statement has no effect or meaning or consequence, other than as a statement. A *perlocutionary* form of speech, or *perlocutionary act,* is more than purely descriptive, but is persuasive, or frightening; the action it performs is causative, or contributory to the action which the listener then takes: 'enter the London marathon, you can easily do it'; 'if you don't see the doctor about that rash soon, it will cover your entire face'. The statement is thus *more than* a 'mere' statement, for it has a causal relationship with the action which follows. The statement is therefore 'acting upon' the listener. An *illocutionary* statement, or *illocutionary act*, is one which, by its very utterance, is indistinguishable from the statement itself. Statements, commands, promises comprise illocutionary acts. If a police officer on traffic duty directs a driver to 'move on', or 'pull over' that is a command from one in authority to one not in authority, and is an illocutionary act. Also, by way of example, when John says to Mary, in a ceremony of marriage, valid according to the relative law, the words 'I do', John is performing an illocutionary act – that of marrying Mary. When Andrea Dworkin and Catharine MacKinnon state 'Pornography ... *is* the graphic sexually explicit subordination of women ...', as they do in the Ordinances, they are claiming that pornography – in its many manifestations – is an *illocutionary act* – it subordinates, and silences women.

For speech to be conceptualised as an act, whether locutionary, perlocutionary or illocutionary, there are certain conditions which must be fulfilled. These conditions are labelled, *felicity conditions*. First, there must be a direct form of communication between the speaker and the listener: if the locutionary, perlocutionary or illocutionary words are not understood by the

---

[83] Austin, JL, *How To Do Things With Words*, 1962, Oxford: OUP.

person to whom they are directed, they cannot assume the status of a speech act. Thus, if, for example, one party thinks that he is getting married, and the other thinks that it is a religious conversion ceremony, the words 'I do' will not be an illocutionary act since there is a mismatch between the parties understanding of the effect of the words.[84] Secondly, in relation to the marriage example, there are certain legal requirements surrounding the ceremony which must be complied with in order for the words 'I do' to have illocutionary effect: the formalities must be adhered to, the parties respectively male and female and single, etc. Also, for a illocutionary act, such as an order or command, to be performed, the person uttering the words must be in a position of authority or superiority for the words to take effect as an act: if the words are simply ignored, they have failed in their primary purpose – to effect a consequential outcome. Thus, for example, if an employer says to an employee 'you are dismissed', it is an illocutionary act; whereas if a fellow employee says to another, 'you are fired', this has no illocutionary effect since the fellow employee lacks the authority to make such a statement meaningfully.

When the anti-pornography Ordinances were challenged in court, one of the arguments put forward was that it was philosophically incorrect to assert that 'pornography ... is the ... subordination of women': it was a philosophical and linguistic 'sleight of hand'[85] – a movement from the argument that pornography causes the insubordination of women (a perlocutionary act), to the argument that pornography is the subordination of women (an illocutionary act).

Catharine MacKinnon argues that speech act theory is central to the legal response to pornography. If pornography remains classified as speech, as it is by the US Supreme Court, it continues to attract the First Amendment protection. If, however, it is reclassified as *action* it loses this protection. In 'Pornography: on morality and politics',[86] MacKinnon asks: '[W]hat is saying "yes" in Congress – a word or an act? What is saying "kill" to a trained guard dog? What is its training? What is saying "you're fired" ... What is a sign that reads "Whites Only"?' Each, correctly classified, is an illocutionary act. So too with pornography: '[P]ornography is not an idea any more than segregation or lynching are ideas, although both institutionalise the idea of the inferiority of one group to another ... In a feminist perspective, pornography is the essence of a sexist social order, its quintessential social act.'[87] This reconceptualisation of pornography is central to MacKinnon's quest to free

---

[84] See *Mehta v Mehta* [1945] 2 All ER 690.
[85] *Per* Judge Barker, *American Booksellers Inc v Hudnut* 598 F Supp (SD Ind 1984), 1316. See Parent, W, 'A second look at pornography and the subordination of women' (1990) 87 Journal of Philosophy 205.
[86] 'Pornography: on morality and politics', in MacKinnon, *op cit*, fn 58.
[87] *Ibid*, MacKinnon, p 204.

pornography from First Amendment protection, and forms the core of her argument in *Only Words*.[88] Pornography *is the act which it performs*: that of subordinating women and denying women an effective right to speak. By its message, pornography constructs women as inferior sexual beings, and by so doing classifies women as unequal. Within the speech act context, pornography is an illocutionary act which subordinates. Consider this analogy, one drawn by MacKinnon herself: the act of lynching a black man, by the Ku Klux Klan, is action. It is not action alone though, because the action it performs – the killing – conveys a message of threat and terror to all black people. For MacKinnon, pornography has this same effect. Thus, by breaking down the distinction between acts and words, actions and ideas, pornography may be reconceptualised in a manner which would enable the United States courts to escape from 'First Amendment logic',[89] and to place constitutional restrictions on its production, distribution and use and to provide remedies for those harmed by pornography.

THE LIBERAL APPROACH: ABSOLUTE AND MODIFIED

From the liberal Millian perspective, the question is whether restrictions on freedom of expression should be allowed on the basis that the material in question causes 'harm' to others. As noted above, this 'harm' principle was adopted by the Williams' Committee in its review of obscenity and censorship.[90] The problem with the 'harm' principle in relation to pornography lies in establishing whether harm is caused, and to whom – and as has been seen, the evidence to date – focusing on the depravity and corruption test, rather than the effect on women – is equivocal.

John Stuart Mill, writing in 1859, argued for the sovereignty of the free individual exercising freedom of conscience, thought and expression 'without impediment from our fellow creatures, so long as what we do does not harm them, even though they should think our conduct foolish perverse, or wrong'.[91] On this basis, without clear proof of harm, there could be no justified legal restriction. Without proof of harm we are free to educate, to criticise, but not to infringe another's liberty by legislating. The inescapable difficulty in relation to pornography is evaluating the harm it causes in a meaningful manner.

Liberal philosopher Ronald Dworkin has considered the question of pornography and 'what to do about it'. Dworkin tackles the problem of

---

[88] *Op cit*, MacKinnon, fn 64.
[89] *Op cit*, MacKinnon, fn 86, p 206.
[90] *Op cit*, Report, fn 4.
[91] Mill, JS, *On Liberty* (1859), 1989, Cambridge: CUP, p 15.

pornography, starting with the statement that: '[I]t is an old problem for liberal theory how far people should have the right to do the wrong thing.'[92] It is Dworkin's contention that an individual's right to moral independence 'requires a permissive legal attitude toward the consumption of pornography in private', but that that right may be circumscribed by a scheme of regulation which guards against those not wishing to be confronted by pornography to be protected from it, provided that the restrictions do not amount to undue hardship or embarrassment for the consumer: a curious trivialisation of the problem of pornography from a feminist perspective.

In 'Liberty and pornography',[93] a review of Catharine MacKinnon's *Only Words*, Dworkin directly assesses radical feminist claims concerning pornography. Dworkin adopts the distinction between *negative liberty* and *positive liberty* advanced by Sir Isiah Berlin.[94] Negative liberty is defined as: 'not being obstructed by others in doing what one might wish to do.' Freedom of speech – without censorship – is a negative liberty. A positive liberty is defined as being:

> ... the power to control or participate in public decisions, including the decision how far to curtail negative liberty. In an ideal democracy – whatever it is – the people govern themselves.

Censorship of pornography[95] – as opposed to restrictions on access – is not justified, Dworkin tells us. His view is best expressed in the following passage:

> Pornography is often grotesquely offensive; it is insulting, not only to women but to men as well. But we cannot consider that a sufficient reason for banning it without destroying the principle that the speech we hate is as much entitled to protection as any other. The essence of negative liberty is freedom to offend, and that applies to the tawdry as well as to the heroic.

Dworkin also rejects the claim that pornography causes measurable harm to women. The evidence he says does not support the claim that there is a link between pornography and sexual violence. Dworkin also rejects the claim that pornography causes 'a more general and endemic subordination of women', or, in other words, that 'pornography makes for inequality'. He further rejects the claim that pornography 'leads to women's *political* as well as economic or social subordination. His interpretation of this claim to political subordination – the idea that pornography is both a consequence of, and cause of, the

---

[92] Dworkin, R, 'Do we have a right to pornography?' (1981) 1 OJLS 177.
[93] *Op cit*, Dworkin, fn 76, pp 12–15; repr in Dwyer, *op cit*, fn 11, pp 113–21.
[94] See Berlin, I, *Four Essays on Liberty*, 1968, Oxford: OUP, p lvi.
[95] As noted above, 'censorship' was not the motivation behind the Ordinances. Rather, the Ordinances sought to prohibit the production and sale of certain materials and to provide civil remedies for those harmed by pornography.

construction of women's identity – is that the claim 'seems strikingly implausible'. Dworkin argues that other forces – such as media advertising – are far more important in defining women than hard core pornography and concludes that, whilst sadistic pornography is 'revolting', it has less importance – given its relative inaccessibility – than the 'subtle and ubiquitous' portrayal of women in the domestic sphere, and that in terms of importance, sadistic pornography 'is greatly overshadowed by these dismal cultural influences' as a causal force.[96] The idea that pornography 'silences' women[97] is dismissed with little analysis. Instead the 'pre-eminent place' of free speech under the Constitution must be defended against all attack.

A number of objections can be raised against Dworkin's approach. First and foremost, the idea of absolute freedom of speech must be set within the United States' constitutional arrangements which have few echoes in the United Kingdom. Whilst the First Amendment to the Constitution ensures a free and vigorous media with the capacity to unravel corruption in government in a manner unparalleled in the United Kingdom, the First Amendment also provides protection for those who espouse racist and sexist views. As Ronald Dworkin comments, the Ku Klux Klan are free to disseminate ideas in the United States whereas under the British Race Relations Act 1976 such 'speech' would incur legal liability. Banging the First Amendment drum may create a superficially impressive noise, but in fact does little to evaluate whether, in a particular context, such as racial and sexual hatred and discrimination, the noise has a firm moral base. Furthermore, Dworkin glosses over the alleged dangers of pornography which are perceived by radical feminists, such as Catharine MacKinnon and Andrea Dworkin, whose work Ronald Dworkin criticises. Dworkin tells us, as seen above, that pornography's arguable damaging effects are overshadowed by the 'dismal cultural influences' of breakfast time television and the advertising industry. It is difficult to argue against Dworkin in relation to advertising: persistent pictures of women showing pride in their cleaning and cooking perpetuates images of women confined to the private sphere of life more appropriate to Victorian times than to the late twentieth century, and Ronald Dworkin is probably correct in arguing that were research to be undertaken into these 'forces', the damage to women's image as equal partners in society would be substantiated. However, to equate pornography, whether hard or soft, with the advertising of washing-up liquid and other

---

[96] *Op cit*, Dwyer, fn 11, p 118.
[97] An idea propounded by, among others, Michelman, F, 'Conceptions of democracy in American constitutional argument: the case of pornography regulation' (1989) 56 Tennessee L Rev 303, which is cited and opposed by Dworkin in 'Liberty and pornography', *op cit*, fn 76. On silencing women through pornography, see, further, below.

domestic aids, it may be argued, is to confuse the insidious and relatively trivial with the overtly damaging.[98]

An alternative interpretation of John Stuart Mill's 'harm' principle[99]

Mill, it will be recalled, cautioned against any restriction on any person's conduct unless that conduct could prove to be harmful to another. Citizens are free to try to educate, to warn, to encourage, but not to prohibit non-harmful-to-others conduct. Mill was particularly concerned with freedom of expression. Consider the following passage:

> This, then, is the appropriate region of human liberty. It comprises, first, the inward domain of consciousness; demanding liberty of conscience, in the most comprehensive sense; liberty of thought and feeling; absolute freedom of opinion and sentiment on all subjects, practical or speculative, scientific, moral, or theological. The liberty of expressing and publishing opinions may seem to fall under a different principle, since it belongs to that part of the conduct of an individual which concerns other people; but, being almost of as much importance as the liberty of thought itself, and resting in great part on the same reasons, is practically inseparable from it.[100]

The priority of liberty over censorship or restriction[101] derives from the potential dangers of the imposition of moral standards by the majority over the minority, a consequence which would harm all members of society. Each individual must be free to determine his or her own morality – nothing could be more dangerous than to have the morality of the majority imposed upon the individual, for that would stultify thought and expression and could turn society into a mindless mass to be manipulated by those with power. Mill makes it clear that he is primarily concerned with liberty of thought and opinion, the exchange of ideas. Central to these are a free press and the English law relating to which Mill described as 'as servile to this day as it was in the time of the Tudors',[102] in order that individuals be free of tyrannical government. In relation to freedom of thought and conscience, Mill writes of Socrates, Jesus Christ and others who were put to death for teaching the new,

---

[98] For a more extensive analysis of Ronald Dworkin's views, see Langton, R, 'Whose right? Ronald Dworkin, women, and pornographers' (1990) 194 Philosophy and Public Affairs 311.

[99] For an in-depth analysis of Mill and pornography, see Wolgast, E, 'Pornography and the tyranny of the majority', in *The Grammar of Justice*, 1987, New York: Cornell UP. (See *Sourcebook*, pp 463–76.)

[100] *Op cit*, Mill, fn 91, p 15.

[101] Censorship is here defined as legal prohibition; restriction as regulation to access to pornography.

[102] *Op cit*, Mill, fn 91, p 19.

the unorthodox, the *inconvenient*. Mill argues cogently for the need for religious toleration, for the toleration of another person's beliefs which may be different from those of the majority. Oppression – such as that suffered by the early Christians – did not prevent the growth of Christianity. Thus, no one person or group, be it a minority or majority, and no one age, can dictate to society what 'is right'.

This priority of freedom of expression so passionately argued for by Mill is that accorded to the press under the First Amendment of the United States Constitution, and which has been used by liberals to advance the argument that freedom of expression encompasses the right to produce and consume pornography. However, Mill was primarily discussing the need for freedom in political debate and freedom of conscience and religion: rights and freedoms fundamental to a healthy democratic society. Freedom of expression and opinion form the basis of 'the mental well being of mankind (on which all their other well being depends)'.[103] Freedom of expression, from the Millian perspective, is the essence of democracy and political life.

The question which immediately needs to be addressed here is whether – and on what grounds – it is justifiable to employ John Stuart Mill's strictures on the primacy of freedom of expression in political and religious life in relation to the production, distribution and consumption of pornography. In considering this question, it is useful to turn to John Stuart Mill's views on women in society. In 1869 Mill's *The Subjection of Women* was published.[104] *The Subjection of Women* represents one of the most powerful pieces of feminist writing of the Victorian, and indeed any, era. Mill writes that the subordination of woman to the power of man has traditionally been one of 'universal custom' with women originally being taken by force and later imprisoned in the family, sold by the father as a chattel to a husband and kept by that husband subject to his total physical, sexual and economic power. Mill states:

> All women are brought up from the very earliest years in the belief that their ideal of character is the very opposite to that of men; not self-will, and government by self-control, but submission, and yielding to the control of others.[105]

Since the abolition of slavery, the position of women in society remained 'an isolated fact' representing a 'relic' of former times. Women had become the slaves of men. Men operate under the fear that if women are educated and trained and allowed to enter the 'public world' of employment and participation in the process of government, women would choose not to marry into such a condition of slavery. Whether Mill is writing of women's

---

[103] *Op cit*, Mill, fn 91, p 53.
[104] Mill, JS, *The Subjection of Women* (1869), 1989, Cambridge: CUP.
[105] *Ibid*, p 132.

subordination within the family, or women's exclusion from public life, or their underrepresentation in the arts, Mill's demand for women's equality shines through. On the basis of the 'abstract right' for equality, Mill demanded nothing less than a social revolution.[106] On this basis, it is submitted that it is inconceivable to argue that Mill would tolerate the subjection of women in pornographic representation on the basis of freedom of expression which he interprets to mean the exchange and development of ideas at an intellectual (rather than base) level. To accept, therefore, Mill's insistence on freedom of expression as one of the most powerful ingredients in a free democracy does not compel us to admit that pornography falls within its ambit and should be given equal protection under the law as political and other debate. From this angle, it could be argued that pornography is not speech, it is not expression within the Millian interpretation of that phrase, and on this basis the Millian harm principle need not be invoked to justify differing treatment of pornography from other instruments of free expression. To reach this conclusion, however, does not necessarily impel us toward the conclusion that the *law* should be utilised to suppress pornography. Whether or not the law should intervene is a necessarily related but separate issue of some complexity which will be given further consideration below.

Whatever the merits of the liberal position, it is not one which has been consistently followed by governments, although governments are not notably consistent in their inconsistencies. Thus, in the United Kingdom certain drugs are proscribed, on the harm principle, whereas others are proscribed in the absence of clear and convincing evidence as to their harmful effects and others are permitted irrespective of the clear evidence that they cause harm.[107] Censorship of television, film and theatre and literature is provided for under English law. There exists also inconsistency and ambivalence in relation to freedom of expression and freedom of association. Taking the latter first, on the grounds of the 'interests of the State', membership and support of proscribed organisations is a criminal offence.[108] In relation to freedom of expression, in addition to the controls provided over film, television and theatre, legal controls exists to restrain bodies or individuals from causing racial hatred.[109] Freedoms are further curtailed in the sphere of employment and public service where employers and service providers are not free to discriminate on the basis of race or sex.[110]

---

[106] *Op cit*, Mill, fn 104, p 194.

[107] Eg, alcohol and tobacco.

[108] See the Prevention of Terrorism Acts 1974–96.

[109] See the Race Relations Act 1976, Public Order and Criminal Justice Act 1994. Contrast this position with that in the United States where such restrictions would be ruled unconstitutional as being contrary to the First Amendment of the Constitution.

[110] See Race Relations Act 1976; Sex Discrimination Act 1975; Equal Pay Act 1976; Treaty of Rome, Art 119, and Directives thereunder.

That there are numerous exceptions to the principle of respect for individual autonomy does not, *per se,* provide justification for such exceptions. If such apparent legal anomalies are justified, the basis for that justification must be sought. One justification offered by Right-wing conservative moralists lies in the protection of the 'moral health' of the nation, which represents an alternative approach to the problem of pornography.

THE CONSERVATIVE APPROACH TO PORNOGRAPHY

The classical conservative stance was advanced in the United Kingdom by Sir (later Lord) Patrick Devlin.[111] Lord Devlin's views were aired after the Wolfenden Committee had reported on the relaxation of the legal regulation of homosexuality.[112] The majority of that Committee's members had endorsed the views expressed nearly a century earlier by the liberal philosopher John Stuart Mill,[113] namely that:

> ... the sole end for which mankind are warranted, individually or collectively, in interfering with the liberty of action of any of their number, is self-protection. That the only purpose for which power can be rightfully exercised over any member of a civilised community, against his will, is to prevent harm to others. His own good, either physical or moral, is not a sufficient warrant.[114]

To Lord Devlin such a liberal approach lacked a necessary dimension, namely that society had an interest over and above that of the individual's personal freedom in the protection of the moral fabric of society. Society, according to Devlin, is held together by an invisible, intangible but nevertheless real, shared morality. Contrary to Mill, therefore, Devlin argued that not only was the law justified in intervening in personal liberty, but it had a *duty* so to do in order to protect society's unifying bonds. The duty of the State to protect its moral fibre, for Devlin, was analogous to the duty of the State to protect against subversion. This demand, however, is not without qualification. For Devlin, the maximum toleration of others should be encouraged: restriction should be justified on the grounds of 'disgust or approbation', not on the mere disapproval of others towards the conduct in question. The issue as to whether or not the limits of society have been reached – in which case legal limitations may be imposed – is to be judged not by some philosopher-king, or the government of the day, but by 'ordinary men and women who represent society in the jurybox'.

---

[111] See Devlin, P, *The Enforcement of Morals,* 1965, Oxford: OUP.
[112] See *The Report of the Committee on Homosexual Offences and Prostitution,* Cmnd 247, 1957, London: HMSO.
[113] On whom see below.
[114] *Op cit,* Mill, fn 91, p 13.

This conservative stance on pornography is adopted by the vocal Moral Right, particularly in the United States of America. From this radical conservative perspective, pornography should be subject to strict censorship laws – a stance in direct conflict with either the classical liberal approach or the radical feminist approach discussed above.

The moral health of the nation, from this perspective, is to be protected from forces which are perceived (even if not proven) to be harmful to the 'moral fabric' of society. In Devlin's view, society – and government as the representative of that society – has as much a duty to protect the moral fabric of society as it does to protect the physical integrity of the nation from subversion or attack.[115]

Devlin's views, however, have been subjected to trenchant criticism. First and foremost, there is the critique of the conservative view from Professor Herbert Hart.[116] In *Law, Liberty and Morality*,[117] Professor Hart responded to Patrick Devlin's thesis. Central to Hart's objection is Devlin's insistence that morality acts as some form of bonding in society – a 'seamless web' – which holds society together and without which, society would 'disintegrate'. Hart concedes the importance of morality, but not a stagnant morality which would ensue from Devlin's approach to its protection. Society, and its morality, change and adapt: it cannot be constrained within the boundaries of a particular time, but rather must be allowed to grow and adapt as time passes. Accordingly, there can be no generalised attempt by the State to freeze society's morality at any point in time. This, however, does not imply that the State has no role to play in the protection of morality. Hart's approach may be understood as liberal but moderately paternalistic. Hart distinguishes between conduct which is carried out in private and conduct which is, at least in part, in the public domain. Members of society have no right, Hart tells us, to be protected from any harm which they may experience through knowing that another person is taking part in some act or practice which is abhorred. However, should that same conduct be indulged in public, where the action in question may be witnessed by others, then restriction on that conduct is justified. In this manner, Hart argues, society may find a middle way between overly intruding upon individual privacy, and protecting 'society' from directly witnessing that conduct.

This approach is in large measure the approach endorsed by the Williams Committee on Obscenity and Film Censorship whose report was published in 1979.[118] This *via media* is subjected to attack on two fronts, at least: the Moral

---

[115] *Op cit*, Devlin, fn 111.
[116] Professor of Jurisprudence, University of Oxford.
[117] Hart, HLA, *Law, Liberty and Morality*, 1965, Oxford: OUP.
[118] *Op cit, Report*, fn 4.

Right calling for complete censorship; radical feminists arguing that it misses the central focus of the problem, namely the equality of women in society.

ALTERNATIVE AND POSTMODERN PERCEPTIONS CONCERNING PORNOGRAPHY

The feminist anti-pornography quest has not been universally welcomed by feminists. Before judgment can be passed on the way forward in relation to pornography, there are a number of considerations which must be taken into account. The first difficulty to be overcome, if law is to be used in the quest to eradicate the harms caused by pornography, is that of definition. Feminist scholars discern a clear distinction between the 'erotic' and the 'pornographic', and it is essential that this distinction be maintained if a movement towards the eradication of non-pornographic representations is to be avoided. The borderline between erotica and pornography is by no means unproblematic. Erotica to Gloria Steinem[119] and Catharine MacKinnon involves the portrayal of intimate relationships within the context of equality (as opposed to domination and submission which is represented in pornography). Diana Russell defines erotica as being 'sexual representations that aim to be sexually arousing, but that are non-abusive and non-sexist'.[120] There remain, however, logical and conceptual difficulties in the analysis of pornography and erotica and the consequent justification for the restriction of the former but not the latter, and the point is of crucial importance if the movement for legal regulation is not to descend down a very slippery slope to the suppression of all forms of sexually explicit materials in a manner which the Moral Right, but not radical feminists against pornography, would advocate.

A further difficulty lies in the argument that radical anti-pornography feminist theory exaggerates pornography's role in the maintenance of women's inequality. This critique, implicit in the traditional liberal insistence on the American First Amendment protection for pornography, entails two differing arguments. The first concern revolves around the differing representations of women which, whilst not pornographic, or even erotic, nevertheless continue to portray women in their stereotypical roles within the private sphere of the family, or as stereotypically sexual beings.[121] The second concern is the charge levelled at radical feminism by other feminists, namely that the radical feminist anti-pornography campaign is one characterised by essentialism, in so far as the radical critique focuses exclusively on heterosexual patriarchal pornographic representation.

---

[119] *Op cit*, Steinem, fn 11, p 29.
[120] Russell, D, 'Pornography and rape: a causal model', in Itzin, *op cit*, fn 10, p 317.
[121] The argument advanced by Dworkin, R, above.

In relation to the first issue, it is undeniable that pornography is by no means the only medium in which women are represented as inferior, submissive, subject. Romantic fiction, 'soap operas', domestic television comedies, television, magazine and billboard advertising and the press all play a role in perpetuating the portrayal of women as little more than domestic, sexual objects. The fashion and beauty industry is also implicated in the myth of femininity and the promotion of heterosexual desirability.[122] Nevertheless, damaging as such representations may be to women's equality in society, none of them carry the power and violence which pornography conveys. Pornography has a defining quality which transcends other representations of women – with its explicit message that women exist for violent sexual abuse imposed by men.

The charge of essentialism – that the anti-pornography campaign is characterised as the concern of white, middle-class, heterosexual women – is levelled by feminists whose focus on women and the law is informed by different criteria. Thus, for example, liberal feminists are opposed to the restriction on freedom of expression. Socialist feminists oppose the campaign as a divergence from the campaign for a society where economic and social conditions respect not just the elite in society. Others, whilst sympathetic to the rationale for the campaign, object on the basis that it distorts feminism through its emphasis on women as sexual objects alone, thus making biological sex the focus of all discrimination in society.

Some lesbian feminists, on the other hand, oppose the anti-pornography campaign for its emphasis on heterosexual relationships, and the apparent exclusion of homosexual relationships. From this perspective, lesbian feminists argue that they are not demeaned or subordinated by heterosexual pornographic representations, and that accordingly the debate concerning pornography is too narrowly constructed, in so far as it fails both to include lesbian sexuality and to encompass possible alternative interpretations of pornography.[123]

While the radical feminist quest to raise the profile of pornography as a matter of urgent political significance and action is both powerful and intuitively appealing, its resonance falls on unreceptive ears in relation to those who hold alternative perspectives about the meaning and significance of pornography. One argument centres on the diversity of pornographic representation. Pornography is not, it is argued, solely the representation of the sexual availability of woman for heterosexual man. Rather, pornographic representations extend to both female and male homosexual representations,

---

[122] See Wolf, N, *The Beauty Myth*, 1991, London: Vintage; Faludi, S, *Backlash: The Undeclared War Against Women*, 1992, London: Vintage.

[123] For a discussion of lesbian pornography, see Rodgerson, G, 'Lesbian erotic exploration', in Segal, L and McIntosh, M (eds), *Sex Exposed: Sexuality and the Pornography Debate*, 1992, London: Virago, p 275.

and thus the arguments about the centrality of portraying women as the victims of, and subordinate to men, cannot be sustained.

Another argument concerns the radical feminist interpretation of pornography. It is argued, against radical feminists, that not all pornography is violent, that not all pornography depicts women in a position of inferiority: pornography has many differing meanings; meanings which are attached to the 'message' by the consumer, and which cannot be categorised in such a limited manner. To portray pornography as depicting (solely) violence, and to argue that these depictions represent and valorise the hatred of women is, from this alternative perspective, misleading. Gayle Rubin, for example, discusses sado-masochist materials. It is Rubin's contention that sado-masochist representations have less to do with violence than with the depiction of 'of ritual and contractual sex play whose *aficionados* go to great lengths in order to do it and to ensure the safety and enjoyment of one another'.[124] If this perception is accurate, the focus on pornography as the primary site of women's degradation, by violent men, appears misguided. Furthermore, it is argued by some lesbian feminists that the radical feminist argument against pornography is essentialist in that it centres on the heterosexual, male dominant/woman subordinate, conceptualisation of women to the exclusion of those with different gender orientations for whom the issue of dominance and subordination does not arise. Anti-anti-pornography theorists also argue, among other things, that pornography can be a means by which women themselves explore their sexuality, and thus pornography becomes not a force for subordination but for sexual experimentation and liberation. Thus, to conceptualise pornography as harm, and no more, is to deny women the right to identify their own sexuality, and to force women to accept the male pornographic representation of woman's sexuality. Moreover, if viewed in this constructive light and if pornography can have positive and liberating effects for women, the conceptualisation of women as the victims of pornography becomes problematic.

In 'Desire and power'[125] Catharine MacKinnon addressed the question whether 'all women are oppressed by heterosexuality'?[126] Her answer is that 'heterosexuality is the dominant gendered form of sexuality in a society where gender oppresses women through sex, sexuality and heterosexuality are essentially the same thing'.[127] Thus, heterosexual sex is an act of dominance

---

[124] Rubin, G, 'Misguided, dangerous and wrong: an analysis of anti-pornography politics', in Assiter, A and Carol, A (eds), *Bad Girls and Dirty Pictures: The Challenge to Radical Feminism*, 1993, London: Pluto Press, p 22. Gayle Rubin's essay was originally submitted as testimony to a hearing on pornography held by the National Organisation for Women in California in 1986.

[125] From MacKinnon, *op cit*, fn 58, p 46.

[126] *Op cit*, MacKinnon, fn 58, p 60.

[127] *Op cit*, MacKinnon, fn 58.

(male) and submission (female).[128] If this is the case, the 'approval', or tolerance, of erotic depictions of sexuality would appear to meet with precisely the same objections that pornography meets: namely depictions of dominance and submission. John Stoltenberg's analysis supports the radical feminist thesis. In Stoltenberg's analysis, pornography, whether heterosexual or homosexual, is deeply homophobic: 'Homophobia is totally rooted in the woman-hating that male supremacy thrives on.'[129] Male supremacy over women is maintained in the stories pornography tells: woman as the unequal other to be used by the dominant male. Pornography constructs masculinity and femininity as power disparity. In gay pornography, the message is the same in Stoltenberg's analysis, for heterosexual masculinity must preserve its virility and through pornographic representations of the gay male in the role of woman, the denigration of woman persists. Thus '... pornography *institutionalises* the sexuality that both embodies and enacts male supremacy'.[130] From this standpoint, if it is accepted that pornography is a powerful means of perpetuating damaging perceptions about women, reinforcing women's inequality, prolonging the emphasis on women as sexual objects, then all women – irrespective of race, class or sexual orientation – are damaged by pornography. The consumers of pornography see one central figure defined in their miserable product: woman – old, young, black, white, poor, rich, heterosexual or lesbian.

Arguments for and against the legal regulation of pornography

Radical feminists have advanced powerful arguments for the regulation of pornography on the basis of the political and social damage to woman's equality. Pornography not only defines women as sexual objects for the use of men but also has a (although not conclusively established or quantified) relationship with sexual crimes against women. Pornography emphasises male sexual and other dominance and thus maintains and supports gender inequality. Pornography, as analysed by Catharine MacKinnon, is a form of sexual harassment, sexual discrimination and sexual hatred directed against women in a manner which is no longer permissible against minority groups in society. Pornography denies women an equal voice in society: by the constant portrayal of women as inferior, as objects, women are denied respect and their claims to equality are silenced under a blanket of disrespect which, in the name of freedom of expression, the law condones. On these bases, the harm is demonstrable, if not scientifically assessable, and there exist strong grounds

---

[128] MacKinnon does not ignore homosexuality here, and points out that such relationships may nevertheless be as gendered as heterosexual relationships.

[129] Stoltenberg, J, 'Pornography, homophobia and male supremacy', in Itzin, *op cit*, fn 10, pp 145, 158.

[130] *Ibid*, p 150.

for pornography's restriction. Indeed, given the strength of the arguments put forward, the onus should not be on women to justify their claim for action under law, but rather on pornographers and pornographic consumers to justify their continued 'right' to produce and consume pornography. If sexual harassment and denigration is for the moment, and for these purposes, considered analogous to racial harassment and denigration, it would be strange (unthinkable) to demand that victims of racial harassment and oppression justify their case, adducing scientific evidence, against such treatment. Why, then, are women in a less favoured position than racial groups in society?

Despite the strength and obviousness of the case for the regulation of pornography, and the intuitive appeal of providing legal remedies for those harmed by pornography, there are arguments against the use of *law* to regulate it. The radical feminist demand, not for censorship, but for the provision of civil remedies for those harmed by pornography, meets with a number of objections. In relation to the Dworkin/MacKinnon Ordinances, Emily Jackson[131] argues that by providing civil remedies for those alleging harm by pornography would require changes in legal thinking. Jackson argues that, first, group actions would have to be facilitated; secondly, that 'harm' would have to be redefined to accommodate the more 'diffuse' type of harm suffered; thirdly, that the doctrine of causation would need revision to include harm caused by a third party, and to accommodate 'speculative decisions' as to the cause of the injury suffered.[132] Nicola Lacey[133] also questions whether law is the appropriate medium for protecting against the harm pornography causes to women. Feminist lawyers, she suggests, are lawyers first, feminists second, by which she means that feminist lawyers – perhaps wrongly or inappropriately – seek a *legal* remedy for the many harms which feminism identifies.[134]

Without denying the rationale for the MacKinnon/Dworkin Ordinances both Jackson and Lacey have accordingly questioned the efficacy of using law as the means of effecting reform. In Emily Jackson's analysis, for example, pornographic representations of women are, as discussed above, but a part of the many forms of stereotypical representations – in the media, advertising, art and literature – which create and sustain sexual inequality. The use of law to prohibit pornography, in one sense, could prove damaging to sexual equality in so far as it leaves the surrounding, the more pervasive and

---

[131] Birkbeck College, University of London.

[132] See Jackson, E, 'The problem with pornography' [1995] Feminist Legal Studies 49. (See *Sourcebook*, pp 476–90.)

[133] Birkbeck College, University of London.

[134] See Lacey, N, 'Theory into practice? Pornography and the public/private dichotomy' in Bottomley, A and Conaghan, J, *Feminist Theory and Legal Strategy*, 1993, Oxford: Basil Blackwell, p 93.

insidious, representations intact, thus suggesting that these are acceptable. In Nicola Lacey's view, while anti-pornography feminist lawyers are credited with having elevated the issue of pornography into the political arena and establishing pornography as a political public – as opposed to private – issue, the emphasis on law as the remedial mechanism for pornography's harms is misplaced and 'the implications of the legislative strategy seem at best, uncertain and at worst, damaging'. Lacey cites several reasons for her opposition to the use of law in this area. First, there is the pragmatic problem of bringing legal action against pornography: the costs involved, the degree of commitment required to undertake the task. Secondly, there is the perceived danger of the Moral Right using such an ordinance to advance its own claims to censorship of sexually explicit literature and art. Thirdly, the likelihood of successful litigation is viewed as slim: the problems of proof and definition again loom large. Fourthly, even if litigation were to succeed how would damages be assessed, how would injunctions be enforced? Fifthly, the position of women working in the pornography industry – outside of coercion which is expressly covered in the MacKinnon/Dworkin Ordinance – would remain unchanged. Turning to the symbolic effects of such a law, Lacey argues that were the practical limitations of the law to prove to be well founded, the law would be perceived as devoid of meaning and significance, or as a 'sop to political sentiment and a way of avoiding the need for more effective political action'. Further, the falsely assumed alliance with the Moral Right forged by anti-pornography feminists might be perceived as movement in favour of repression, to the detriment of feminism. For Lacey, the emphasis on law exaggerates the potential utility of law, as opposed to political debate and pressure. As she puts it, feminist lawyers are prone to thinking that for every problem there must be a legal – as opposed to another – form of redress.[135]

CONCLUSION

As has been seen, pornography, from the standpoint of radical feminists, is a political issue. Co-existing with its ugly relatives – sexual harassment, sexual discrimination, sexual hatred and violence and prostitution – pornography represents a powerful image of man as politically and sexually dominant and woman as politically and sexually inferior. On this analysis, a society

---

[135] *Op cit*, Lacey, fn 134, p 93. See, also, Mary Joe Frug's critique of the Ordinance campaign: 'The political of postmodern feminism: lessons from the anti-pornography campaign', in Frug, M, *Postmodern Legal Feminism*, 1991, London: Routledge, Chapman and Hall. See, also, Smart, C, 'The problem of pornography', in *Feminism and the Power of Law*, 1989, London: Routledge and Kegan Paul; for Catharine MacKinnon's (1985) response to feminist lawyers' opposition to legal action on pornography, see 'On collaboration', in MacKinnon, *op cit*, fn 58, Chapter 15.

committed to genuine gender equality would find no room for pornography. Whether, however, law is the appropriate instrument for changing social mores, has been revealed as a far more questionable issue. It may be that the limits of law in terms of effecting changed social mores are reached when the law condemns and restricts the production and availability of pornography through regulation: social not legal change is, from this perspective, a prerequisite for changing the meaning and effects of pornography. However, if 'the problem of pornography' is not conceptualised as an issue of woman's status, woman's equality, but regarded as an aspect of the expression and representation of human sexuality, in all its many manifestations, the argument for any form of regulation – other than for the protection of children or sex workers against unlawful violence – falls away. On either interpretation, pornography represents intractable difficulties for feminism. Too great a focus on pornography, and too great an emphasis on law as the solution to the problem howsoever defined, not only invites failure, but also reinforces the notion of women as victim, women as unequal. Moreover, the intense feminist debate concerning pornography, on which no consensus is likely to prove forthcoming, detracts important energies from alternative analyses of women's remaining inequalities in society.

PROSTITUTION AND LAW: AN OUTLINE

[P]rostitution is part of the exercise of the law of male sex-right, one of the ways in which men are ensured access to women's bodies.[136]

Conceptually, prostitution is closely allied to pornography. Both involve the core idea of women as nothing more than sexual objects for use by men, and thus uphold the patriarchal power of man over subordinate woman. Both industries prey on weak and economically vulnerable women. Both pornography and prostitution debase and demean women in the eyes of society. And yet, neither pornography nor prostitution are amenable to regulation by law which would successfully eradicate the dangerous message which they convey, without involving repression and censorship, which no-one – other than those on the conservative Moral Right – would countenance. Both thus exist as conundrums for feminist scholars who seek an end to the discrimination and inequality against women which pornography and prostitution promote and protect.

A brief introduction to prostitution is included in this chapter on the basis that prostitution may be conceptualised as violence and discrimination against women and thus analogous to pornographic representations. Whilst the United Nations Declaration on the Elimination of All Forms of

---

[136] Pateman, C, *The Sexual Contract*, 1988, London: Polity, p 194.

Discrimination Against Women 1983, extracted in Chapter 11, clearly includes forcible prostitution in its definition of prohibited violence against women, it may be contended that any form of prostitution – 'voluntary' or forcible – is a representation of violence against women and the image of women in society, and a further manifestation of patriarchy.

Prostitution is juridically conceived in the United Kingdom, as in other jurisdictions, as a contractual matter between the commissioning man and the freely consenting woman. The official standpoint, adopted by the Wolfenden Committee of 1957, was that prostitution, being a matter of private morality, was 'not the law's business'.[137] Thus prostitution is not an offence under law. It does not follow, however, that the law does not regulate prostitution. It is a criminal offence, under English law, for a woman to solicit for the purposes of prostitution,[138] or for a man to solicit a woman for the purpose of prostitution,[139] from a motor vehicle while it is in a street of public place; or in a street while in the immediate vicinity of a motor vehicle that he has just got out of.[140] Any known prostitute is thus liable to be arrested merely for being on the street. Where the woman is carrying condoms these may be used as evidence of prostitution. If a prostitute shares accommodation with another prostitute, she can be charged with brothel-keeping.[141] Furthermore, it is a criminal offence for a man or woman to live on immoral earnings.[142] Thus, while prostitution is not unlawful in England and Wales, almost every activity associated with it is unlawful.

In the United Kingdom, licensed brothels, escort agencies and massage parlours proliferate in large cities. In addition, organised crime and individual opportunistic pimps control women prostitutes. Drug addiction[143] and single motherhood force women, and increasingly young homeless girls, into prostitution, selling their sexual services to maintain a drug habit, their children, or both. Requiring no qualifications, immunity from the tax system, and flexible hours, make the option of prostitution a viable means of earning a living, with the attendant risks of violence and the risk to health.

---

[137] *Report of the Committee on Homosexuality and Prostitution*, 1957, London: HMSO.

[138] Street Offences Act 1959, s 1(1).

[139] See Cohen, M, 'Soliciting by men' [1982] Crim LR 349.

[140] Sexual Offences Act 1985, s 1. The Act has proved unsuccessful, principally due to the evidential burden. See Edwards, S, 'The kerb-crawling fiasco' (1987) 137 NLJ 1209.

[141] Sexual Offences Act 1956, s 33.

[142] Sexual Offences Act 1956, s 30. The offence applies to both men and women: *R v Puckerin* (1990) 12 Cr App R (S) 602. Any person knowingly entering into a contract with a prostitute, eg, a taxi-driver driving a prostitute to visit a client, may be found guilty (see *R v Ferrugia* (1979) 69 Cr App R 108), as could a landlord renting property to a prostitute.

[143] In 1994, a survey conducted at a Glasgow Drop-in Centre for female prostitutes, 44 of the 51 respondents were injecting drug users: (1994) 308 BMJ 538.

Alternative legal responses to prostitution

As seen above, while prostitution is not unlawful in England and Wales, a number of associated criminal offences exist. Debate about prostitution, and the appropriate State response to it, revolves primarily around the issue of State regulation. In Holland, and in Vancouver, there are designated 'toleration zones' in which prostitutes may ply their trade. However, wherever such zoning is attempted, it is attended by problems. On the one hand, it enables the authorities to designate areas in which prostitution would create least public nuisance and complaint. On the other hand, evidence reveals that designation of 'strolls', while allowing some prostitutes to be self-employed, has the effect that other prostitutes, because of potential overcrowding and competition, set up patrols in other, non-designated, areas where they were vulnerable to control by pimps.[144] In West Germany, Nevada and Melbourne,[145] among other places, legalised brothels have been introduced. From the point of view of the authorities, legalising brothels brings prostitution under greater official control; enables the State to enforce strict health check requirements; and to collect revenue from prostitution through licensing fees and taxation of earnings. However, while the case for State-licensed brothels may be argued from the point of view of control to reduce the nuisance of prostitution on the streets, and on the basis of ensuring the health of prostitutes, there exist counter-arguments. Nina Lopez-Jones, for example, argues that State-regulated brothels, 'have increased police powers and institutionalised pimping by the State, making it harder for women to keep their earnings or to bargain to determine their working conditions'.[146] State brothels also control the number of officially 'recognised' prostitutes, increasing competition, and permitting State control over those who may be permitted to work in the brothel, thus discriminating against those deemed to be 'unsuitable'. Where, as in Melbourne, the introduction of licensed brothels is combined with making street prostitution illegal, the effect is to force the most vulnerable prostitutes who cannot gain admission to licenced brothels into criminal activity on the streets, or into illegal brothels.

Competing arguments concerning prostitution

Prostitution may be conceptualised in a number of differing ways, as indeed it has been by feminists. On the one hand, the freedom of contract approach

---

[144] See Lowman, J, 'Street prostitution control: some Canadian reflections on the Finsbury Park experience' (1992) 32 Br J Crim 1; see in reply, Matthews, R, 'Regulating street prostitution and kerb-crawling: a reply to John Lowman' (1992) 32 Br J Crim 18.
[145] Street prostitution in Melbourne is illegal, although evidence shows that that has not eradicated street prostitution.
[146] Lopez-Jones, N, 'Legalising brothels' (1992) 142 NLJ 594.

may be preferred as allowing women autonomy and free choice in their lifestyles and occupations. The law's limited approach to prostitution, especially allied with enforcement problems associated with the limited regulation of prostitution, appeals to those advancing this approach. For many prostitutes, their trade in their bodies represents the only means of escaping from the poverty trap of unemployment, or low employment. That such 'sex workers' are more vulnerable to violence and exploitation – whether by clients or pimps – is the principal cause for concern, but one which could be remedied not by increasing legal regulation, let alone prohibition, but by legitimising the industry and providing formal State support for sex workers, through the provision of licensed safe premises designated for prostitution, complete with health checks for sex workers.

This liberal, rights-based, contractual conceptualisation of prostitution carries with it a number of difficulties.[147] To view a woman's 'right' to lease her body as a right to enter into a contract of employment, or contract for the provision of services, confuses a woman's right to physical integrity with the provision of a commercial product, as if submitting to paid sex is the same as supplying soap powder in a supermarket. Soap powders do not have personalities, individuality, intellectual capacity, rights to autonomy, freedom and respect: women do. Conceptualising woman as a product, on sale and for sale, conceals the true nature of the contract in question: that of the purchase of a woman by a man, a capitalist transaction in the 'free' marketplace. Given that the practice of wife-sale, discussed in Chapter 2, was eradicated by the nineteenth century, prostitution represents the last blatant vestige of the power of money, in the hands of man, to purchase a woman, her body, her self. Defenders of the contractarian model of prostitution, argue that this argument is flawed. What is on offer, they argue, is not the woman, or even her body, but the use of her sexual services. Moreover, the woman in question enters this contract voluntarily: there is no coercion and she may contract out.[148] To take the argument further, the woman has a *right* to offer and to sell her services in this way. To argue in any other manner concerning prostitution, is to argue against an individual's right to freedom.[149] However, as Carole Pateman's analysis makes clear, the prostitute's work is unlike other

---

[147] As a matter of law, the prostitution contract is unlawful: 'It is well settled that a contract which is made upon a sexually immoral consideration or for a sexually immoral purpose is against public policy and is illegal and unenforceable. The fact that it does not involve or may not involve the commission of a criminal offence in no way prevents the contract being illegal, being against public policy and therefore being unenforceable.' Ackner LJ in *Register of Companies ex p Attorney General* [1991] BCLC 476. See, also, *Inland Revenue Commissioners v Aken* [1990] 1 WLR 1374.

[148] This argument is much weakened when a woman is controlled by a pimp who exerts a patriarchal control over her time and activities.

[149] See Ericcson, L, 'Charges against prostitution: an attempt at a philosophical assessment' (1980) 90 Ethics 335.

workers' employment. Prostitution, Pateman argues, is part of the age-old sexual contract:

> Once the story of the sexual contract has been told, prostitution can be seen as a problem about *men*. The problem of prostitution then becomes encapsulated in the question why men demand that women's bodies are sold as commodities in the capitalist market. The story of the sexual contract also supplies the answer; prostitution is part of the exercise of the law of male sex-right, one of the ways in which men are ensured access to women's bodies.[150]

An alternative to the rights-based, contractarian, human rights based argument also invokes human rights. The human right to contract is here pitted against the human right not to be degraded and sexually violated, and the more general right of women not to be subordinated or discriminated against, but to be accorded equality and respect. However, there are problems with this line of argument: evidence suggests that for many women prostitutes, despite the economic coercion which leads them into prostitution, and despite the inherent risks of their trade, prostitution represents the only available means by which to support themselves (and their children). From the perspective of the prostitute, therefore, the right which assumes priority over the right to physical integrity, is the right to act as an independent economic agent, in order to preserve her own economic viability. To assert, therefore, that prostitution is wrong – from a moral perspective situated on perceptions about women's rights to physical integrity – is to assume a moral, and conservative, high-ground which would be interpreted as unwanted and unnecessary 'paternalism'. Furthermore, defining prostitution and its consequences; combining definition, effect and moral argument, in order to come to a conclusion about the appropriate response to prostitution, from a postmodern perspective, is redolent of essentialism and universalism. It is for reasons such as these that prostitution, as with pornography, represents such an intractable problem for feminist analysis.

---

[150] *Op cit*, Pateman, fn 136, pp 193–94.

BIBLIOGRAPHY

Abel, E and Abel, EK (eds), *The Signs Reader: Women, Gender and Scholarship*, 1978, Chicago: Chicago UP.

Adler, Z, *Rape on Trial*, 1987, London: Routledge.

Allott, A, *The Limits of Law*, 1980, London: Butterworths.

Anderson, M et al (eds), *The Social and Political Economy of the Household*, 1994, New York: OUP.

Anderson, W (ed), *The Fontana Postmodernism Reader*, 1996, London: Fontana.

Arblaster, A, *The Rise and Decline of Western Liberalism*, 1994, Oxford: Basil Blackwell.

Archbold, JF, *Criminal Law Practice and Proceedings*, Richardson, PJ (ed), 1997, London: Sweet & Maxwell.

Arditti, R, Klein, R and Minden, S (eds), *Test-tube Women*, 1984, London: Pandora.

Arendt, H, *The Human Condition*, 1958, Chicago: Chicago UP.

Aristotle, *The Nicomachean Ethics*, Ross, D (trans), 1925, Oxford: OUP.

Aristotle, *The Politics*, Sinclair, TA (trans), 1962, London: Penguin.

Assiter, A and Carol, A (eds), *Bad Girls and Dirty Pictures: The Challenge to Radical Feminism*, 1993, London: Pluto.

Atkins, S and Hoggett, B, *Women and the Law*, 1984, Oxford: Basil Blackwell.

Austin, J, *The Province of Jurisprudence Determined* (1832), 1954, London: Weidenfeld and Nicholson.

Austin, JL, *How To Do Things With Words*, 1962, Oxford: OUP.

Bacon, *Abridgement of the Law*, 1736, Tit baron and Feme (B).

Bainham, A, 'Handicapped girls and judicial parents' (1987) 103 LQR 334.

Bainham, A, 'The balance of power in family decisions' [1986] CLJ 262.

Bainham, A, 'The judge and the competent minor' (1992) 108 LQR 194.

Barker-Benfield, GJ, *Horrors of the Half-Known Life: Male Attitudes Toward Women and Sexuality in Nineteenth Century America*, 1976, New York: Harper and Row.

Barnett, H, *Constitutional & Administrative Law*, 2nd edn, 1998, London: Cavendish Publishing.

Barnett, H, *Sourcebook on Feminist Jurisprudence*, 1997, London: Cavendish Publishing.

Bartlett, K, 'Feminist legal methods' (1990) 100 Harv L Rev 829.

Bartlett, KT and Kennedy, R (eds), *Feminist Legal Theory: Readings in Law and Gender*, 1991, Boulder: Westview.

Baudelaire, CP, *The Painter of Modern Life*, (1863), Mayne, J, 1964, London: Phaidon.

Bender, L, 'A lawyer's primer on feminist theory and tort' (1988) 38 J Legal Educ 3.

Bender, L, 'From gender difference to feminist solidarity: using Carol Gilligan and an ethic of care in law' (1990) 15 Vermont L Rev 1.

Benhabib, S and Cornell, D (eds), *Feminism as Critique: Essays on the Politics of Gender in Late-Capitalist Societies*, 1987, London: Polity.

Bentham, J, *Introduction to the Principles of Morals and Legislation* (1789), Burns, JH and Hart, HLA (eds), 1977, London: Athlone.

Bentham, J, *A Fragment on Government* (1776), 1948, Oxford: Basil Blackwell.

Berlin, I, *Four Essays on Liberty*, 1968, Oxford: OUP.

Birkett Committee, *Report of the Committee of Inquiry into Abortion*, 1939, London: HMSO.

Bishop, S and Weinzweig, M (eds), *Philosophy and Women*, 1979, Belmont, California: Wadsworth.

Blackstone, W, *Commentaries on the Laws of England 1765–69*, 1978, New York: Garland.

Bock, G and James, S, *Beyond Equality and Difference*, 1992, London: Routledge.

Boldhar, J, 'The right to reproduce' (1989) 63 Law Inst J 708

Bordo, S, *Unbearable Weight: Feminism, Western Culture and the Body*, 1993, Berkeley, California: California UP.

Bottomley, A (ed), *Feminist Perspectives on the Foundational Subjects of Law*, 1996, London: Cavendish Publishing.

Bottomley, A and Conaghan, J, *Feminist Theory and Legal Strategy*, 1993, Oxford: Basil Blackwell.

Bouchard, D (ed), *Language, Counter-Memory, Practice: Selected Essays and Interviews*, 1977, Oxford: Basil Blackwell.

Bourne, A, 'Abortion and the Law' (1938) 2 BMJ 254.

Brazier, M, *Medicine, Patients and the Law*, 2nd edn, 1992, Harmondsworth: Penguin.

Brinton, M, *Women and the Economic Miracle: Gender and Work in Postwar Japan*, 1993, Berkeley, California: California UP.

Brownmiller, S, *Against Our Will: Men, Women and Rape*, 1975, New York: Simon & Schuster.

Bibliography

Burke, C, Schor, N and Whitford, M (eds), *Engaging with Irigaray: Feminist Philosophy and Modern European Thought*, 1994, New York: Columbia UP.

Butler, J, *Gender Trouble: Feminism and the Subversion of Identity*, 1990, New York: Routledge.

Cain, P, 'Feminist jurisprudence: grounding the theories' (1989) Women's LJ 191.

Campbell, J, *The Masks of God: Oriental Mythology*, 1962, New York: Viking.

Castiglioni, A, *A History of Medicine* (1941), 2nd edn, 1958, Alfred A Knopf.

Chan, J, *Wild Swans: Three Daughters of China*, 1991, London: HarperCollins.

Charlesworth, H, Chinkin, C and Wright, S, 'Feminist approaches to international law' (1991) 85 AJIL 613.

Chodorow, N, *Femininities, Masculinities, Sexualities: Freud and Beyond*, 1994, London: Free Association Books.

Chodorow, N, *The Reproduction of Mothering: Psychoanalysis and the Sociology of Gender*, 1978, Berkeley, California: California UP.

Cica, N, 'Sterilising the intellectually disabled' (1993) 1 Med L Rev 186.

Cohen, I, *The Newtonian Revolution*, 1980, Cambridge: CUP.

Cohen, M, 'Soliciting by men' [1982] Crim LR 349.

Cohn, N, *Europe's Inner Demons*, 1975, London: Chatto, Heinemann.

Cohen, N, 'Reaping rich rewards from the profits of pornography' (1989) *The Independent*, 19 December.

Colletti, L (ed), *Early Writings*, 1975, London: Penguin.

Collins English Dictionary, 3rd edn, 1991, London: HarperCollins.

Collins, H, *Marxism and Law*, 1982, Oxford: Clarendon.

Cook, R (ed), *Human Rights of Women: National and International Perspectives*, 1994, Pennsylvania: Pennsylvania UP.

Corea, G et al (eds), *Man-made Women: How New Reproductive Technologies Affect Women*, 1985, London: Hutchinson.

Cornell, D, *Beyond Accommodation: Ethical Feminism Deconstruction, and the Law*, 1991, London: Routledge.

Cornell, D, 'Beyond tragedy and complacency' (1987) 81 Northwestern University L Rev 693.

Cornell, D, 'The doubly prized world: myth, allegory and the feminine' (1990) 75 Cornell L Rev 644.

Cornell, D, *The Imaginary Domain*, 1995, London: Routledge.

Cornell, D, *The Philosophy of the Limit*, 1992, London: Routledge.

Cornell, D, 'Sexual difference, the feminine, and equivalency: a critique of MacKinnon's *Toward a Feminist Theory of the State*' (1990) 100 Yale LJ 2247.

Cornell, D, *Transformations: Recollective Imagination and Sexual Difference*, 1993, London: Routledge.

Cotterrell, RBM, *Law's Community*, 1995, Oxford: Clarendon.

Cotterrell, RBM, *The Sociology of Law: An Introduction*, 1985, London: Butterworths.

Crenshaw, K, 'Race, reform and retrenchment: transformation and legitimation in anti-discrimination law' (1988) 101 Harv L Rev 1331.

Cretney, S, 'Gillick and the concept of legal capacity' (1989) 105 LQR 356.

Cretney, S and Masson, J, *Principles of Family Law*, 5th edn, 1990, London: Sweet & Maxwell.

Cretney, S and Masson, J, *Principles of Family Law*, 6th edn, 1997, London: Sweet & Maxwell.

Dale, A and Glover, J, *An Analysis of Women's Employment Patterns in the UK, France and the USA*, 1990, London Employment Department Group, Research Paper 75.

Daly, M, *Beyond God the Father: Toward a Philosophy of Women's Liberation*, 1973, London: The Women's Press.

Daly, M, *Gyn/Ecology: the Metaethics of Radical Feminism*, 1979, London: The Women's Press.

de Beauvoir, S, *The Second Sex* (1949), Parshley, H (ed and trans), 1989, London: Picador.

Dell, S, *Murder Into Manslaughter*, 1984, Institute of Psychiatry, Maudsley Monographs, Oxford: OUP.

d'Entrèves, AP, *Natural Law*, 2nd edn, 1970, London: Hutchinson.

Department of Health, *Departmental Report*, 1994, London: HMSO.

Derrida, J, *Dissemination*, 1972, Paris: Éditions du Seuil.

Derrida, J, *Of Grammatology*, 1976, Baltimore: Johns Hopkins UP.

Derrida, J, *Speech and Phenomena, and Other Essays on Husserl's Theory of Signs*, 1973, Chicago, Illinois: Northwestern UP.

Derrida, J, *Writing and Difference*, 1978, London: Routledge and Kegan Paul.

Devlin, P, *The Enforcement of Morals*, 1965, Oxford: OUP.

Dex, S and Shaw, L, *British and American Women at Work*, 1986, London: Macmillan.

Bibliography

Dinnerstein, D, *Rocking the Cradle,* 1978, London: Souvenir.

Dobash, R and Dobash, R, 'The nature and antecedents of violent events' (1984) 24 Br J Crim 269.

Dobash, R and Dobash, R, *Violence Against Wives: A Case Against the Patriarchy,* 1979, New York: Free Press.

Dobash, R and Dobash, R, *Women, Violence and Social Change,* 1992, New York: Routledge.

Douglas, G, 'The retreat from Gillick' (1992) 55 MLR 569.

Dresser, R, 'Feeding the hungry artist: legal issues in treating anorexia' (1984) 2 Wisconsin L Rev 297.

Duchen, C, *Feminism in France: From May '68 to Mitterand,* 1986, London: Routledge and Kegan Paul.

Duncan, S, 'Law as literature: deconstructing the legal text' (1994) 5.1 Law and Critique.

Duncan, S, 'Law's sexual discipline: visibility, violence and consent' (1995) 22.3 JLS 326.

Durkheim, E, *Suicide* (1858), 1951, Glencoe, Illinois: Free Press.

Dworkin, A, 'Liberty and pornography' (1993) *The New York Review of Books,* 21 October.

Dworkin, A, *Life and Death: Unapologetic Writings on the Continuing War Against Women,* 1997, London: Virago.

Dworkin, A, *Pornography: Men Possessing Women,* 1981, London: The Women's Press.

Dworkin, R, 'Do we have a right to pornography?' (1981) 1 OJLS 177.

Dworkin, R, 'The future of abortion' (1989) New York Review of Books, 28 September.

Dworkin, R, *Law's Empire,* 1986, London: Fontana.

Dworkin, R, *A Matter of Principle,* 1986, Oxford: OUP.

Dworkin, R, *Taking Rights Seriously,* 1977, London: Duckworth.

Dwyer, S, *The Problem of Pornography,* 1995, Belmont, California: Wadsworth.

Edwards, S, 'Battered women who kill' (1990) 5 NLJ 1380.

Edwards, S, 'The kerb-crawling fiasco' (1987) 137 NLJ 1209.

Edwards, S, *Sex and Gender in the Legal Process,* 1996, London: Blackstone.

Eekelaar, J, 'The emergence of children's rights' [1986] 6 OJLS 161.

Eekelaar, JM and Katz, SN, *Family Violence,* 1978, Toronto: Butterworths.

Ehrlich, E, *The Fundamental Principles of the Sociology of Law* (1936), 1975: New York: Arno.

Engels, F, *The Origins of the Family, Private Property and the State* (1884), 1940, London: Lawrence & Wishart.

'Entire village sterilised' (1978) India Now, August.

Ericcson, L, 'Charges against prostitution: an attempt at a philosophical assessment' (1980) 90 Ethics 335.

Ewen, L, *Witch Hunting and Witch Trials* (1929), 1971, Frederick Miller.

Ewing, C, *Battered Women Who Kill: Psychological Self-defence as Legal Justification*, 1987, Lexington Books, DC Heath.

Faludi, S, *Backlash: The Undeclared War Against Women*, 1992, London: Vintage.

Figes, K, *Because of Her Sex*, 1995, London: Pan.

Finnis, JM, *Natural Law and Natural Rights*, 1980, Oxford: Clarendon.

Firestone, S, *The Dialectic of Sex: The Case for a Feminist Revolution*, 1974, New York: Bantam.

Fish, S, *There's No Such Thing as Free Speech, and It's a Good Thing, Too*, 1993, Oxford: OUP.

Fishburne Collier, J and Junko Yanagisako, S (eds), *Gender and Kinship: Essays Toward a Unified Analysis*, 1987, Stanford: Stanford UP.

Fortin, J, 'Can you ward a foetus?' (1988) 51 MLR 768.

Foster, H (ed), *The Anti-Aesthetic: Essays on Postmodern Culture*, 1983, Washington: Port Townsend.

Foster, P, *Women and the Health Care Industry: An Unhealthy Relationship?*, 1995, Buckingham: Open University.

Foucault, M, *Discipline and Punish: The Birth of the Prison*, Sheridan Smith, A (trans), Harmondsworth: Penguin.

Foucault, M, *History of Sexuality*, 1990, London: Penguin.

Foucault, M, *Language, Counter-Memory, Practice: Selected Essays and Interviews*, 1977, New York: Cornell UP.

Foucault, M, *Madness and Civilization: A History of Insanity in the Age of Reason*, 1971, London: Routledge.

Foucault, M, *Power/Knowledge*, 1972, New York: Pantheon.

Foucault, M, *Power/Knowledge: Selected Interviews and other Writings, 1972–77*, 1980, Brighton: Harvester.

Foucault, M, *The Archaeology of Knowledge and the Discourse on Language*, Sheridan Smith, A (trans), 1972, London: Tavistock.

Bibliography

Frazer, E and Lacey, N, *The Politics of Community: A Feminist Critique of the Liberal-Communitarian Debate*, 1993, Hemel Hempstead: Harvester.

Freeman, M, 'Violence against women: does the legal system provide solutions or itself constitute the problem?' (1980) 7 British JL Soc 215.

Freeman, M, *Lloyd's Introduction to Jurisprudence* (1994) 6th edn, London: Sweet & Maxwell.

Freud, S, *New Introductory Lectures on Psychoanalysis*, 1933, London: WW Norton.

Frost, N, 'Food for thought: Dresser on anorexia' (1984) 2 Wisconsin L Rev 375.

Frothingham, OB, 'The real case of the "remonstrants" against woman suffrage' (1890) 11 The Arena 176.

Frug, M, *Postmodern Legal Feminism*, 1992, London: Routledge, Chapman and Hall.

Fuller, L, 'Positivism and fidelity to law – a reply to Professor Hart' (1958) 71 Harv L Rev 630.

Gabe, J (ed), *Mental Illness: The Fundamental Facts*, 1993, London: Mental Health Foundation.

Gabe, J (ed), *Understanding Tranquiliser Use*, 1991, London: Routledge.

Galsworthy, J, *The Man of Property (The Forsyte Chronicles, I)* (1906), 1951, London: Penguin.

Gewirth, A, 'Rights and virtues' (1988) 38 Review of Metaphysics.

Gilligan, C, 'Getting civilized' (1992) LXIII Fordham L Rev 17.

Gilligan, C, *In A Different Voice: Psychological Theory and Women's Development*, 1982, Cambridge, Mass: Harvard UP.

Gostin, L (ed), *Civil Liberties in Conflict*, 1988, London: Routledge.

Griffin, S, *Rape: The Power of Consciousness*, 1979, New York: Harper & Row.

Grosz, E, *Sexual Subversions: Three French Feminists*, 1989, London: Allen & Unwin.

Hale, Sir M, *The History of the Pleas of the Crown* (1736), 1971, London: London Professional Books.

Hamilton, E and Cairns, H (eds), *Plato: The Collected Dialogues*, 1963, Ewing, New Jersey: Princeton UP.

Harding, S, *The Science Question in Feminism*, 1986, New York: Cornell UP.

Hardy, T, *The Mayor of Casterbridge* (1886), 1975, London: Macmillan.

Harman, H, *Trying for a Baby: A Report on the Inadequacy of NHS Infertility Services*, 1990, London: HMSO.

Harris, A, 'Race and essentialism in feminist legal theory' (1990) 42 Stanford L Rev 581.

Hart, HLA, *The Concept of Law*, 1961, Oxford: OUP.

Hart, HLA, *The Concept of Law*, 1961, 2nd edn, 1994, Oxford: OUP.

Hart, HLA, *Law, Liberty and Morality*, 1965, Oxford: OUP.

Hart, HLA, 'Positivism and the separation of morals' (1958) 71 Harv L Rev 593.

Hartmann, B, *Reproductive Rights and Wrongs: The Global Politics of Population Control*, 1995, Boston, Mass: South End.

Hartsock, N, *Money, Sex and Power: Toward a Feminist Historical Materialism*, 1983, London: Longman.

Hartsock, N, 'Rethinking modernism: minority vs majority theories' (1987) 7 Cultural Critique 187.

Hegel, G, *The Phenomenology of Spirit* (1807), Miller, AV (trans), 1977, New York: OUP.

Hegel, G, *Philosophy of Right* (1821), Knox, T (trans), 1952, Oxford: OUP.

Hegel, G, *Science of Logic* (1812–16), Miller, AV (trans), 1969, London: Allen & Unwin.

Heinze, E, 'Discourses of sex: classical, modernist, post-modernist' (1998) 67 Nordic Journal of International Law 37.

Hester, M, *Lewd Women and Wicked Witches: A Study of the Dynamics of Male Domination*, 1992, London: Routledge and Kegan Paul.

Hirsch, M and Fox Keller, E (eds), *Conflicts in Feminism*, 1990, London: Routledge.

Hobbes, T, *De Cive*, repr 1972, Garden City: Doubleday & Co.

Hobbes, T, *De Corpore Politico*.

Hobbes, T, *The Leviathan* (1651), Tuck, R (ed), 1991, Cambridge: CUP.

Hoggett, B, Pearl, D, Cooke, E and Bates, P, *The Family, Law and Society: Cases and Materials*, 4th edn, 1996, London: Butterworths.

Home Office, *Criminal Statistics 1994*, Cm 3020, London: HMSO.

Home Office, *Criminal Statistics England and Wales 1983–94, Criminal Statistics Supplementary Tables*, Vol 2, 1983–94, London: HMSO.

Home Office, *Criminal Statistics: England and Wales, 1995*, Cm 3421, 1996, London: The Stationery Office.

Home Office, *Domestic Proceedings: England and Wales*, 1983–92, Home Office Statistical Bulletin, London: HMSO.

Home Office, *The Effect of Video Violence on Young Offenders*, 1998, London: Home Office.

Home Office, *Gender and the Criminal Justice System*, 1992, Home Office, London: HMSO.

Home Office, *Health and Personnel Social Services Statistics for England*, 1992, London: HMSO.

Home Office, *Report of the Commissioner of Police of the Metropolis*, London: HMSO.

Home Office, *The Report of the Committee on the Age of Majority* (the Latey Report), Cmnd 3342, 1967, London: HMSO.

Home Office, *The Report of the Committee on Homosexual Offences and Prostitution*, Cmnd 247, 1957, London: HMSO.

Home Office, *Report of the Committee on Homosexuality and Prostitution*, 1957, London: HMSO.

Home Office, *Sexual Offences*, Cmnd 9213, 1984, London: HMSO.

hooks, b, *Feminist Theory: From Margin to Center*, 1984, Boston: South End Press.

hooks, b, *Yearning: Race, Gender, and Cultural Politics*, 1991, Boston: South End.

Hordern, J, *Provocation and Responsibility*, 1992, Oxford: Clarendon.

Hordern, J, 'Sex violence and sentencing in provocation cases' [1989] Crim LR 546.

Houghton, N, *The Victorian Frame of Mind*, 1957, New Haven: Yale UP.

House of Commons, *Report of the Select Committee on Violence in Marriage*, HC 553, 1974–75.

Howitt, D and Cumberbatch, G, *Pornography: Impacts and influences*, 1990, London: Home Office.

Hume, D, *An Enquiry Concerning the Principles of Morals* (1751), Selby Bigge, LA (ed), 3rd edn, rev Nidditch, PH, 1902, Oxford: Clarendon.

Hume, D, *History of England* (1778), 1983, Indianapolis: Library Classics.

Hume, D, *A Treatise of Human Nature* (1740), 1938, Cambridge: CUP.

Hunt, A, *Reading Dworkin Critically*, 1992, Oxford: Berg.

Hunt, A, *The Sociological Movement in Law*, 1978, London: Macmillan.

Hunt, L, *The Invention of Pornography*, 1993, New York: Zone.

Institute of Law Research and Reform (Edmonton, Alberta), *Sterilization Decisions: Minors and Mentally Incompetent Adults*, 1988.

Irigaray, L, *Sexes et Parentés*, Macey, D (trans), 1993, New York: Columbia UP.

Irigaray, L, *Speculum of the Other Woman*, Gill, G, (trans), 1985, New York: Cornell UP.

Irigaray, L, *Le Temps de la Différence*, 1989, published in English as *Thinking the Difference: For a Peaceful Revolution*, Montin, K (trans), 1994, London: Athlone.

Irigaray, L, *This Sex Which Is Not One*, Porter, C and Burke, C (trans), 1985, New York: Cornell UP.

Itzin, C (ed), *Pornography: Women, Violence and Civil Liberties: A Radical New View*, 1992, Oxford: OUP.

Jackson, E, 'The problem with pornography' [1995] Feminist Legal Studies 49.

Jaggar, A, *Feminist Politics and Human Nature*, 1983, New Jersey: Rowman and Littlefield.

Jowell, R, Witherspoon, S and Brook, L (eds), *British Social Attitudes, the Fifth Report*, 1988.

Jowell, R, Witherspoon, S and Brook, L (eds), *British Social Attitudes: Special International Report*, 1989, Aldershot: Gower.

Kairys, D (ed), *The Politics of Law: A Progressive Critique*, 1982, New York: Pantheon.

Kant, I, *Critique of Practical Reason* (1788), White Beck, L (trans), 1949, Chicago: Chicago UP.

Kant, I, *Critique of Pure Reason* (1781), Kemp-Smith, N (trans), 1965, New York: St Martins.

Karkal, M, 'Abortion laws and the abortion situation in India' [1991] 4 Reproductive and Genetic Engineering 3.

Kelsen, H, *The General theory of Law and State*, 1961, New York: Russell.

Kelsen, H, *The Pure Theory of Law*, 1967, California: California UP.

Kennedy, H, *Eve Was Framed*, 1992, London: Vintage.

Kennedy, I, 'Husband denied a say in abortion decision' 42 MLR 324.

Kennedy, I, *Treat Me Right: Essays in Medical Law and Ethics*, 1994, Oxford: OUP.

Kennedy, I and Lee, S, 'This rush to judgment' (1987) *The Times*, 1 April.

Kenny, C, 'Wife selling in England' (1920) 45 LQR 496.

Bibliography

Kolder, V, Gallagher, J and Parsons, M, 'Court-ordered obstetrical interventions' (1987) 316 New England Journal of Medicine 1192.

Kramer, H and Sprenger, J, *The Malleus Maleficarum* (1928), Summers, Rev M (trans), 1971, New York: Dover.

Kymlicka, W, *Liberalism, Community and Culture*, 1989, Oxford: OUP.

Lacey, N, 'Feminist legal theory: beyond neutrality' [1995] CLP 1.

Lacey, N, 'Theories of justice and the welfare state' (1992) 1 Social and Legal Studies 323.

Laird, V, 'Reflections on *R v R*' (1991) 55 MLR 386.

Langton, R, 'Whose right? Ronald Dworkin, women, and pornographers' (1990) 194 Philosophy and Public Affairs 311.

Larner, C, *Witchcraft and Religion*, 1984, Oxford: Basil Blackwell.

Laski, H, *The Rise of European Liberalism*, 1936, London: Allen & Unwin.

Laslett, P (ed), *Sir Robert Filmer, Patriarcha and Other Political Works of Sir Robert Filmer*, 1949, Oxford: Basil Blackwell.

Law Commission, *Criminal Law: Rape Within Marriage*, Law Com No 205, 1992, London: HMSO.

Law Commission, *Facing the Future: A Discussion Paper on the Ground for Divorce*, Law Com No 170, 1998, London: HMSO.

Law Commission, *Family Law: The Ground for Divorce*, Law Com No 192, 1990, London: HMSO.

Law Commission, *Mental Incapacity*, Law Com No 231, 1995, London: HMSO.

Law Commission, *Rape Within Marriage*, Working Paper No 116, 1990, London: HMSO.

Law Commission, *Report on Domestic Violence and Occupation of the Family Home*, Law Com No 107, 1992.

Law Commission Working Paper, No 116, 1990.

Lederer, L (ed), *Take Back the Night: Women and Pornography*, 1980, New York: William Morrow.

Lee, L, 'Legal implications of the world population plan of action' (1974) 9 Journal of International Law and Economics 375.

Lester, A and Bindman, G, *Race and Law*, 1972, London: Penguin.

Levi-Strauss, C, *The Savage Mind*, 1966, London: Weidenfeld and Nicolson.

Litteton, C, 'In search of a feminist jurisprudence' (1987) 10 Harvard Women's LJ 1.

Lloyd, G, *The Man of Reason: 'Male' and 'Female' in Western Philosophy*, 1984, London: Methuen.

Locke, J, *Two Treatises on Government* (1690), 1924, New York: JM Dent.

Longstaff, L and Neale, A, 'The convicted rapist feels unlucky – rarely guilty' (1997) *The Times*, 18 November.

Lopez-Jones, N, 'Legalising brothels' (1992) 142 NLJ 594.

Lorde, A, *Sister Outsider*, 1984, Trumansburg: Crossing.

Lowe, N, 'Wordship and abortion preventions' (1980) 96 LQR 29.

Lowman, J, 'Street prostitution control: some Canadian reflections on the Finsbury Park experience' (1992) 32 Br J Crim 1.

Lyndon Shanley, M and Pateman, C (eds), *Feminist Interpretations and Political Theory*, 1988, London: Polity.

Lyotard, J-F, *The Postmodern Condition: A Report on Knowledge*, Bennington, G and Massumi, B (trans), 1984, Manchester: Manchester UP.

MacFarlane, A, *Witchcraft in Tudor and Stuart England, a Regional and Comparative Study*, 1970, London: Routledge and Kegan Paul.

MacIntyre, A, *After Virtue: A Study in Moral Theory*, 2nd edn, 1984, London: Duckworth.

MacIntyre, A, *Whose Justice, Which Rationality?*, 1988, London: Duckworth.

MacKinnon, C, *Feminism Unmodified: Discourses on Life and Law*, 1987, Cambridge, Mass: Harvard UP.

MacKinnon, C, *Only Words*, 1994, London: HarperCollins.

MacKinnon, C, *Sexual Harassment of Working Women*, 1979, New Haven: Yale UP.

MacKinnon, C, *Toward a Feminist Theory of the State*, 1989, Cambridge, Mass: Harvard UP.

Mahoney, M, 'Legal images of battered women: redefining the issue of separation' (1991) 90 Michigan L Rev 1.

Maidment, S, 'The law's response to marital violence in England and the USA' 26 ICLQ 403.

Maine, H, *Ancient Law*, 1972, London: JM Dent.

Malinowski, B, *Sex and Repression in Savage Society*, (1927), 1960, London: Routledge and Kegan Paul.

Malos, E (ed), *The Politics of Housework*, 1980, London: Alison and Busby.

Marks, E and de Courtivron, I (eds), *New French Feminism*, 1984, New York: Schocken.

Martin, E, *The Woman in the Body: A Cultural Analysis of Reproduction*, 1987, Buckingham: Open University.

Marx, K, *Capital*, Vol I, 1967, New York: International Publishers.

Marx, K, *The Communist Manifesto* (1848), Wayne, J (ed), 1987, Toronto: Canadian Scholars.

Marx, K and Engels, F, *The German Ideology*, Arthur, C (ed), 1970, New York: International Publishers.

Matsuda, M, 'Liberal jurisprudence and abstracted visions of human nature: a feminist critique of Rawls' *A Theory of Justice*' (1986) 16 New Mexico L Rev 613.

Matthews, R, 'Regulating street prostitution and kerb-crawling: a reply to John Lowman' (1992) 32 Br J Crim 18.

McElroy, W (ed), *Freedom, Feminism and the State*, 1982, USA: Cato Institute.

Menafee, S, *Wives for Sale*, 1981, Oxford: OUP.

Menkel-Meadow, C, 'Portia in a different voice: speculations on a woman's lawyering process' [1985] Berkeley Woman's LJ 39.

Merquior, J, *Foucault*, 1985, London: Fontana.

Michelman, F, 'Conceptions of democracy in American constitutional argument: the case of pornography regulation' (1989) 56 Tennessee L Rev 303.

Mill, JS, *On Liberty* (1859), 1989, Cambridge: CUP.

Mill, JS, *Representative Government* (1865), 1958, Indianapolis: Bobbs-Merrill.

Mill, JS, *The Subjection of Women* (1869), 1989, Cambridge: CUP.

Millett, K, *Sexual Politics* (1972), 1977, London: Virago.

Milunsky, A and Annas, G (eds), *Genetics and the Law – III*, 1985, Aldershot: Dartmouth.

Moi, T (ed), *French Feminist Thought: A Reader*, 1987, Oxford: Blackwells.

Moi, T, *Sexual/Textual Politics*, 1985, London: Methuen.

Moller Okin, S, 'Justice and gender' (1987) 16 Philosophy and Public Affairs 42.

Moller Okin, S, *Justice, Gender and the Family*, 1989, New York: Basic Books.

Moller Okin, S, *Women in Western Political Thought*, 1979, Ewing, New Jersey: Princeton UP.

Monter, E, *Witchcraft in France and Switzerland*, 1976, New York: Cornell UP.

Morley, R and Mullender, A, (1992) 6 International Journal of Law and the Family 265.

Morrison, W, *Jurisprudence: From the Greeks to Post-modernism*, 1997, London: Cavendish Publishing.

Mosse, J and Heaton, J, *The Fertility and Contraception Book*, 1990, London: Faber & Faber.

Mossman, MJ, 'Feminism and legal method: the difference it makes' (1987) Wisconsin Women's LJ.

Mulhall, S and Smith, A, *Liberals and Communitarian*, 2nd edn, 1995, Oxford: Basil Blackwell.

Naffine, N, *Law and the Sexes*, 1990, Sydney: Allen & Unwin.

Naffine, N, 'Possession: erotic love in the law of rape' (1994) 57 MLR 10.

Naffine, N and Owens, R (eds), *Sexing the Subject of Law*, 1997, London: LBS Information Services/Sweet & Maxwell.

Nesbit, R, *History of the Idea of Progress*, 1980, New York: Basic Books.

Nicholson, L (ed), *Feminism/Postmodernism*, 1990, London: Routledge.

Norrie, A (ed), *Closure or Critique: New Directions in Legal Theory*, 1993, Edinburgh: Edinburgh UP.

Norrie, S, *Family Planning Practice and the Law*, 1991 Aldershot: Dartmouth.

O'Donovan, K, 'Law's knowledge: the judge, the expert, the battered woman, and her syndrome' (1993) 20 JLS 427.

O'Donovan, K, *Sexual Divisions in Law*, 1985, London: Weidenfeld and Nicolson.

Oakley, A and Mitchell, J (eds), *The Rights and Wrongs of Woman*, 1976, London: Penguin.

Olsen, F, 'The family and the market: a study of ideology and legal reform' (1983) 96 Harv L Rev 7.

Olsen, F, 'Feminism and critical legal theory: an American perspective' (1990) 18 Int J Soc L 199.

Orbach, S, *Fat is a Feminist Issue*, 1993, Harmondsworth, Penguin.

Orbach, S, *Hunger Strike: The Anorexic's Struggle as a Metaphor for Our Age*, 1993, Harmondsworth: Penguin.

Pagels, EH, 'What became of God the mother? Conflicting images of God in early Christianity', in Abel, E and Abel, EK (eds), *The Signs Reader: Women, Gender and Scholarship*, 1978, Chicago: University of Chicago Press.

Pahl, J (ed), *Private Violence and Public Policy. The Needs of Battered Women and the Response of the Public Services*, 1985, London: Routledge and Kegal Paul.

Bibliography

Palmer, R, *Anorexia Nervosa*, 2nd edn, 1988, London: Penguin.

Parent, W, 'A second look at pornography and the subordination of women' (1990) 87 Journal of Philosophy 205.

Parsons, T, Bales, J, Olds, M, Zelditch, P and Slater, E, *Family, Socialisation, and Interaction Process*, 1955, New York: Free Press.

Parsons, T, *Societies: Evolutionary and Comparative Perspectives*, 1966, New Jersey: Prentice Hall.

Pateman, C and Grosz, E (eds), *Feminist Challenges: Law and Social Theory*, 1986, London: Allen & Unwin.

Pateman, C, *The Sexual Contract*, 1988, London: Polity Press.

Patterson, D (ed), *Postmodernism and Law*, 1994, Aldershot: Dartmouth.

Pizzey, E, *Scream Quietly or the Neighbours Will Hear*, 1974, London: Penguin.

Plato, *The Republic*, Lee, D (trans), 2nd edn, 1974, London: Penguin.

Plaza, M, '"Phallomorphic power" and the psychology of "woman": a patriarchal vicious circle' (1980) 1 Feminist Issues 73.

Power Cobbe, F, *Wife Torture in England*, 1878.

Ravindran, 'Women and the politics of population' [1991] 4 Reproductive and Genetic Engineering 3.

Rawls, J, 'The idea of an overlapping consensus' (1987) 7 OJLS 1.

Rawls, J, 'Justice as fairness: political not metaphysical' (1985) 14 Philosophy and Public Affairs 3.

Rawls, J, 'Kantian constructivism in moral theory' (1985) Journal of Philosophy 77.

Rawls, J, *Politician Liberalism*, 1993, New York: Columbia UP.

Rawls, J, 'The priority of the right and ideas of the good' (1988) 17 Philosophy and Public Affairs 251.

Rawls, J, *A Theory of Justice*, 1972, Oxford: OUP.

Reiss, H (ed), *Kant's Political Writings*, 1977, Cambridge: CUP.

Rich, A, *Of Woman Born: Motherhood as Experience and Institution*, 1976, New York: WW Norton.

Richlin, A (ed), *Pornography and Representation in Ancient Rome*, 1992, New York: OUP.

Robbins, RH, *The Encyclopedia of Witchcraft and Demonology*, 1959, London: Peter Nevill.

Rorty, A (ed), *Explaining Emotions*, 1980, Berkeley, California: California UP.

Rosaldo, M, 'The use and abuse of anthropology: reflections on feminism and cross-cultural understanding' (1980) 5, 3 Signs: Journal of Women and Culture in Society 389.

Rosaldo, M and Lamphere, L (eds), *Women, Culture and Society*, 1974, Stanford: Stanford UP.

Rousseau, J-J, *Emile* (1762), Bloom, A (trans), 1991, Harmondsworth: Penguin.

Rousseau, J-J, *The Social Contract* (1762), 1913, New York: JM Dent.

Rowbotham, S, *A Century of Women: The History of Women in Britain and the United States*, 1997, New York: Viking.

Rubin, E, *Abortion, Politics, and the Courts: Roe v Wade and its Aftermath*, 1987, New York: Greenwood.

Russo, A, 'Conflicts and contradictions among feminists over issues of pornography and sexual freedom' (1987) 102 Women's Studies International 103.

Sachs, A and Hoff Wilson, J, *Sexism and the Law*, 1978, Oxford: Martin Robertson.

Sandel, M, *Liberalism and the Limits of Justice*, 1982, Cambridge: CUP.

Savage, W, *A Savage Enquiry: Who Controls Childbirth?*, 1986, London: Virago.

Schlag, P, 'The problem of the subject' (1991) 69 Texas L Rev 1627.

Seccombe, I and Ball, J, *Motivation, Morale and Mobility: A Profile of Qualified Nurses in the 1990s*, 1992, London: Institute of Manpower Studies.

Segal, L, *Is the Future Female: Troubled Thoughts on Contemporary Feminism*, 1987, London: Virago.

Segal, L and McIntosh, M (eds), *Sex Exposed: Sexuality and the Pornography Debate*, 1992, London: Virago.

Shapiro, S, Schlesinger, E and Nesbitt, R, *Infant, Perinatal, Maternal and Childhood Mortality in the United States*, 1968, Cambridge, Mass: Harvard UP.

Sheldon, S, *Beyond Control*, 1997, London: Pluto.

Sheldon, S, 'Who is the mother to make the judgment? Construction of women in English abortion law' [1993] 1 Feminist Legal Studies 3.

Simmel, G, *Conflict and the Web of Group Affiliations*, 1955, New York: Macmillan.

Simms, M (ed), *Australian Women and the Political System*, 1984, Melbourne: Longman.

Smart, C, *Feminism and the Power of Law*, 1989, London: Routledge and Kegan Paul.

Bibliography

Smart, C, *Law, Crime and Sexuality: Essays in Feminism*, 1995, London: Sage.

Smart, C, *The Ties That Bind: Law, Marriage and the Reproduction of Patriarchal Relations*, 1984, London: Routledge and Kegan Paul.

Smith, TV, *The American Philosophy of Equality*, 1927, Chicago: Chicago UP.

Sommerville, JP, *Thomas Hobbes. Political Ideas in Historical Context*, 1972, Basingstoke: Macmillan.

Spelman, E, *Inessential Woman: Problems of Exclusion in Feminist Thought*, 1990, London: The Women's Press.

Spencer, H, *Principles of Sociology*, 1892–93, New York: D Appleton.

Spender, D (ed), *Feminist Theorists*, 1983, London: The Women's Press.

Stanki, B, 'Book review: *Women, Violence and Social Change* (1993) Br J Crim 449.

Stanton, A and Stanton, C, *The History of Woman Suffrage*, 1881, New York: Fowler & Wells; repr 1969, New York: Arno and New York Times.

Stanworth, M (ed), *Reproductive Technologies: Gender, Motherhood and Medicine*, 1987, Cambridge: Polity.

Steele Commage, H (ed), *Documents of American History*, 1956, New York: Appleton-Century-Crofts.

Stockman, N, Bonney, N and Xuewen, S, *Women's Work in East and West: The Dual Burden of Employment and Family Life*, 1995, London: UCL Press.

Stockton, N, Bonney, N and Xuewen, S, *Women's Work in East and West*, 1995, London: UCL Press.

Stone, L, *Road to Divorce: England 1530–1987*, 1992, Oxford: OUP.

Strachey, R, *The Cause* (1928), 1978, London: Virago.

Strachey, R, *Millicent Garrett Fawcett*, 1951, London: John Murray.

Stubbs, J (ed), *Women, Male Violence and the Law*, 1994, Sydney: Institute of Criminology, Monograph Series No 6.

Sumner, W, *Folkways* (1906), 1940, Boston, Mass: Ginn.

Swanson, J, *The Public and the Private in Aristotle's Political Philosophy*, 1992, New York: Cornell UP.

Taylor, B, *Modernism, Post-modernism, Realism: a Critical Perspective for Art*, 1987, Winchester.

Taylor, C, *Philosophical Papers*, Vol 2, 1985, Cambridge: CUP.

Taylor, C, *Sources of the Self*, 1990, Cambridge: CUP.

Temkin, J, *Rape and the Legal Process*, 1987, London: Sweet & Maxwell.

Temkin, J, 'Sexual history evidence – the ravishment of section 2' [1993] Crim LR 3.

Thomas, K, *Religion and the Decline of Magic*, 1971, London: Weidenfeld and Nicolson.

Thornton, M (ed), *Public and Private: Feminist Legal Debates*, Melbourne: OUP.

Thornton, R, 'Multiple keyholders – wardship and consent to medical treatment' [1992] CLJ 34.

United Nations Report, *The World's Women 1970–90*, 1991, London: HMSO.

United Nations Report, *The World's Women 1995: Trends and Statistics*, 1995, London: HMSO.

United Nations Report, *Violence Against Women in the Family*, 1989, (United Nations Sales No E.89.IV.5).

US Department of Justice, *Sourcebook of Criminal Justice Statistics*, 1988.

Venkatachalam, R and Viji, S, *Female Infanticide*, 1993, New Delhi: Har-Anand.

von Savigny, K, *On the Vocation of Our Age for Legislation and Jurisprudence*, 1831, Hayward A (trans), 1975, New York: Arno.

Walker, L, *The Battered Woman Syndrome*, 1984, New York: Springer.

Wallace, A, *Homicide: the Social Reality*, 1986, Sydney: NSW Bureau of Crime Statistics and Research.

Warnock Committee, *Report of the Committee of Inquiry into Fertilisation and Embryology*, Cmnd 9314, 1984, London: HMSO.

Warnock, M, *A Question of Life*, 1985, Oxford: Basil Blackwell.

Wasik, M, 'Cumulative provocation and domestic killing' [1982] Crim LR 29.

Weber, M (1864–1920), *Economy and Society*, 1987, Berkeley: California: California UP.

West, R, 'Jurisprudence and gender' (1988) 55 Chicago UL Rev 1.

West, R, 'The difference in women's hedonic lives: a phenomenological critique of feminist legal theory' (1987) 3 Wisconsin Women's LJ.

West, R, *Narrative, Authority and Law*, 1993, Michigan UP.

Whitford, M (ed), *The Irigaray Reader*, 1991, Oxford: Basil Blackwell.

Whitford, M, *Luce Irigaray: Philosophy in the Feminine*, 1991, London: Routledge.

Whitmarsh, A, *Social Focus on Women*, 1995, London: HMSO.

Whitford, M, 'Speaking as a woman: Luce Irigaray and the female imaginary' (1986) 43 Radical Philosophy 3.

Bibliography

Williams Committee, *Report of the Committee on Obscenity and Film Censorship*, Cmnd 7772, 1979, London: HMSO.

Williams, G, 'The *Gillick* saga' (1985) 135 NLJ 1156 and 1179.

Williams, P, *The Alchemy of Race and Rights*, 1991, Cambridge, Mass: Harvard UP.

Wilson, M and Daly, M, 'Spousal homicide' (1994) 148 Juristat Service Bulletin, Canadian Centre for Justice Statistics.

Wolf, N, *The Beauty Myth*, 1991, London: Vintage.

Wolgast, E, *The Grammar of Justice*, 1987, New York: Cornell UP.

Wollstonecraft, M, *Vindication of the Rights of Women* (1792), 1967, New York: WW Norton.

Young, A, 'Conjugal homicide and legal violence: a comparative analysis' (1993) 31 Osgoode Hall LJ 761.

Young, I, 'The ideal of community and the politics of difference' (1986) 12 Social Theory and Practice 1.

INDEX

Abortion, 69, 217, 230–32, 234
  Roe v Wade, 107, 230, 235, 236, 237, 238, 239
Abortion Act 1967, 21, 69, 217
Abortion Law
  Reform Association, 231
Abortion rights, 229–40
  natural father, 233
  United States, 234–40, 244
Aeschylus,
  Oresteia, 153
Age of modernity, 95–96, 177–78
American Medical Association, 47
American Realist school, 108
American Woman
  Suffrage Association, 44
Ancient Greece,
  natural law, 89–90
  public/private distinction, 123
Anderson, Elizabeth Garrett, 46
Anorexia nervosa,
  non-consensual treatment, 244–49
Anthony, Susan B, 44
Aquinas, St Thomas, 92
Aretino, Pietro, 282
Aristotle, 3, 6, 35, 83, 88–89, 166, 257
  ideal state, 88
  The Politics, 57, 88–89
Arranged marriage, 78
Asquith, 42
Augustine, 91
Austin, JL, 184, 299
Austin, John, 100
Australia, 76
  battered woman
    syndrome, 274–75
  pornography, 284, 285
  sterilisation, 223

B v Croydon Health Authority, 245
Bacon, 65
  Abridgement of the Law, 57
Bartlett, Katharine, 21
Battered woman syndrome, 23, 257, 270–73
  Australia, 274–75

Canada, 273–74
Baudelaire, 177
Beal v Doe, 236
Beauvoir, Simone de, 71, 150, 158
  The Second Sex, 3–4, 14–16, 30, 147
Bender, Leslie, 25, 26
Berlin, Sir Isiah, 302
Blackmun, J, 230
Blackstone, Sir William, 65, 258
  *Commentaries on the Laws
    of England 1765–69*, 35, 259
Blackwell, Elizabeth, 46
Bonney, N, 51–53, 71
Bordo, Susan, 196, 198, 200
Bradwell v Illinois, 24
British Central Statistical
  Office Report 1995, 53–55
*Brown v Board of
  Education of Topeka*, 37, 106, 293
Brownmiller, Susan, 275
Butler, Josephine, 39
Butler, Judith, 16

C v S, 233
Caesarean section,
  court ordered, 223–26
Cain, Patricia, 78, 194
Cameron, Deborah, 289
Canada,
  battered woman
    syndrome, 273–74
  pornography, 284, 285, 286, 288
  sterilisation case law, 220–21
Canadian Attorney General
  Commission on Pornography, 288
Canadian Criminal
  Code, s 163(8), 283
Cat and Mouse Act, 42, 43
Cave, Bertha, 49
Charlesworth, Hilary, 69, 244
Child custody, 63
Child law, 68
Childcare, 52, 54
Children Act 1989, 68, 126, 200
China, 71

footbinding,	31–32	Descartes, Rene,	95
population control,	241	Devlin, Lord Patrick,	307–08
work patterns,	51–54	*Diamond v Charles*,	237
Chinkin, Christine,	244	Diminished responsibility,	268–69
Chodorow, Nancy,	143–45	Divine Right of Kings,	58
Chorlton v Lings,	24, 40	Divorce,	62–63
Christian natural law,	90–92	Divorce Reform Act 1857,	62
Cicero,	90	Dobash, R & Dobash, R,	73, 257
City of Akron v Akron Center for Reproductive Health,	237, 238	Domestic Proceedings and Magistrates' Courts Act 1978,	255, 262
Civil War,	96–97	Domestic violence,	22–23, 66, 72–74, 258, 261–66, 270
Cixous, Helene,	147		
CLS *See* Critical Legal Studies		United Kingdom statistics,	255
Communitarian philosophy,	115–16	Domestic Violence and Matrimonial Proceedings Act 1976,	255, 262
Contagious Diseases Acts,	39		
Contraception,	234		
Cornell, Drucilla,	115, 156, 159–61, 173–76	Dominance theory,	165–73
Corpus Iuris Civilis,	90	Dunant, Henri,	49
Court of Justice of the European Communities,	10	Duncan, Sheila,	277
		Durkheim, Emile,	30
CR v United Kingdom,	66	Dworkin, Andrea,	11, 103, 167–68, 203, 299, 303
Crenshaw, Kimberlè,	193–94, 204		
Crimea War,	48		
Criminal conversation,	61–62	model anti-pornography ordinance,	295–97, 313
Criminal Justice Act 1991,	278		
Criminal Justice and Public Order Act 1994,	261	*Pornography: Men Possessing Women*,	291–92
Criminal Law Revision Committee,	260	Dworkin, Ronald,	103, 104–10, 298, 301–04
Critical Legal Studies,	108, 180, 188–94, 200–04	*Law's Empire*,	105, 190
		Taking Rights Seriously,	104
Cromwell, Oliver,	96	Dworkin-MacKinnon Model Anti-Pornography Ordinance,	295–97, 313
Daly, Mary,	91, 216		
Gyn/Ecology,	32, 33, 34		
Davidson, Emily Wilding,	42		
Davies, Emily,	45	East London Federation of Suffragettes,	42
Davies, Margaret,	206	Education,	45–49
Declaration of Sentiments,	43	*Edwards v AG for Canada*,	24
Deconstruction,	204–07	Edwards, Susan,	269
Deep Throat,	296	Ehrlich, Eugen,	36–38
Department of Health v JWB and SWB,	223	*Fundamental Principles of the Sociology of Law*,	37
Derrida, Jacques,	15, 48, 160, 181, 185–87	Employment,	51–55

Index

Engels, Friedrich, 29, 135, 139
*The Origins of the Family,
Private Property
and the State,* 137, 138
English Bill of Rights, 97
Englishwomen's Journal, The, 45
Enlightenment, 95–96, 97, 98, 177
Equal Pay Act 1970, 126
Equal Pay Act 1975, 37
Equality, 70–76
Erotica, 309
Espionage Act, USA, 50
Essentialism, 310
  Critical Legal Studies, 189–94
  Luce Irigaray, 158–59
  patriarchy and, 76–78
  radical feminism, 173–76
Ethnic minorities, 77–78
European Convention of
Human Rights and
Fundamental Freedoms,
Article 7, 260
European witch-murders, 33–34
Ewing, Charles P, 271
Exclusion order, 263

Faludi, Susan, 11–12
Family Homes and Domestic
Violence Bill 1994, 262
Family Law Act 1969 s 8, 246
Family Law Act 1996, 262
Fawcett, Millicent Garrett, 41–42
Female circumcision, 32
Feminine symbolism, 91
Feminism,
  first phase, 5
  French, 146–48
  second phase, 5
  third phase, 7
  United States of America, 10
Feminist developmental
  theories, 143–45
Filmer, Sir Robert, 59
Firestone, Shulamith, 6, 153, 164
First World War, 49–50

Fish, Stanley
*There's No Such Thing
as Free Speech, and
It's a Good Thing, Too,* 298
Flax, Jane, 198
Foetal rights, 232–33
Foster, Peggy, 227
Foucault, Michel, 181, 182–83
Franchise, the,
  United Kingdom, 40–43
  United States, 43–45
Frazer, Elizabeth, 289
Freedom of speech
  See United States
French feminism, 146–48
French, In re 24
Freud, Sigmund, 99, 148, 149, 151, 152
Frothingham, Octavius B, 44
Frug, Mary Joe, 199
Fuller, Lon, 93

Gender construction, 195–200
Gender debate, 14–19
George, Lloyd, 42
Ghandi, Indira, 242
*Gillick v West Norfolk and
Wisbech Area
Health Authority,* 247, 248
Gilligan, Carol, 25, 26, 108, 170
  In a Different Voice, 143, 145–46
Girton College, Cambridge, 45
Gnostic scripture, 91
Gordon, Robert, 189
Greek philosophers, 83–89
Grosz, Elizabeth, 148, 152, 156, 157, 159
Guardianship Act 1973, 63
Guardianship of
  Infants Act 1925, 63
Gynaecology, 215

Hale, Sir Matthew, 259
*The History of the
Pleas of the Crown,* 65
Hardy, Thomas
  The Mayor of Casterbridge, 34

Introduction to Feminist Jurisprudence

Harris v McRae,	236	Irigaray, Luce,	72, 86, 143,
Harris, Angela,	192		145, 147, 148–59,
Hart, HLA,	93, 100, 101		170, 172, 174–76,
The Concept of Law,	101–02,		195, 230
	105, 190	essentialism,	158–59
Law, Liberty and Morality,	308	*Sexes et Parentés*,	57, 157
Hartsock, Nancy,	137–38	*Sexual Differences*,	151
Hawkins, J,	260	*Speculum of the Other Woman*,	149
Hegel, Georg Wilheim Friedrich,	97	*This Sex Which Is Not One*,	154, 155
Philosophy of Right,	93		
Heidegger, Martin,	185	Jackson, Emily,	313
Hester, Marianne,	34, 216	James VI,	33–34
Hickey,	275	Japan,	71
Hindu suttee,	33, 241	work patterns,	51–54
Hirani v Hirani,	78	*Jefferson v Giffin Spalding County Hospital*,	232
Hobbes, Thomas,	110	Jex-Blake, Sophia,	46
Elements of Law,	58	Judicial Studies Board	
Leviathan,	58	*Handbook on Ethnic Minority Issues*,	77–78
Hodgson v Minnesota,	238	Justice	
Homicide Act 1957,	267	principles,	112–15
Homosexuality,	68–69		
Hordern, Jeremy,	266–67	Kant, Immanuel,	95, 97
Human fertilisation and embryology		Kelsen, Hans,	100
Warnock Committee,	227–28, 233	Kennedy, Duncan,	189
Human Fertilisation and Embryology Act 1990,	228	Kennedy QC, Helena,	74, 279
Hume, David,	97, 99	Kerruish, Valerie,	109
Hunt, Alan,	109, 110	Kramer, H & Sprenger, J,	
Hutchinson, Allan C,	109	*The Malleus Maleficarum*,	33
		Kristeva, Julia,	147, 196
Ibrams and Gregory,	267	Lacan, Jacques,	148, 149, 151, 152, 181
In re French,	24		
India,		Lacey, Nicola,	108, 313, 314
population control,	241, 242	Lady of the Lamp,	48
Inequality,	70–76	LAPS test,	286
Infertility treatment,	227–29	Law Commission,	
Inland Revenue Commissioners v Aken,	318	*Criminal Law: Rape Within Marriage*,	260
International Conference on Population and Development, Report 1994,	240	Legal methods,	19–27
		Legal positivism *See* Positivism	
International Labour Organisation,	50	Legal profession,	49
International Red Cross,	49	Legal rights,	202–04
Interpretation Act 1889,	24, 40	Lesbian feminism,	78

Index

Levi–Strauss, Claude, 152, 181
Liberalism, 96–99, 121–27, 258–59
  communitarian critique, 115–16
  feminist critique, 127–34
Life, 232
Lloyd, Genevieve, 84, 91
Locke, John, 59, 110
  Second Treatise, 59–60
Longstaff, Lisa, 278
Lopez–Jones, Nina, 317
Lorde, Audrey, 20
Lyotard, Jean–Francois, 181, 183–84
  The Postmodern Condition: A Report on Knowledge, 184

MacKinnon, Catharine, 11, 18, 73, 74, 75, 103, 130, 132–34, 160, 173–76, 189, 192, 194, 203, 257, 284, 291, 292, 309, 311–12
  dominance theory, 165–73
  Feminism Unmodified: Discources on Life and Law, 165, 172
  model anti–pornography ordinance, 295–97, 313
  Only Words, 294, 302
  speech act theory, 299–301
Maher v Roe, 236
Mahoney, Martha, 73
Maine, Sir Henry, 61
Maintenance of Wives Act 1886, 63
Malinovski, Bradislaw, 29
Malleus Maleficarum, The, 33
Manchester Women's Suffrage Committee, 40
Mansfield, Arabella, 49
Marchiano, Linda, 296
Marital rape, 65–66, 127, 259–61
  See also Rape
Marriage, 35
Martin, Emily, 218

Martineau, Hariett, 39
Marx, Karl, 9, 135, 136, 139, 140
Marx, Karl and Engels, Friedrich,
  The German Ideology, 138
Marxism, 19–20
Marxist-Socialist feminism, 135–41
Matrimonial Causes Act 1973, 67
Matsuda, Mari J, 113, 114
May Movement, 147
Medicaid, 235
Medical profession, 46–49, 213–218
Medical treatment,
  anorexia nervosa, 244–49
  consent of minor, 246–49
  medically incompetent person, 225–26
  right to refuse, 220–25
Medicine, 46–49
Mehta v Mehta, 300
Menkel-Meadow, Carrie, 25–26
Mental Health Act 1983, 225–26, 245
Mental Health Act 1995 s 3, 226
Meritor Savings Bank, FSB v Vinson, 171
Merquior, JG, 147
Midwifery, 47–48
Mill, Harriet Taylor, 40
Mill, John Stuart, 40, 60–61, 98, 259
  'harm' principle, 301, 304–07
  On Liberty, 122–23, 307
  The Subjection of Women, 41, 305
Miller v California, 286
Millet, Kate, 70
Minneapolis Civil Rights Ordinance, 295
Minors,
  consent to treatment, 247–49
Missouri v Ashcroft, 237
Modernity, 95–96, 177–78
Molestation, definition, 262–63
Montesquieu, 98
Moral Right, 236, 308, 309, 314

Morrison, Carrie,	49	Olsen, Frances,	201, 211
Morrison, Wayne,	187		
Mossman, Mary Jane,	24	Pagels, Elaine,	91
Mothering,	144	Pankhurst, Christabel,	42
Mouvement de Liberation des Femmes,	147	Pankhurst, Emmeline,	42–43
		Pankhurst, Sylvia,	42
Naffine, Ngaire,	5, 72	Parliament (Qualification of Women) Act 1918,	43
National American Woman Suffrage Association,	44	Parsons, Talcott,	51
		Part-time work,	53
National Union of Societies for Equal Citizenship,	50	Pateman, Carole,	113–14, 318–19
National Union of Women's Suffrage Societies (NUWSS),	41	Patriarchy, arranged marriage,	78
		essentialism, and,	76–78
National Woman Suffrage Association,	44	explanation,	57–70
		lawful,	61–63
Natural father, abortion rights,	233	private,	63–70
		public,	64
Natural law, ancient Greece and Rome,	89–90	Paul, St,	90
Christian,	90–91	Pay,	53, 54, 141
positive law, and,	92–93	Pennsylvania Abortion Control Act 1982,	238
Nazism,	178	*Persons* case,	24
Neale, Anne,	278	Picasso,	
Netherlands Advisory Committee on Human Rights and Foreign Policy 1992,	253	*Guernica*,	177
		Pizzey, Erin,	256
		Scream Quietly or the Neighbours Will Hear,	261
Nietzsche,	182	*Planned Parenthood of Southeastern Pennsylvania v Casey*,	238, 239
Nightingale, Florence,	48		
Non-molestation order,	262–63		
		Planned Parenthood v Danforth,	236
O'Donovan, Katherine,	258		
Sexual Divisions in Law,	128–32	Plato,	3, 83, 166
Oakley, Ann,	216	ideal state,	84–87
Obscenity		*The Republic*,	84–87, 125
See Pornography		*Timaeus*,	84
Obscenity and Film Censorship Report 1979,	282, 283, 287–88	*Plessey v Ferguson*,	293
		Pope v Illinois,	286
		Popular Health Movement,	47
Obstetrics,	215	Population control,	241–44
Oedipal complex,	152–53	Pornography,	75–76, 171–72, 175, 203
Offences Against the Persons Act 1861,	231	anti-pornography campaign,	309–12
Office of Planned Parenthood,	234	anti-pornography ordinance,	295–96, 300, 313
Okin, Susan Moller,	58		
Justice, Gender and the Family,	113	Commission on Pornography,	288

Index

conservative approach,	307–09	*R v Puckerin*,	316
definitions,	282–84	*R v R*,	66, 127, 260
empirical evidence,	287–89	*R v Thornton*,	22, 272
evolution,	281–82	Race Relations Act 1968,	37
First Amendment protection,	296, 297–98, 300, 309	Race Relations Act 1976,	293, 303
		Racial discrimination,	264–65
freedom of speech,	297–98	pornography,	293–95
'harm' principle,	301–04	Radbruch, Gustav,	93
legal regulation,	284–87, 312–14	Radical feminism,	163–76
		essentialism,	173–76
liberal approach,	301–04	pornography,	291–92
racial discrimination,	293–95	Rape,	206, 254
radical feminism,	291–92	definition,	277
speech act theory,	299–301	marital,	65–66, 127, 259–61
Positivism,	92–93, 99–110	wartime,	254
Postmodernism,	178–87, 195–207	women on trial,	275–79
Poststructuralism,	185–87	Rawls, John	
Principles of justice,	112–15	*A Theory of Justice*,	110–16, 190
Prisoner's (Temporary Discharge for Ill-health) Act 1913,	42, 43	*Re Andrews*,	63
		Re B (A Minor) (Wardship: Sterilisation),	221
Privatisation public service provision,	67–70	*Re D*,	220
Property,	61, 62	*Re Eve*,	220
protection of rights,	263	*Re F (in utero)*,	233
Prostitution,	315–19	*Re F (Mental Patient: Serilisation)*,	222–23
trafficking of women,	253		
Provocation,	206, 266–68	*Re KB (Adult) (Mental Patient: Medical Treatment)*,	246
Psychoanalyse et Politique,	147	*Re M (A Minor) (Care order: threshold conditions)*,	68
Psychological theory,	145–46	*Re MB*,	224–25
Public Order Act 1986,	293	*Re Paton v British Pregnancy Advisory Service Trustees*,	233
R v Ahluwalia,	22, 272	*Re R (A Minor) (Wardship: Medical Treatment)*,	248
R v Ballard,	266		
R v Bourne,	231	*Re T (Refusal of Treatment)*,	224
R v Brown,	277	*Re W (A Minor) (Medical Treatment: Court's Jurisdiction)*,	246, 248
R v Butler,	286, 290		
R v Camplin,	276	*Regents of the University of California v Bakke*,	106
R v Duffy,	266		
R v Ferrugia,	316	*Register of Companies ex p Attorney General*,	318
R v Hicklin (1868),	285		
R v Human Fertilisation and Embryology Authority ex p Blood,	228	Representation of the People Act 1867,	40
		Representation of the People Act 1918,	43
R v Lavallee,	273–74		
R v Linekar,	276	Reproduction,	216–18
R v Morgan,	276–77		

Reproductive rights,	240	*Simpoulos v Virginia*,	237
Republic of Ireland, abortion,	69	*Singh v Singh*,	78
		Smart, Carol,	7
Revolution,	44	Social contract theory,	110–16
Rights,	202–04	Society for Protection of the Unborn Child,	232
to vote,	40–45		
Roe v Wade,	107, 230, 235, 236, 237, 238, 239	Speech act theory,	299–301
		Spelman, Elizabeth,	88
		Inessential Woman: Problems of Exclusion in Feminist Thought,	190–92
Roman Catholic Church,	243		
abortion,	236		
Rosaldo, Michelle Zimbalist,	30–31	Spencer, Herbert,	30
Rosenau, Pauline Marie,	187	St George's Healthcare National Health Service Trust v S,	225
Roth v United States,	283, 286		
Rousseau, Jean-Jacques,	97, 98	St Paul,	90
Rubin, Gayle,	311	Stanton, Elizabeth Cady,	
Russell, Diana,	309	*The History of Woman Suffrage*,	44
Rust v Sullivan,	236	Stanworth, Michelle,	227
		Steinem, Gloria,	309
Sade, Marquis de,	282	Sterilisation,	219–20, 234
Savigny, Karl von,	36–38	case law,	220–23
Schor, Naomi,	158	non-voluntary,	243–44
Science,	46–49	Stockman, N,	51–53, 71
Scottish Petition of Right,	97	Stoltenberg, John,	312
Sears v Equal Employment Opportunities Commission,	130	Stone, Lawrence,	35, 62
		Stubbs, Julia,	274
Second World War,	49–50, 93	Suffrage movement,	41–43
		Sumner, William Graham,	36–38
Secretary of State for Home Department v Robb,	246	*Sun, The*,	294
		SW v United Kingdom,	66
Seligman, Martin,	271	Symposium on Law and Population 1974,	243
Sex discrimination,	133		
Sex Discrimination Act 1970,	37		
Sex Discrimination Act 1975,	75, 126	*Tameside and Glossop Acute Services Trust v CH*,	226
Sex Disqualification Act 1919,	49	Temkin, Jennifer,	278
Sexual abuse,	253	*Thornburgh v American College of Obstetricians*,	237
of children,	171		
Sexual discrimination,	264–65	Tolmie, Julia,	274
Sexual harassment,	74–75, 171, 296–97	Trafficking of women,	253
		Treaty of Rome 1957 Article 119,	127
Sexual Offences Act 1956, amended 1994,	277		
Sexual Offences (Amendment) Act 1976,	260, 278	United Nations Declaration on the Elimination of All Forms of Discrimination against Women 1983,	316
Simmel, Georg,	30		

Index

United Nations Declaration
  on the Elimination of
  Violence Against Women, 251, 254
United Nations Report
  The World's Women 1970–90, 252–54
  *Violence Against Women
    in the Family,* 254
United States
  abortion, 69, 107, 217,
    234–40, 244
  anti-pornography
    ordinances, 295–97
  foetal rights, 232
  Fourteenth Amendment, 43–44
  inequality, 71
  medicine, 47
  pornography, 75–76, 293,
    297–98
  legal regulation, 284, 285–86
  right to vote, 43–45
  rights, 203, 297–98
  segregation, 37
  sexual harassment, 296–97
  women of colour, 76–77
  work patterns, 51–54
United States v Bennett (1879), 285
*United States v One Book
  Called Ulysses,* 286
United States' Attorney General
  Commission on Pornography, 288

Veil of ignorance, 111–12
Violence,
  domestic,
    See Domestic violence
  gender-based, 35–36,
    251–54
  explanation, 256–58
  international data, 252
  physical, 72–74
Voltaire, 98

Walker, Lenore, 270–71
Warnock Committee
  Report, 227–28, 233
Wasik, Martin, 267
Weber, Max, 51, 178
West, Robin, 134, 167
Westminster Review, 40
Whitford, Margaret, 148, 149, 154,
  158–59

Wife sale, 34–35
*William Webster v
  Reproductive Health Services,* 237
Williams, Ivy, 49
Williams, Patricia, 192–93
  *The Alchemy of Race
    and Rights,* 76–77
Williams Committee on
  Obscenity and
  Film Censorship, 282, 283,
    287–88, 301, 308
Witchcraft, 33–34
Wittgenstein, 184
Wolfenden Committee, 316
Wollestonecraft, Mary, 124
  *Vindication of the
    Rights of Women,* 38, 98
Woman as 'Other', 15–19, 71,
  149–57,
  166
  See also Beauvoir, Simone de
Women,
  invisibility of, 65–68
  legal profession, 49
  medicine, 46–49
  Parliament, in, 64
  position in
    contemporary society, 51–55
  property on marriage, 62
  right to vote, 40–45
  science, 46–49
Women's Advisory Committee, 50
Women's Army Auxiliary Corps, 50
Women's Co-operative Guild, 50
Women's Land Army, 50
Women's rights, 38–40
Women's Royal Air Force, 50
Women's Royal Naval Service, 50
Women's Union for
  Parliamentary Suffrage, 42
Work patterns, 51–55
World Health Organisation, 229, 234
Wright, Shelley, 244

Xuewen, S, 51–53, 71

Young Women Lawyers Group, 265
Young, Iris, 116